The Civilizing Process

Norbert Elias

THE CIVILIZING PROCESS

The History of Manners

Translated by Edmund Jephcott

URIZEN BOOKS   **NEW YORK**

The author and publishers wish to thank Professor Johan Goudsblom for rendering invaluable assistance in preparing the English text.

Originally published as **Uber den Prozess der Zivilisation** in 1939 by Haus zum Falken, Basel.

© Norbert Elias

This translation © Urizen Books New York 1978

ISBN 0-916354-32-6

Dedicated to the Memory of My Parents
Hermann Elias, d. Breslau 1940
Sophie Elias, d. Auschwitz 1941 (?)

Sociogenetic and Psychogenetic Investigations

Table of Contents
(*Vol. 1*)

CHAPTER TWO

Preface*

Central to this study are modes of behavior considered typical of Western civilized man. The problem they pose is simple enough. Western man has not always behaved in the manner we are accustomed to regard as typical or as the hallmark of "civilized" man. If a member of present-day Western civilized society were to find himself suddenly transported into a past epoch of his own society, such as the medieval-feudal period, he would find there much that he esteems "uncivilized" in other societies today. His reaction would scarcely differ from that produced in him at present by the behavior of people in feudal societies outside the Western world. He would, depending on his situation and inclinations, be either attracted by the wilder, more unrestrained and adventurous life of the upper classes in this society, or repulsed by the "barbaric" customs, the squalor and coarseness that he encountered there. And whatever he understands by his own "civilization," he would at any rate feel quite unequivocally that society in this past period of Western history was not "civilized" in the same sense and to the same degree as Western society today.

This state of affairs may seem obvious to many people, and it might appear unnecessary to refer to it here. But it necessarily gives rise to questions which cannot with equal justice be said to be clearly present in the consciousness of living generations, although these questions are not without importance for an understanding of ourselves. How did this change, this "civilizing" of the West, actually happen? Of what did it consist? And what were its causes or motive forces? It is to the solution of these main questions that this study attempts to contribute.

*The Introduction to the 1968 German edition can be found on p. 221

To facilitate understanding of this book, and thus as an introduction to the questions themselves, it seems necessary to examine the different meanings and evaluations assigned to the concept of "civilization" in Germany and France. This inquiry makes up the first chapter. It may help the reader to see the concepts of *Kultur* and *civilisation* as somewhat less rigidly and self-evidently opposed. And it may also make a small contribution toward improving the German historical understanding of the behavior of Frenchmen and Englishmen, and the French and English understanding of the behavior of Germans. But in the end it will also serve to clarify certain typical features of the civilizing process.

To gain access to the main questions, it is necessary first to obtain a clearer picture of how the behavior and affective life of Western peoples slowly changed after the Middle Ages. To show this is the task of the second chapter. It attempts as simply and clearly as possible to open the way to an understanding of the *psychical* process of civilization. It may be that the idea of a psychical process extending over many generations appears hazardous and dubious to present-day historical thinking. But it is not possible to decide in a purely theoretical, speculative way whether the changes in psychical makeup observable in the course of Western history took place in a particular order and direction. Only a scrutiny of documents of historical experience can show what is correct and what is incorrect in such theories. That is why it is not possible here, when knowledge of this documentary material cannot be presupposed, to give a brief preliminary sketch of the structure and central ideas of the whole book. They themselves take on a firmer form only gradually, in a continuous observation of historical facts and a constant checking and revision of what has been seen previously through what entered later into the field of observation. And thus the individual parts of this study, its structure and method, will probably be completely intelligible only when they are perceived in their entirety. It must suffice here, to facilitate the reader's understanding, to pick out a few problems.

The second chapter contains a number of series of examples. They serve to show development in an accelerated fashion. In a few pages we see how in the course of centuries the standard of human behavior on the same occasion very gradually shifts in a specific direction. We see people at table, we see them going to bed or in hostile clashes. In these and other elementary activities the manner in which the individual behaves and feels slowly changes. This change is in the direction of a gradual "civilization," but only historical experience makes clearer what this word actually means. It shows, for example, the decisive role played in this civilizing process by a very specific change in the feelings of shame and delicacy. The standard of what society demands and prohibits changes; in conjunction with this, the threshold of socially instilled displeasure and fear moves; and the question of sociogenic fears thus emerges as one of the central problems of the civilizing process.

Very closely related to this is a further range of questions. The distance in behavior and whole psychical structure between children and adults increases in the course of the civilizing process. Here, for example, lies the key to the question of why some peoples or groups of peoples appear to us as "younger" or "more childlike," others as "older" or "more grown-up." What we are trying to express in this way are differences in the kind and stage of the civilizing process that these societies have attained; but that is a separate question which cannot be included within the framework of this study. The series of examples and the interpretations of them in the second chapter show one thing very clearly: the specific process of psychological "growing up" in Western societies, which frequently occupies the minds of psychologists and pedagogues today, is nothing other than the individual civilizing process to which each young person, as a result of the social civilizing process over many centuries, is automatically subjected from earliest childhood, to a greater or lesser degree and with greater or lesser success. The psychogenesis of the adult makeup in civilized society cannot, therefore, be understood if considered independently of the sociogenesis of our "civilization." By a kind of basic "sociogenetic law"** the individual, in his short history, passes once more through some of the processes that his society has traversed in its long history.

** This expression should not be understood to mean that all the individual phases of a society's history are reproduced in the history of the civilized individual. Nothing would be more absurd than to look for an "agrarian feudal age" or a "Renaissance" or a "courtly-absolutist period" in the life of the individual. All concepts of this kind refer to the structure of whole social groups.

What must be pointed out here is the simple fact that even in civilized society no human being comes into the world civilized, and that the individual civilizing process that he compulsorily undergoes is a function of the social civilizing process. Therefore, the structure of the child's affects and consciousness no doubt bears a certain resemblance to that of "uncivilized" peoples, and the same applies to the psychological stratum in grown-ups which, with the advance of

---

It is the purpose of the third chapter, which constitutes the greater part of the second volume [to be published in English in 1978], to make certain processes in this long history of society more accessible to understanding. It attempts, within a number of precisely defined areas, to clarify how and why in the course of its history the structure of Western society continuously changes, and points at the same time to an answer to the question of why, in the same areas, the standard of behavior and the psychical makeup of Western peoples change.

We see, for example, the social landscape of the early Middle Ages. There is a multitude of greater and smaller castles; even the town settlements of earlier times have become feudalized. Their centers too are formed by the castles and estates of lords from the warrior class. The question is: What are the sets of social relationships that press toward the development of what we call the "feudal system"? The attempt is made to demonstrate some of these "mechanisms of feudalization." We see further how, from the castle landscape, together with a number of free, urban craft and commercial settlements, a number of larger and richer feudal estates slowly emerge. Within the warrior class itself a kind of upper stratum forms more and more distinctly; their dwelling places are the real centers of minnesong and the lyrics of the troubadours, on the one hand, and of *courtois* forms of behavior on the other. If earlier in the book the *courtois* standard of conduct is placed at the starting point of a number of sequences of examples giving a picture of the subsequent change of psychical makeup, here we gain access to the sociogenesis of these *courtois* forms of behavior themselves.

Or we see, for example, how the early form of what we call a "state" develops. In the age of absolutism, under the watchword of *civilité*, behavior moves very perceptibly toward the standard that we denote today by a derivative of the word *civilité* as "civilized" behavior. It therefore seems necessary, in elucidating this civilizing process, to obtain a clearer picture of what gave rise to the absolutist regimes and therefore to the absolutist state. It is not only the observation of the past that points in this direction; a wealth of contemporary observations suggest strongly that the structure of civilized behavior is

---

civilization, is subjected to more or less heavy censorship and consequently finds an outlet in dreams, for example. But since in our society each human being is exposed from the first moment of life to the influence and the molding intervention of civilized grown-ups, he must indeed pass through a civilizing process in order to reach the standard attained by his society in the course of its history, but not through the individual historical phases of the social civilizing process.

closely interrelated with the organization of Western societies in the form of states. The question, in other words, is: How did the extremely decentralized society of the early Middle Ages, in which numerous greater and smaller warriors were the real rulers of Western territory, become one of the internally more or less pacified but outwardly embattled societies that we call states? Which dynamics of human interdependencies push toward the integration of ever larger areas under a relatively stable and centralized government apparatus?

It may perhaps seem at first sight an unnecessary complication to investigate the genesis of each historical formation. But since every historical phenomenon, human attitudes as much as social institutions, did actually once "develop," how can modes of thought prove either simple or adequate in explaining these phenomena if, by a kind of artificial abstraction, they isolate the phenomena from their natural, historical flow, deprive them of their character as movement and process, and try to understand them as static formations without regard to the way in which they have come into being and change? It is not theoretical prejudice but experience itself which urges us to seek intellectual ways and means of steering a course between the Scylla of this "statism," which tends to express all historical movement as something motionless and without evolution, and the Charybdis of the "historical relativism" which sees in history only constant transformation, without penetrating to the order underlying this transformation and to the laws governing the formation of historical structures. That is what is attempted here. The sociogenetic and psychogenetic investigation sets out to reveal the *order* underlying historical *changes*, their mechanics and their concrete mechanisms; and it seems that in this way a large number of questions that appear complicated or even beyond understanding today can be given fairly simple and precise answers.

For this reason, this study also inquires into the sociogenesis of the state. There is, to take one aspect of the history of the state's formation and structure, the problem of the "monopoly of force." Max Weber pointed out, mainly for the sake of definition, that one of the constitutive institutions required by the social organization we call a state is a monopoly in the exercise of physical force. Here the attempt is made to reveal something of the concrete historical processes that, from the time when the exercise of force was the privilege of a host of rival warriors, gradually impelled society toward this centralization and monopolization of the use of physical violence and its instruments. It can be shown that the tendency to form such monopolies in this past epoch of our history is neither easier nor more difficult to understand than, for example, the strong tendency toward monopolization in our own epoch. And it is then not difficult to understand that with this monopolization of physical violence as the point of intersection of a multitude of social interconnections, the whole apparatus which shapes the individual, the mode of operation of the social demands and prohibitions which mold his social makeup, and above all the kinds of fear that play a part in his life are decisively changed.

Finally, the concluding "Sketch of a Theory of Civilization" underlines once more the connections between changes in the structure of society and changes in the structure of behavior and psychical makeup. Much of what could only be hinted at earlier, in depicting concrete historical processes, is now stated explicitly. We find here, for example, a short sketch of the structure of the fears experienced as shame and delicacy, as a kind of theoretical summing-up of what previously emerged of itself from the study of historical documents; we find an explanation of precisely why fears of this kind play an especially important role in the advance of the civilizing process; and at the same time, some light is shed on the formation of the "superego" and on the relation of the conscious and unconscious impulses in the psyche of civilized man. Here an answer is given to the question of historical processes; the question of how all these processes, consisting of nothing but the actions of individual people, nevertheless give rise to institutions and formations which were neither intended nor planned by any single individual in the form they actually take. And finally, in a broad survey, these insights from the past are combined into a single picture with experiences from the present.

This study therefore poses and develops a very wide-ranging problem; it does not pretend to solve it.

It marks out a field of observation that has hitherto received relatively little attention, and undertakes the first steps toward an explanation. Others must follow.

Many questions and aspects which presented themselves in the course of this study I deliberately did not pursue. It was not so much my purpose to build a general theory of civilization in the air, and then afterward find out whether it agreed with experience; rather, it seemed the primary task to begin by regaining within a limited area the lost perception of the process in question, the peculiar transformation of human behavior, then to seek a certain understanding of its causes, and finally to gather together such theoretical insights as have been encountered on the way. If I have succeeded in providing a tolerably secure foundation for further reflection and research in this direction, this study has achieved everything it set out to achieve. It will need the thought of many people and the cooperation of different branches of scholarship, which are often divided by artificial barriers today, gradually to answer the questions that have arisen in the course of this study. They concern psychology, philology, ethnology, and anthropology no less than sociology or the different special branches of historical research.

However, the issues raised by the book have their origin less in scholarly tradition, in the narrower sense of the word, than in the experiences in whose shadow we all live, experiences of the crisis and transformation of Western civilization as it had existed hitherto, and the simple need to understand what this "civilization" really amounts to. But I have not been guided in this study by the idea that our civilized mode of behavior is the most advanced of all humanly possible modes of behavior, nor by the opinion that "civilization" is the worst form of life and one that is doomed. All that can be seen today is that with gradual civilization a number of specific civilizational difficulties arise. But it cannot be said that we already understand why we actually torment ourselves in this way. We feel that we have got ourselves, through civilization, into certain entanglements unknown to less civilized peoples; but we also know that these less civilized peoples are for their part often plagued by difficulties and fears from which we no longer suffer, or at least not to the same degree. Perhaps all this can be seen somewhat more clearly if it is understood how such civilizing processes actually take place. At any rate, that was one of the wishes with which I set to work on this book. It may be that, through clearer understanding, we shall one day succeed in making accessible to more conscious control these processes which today take place in and around us not very differently from natural events, and which we confront as medieval man confronted the forces of nature.

I myself was obliged in the course of this study to revise my thinking on a large number of points, and I cannot spare the reader from becoming acquainted with a number of unfamiliar aspects and expressions. Above all, the nature of historical processes, of what might be called the "developmental mechanics of history," has become clearer to me, as has their relation to psychical processes. Terms such as socio- and psychogenesis, affective life and instinct-molding, external and internal compulsions, embarrassment threshold, social power, monopoly mechanism, and a number of others give expression to this. But the least possible concession has been made of the necessity to express new things that have become visible by new words.

So much for the subject of this book.

For the present study and for a number of necessary preliminary investigations, I have received advice and support from many sides. It is my wish here to thank expressly all the people and institutions that have helped me.

The enlargement of my *Habilitationschrift* and an extended study of nobility, royalty, and courtly society in France which is the basis of the present book, was made possible by the support of the Steun-Fond of Amsterdam. My thanks are due to this foundation, and to Professor Frijda of Amsterdam and Professor Bouglé of Paris for the great kindness and interest they showed me during my work in Paris.

For the period of my work in London I received the generous support of Woburn House, London. To it and above all to Professor Ginsberg of London, Professor H. Loewe of Cambridge, and A. Makower, M.A., of London I owe very great thanks. Without their help my work would not have come to fruition. Professor K. Mannheim of London I thank for the help and advice he gave me. And I am not least indebted to my friends Gisèle Freund, D.Phil., Paris; M. Braun, D.Phil., Ph.D., Cambridge; A. Glücksmann, D.Med., Cambridge; H. Rosenhaupt, D.Phil., Chicago; and R. Bonwit, London, for their help and for the discussions in which many things were made clear to me, and I thank them.

September, 1936   Norbert Elias

Chapter One
On the Sociogenesis of the Concepts "Civilization" and "Culture"

Part One

Sociogenesis of the Difference Between Kultur *and* Zivilisation *in German Usage*

I

Introduction

1. The concept of "civilization" refers to a wide variety of facts: to the level of technology, to the type of manners, to the development of scientific knowledge, to religious ideas and customs. It can refer to the type of dwelling or the manner in which men and women live together, to the form of judicial punishment, or to the way in which food is prepared. Strictly speaking, there is almost nothing which cannot be done in a "civilized" or an "uncivilized" way; hence, it always seems somewhat difficult to summarize in a few words everything that can be described as civilization.

But when one examines what the general function of the concept of civilization really is, and what common quality causes all these various human attitudes and activities to be described as civilized, one starts with a very simple discovery: this concept expresses the self-consciousness of the West. One could even say: the national consciousness. It sums up everything in which Western society of the last two or three centuries believes itself superior to earlier societies or "more primitive" contemporary ones. By this term Western society seeks to describe what constitutes its special character and what it is proud of: the level of *its* technology, the nature of *its* manners, the development of *its* scientific knowledge or view of the world, and much more.

2. But "civilization" does not mean the same thing to different Western nations. Above all, there is a great difference between the English and French use of the word, on the one hand, and the German use of it, on the other. For the former, the concept sums up in a single term their pride in the significance of their own nations for the progress of the West and of mankind. But in German usage, *Zivilisation* means something which is indeed useful, but nevertheless only a value of the second rank, comprising only the outer appearance of human beings, the surface of human existence. The word through which Germans interpret themselves, which more than any other expresses their pride in their own achievement and their own being, is *Kultur*.

3. A peculiar phenomenon: Words like the English and French "civilization" or the German *Kultur* appear completely clear in the internal usage of the society to which they belong. But the way in which a piece of the world is bound up in them, the manner in which they include certain areas and exclude others as a matter of course, the hidden evaluations which they implicitly bring with them, all this makes them difficult to define for any outsider.

The French and English concept of civilization can refer to political or economic, religious or technical, moral or social facts. The German concept of *Kultur* refers essentially to intellectual, artistic, and religious facts, and has a tendency to draw a sharp dividing line between facts of this sort, on the one side, and political, economic, and social facts, on the other. The French and English concept of civilization can refer to accomplishments, but it refers equally to the attitudes or "behavior" of people, irrespective of whether or nor they have accomplished anything. In the German concept of *Kultur*, by contrast, the reference to "behavior," to the value which a person has by virtue of his mere existence and conduct, without any accomplishment at all, is very minor. The specifically German sense of the concept of *Kultur* finds its clearest expression in its derivative, the adjective *kulturell*, which describes the value and character of particular human products rather than the intrinsic value of a person. But this word, the concept embodied in *kulturell*, cannot be exactly translated into French and English.

The word *kultiviert* (cultivated) is very close to the Western concept of civilization. To some extent, it represents the highest form of being civilized. Even people and families who have accomplished nothing *kulturell* can be *kultiviert*. Like the term "civilized," *kultiviert* refers primarily to the form of people's conduct or behavior. It describes a social quality of people, their housing, their manners, their speech, their clothing, unlike *kulturell*, which does not refer directly to people themselves, but exclusively to particular human accomplishments.

4. Another difference between the two concepts is very closely bound up with this. "Civilization" describes a process or at least the result of a process. It refers to something which is constantly in motion, constantly moving "forward." The German concept of *Kultur*, in current usage, has a different relation to motion. It refers to human products which are there like "flowers of the field,"[1] to works of art, books, religious or philosophical systems, in which the individuality of a people expresses itself. The concept of *Kultur* delimits.

To a certain extent, the concept of civilization plays down the national differences between peoples; it emphasizes what is common to all human beings or—in the view of its bearers—should be. It expresses the self-assurance of peoples whose national boundaries and national identity have for centuries been so fully established that they have ceased to be the subject of any particular discussion, peoples which have long expanded outside their borders and colonized beyond them.

In contrast, the German concept of *Kultur* places special stress on national differences and the particular identity of groups; primarily by virtue of this, it has acquired in such fields as ethnological and anthropological research a significance far beyond the German linguistic area and the situation in which the concept originated. But that situation is the situation of a people which, by Western standards, arrived at political unification and consolidation only very late, and from whose boundaries, for centuries and even down to the present, territories have again and again crumbled away or threatened to crumble away. Whereas the concept of civilization has the function of giving expression to the continuously expansionist tendency of colonizing groups, the concept of *Kultur* mirrors the self-consciousness of a nation which had constantly to seek out and constitute its boundaries anew, in a political as well as a spiritual sense, and again and again had to ask itself: "What is really our identity?" The orientation of the German concept of culture, with its tendency toward demarcation and the emphasis on and detailing of differences between groups, corresponds to this historical process. The questions "What is really French? What is really English?" have long since ceased to be a matter of much discussion for the French and English. But for centuries the question "What is really German?" has not been laid to rest. One answer to this question—one among others—lies in a particular aspect of the concept of *Kultur*.

5. Thus the national self-images represented by concepts such as *Kultur* and "civilization" take very different forms. But however different the self-image of the Germans, who speak with pride of their *Kultur*, and that of the French and English, who think with pride of their "civilization," they all regard it as completely self-evident that theirs is the way in which the world of men as a whole wants to be viewed and judged. The German can perhaps try to explain to the French and English what he means by the concept of *Kultur*. But he can communicate hardly anything of the specific national background and the self-evident emotional values which envelop the word for him.

The Frenchman or Englishman can perhaps tell the German what elements make the concept of civilization the sum of the national self-image. But however reasonable and rational this concept may appear to them, it too grows out of a specific set of historical situations, it too is surrounded by an emotional and traditional atmosphere which is hard to define but which nevertheless represents an integral part of its meaning. And the discussion really becomes futile when the German tries to show the Frenchman and Englishman why the concept of *Zivilisation* does indeed represent a value for him, but only one of the second rank.

6. Concepts like these two have something of the character of those words which from time to time make their appearance in some narrower group, such as a family or a sect, a school class or an association, and which say much to the initiate and little to the outsider. They take form on the basis of common experiences. They grow and change with the group whose expression they are. The situation and history of the group are mirrored in them. And they remain colorless, they never become fully alive for those who do not

---

share these experiences, who do not speak from the same tradition and the same situation.

The concepts of *Kultur* and "civilization," to be sure, bear the stamp not of sects or families but of whole peoples, or perhaps only of certain classes of these peoples. But in many respects what is true of the specific words of smaller groups is also true of them: they are primarily used by and for people who share a particular tradition and a particular situation.

Mathematical concepts can be separated from the group which uses them. Triangles may be explicable without reference to historical situations. Concepts such as "civilization" and *Kultur* are not. It may be that particular individuals formed them from the existing linguistic material of their group, or at least gave them new meaning. But they took root. They established themselves. Others picked them up in their new meaning and form, developing and polishing them in speech or writing. They were tossed back and forth until they became efficient instruments for expressing what people had jointly experienced and wanted to communicate about. They became fashionable words, concepts current in the everyday speech of a particular society. This shows that they met not merely individual but collective needs for expression. The collective history has crystallized in them and resonates in them. The individual finds this crystallization already in their possibilities of use. He does not know very precisely why this meaning and this delimitation are bound up with the words, why exactly this nuance and that new possibility can be drawn from them. He makes use of them because it seems to him a matter of course, because from childhood he learns to see the world through the lens of these concepts. The social process of their genesis may be long forgotten. One generation hands them on to another without being aware of the process as a whole, and the concepts live as long as this crystallization of past experiences and situations retains an existential value, a function in the actual being of society—that is, as long as succeeding generations can hear their own experiences in the meaning of the words. The terms gradually die when the functions and experiences in the actual life of society cease to be bound up with them. At times, too, they only sleep, or sleep in certain respects, and acquire a new existential value from a new social situation. They are recalled then because something in the present state of society finds expression in the crystallization of the past embodied in the words.

II

The Development of the Antithesis of
Kultur and *Zivilisation*[2]

7. It is clear that the function of the German concept of *Kultur* took on new life in the year 1919, and in the preceding years, partly because a war was waged against Germany in the name of "civilization" and because the self-image of the Germans had to define itself anew in the situation created by the peace treaty.

But it is just as clear, and can be proved, that to a certain extent the historical situation of Germany after the war only gave a new impulse to an antithesis which had long found expression through these two concepts, even as far back as the eighteenth century.

It seems to have been Kant who first expressed a specific experience and antithesis of his society in related concepts. In 1784 he wrote in his *Ideas on a Universal History from the Point of View of a Citizen of the World*: "Cultivated to a high degree by art and science, we are civilized to the point where we are overburdened with all sorts of social propriety and decency. . . ."

"The idea of morality," he added, "is a part of culture. But the application of this idea, which results only in the similitude of morality in the love of honor and in outward decency, amounts only to civilizing."

Related as this formulation of the antithesis already seems, in the moment of its genesis, to our formulation, its concrete point of departure in the experiences and situation in the late eighteenth century, though not without a historical connection to the experiences on which its present-day use rests, is nevertheless significantly different. The contraposition here, where the spokesmen of the developing German bourgeoisie, the middle-class German intelligentsia,[3] still speak in large part "from the point of view of a citizen of the world," relates only vaguely and at best secondarily to a national contrast. Its primary aspect is an internal contrast within the society, a social contrast which nevertheless bears within itself in a significant way the germ of the national contraposition: the contrast between the courtly nobility, predominantly French-speaking and "civilized" on the French model, and a German-speaking, middle-class stratum of intelligentsia recruited chiefly from the bourgeois "servers of princes" or officials in the broadest sense, and occasionally also from the landed nobility.

This latter is a stratum far removed from political activity, scarcely thinking in political terms and only tentatively in national ones, whose legitimation consists primarily in its intellectual, scientific, or artistic *accomplishments*. Counterposed to it is an upper class which "accomplishes" nothing in the sense in which the others do, but for which the shaping of its distinguished and distinctive *behavior* is central to its self-image and self-justification. And this is the class which Kant has in mind when he speaks of being "civilized to the point where we are overburdened," of mere "social propriety and decency," of "the similitude of morality in the love of honor." It is in the polemic of the stratum of German middle-class intelligentsia against the etiquette of the ruling courtly upper class that the conceptual contraposition of *Kultur* and *Zivilisation* originates in Germany. But this polemic is older and broader than its crystallization in these two concepts.

8. It can be traced long before the middle of the eighteenth century, even if only as an undertone in thought much more muted than after the middle of the century. A good idea of this can be obtained from the articles on *Hof, Höflichkeit,* and *Hofmann* (Court, Courtesy, Courtier), too long to be reproduced here in full, in the *Zedler Universal Lexicon* of 1736.[4]

Courtesy undoubtedly gets its name from the court and court life. The courts of great lords are a theater where everyone wants to make his fortune. This can only be done by winning the favor of the prince and the most important people of his court. One therefore takes all conceivable pains to make onself agreeable to them. Nothing does this better than making the other believe that we are ready to serve him to the utmost of our capacity under all conditions. Nevertheless, we are not always in a position to do this, and may not want to, often for good reasons. Courtesy serves as a substitute for all this. By it we give the other so much reassurance, through our outward show, that he has a favorable anticipation of our readiness to serve him. This wins us the other's trust, from which an affection for us develops imperceptibly, as a result of which he becomes eager to do good to us. This is so common with courtesy that it gives a special advantage to him who possesses it. To be sure, it should really be ability and virtue which earn us people's esteem. But how few are the correct judges of these two! And how many fewer hold them worthy of honor! People, all too concerned with externals, are far more moved by what reaches their senses externally, especially when the accompanying circumstances are such as particularly affect their will. This works out exactly in the case of a courtier.

Simply, without philosophical interpretation and in clear relation to specific social configurations, the same antithesis is here expressed which eventuates in Kant, refined and deepened, in the contraposition of culture and civilization: deceptive external "courtesy" and true "virtue." But the author only speaks of this in passing, with a sigh of resignation. After the middle of the century the tone gradually changes. The self-legitimation of the middle classes by virtue and accomplishment becomes more precise and emphatic, and the polemic against the external and superficial manners to be found in the courts becomes more explicit.

III

Examples of Courtly Attitudes in Germany

9. It is not easy to speak of Germany in general, since at this time there are special characteristics in each of the many states. But only a few are eventually decisive for the development of the whole; the rest follow. And certain general phenomena present themselves more or less clearly everywhere.

To begin with, there is the depopulation and the dreadful economic devastation of the country after the Thirty Years War. In the seventeenth century, and even still in the eighteenth, Germany and in particular the German bourgeoisie are poor by French and English standards. Trade, and especially the foreign trade which was highly developed in parts of Germany in the sixteenth century, is in ruins. The huge wealth of the great mercantile houses is destroyed, partly by the shift in trade routes due to the overseas discoveries, and partly as a direct consequence of the long chaos of the war. What is left is a small-town bourgeoisie with narrow horizons, living essentially by supplying local needs.

There is not much money available for luxuries such as literature and art. In the courts, wherever there is enough money to do so, people inadequately imitate the conduct of the court of Louis XIV and speak French. German, the language of the lower and middle classes, is unwieldy and awkward. Leibniz, Germany's only courtly philosopher, the only great German of this time whose name wins acclaim in wider courtly circles, writes and speaks French or Latin, seldom German. And the language problem, the problem of what could be done with this awkward German language, occupies him as it has occupied many others.

French spreads from the courts to the upper layer of the bourgeoisie. All *honnêtes gens* (decent people), all people of "consequence" speak it. To speak French is the status symbol of all the upper classes.

In 1730, Gottsched's bride writes her betrothed: "Nothing is more plebeian than to write letters in German."[5]

If one speaks German, it is considered good form to introduce as many French words as possible. In 1740, E. de Mauvillon writes in his *Lettres Françoises et Germaniques*: "It is only a few years since one did not say four words of German without two of French." That was *le bel usage* (good usage).[6] And he has more to say about the barbaric quality of the German language. Its nature, he says, is "d'être rude et barbare" (to be rude and barbarous).[7] There are the Saxons, who assert "qu'on parle mieux l'Allemand en Saxe, qu'en aucun autre endroit de l'Empire" (German is spoken better in Saxony than in any other part of the Empire). The Austrians make the same assertion in regard to themselves, as do the Bavarians, the Brandenburgers, and the Swiss. A few scholars, Mauvillon continues, want to establish rules of grammar, but "il est difficile, qu'une Nation, qui contient dans son sein tant de Peuples indépendans les uns des autres, se soumette aux décisions d'un petit nombre des Savans" (it is difficult for a nation that embraces so many peoples independent of one another to submit to the decisions of a small number of savants).

Here as in many other fields, a small, powerless, middle-class intelligentsia falls heir to tasks which in France and England were undertaken largely by the court and the aristocratic upper class. It is learned middle-class "servers of princes" who first attempt to create, in a particular intellectual class, models of what German is, and thus to establish at least in this intellectual sphere a German unity which does not yet seem realizable in the political sphere. The concept of *Kultur* has the same function.

But at first most of what he sees in Germany appears crude and backward to Mauvillon, an observer grounded in French civilization. He speaks of the literature as well as the language in these terms:

"Milton, Boileau, Pope, Racine, Tasso, Molière, and practically all poets of consequence have been translated into most European languages; your poets, for the most part, are themselves only translators."

He goes on: "Name me a creative spirit on your Parnassus, name me a German poet who has drawn from his own resources a work of some reputation; I defy you to."[8]

10. One might say that this was the unauthoritative opinion of a badly oriented Frenchman. But in 1780, forty years after Mauvillon and nine years before the French Revolution, when France and England have already passed through decisive phases of their cultural and national development, when the languages of the two Western countries have long since found their classic and permanent form, Frederick the Great publishes a work called *De la littérature allemande*,[9] in which he laments the meager and inadequate development of German writing, makes approximately the same assertions about the German language as Mauvillon, and explains how in his opinion this lamentable situation may be remedied.

Of the German language he says: "I find a half-barbarous language, which breaks down into as many different dialects as Germany has provinces. Each local group is convinced that its patois is the best." He describes the low estate of German literature and laments the pedantry of German scholars and the meager development of German science. But he also sees the reasons for it: he speaks of Germany's impoverishment as a result of continuous wars, and of the inadequate development of trade and bourgeoisie.

"It is," he says, "not to the spirit or the genius of the nation that one must attribute the slight progress we have made, but we should lay the blame only on a succession of sad events, a string of wars which have ruined us and left us poor in men as well as money."

He speaks of the slowly beginning recovery of prosperity: "The Third Estate no longer languishes in shameful degradation. Fathers educate their children without going into debt. Behold, a beginning has been made in the happy revolution which we await." And he prophesies that with growing prosperity there will also come a blossoming of German art and science, a civilizing of the Germans which will give them an equal place among the other nations: this is the happy revolution of which he speaks. And he compares himself to

Moses, who saw the new blossoming of his people approaching without experiencing it.

11. Was Frederick right? A year after the appearance of his work, in 1781, Schiller's *Die Räuber* and Kant's *Critique of Pure Reason* appeared, to be followed in 1787 by Schiller's *Don Carlos* and Goethe's *Iphigenie*. There followed the whole blossoming of German literature and philosophy which we know. All of this seems to confirm his prediction.

But this new blooming had been long in preparation. The German language did not achieve its new expressive power in two or three years. In 1780, when *De la littérature allemande* appeared, this language had long ceased to be the half-barbaric "patois" of which Frederick speaks. A whole collection of works to which today, in retrospect, we assign considerable importance had already appeared. Goethe's *Götz von Berlichingen* had been produced seven years earlier, *Werther* was in circulation, Lessing had already published the major part of his dramatic and theoretical works, including *Laokoon* in 1766 and *Die Hamburgische Dramaturgie* in 1767. Frederick died in 1781, a year after the appearance of his work. Klopstock's writings had been published much earlier; his *Messias* appeared in 1748. This is without counting Herder, the *Sturm und Drang* plays, and a whole collection of widely read novels such as Sophie de la Roche's *Das Fräulein von Sternheim*. There had long since developed in Germany a class of buyers, a bourgeois public—even if still a relatively small one—which was interested in such works. Waves of great intellectual excitement had flowed over Germany and found expression in articles, books, plays, and other works. The German language had become rich and flexible.

Of all this Frederick gives no hint in his work. He either does not see it or assigns it no significance. He mentions a single work of the young generation, the greatest work of the period of *Sturm und Drang* and enthusiasm for Shakespeare, *Götz von Berlichingen*. He mentions it, characteristically, in connection with the education and forms of entertainment of the *basses classes*, the lower strata of the population:

To convince yourself of the lack of taste which has reigned in Germany until our day, you only need go to the public spectacles. There you will see presented the abominable works of Shakespeare, translated into our language; the whole audience goes into raptures when it listens to these ridiculous farces worthy of the savages of Canada. I describe them in these terms because they sin against all the rules of the theater, rules which are not at all arbitrary.

Look at the porters and gravediggers who come on stage and make speeches worthy of them; after them come the kings and queens. How can such a jumble of lowliness and grandeur, of buffoonery and tragedy, be touching and pleasing?

One can pardon Shakespeare for these bizarre errors; the beginning of the arts is never their point of maturity.

But then look at *Götz von Berlichingen* making its appearance on stage, a detestable imitation of these bad English pieces, while the public applauds and enthusiastically demands the repetition of these disgusting stupidities.

And he continues: ''After having spoken of the lower classes, it is necessary for me to go on with the same frankness in regard to the universities.''

12. The man who speaks thus is the man who did more than any of his contemporaries for the political and economic development of Prussia and perhaps indirectly for the political development of Germany. But the intellectual tradition in which he grew up and which finds expression through him is the common tradition of Europe's ''good society,'' the aristocratic tradition of prenational court society. He speaks its language, French. By the standard of its taste he measures the intellectual life of Germany. Its prescribed models determine his judgment. Others of this society have long spoken of Shakespeare in a way altogether similar to his. Thus, in 1730, Voltaire gave expression to very similar thoughts in the *Discours sur la tragédie*, which introduces the tragedy *Brutus*: ''I certainly do not pretend to approve the barbarous irregularities with which it [Shakespeare's tragedy *Julius Caesar*] is filled. It is only surprising that there are not more in a work composed in an age of ignorance by a man who did not even know Latin and had no teacher except his own genius.''

What Frederick the Great says about Shakespeare is, in fact, the standard opinion of the French-speaking upper class of Europe. He does not ''copy'' or ''plagiarize'' Voltaire; what he writes is his sincere personal opinion. He takes no pleasure in the rude and uncivilized jests of gravediggers and similar folks, the more so if they are mixed in with the great tragic sentiments of princes and kings. He feels that all of this has no clear and concise form; these are the "pleasures of the lower classes." This is the way in which his comments are to be understood; they are no more and no less individual than the French language he uses. Like it, they bear witness to his membership in a particular society. And the paradox that while his politics were Prussian his aesthetic tradition was French (or, more precisely, absolutist-courtly) is less great than present-day concepts of national uniformity may suggest. It is bound up with the special structure of this court society, whose political institutions and interests were multifariously fissured, but whose social stratification was into estates whose taste, style, and language were by and large the same throughout Europe.

The peculiarities of this situation occasionally produced inner conflicts in the young Frederick, as he slowly became aware that the interests of the ruler of Prussia could not always be brought into accord with reverence for France and adherence to courtly customs.[10] Throughout his life they produced a certain disharmony between what he did as a ruler and what he wrote and published as a human being and philosopher.

The feelings of the German bourgeois intelligentsia toward him were also sometimes correspondingly paradoxical. His military and political successes gave their German self-awareness a tonic it had long lacked, and for many he became a national hero. But his attitude in matters of language and taste, which found expression in his work on German literature though by no means there alone, was exactly what the German intelligentsia, precisely as a *German* intelligentsia, had to fight against.

Their situation had its analogue in almost all the greater German states and in many of the smaller ones. At the top almost everywhere in Germany were individuals or groups of men who spoke French and decided policy. On the other side, there was a German-speaking intelligentsia, who by and large had no influence on political developments. From their ranks, essentially, came the men on whose account Germany has been called the land of poets and thinkers. And from them concepts such as *Bildung* and *Kultur* received their specifically German imprint and tenor.

IV

The Middle Class and the Court Nobility in Germany

13. It would be a special project (and a very fascinating one) to show how much the specific spiritual condition and ideals of a courtly-absolutist society found expression in classical French tragedy, which Frederick the Great counterposes to the Shakespearean tragedies and *Götz*. The importance of good form, the specific mark of every genuine "society"; the control of individual feelings by reason, a vital necessity for every courtier; the reserved behavior and elimination of every plebeian expression, the specific mark of a particular stage on the road to "civilization"—all this finds its purest expression in classical tragedy. What must be hidden in court life, all vulgar feelings and attitudes, everything of which "one" does not speak, does not appear in tragedy either. People of low rank, which for this class also means of base character, have no place in it. Its form is clear, transparent, precisely regulated, like etiquette and court life in general.[11] It shows the courtly people as they would like to be and, at the same time, as the absolute prince wants to see them. And all who lived under the impress of this social situation, be they English or Prussian or French, had their taste forced into the same pattern. Even Dryden, next to Pope the best-known courtly poet of England, wrote about earlier English drama very much in the vein of Frederick the Great and Voltaire in the epilogue to the *Conquest of Granada*:

> Wit's now arrived to a more high degree;
> Our native language more refined and free,
> Our ladies and our men now speak more wit
> In conversation, than those poets writ.

The connection with social stratification is particularly clear in this aesthetic judgment. Frederick, too, defends himself against the tastelessness of juxtaposing on the stage the "tragic grandeur" of princes and queens and the "baseness" of porters and gravediggers. How could he have understood and approved a dramatic and literary work which had central to it precisely the struggle against class differences, a work which was intended to show that not merely the sorrows of princes and kings and the courtly aristocracy but those of people lower on the social scale have their greatness and their tragedy.

In Germany, too, the bourgeoisie slowly becomes more prosperous. The King of Prussia sees this and promises himself that it will lead to an awakening of art and science, a "happy revolution." But this bourgeoisie speaks a different language from the king. The ideals and taste of the bourgeois youth, the models for its behavior, are almost the opposite of his.

In *Dichtung und Wahrheit* (*Poetry and Truth*), Book 9, Goethe writes: "In Strasbourg, on the French border, we were at once freed from the spirit of the French. We found their way of life much too ordered and too aristocratic, their poetry cold, their criticism destructive, their philosophy abstruse and unsatisfying."

He writes *Götz* from this mood. How could Frederick the Great, the man of enlightened, rational absolutism and aristocratic-courtly taste, have understood it? How could the King have approved the dramas and theories of Lessing, who praises in Shakespeare precisely what Frederick condemns: that his works fit the taste of the people far more than do the French classics?

"If someone had translated the masterpieces of Shakespeare . . . for our Germans, I know well that it would have a better result than thus making them acquainted with Corneille or Racine. In the first place, the people would take far more delight in him than in them."

Lessing writes this in his *Letters Concerning the Most Recent Literature* (part I, letter 17), and he demands and writes bourgeois dramas, appropriate to the newly awakening self-consciousness of the bourgeois classes, because courtly people do not have the exclusive privilege to be great. "This hateful distinction which men have made between themselves," he says, "is not known to nature. She parcels out the qualities of the heart without any preference for the nobles and the rich."[12]

The whole literary movement of the second half of the eighteenth century is the product of a social class—and, accordingly, of aesthetic ideals—in opposition to Frederick's social and aesthetic inclinations. Thus, they have nothing to say to him, and he therefore overlooks the vital forces already active around him and condemns what he cannot overlook, like *Götz*. This German literary movement, whose exponents include Klopstock, Herder, Lessing, the poets of *Sturm und*

Drang (Storm and Stress), the poets of "sensibility," and the circle known as the *Göttinger Hain*, the young Goethe, the young Schiller, and many others, is certainly no political movement. With isolated exceptions, one finds in Germany before 1789 no idea of concrete political action, nothing reminiscent of the formation of a political party or a political party program. One does find, particularly in Prussian officialdom, proposals and also the practical beginning of reforms in terms of enlightened absolutism. In philosophers such as Kant one finds the development of general basic principles which are, in part, in direct opposition to the prevailing conditions. In the writings of the young generation of the *Göttinger Hain* one finds expressions of wild hatred of princes, courts, aristocrats, Frenchifiers, courtly immorality, and intellectual frigidity. And everywhere among middle-class youth one finds vague dreams of a new united Germany, of a "natural" life—"natural" as opposed to the "unnatural" life of court society—and again and again an overwhelming delight in their own exuberance of feeling.

Thoughts, feelings—nothing which was able in any sense to lead to concrete political action. The structure of this absolutist society of petty states offered no opening for it. Bourgeois elements gained self-assurance, but the framework of the absolute states was completely unshaken. The bourgeois elements were excluded from any political activity. At most, they could "think and write" independently; they could not act independently.

In this situation, writing becomes the most important outlet. Here the new self-confidence and the vague discontent with what exists find a more or less covert expression. Here, in a sphere which the apparatus of the absolute states had surrendered to a certain extent, the young middle-class generation counterposed its new dreams and oppositional ideas, and with them the German language, to the courtly ideals.

As has been said, the literary movement of the second half of the eighteenth century is not a political one, but in the fullest sense of the word it is the expression of a social movement, a transformation of society. To be sure, the bourgeoisie as a whole did not yet find expression in it. It was at first the expression of a sort of bourgeois vanguard, what is here described as the middle-class intelligentsia: many individuals in the same position and of similar social origin scattered throughout the country, individuals who understood one another because they were in the same position. Only occasionally do individuals of this vanguard find themselves together in some place as a group, for a shorter or longer time; often they live in isolation or solitude, an elite in relation to the people, persons of the second rank in the eyes of the courtly aristocracy.

Again and again one can see in these works the connection between this social situation and the ideals of which they speak: the love of nature and freedom, the solitary exaltation, the surrender to the excitement of one's own heart, unhindered by "cold reason." In *Werther*, whose success shows how typical these sentiments were of a particular generation, it is occasionally said quite unequivocally.

In the letter of December 24, 1771, one reads: "The resplendent misery, the boredom among the detestable people gathered together here, the competition for rank among them, the way they are constant-ly looking for a chance to get a step ahead of one another. . . ."

And under January 8, 1772: "What sort of people are these whose whole soul is rooted in ceremonial, and whose thoughts and desires the year round are centered on how they can move up a chair at table."

Under March 15, 1772: "I gnash my teeth . . . I eat at the Count's house and after dinner we walk back and forth in the great park. The social hour approaches. I think, God knows, about nothing." He remains, the nobles arrive. The women whisper, something circulates among the men. Finally the Count, somewhat embarrassed, asks him to leave. The nobility feel insulted at seeing a bourgeois among them.

" 'You know,' " says the Count, " 'I notice that the company is displeased at seeing you here. ' . . . I stole away from the distin-guished company, and drove to M., to watch the sunset from the hill there while reading in my Homer the noble song of how Ulysses was hospitably received by the excellent swineherds."

On the one hand, superficiality, ceremony, formal conversation; on the other, inwardness, depth of feeling, immersion in books, develop-ment of the individual personality. It is the same contrast which is ex-pressed by Kant in the antithesis between *Kultur* and civilization, relating to a very specific social situation.

In *Werther*, Goethe also shows particularly clearly the two fronts between which the bourgeoisie lives. "What irritates me most of all," we read in the entry of December 24, 1771, "is our odious bourgeois situation. To be sure, I know as well as any other how necessary class differences are, how many advantages I owe to them myself, only

they should not stand directly in my way.'' Nothing better characterizes middle-class consciousness than this statement. The doors
below must remain shut. Those above must open. And like any other
middle class, this one was imprisoned in a peculiarly middle-class
way: it could not think of breaking down the walls that blocked the
way up, for fear that those separating it from the lower strata might
also give way in the assault.

The whole movement was one of upward mobility: Goethe's great-
grandfather was a blacksmith,[13] his grandfather a tailor, then an
innkeeper with a courtly clientele and courtly-bourgeois manners.
Already well-to-do, his father becomes an imperial councellor, a rich
bourgeois of independent means, with a title. His mother is the
daughter of a Frankfurt patrician family.

Schiller's father was a surgeon, later a badly paid major; his
grandfather, great-grandfather, and great-great-grandfather were bak-
ers. From similar social origins, now closer, now farther off, from the
crafts and the middle administration, come Schubart, Bürger, Winkelmann, Herder, Kant, Friedrich August Wolff, Fichte, and many
other members of this movement.

14. There was an analogous movement in France. There, too, in
conjunction with a similar social change, a profusion of outstanding
people emerged from middle-class circles. They include Voltaire and
Diderot. But in France these talents were received and assimilated
without great difficulty by the large court society of Paris. In Germany, on the other hand, sons of the rising middle class who were
distinguished by talent and intelligence were debarred, in their great
majority, from courtly-aristocratic life. A few, like Goethe, achieved
a kind of elevation to these circles. But aside from the fact that the
court at Weimar was small and relatively poor, Goethe was an exception. By and large, the walls between the middle-class intelligentsia and the aristocratic upper class in Germany remained, by Western
standards, very high. In 1740 the Frenchman Mauvillon notes that
''one observes in the German gentleman an air that is haughty to the
point of arrogance. Swollen with a lineage the length of which they are
always ready to prove, they despise anyone not similarly endowed.
Seldom,'' he continues, ''do they contract *mésalliances*. But no less
seldom are they seen behaving simply and amiably toward middle-
class people. And if they spurn connubiality with them, how much
less do they seek out their company, whatever their merit may be.''[14]

THE CIVILIZING PROCESS

In this particularly sharp social division between nobility and middle class, to which countless documents bear witness, a decisive factor was no doubt the relative indigence of both. This impelled the nobles to cut themselves off, using proof of ancestry as the most important instrument for preserving their privileged social existence. On the other hand, it blocked to the German middle class the main route by which in the Western countries bourgeois elements rose, intermarried with, and were received by the aristocracy: through money.

But whatever the causes—doubtless highly complex—of this very pronounced separation, the resulting low degree of fusion between the courtly-aristocratic models and values based on intrinsic worth, on the one hand, and the bourgeois models and values based on achievement, on the other, protractedly influenced the German national character as it emerged from now on. This division explains why a main linguistic stream, the language of educated Germans, and almost the entire recent intellectual tradition deposited in literature received their decisive impulses and their stamp from a middle-class intellectual stratum which was far more purely and specifically middle-class than the corresponding French intelligentsia and even than the English, the latter seeming to occupy an intermediate position between those of France and Germany.

The gesture of self-isolation, the accentuation of the specific and distinctive, which was seen earlier in the comparison of the German concept of *Kultur* with Western "civilization," reappears here as a characteristic of German historical development.

It was not only externally that France expanded and colonized early in comparison with Germany. Internally, too, similar movements are frequently seen throughout her more recent history. Particularly important in this connection is the diffusion of courtly-aristocratic manners, the tendency of the courtly aristocracy to assimilate and, so to speak, colonize elements from other classes. The social pride of the French aristocracy is always considerable, and the stress on class differences never loses its importance for them. But the walls surrounding them have more openings; access to the aristocracy (and thus the assimilation of other groups) plays a far greater role here than in Germany.

The most vigorous expansion of the German empire occurs, by contrast, in the Middle Ages. From this time on, the German Reich diminishes slowly but steadily. Even before the Thirty Years War and more so after it, German territories are hemmed in on all sides, and strong pressure is exerted on almost all the external frontiers. Correspondingly, the struggles within Germany between the various social groups competing for the limited opportunities and for survival, and therefore the tendencies toward distinctions and mutual exclusiveness, were generally more intense than in the expanding Western countries. As much as the fragmentation of the German territory into a multiplicity of sovereign states, it was this extreme isolation of large parts of the nobility from the German middle class that stood in the way of the formation of a unified, model-setting, central society, which in other countries attained decisive importance at least as a stage on the way to nationhood, setting its stamp in certain phases on language, on the arts, on the manners, and on the structure of emotions.

V

Literary Examples of the Relationship of the German Middle-Class Intelligentsia to the Court

15. The books of the middle classes which had great public success after the mid-eighteenth century—that is, in the period when these classes were gaining in prosperity and self-assurance—show very clearly how strongly this dissimilarity was felt. They also demonstrate that the differences between the structure and life of the middle class, on the one hand, and the courtly upper class, on the other, were matched by differences in the structure of behavior, emotional life, aspirations, and morality; they show—necessarily one-sidedly—how these differences were perceived in the middle-class camp.

An example of this is the well-known novel by Sophie de la Roche, *Das Fräulein von Sternheim*,[15] which made the authoress one of the most celebrated women of her time. "My whole ideal of a young woman," wrote Caroline Flachsland to Herder after reading *Sternheim*, "gentle, delicate, charitable, proud, virtuous, and deceived. I have spent precious, wonderful hours reading the book. Alas, how far I still am from my ideal, from myself."[16]

The curious paradox residing in the fact that Caroline Flachsland, like many others of similar makeup, loves her own suffering—that she includes being deceived, along with charity, pride, and virtue, among the features of the ideal heroine whom she wishes to resemble—is highly characteristic of the emotional condition of the middle-class intelligentsia, and particularly of the women among them, in the age of sensibility. The middle-class heroine is deceived by the aristocratic courtier. The warning, the fear of the socially superior "seducer" who cannot marry the girl because of the social discrepancy, and the secret wish for his approach, the fascination that lies in the idea of penetrating the closed and dangerous circle, finally the identifying empathy with the deceived girl: all this is an example of the specific ambivalence besetting the emotional life of middle-class people—and not only women—with regard to the aristocracy. *Das Fräulein von Sternheim* is, in this respect, a feminine counterpart of *Werther*. Both works point to specific entanglements of their class, which find expression in sentimentality, sensibility, and related shades of emotion.

The problem presented in the novel: A high-minded country girl, from a family of landed gentry with bourgeois origins, arrives at court. The Prince, related to her on her mother's side, desires her as his mistress. Having no other escape, she seeks refuge with the "scoundrel" of the novel, an English lord living at the court, who speaks just as many middle-class circles would have imagined an "aristocratic seducer" to speak, and who produces a comic effect because he utters middle-class reproaches to his type as his own thoughts. But from him, too, the heroine preserves her virtue, her moral superiority, the compensation for her class inferiority, and dies.

This is how the heroine, Fräulein von Sternheim, the daughter of an ennobled colonel, speaks:[17]

To see how the tone, the modish spirit of the court suppresses the noblest movements of a heart admirable)| y nature, to see how avoiding the sneers of the ladies and gentlemen of fashion means laughing and agreeing with them, fills me with contempt and pity. The thirst for amusement, for new finery, for admiration of a dress, a piece of furniture, a new noxious dish— oh, my Emilie, how anxious and sick my soul grows. . . . I will not speak of the false ambition that hatches so many base intrigues, grovels before vice ensconced in prosperity, regards virtue and merit with contempt, and unfeelingly makes others wretched.

"I am convinced, Aunt," she says after a few days of court life, "that life at court does not suit my character. My taste, my inclinations, diverge from it in every way. And I confess to my gracious aunt that I would leave more happily than I came."

"Dearest Sophie," her aunt tells her, "you are really a most charming girl, but the old vicar has filled your head with pedantic ideas. Let go of them a little."[18]

In another place Sophie writes: "My love of Germany has just involved me in a conversation in which I sought to defend the merits of my Fatherland. I talked so zealously that my aunt told me afterward hat I had given a pretty demonstration of being the granddaughter of a professor. . . . This reproach vexed me. The ashes of my father and grandfather had been offended."

The clergyman and the professor—these are indeed two of the most important representatives of the middle-class administrative intelligentsia, two social figures who played a decisive part in the formation and diffusion of the new German educated language. This example shows quite clearly how the vague national feeling of these circles, with its spiritual, nonpolitical leanings, appears as bourgeois to the aristocracy at the petty courts. At the same time, both the clergyman and the professor point to the social center most important in fashioning and disseminating the German middle-class culture: the university. From it generation after generation of students carried into the country, as teachers, clergymen, and middle-rank administrators, a complex of ideas and ideals stamped in a particular way. The German university was, in a sense, the middle-class counterweight to the court.

Thus it is in words with which the pastor might thunder against him from the pulpit that the court scoundrel expressed himself in the middle-class imagination:[19]

> You know that I have never granted love any other power than over my senses, whose most delicate and lively pleasures it affords. . . . All classes of beauty have pandered to me. . . . I grew sated with them. . . . The moralists . . . may have their say on the fine nets and snares in which I have captured the virtue and pride, the wisdom and the frigidity, the coquetry and even the piety of the whole feminine world. . . . Amour indulged my vanity. He brought forth from the most wretched corner of the countryside a colonel's daughter whose form, mind, and character are so charming that . . .

Twenty-five years later, similar antitheses and related ideals and problems can still earn a book success. In 1796, *Agnes von Lilien*,[20] by Caroline von Wolzogen, appeared in Schiller's *Horen*. In this novel the mother, of the high aristocracy, who must for mysterious reasons have her daughter educated outside the court circle, says:

> I am almost thankful for the prudence that compels me to keep you far from the circle in which I became unhappy. A serious, sound formation of the mind is rare in high society. You might have become a little doll that danced to and fro at the side of opinion.

And the heroine says of herself:[21]

> I knew but little of conventional life and the language of worldly people. My simple principles found many things paradoxical to which a mind made pliable by habit is reconciled without effort. To me it was as natural as that night follows day to lament the deceived girl and hate the deceiver, to prefer virtue to honor and honor to one's own advantage. In the judgment of this society I saw all these notions overturned.

She then sketches the prince, a product of French civilization:[22]

> The prince was between sixty and seventy, and oppressive to himself and others with the stiff, old French etiquette which the sons of German princes had learned at the court of the French king and transplanted to their own soil, admittedly in somewhat reduced dimensions. The prince had learned through age and habit to move almost naturally under this heavy armor of ceremony. Toward women he observed the elegant, exaggerated courtesy of the bygone age of chivalry, so that his person was not unpleasing to them, but he could not leave the sphere of fine manners for an instant without becoming insufferable. His children . . . saw in their father only the despot.
>
> The caricatures among the courtly people seemed to me now ridiculous, now pitiable. The reverence that they were able, on the appearance of their lord, to summon instantly from their hearts to their hands and feet, the gracious or angry glance that passed through their bodies like an electric shock . . . the immediate compliance of their opinions to the most recent utterance from the princely lips, all this I found incomprehensible. I seemed to be watching a puppet theater.

Courtesy, compliance, fine manners, on the one hand, sound education and preference of virtue to honor, on the other: German literature in the second half of the eighteenth century is full of such antitheses. As late as October 23, 1828, Eckermann says to Goethe:

"An education as thorough as the Grand-Duke appears to have had is doubtless rare among princely personages." "Very rare," Goethe replies. "There are many, to be sure, who are able to converse cleverly on any subject, but they do not possess their learning inwardly, and merely tickle the surface. And it is no wonder, if one thinks of the appalling diversions and truncations that court life brings with it."

On occasion he uses the concept of *Kultur* quite expressly in this context. "The people around me," he says, "had no idea of scholarship. They were German courtiers, and this class had not the slightest *Kultur*."[23] And Knigge once observes explicitly: "Where more than here [in Germany] did the courtiers form a separate species."

16. In all these statements a quite definite social situation is reflected. It is the same situation that is discernible behind Kant's opposition of *Kultur* to civilization. But even independently of these concepts, this phase and the experiences deriving from it imprinted themselves deeply in the German tradition. What is expressed in this concept of *Kultur*, in the antithesis between depth and superficiality and in many related concepts, is primarily the self-image of a middle-class intellectual stratum. This is a relatively thin layer scattered over the whole area, and therefore individualized to a high degree and in a particular form. It does not constitute, as does the court, a closed circle, a "society." It is composed predominantly of administrators, of civil servants in the broadest sense of the word—that is, of people who directly or indirectly derive their income from the court, but who, with few exceptions, do not themselves belong to courtly "good society," to the aristocratic upper class. It is a class of intellectuals without a broad middle-class background. The commercial professional bourgeoisie, who might have served as a public for the writers, is relatively undeveloped in most German states in the eighteenth century. The rise to prosperity is only beginning in this period. The German writers and intellectuals are therefore floating in the air to some extent. Mind and books are their refuge and their domain, achievements in scholarship and art their pride. Scope for political activity, political goals, scarcely exists for this class. Commerce and the economic order are for them, in keeping with the structure of their life and society, marginal concerns. Trade, communications, and industry are comparatively undeveloped and still need, for the most part, protection and promotion by mercantilist policy rather than

liberation from its constraints. What legitimizes this eighteenth-century middle-class intelligentsia to itself, what supplies the foundation of its self-image and pride, is situated beyond economics and politics. It exists in what is called for precisely this reason *das rein Geistige* (the purely spiritual), in books, scholarship, religion, art, philosophy, in the inner enrichment, the intellectual formation (*Bildung*) of the individual, primarily through the medium of books, in the personality. Accordingly, the watchwords expressing this self-image of the German intellectual class, terms such as *Bildung* and *Kultur*, tend to draw a sharp distinction between accomplishments in the areas just mentioned, between this purely spiritual sphere as the only one of genuine value, and the political, economic, and social sphere, in complete contrast to the watchwords of the rising bourgeoisie in France and England. The peculiar fate of the German bourgeoisie, its long political impotence, and the late unification of the nation acted continuously in one direction, reinforcing concepts and ideals of this kind. Thus the development of the concept *Kultur* and the ideals it embodied reflected the position of the German intelligentsia without a significant social hinterland, which, being the first bourgeois formation in Germany, developed an expressly bourgeois self-image, specifically middle-class ideas, and an arsenal of trenchant concepts directed against the courtly upper class.

Also in keeping with their situation was what this intelligentsia saw as most to be opposed in the upper class, as the antithesis of *Bildung* and *Kultur*. The attack is directed only infrequently, hesitantly, and usually resignedly against the political or social privileges of the courtly aristocracy. Instead, it is directed predominantly against their human behavior.

A very illuminating description of the difference between this German intellectual class and its French counterpart is likewise to be found in Goethe's conversations with Eckermann: Ampère has come to Weimar. (Goethe did not know him personally but had often praised him to Eckermann.) To everyone's astonishment the celebrated Monsieur Ampère turns out to be a "cheerful youth of some twenty years." Eckermann expresses surprise, and Goethe replies (Thursday, May 3, 1827):

It has not been easy for you on your heath, and we in middle Germany have had to buy dearly enough such little wisdom as we possess. For at bottom we lead an isolated, miserable life! Very little culture comes to us from the people itself, and all our men of talent are scattered across the country. One is in Vienna, another in Berlin, another in Königsberg, another in Bonn or Düsseldorf, all separated from each other by fifty or a hundred miles, so that personal contact or a personal exchange of ideas is a rarity. I feel what this means when men like Alexander von Humboldt pass through, and advance my studies further in a single day than I would otherwise have traveled in a year on my solitary path.

But now imagine a city like Paris, where the outstanding minds of the whole realm are gathered in a single place, and in their daily intercourse, competition, and rivalry teach and spur each other on, where the best from every sphere of nature and art, from the whole surface of the earth, can be viewed at all times. Imagine this metropolis where every walk over a bridge or across a square summons up a great past. And in all this do not think of the Paris of a dull, mindless epoch, but the Paris of the nineteenth century, where for three generations, through men like Molière, Voltaire, and Diderot, such a wealth of ideas has been put into circulation as is not found anywhere else on the entire globe, and you will understand that a good mind like Ampère, having grown up in such plenitude, can very well amount to something in his twenty-fourth year.

Further on, Goethe says with reference to Mérimée: "In Germany we cannot hope to produce such mature work when still so young. This is not the fault of the individual, but of the cultural state of the nation, and the great difficulty that we all experience in making our way in isolation."

From such statements, which in this introductory context must suffice as documentation, it is very clear how the political fragmentation of Germany is connected to a quite specific structure, both of the German intellectual class and of its social behavior and way of thinking. In France the members of the intelligentsia are collected in one place, held together within a more or less unified and central "good society"; in Germany, with its numerous, relatively small capitals, there is no central and unified "good society." Here the intelligentsia is dispersed over the entire country. In France conversation is one of the most important means of communication and, in addition, has been for centuries an art; in Germany the most important means of communication is the book, and it is a unified written language, rather than a unified spoken one, that this German intellectual class develops. In France even young people live in a milieu of rich and stimulating intellectuality; the young member of the German middle class must work his way up in relative solitude and isolation. The mechanisms of social advancement are different in both countries. And finally, this statement of Goethe's also shows very clearly what a middle-class intelligentsia without social hinterland really means. Earlier a passage was quoted in which he attributed little culture to the courtiers. Here he says the same of the common people. *Kultur* and *Bildung* are the watchwords and characteristics of a thin intermediate stratum that has risen out of the people. Not only the small courtly class above it, but even the broader strata below still show relatively little understanding for the endeavors of their own elite.

However, precisely this underdevelopment of the broader, professional bourgeois classes is one of the reasons why the struggle of the middle-class vanguard, the bourgeois intelligentsia, against the courtly upper class is waged almost entirely outside the political sphere, and why the attack is directed predominantly against the conduct of the upper class, against general human characteristics like "superficiality," "outward politeness," "insincerity," and so on. Even the few quotations that were used here show these connections extremely clearly. Admittedly, it is only rarely and without great emphasis that the attack focuses on specific concepts antithetical to those which served as self-legitimization for the German intellectual class, concepts such as *Bildung* and *Kultur*. One of the few specific counter-concepts is "civilization" in the Kantian sense.

VI

The Recession of the Social and the Advance of the National Element in the Antithesis of *Kultur* and *Zivilisation*

17. Whether the antithesis is expressed by these or other concepts, one thing is always clear: the contraposition of particular human characteristics which later serve primarily to express a national antithesis here appears primarily as the expression of a social antithesis. As the experience underlying the formulation of pairs of opposites such as "depth" and "superficiality," "honesty" and "falsity," "outward politeness" and "true virtue," and from which, among other things, the antithesis between *Zivilisation* and *Kultur* grows up,

we find at a particular phase of German development the tension between the middle-class intelligentsia and the courtly aristocracy. Certainly, there is never a complete lack of awareness that courtliness and French are related entities. G. C. H. Lichtenberg expresses this very clearly in one of his aphorisms, in which he speaks of the difference between the French *promesse* and the German *Versprechung* (Part 3, 1775-1779[24]). "The latter is kept," he says, "and not the former. The usefulness of French words in German. I am surprised that it has not been noticed. The French word gives the German idea with an admixture of humbug, or in its court meaning . . . . An invention (*Erfindung*) is something new and a *découverte* something old with a new name. Columbus discovered (*entdeckte*) America and it was Americus Vesputius's *découverte*. Indeed, *goût* and taste (*Geschmack*) are almost antithetical, and people of *goût* seldom have much taste."

But it is only after the French Revolution that the idea of the German courtly aristocracy unmistakably recedes, and the idea of France and the Western powers in general moves toward the foreground in the concept of "civilization" and related ideas.

One typical example: in 1797 there appeared a small book by the French émigré Menuret, *Essay sur la ville d'Hambourg*. A citizen of Hamburg, Canon Meyer, writes the following commentary on it:

> Hamburg is still backward. After a famous epoch (famous enough, when swarms of emigrants are settling here), it has made progress (really?); but to increase, to complete I do not say its happiness (that would be addressing his God) but its civilization, its advance in the career of science and art (in which, as you know, we are still in the North), in that of luxury, comfort, frivolity (his special field!) it still needs a number of years, or events which draw to it new throngs of foreigners (provided they are not more swarms of his civilized compatriots) and an increase of opulence.

Here, therefore, the concepts "civilized" and "civilization" are already quite unequivocally linked with the image of the Frenchman.

With the slow rise of the German bourgeoisie from a second-rank class to the bearer of German national consciousness, and finally— very late and conditionally—to the ruling class, from a class which was first obliged to perceive or legitimize itself primarily by contrasting itself to the courtly-aristocratic upper class, and then by defining itself against competing nations, the antithesis between *Kultur* and *Zivilisation*, with all its accompanying meanings, changes in significance and function: *from a primarily social it becomes a primarily national antithesis.*

And a parallel development is undergone by what is thought specifically German: here, likewise, many originally middle-class social characteristics, imprinted in people by their social situation, become national characteristics. Honesty and sincerity, for example, are now opposed as German characteristics to dissimulating courtesy. But sincerity, as it is used here, originally emerged as a specific trait of the middle-class person, in contrast to the worldling or courtier. This, too, is seen clearly in a conversation between Eckermann and Goethe.

"I usually carry into society," says Eckermann on May 2, 1824, "my personal likes and dislikes and a certain need to love and be loved. I seek a personality conforming to my nature; to that person I should like to give myself entirely and have nothing to do with the others."

"This natural tendency of yours," Goethe answers, "is indeed not of a sociable kind; yet what would all our education be if we were not willing to overcome our natural tendencies. It is a great folly to demand that people should harmonize with us, I have never done so. I have thereby attained the ability to converse with all people, and only thus is knowledge of human character gained, as well as the necessary adroitness in life. For with opposed natures one must take a grip on oneself if one is to get on with them. You ought to do likewise. There's no help for it, you must go into society. No matter what you say."

The sociogenesis and psychogenesis of human behavior are still largely unknown. Even to raise the questions may seem odd. It is nevertheless observable that people from different social units behave differently in quite specific ways. We are accustomed to take this for granted. We speak of the peasant or the courtier, of the Englishman or the German, of the medieval man or the man of the twentieth century, and we mean that the people of the social units indicated by such concepts behave uniformly in a specific manner which transcends all individual differences when measured against the individuals of a contrasting group: for example, the peasant behaves in many respects differently from the courtier, the Englishman or Frenchman from the German, and the medieval man from the man of the twentieth century, no matter how much else they may have in common as human beings.

Modes of behavior differing in this way are apparent in the conversation just quoted between Eckermann and Goethe. Goethe is certainly a man individualized to a particularly high degree. As a result of his social destiny, modes of behavior with different social origins merge in him into a specific unity. He, his opinions, and his behavior are certainly never entirely typical of any of the social groups and situations through which he has passed. But in this quotation he speaks quite expertly as a man of the world, as a courtier, from experiences which are necessarily foreign to Eckermann. He perceives the compulsion to hold back one's own feelings, to suppress antipathies and sympathies, which is inherent in court life, and which is often interpreted by people of a different social situation, and therefore with a different affect structure, as dishonesty or insincerity. And with a degree of consciousness that distinguishes him as a relative outsider from all social groups, he emphasizes the beneficial, human aspect of his moderation of individual affects. His comment is one of the few German utterances of this time to acknowledge something of the social value of "courtesy" and to say something positive about social adroitness. In France and England, where "society" played a far greater role in the overall development of the nation, the behavioral tendencies he speaks of also play—though less consciously than in his case—a far more important part. And ideas of a similar kind, including the notion that people should seek to harmonize with and show consideration for each other, that the individual may not always give way to his emotions, recur quite frequently, with the same specifically social meaning as in Goethe, in the court literature of France, for example. As a reflection, these thoughts were the individual property of Goethe. But related social situations, life in the *monde*, led everywhere in Europe to related precepts and modes of behavior.

Similarly, the behavior which Eckermann describes as his own is—as compared to the outward serenity and amiability concealing opposed feelings that is first developed in this phase in the courtly-aristocratic world—clearly recognizable as originating from the small-town, middle-class sphere of the time. And it is certainly found not only in Germany in this sphere. But in Germany, owing to the particularly pure representation of the middle-class outlook by the intelligentsia, these and related attitudes become visible to an exceptional degree in literature. And they recur in this relatively pure form produced by the sharper, more rigorous division between courtly and middle-class circles, above all in the national behavior of the Germans.

The social units that we call nations differ widely in the personality structure of their members, in the schemata by which the emotional life of the individual is molded under the pressure of institutionalized tradition and of the present situation. What is typical in the behavior described by Eckermann is a specific form of "economy of affects," the open admission of individual inclination that Goethe considers unsociable and contrary to the affect formation necessary for "society."

For Nietzsche, many decades later, this attitude had long been the typical national attitude of Germans. Certainly, it has undergone modifications in the course of history, and no longer has the same social purpose as at Eckermann's time. Nietzsche ridicules it: "The German," he says in *Beyond Good and Evil* (Aphorism 244), "loves 'sincerity' and 'uprightness.' How comforting it is to be sincere and upright. It is today perhaps the most dangerous and deceptive of all the disguises in which the German is expert, this confidential, obliging, German honesty that always shows its cards. The German lets himself go, looking the while with trustful blue empty German eyes—and foreigners immediately mistake him for his nightshirt." This—leaving aside the one-sided value judgment—is one of the many illustrations of how, with the slow rise of the middle classes, their specific social characteristics gradually become national characteristics.

And the same is clear from the following judgment of Fontane on England, to be found in *Ein Sommer in London* (Dessau, 1852):

> England and Germany are related in the same way as form and content, appearance and reality. Unlike things, which in no other country in the world exhibit the same solidity as in England, people are distinguished by form, their most outward packing. You need not be a gentleman, you must only have the means to appear one, and you are one. You need not be right, you must only find yourself within the forms of rightness, and you are right. . . . Everywhere appearance. Nowhere is one more inclined to abandon oneself blindly to the mere luster of a name. The German lives in order to live, the Englishman to represent. The German lives for his own sake, the Englishman for the sake of others.

It is perhaps necessary to point out how exactly this last idea coincides with the antithesis between Eckermann and Goethe: "I give open expression to my personal likes and dislikes," says Eckermann. "One must seek, even if unwillingly, to harmonize with others," argues Goethe.

"The Englishman," Fontane observes, "has a thousand comforts, but no comfort. The place of comfort is taken by ambition. He is always ready to receive, to give audiences. . . . He changes his suit three times a day; he observes at table—in the sitting room and drawing room—certain prescribed laws of propriety. He is a distinguished man, a phenomenon that impresses us, a teacher from whom we take lessons. But in the midst of our wonderment is mixed an infinite nostalgia for our petty-bourgeois Germany, where people have not the faintest idea how to represent, but are able so splendidly, so comfortably and cozily, to live."

The concept of "civilization" is not mentioned here. And the idea of German *Kultur* appears in this account only from afar. But we see from it, as from all these reflections, that the German antithesis between *Zivilisation* and *Kultur* does not stand alone; it is part of a larger context. It is an expression of the German self-image. And it points back to differences of self-legitimization, of character and total behavior, that first existed preponderantly, even if not exclusively, between particular German classes, and then between the German nation and other nations.

Part Two

Sociogenesis of the Concept of Civilisation *in France*

I

Introduction

1. It would be incomprehensible that, in the German antithesis of genuine *Bildung* and *Kultur* on the one hand and mere outward *Zivilisation* on the other, the internal social antithesis should recede and the national become dominant, had not the development of the French bourgeoisie followed, in certain respects, exactly the opposite course from the German.

In France the bourgeois intelligentsia and the leading groups of the middle class were drawn relatively early into court society. The German nobility's old means of distinction, the proof of ancestry—which later, in a bourgeois transformation, took on new life in German racial legislation—was certainly not entirely absent in the French tradition, but particularly after the establishment and consolidation of the "absolute monarchy," it no longer played a very decisive role as a barrier between the classes. The permeation of bourgeois circles by specifically aristocratic traditions (which in Germany, with the more rigorous separation of the classes, had a deep effect only in certain spheres such as the military, being elsewhere very limited) had quite different proportions in France. Here, as early as the eighteenth century, there was no longer any considerable difference of manners between the leading bourgeois groups and the courtly aristocracy. And even if, with the stronger upsurge of the middle class from the mid-eighteenth century onward—or, stated differently, with the enlargement of aristocratic society through the increased assimilation of leading middle-class groups—behavior and manners slowly changed, this happened without rupture as a direct continuation of the courtly-aristocratic tradition of the seventeenth century. Both the courtly bourgeoisie and the courtly aristocracy spoke the same language, read the same books, and had, with particular gradations, the same manners. And when the social and economic disproportionalities burst the institutional framework of the *ancien régime*, when the bourgeoisie became a nation, much of what had originally been the specific and distinctive social character of the courtly aristocracy and then also of the courtly-bourgeois groups, became, in an ever-widening movement and doubtless with some modification, the national character. Stylistic conventions, the forms of social intercourse, affect-molding, esteem for courtesy, the importance of good speech and conversation, articulateness of language and much else—all this is first formed in France within courtly society, then slowly changes, in a continuous diffusion, from a social into a national character.

Here, too, Nietzsche saw the difference very clearly. "Wherever there was a court," he says in *Beyond Good and Evil* (Aphorism 101), "there was a law of right speaking, and therefore also a law of style for all who wrote. Courtly language, however, is the language of the courtier who has no special subject, and who even in conversation on scholarly matters prohibits all technical expressions because they smack of specialization; this is why, in countries with a courtly culture, the technical term and everything that betrays the specialist is a stylistic blemish. Now that all courts have become caricatures . . . one is surprised to find even Voltaire very particular on this point. The fact is that we are all emancipated from court taste, while Voltaire was its consummation!"

In Germany the aspiring middle-class intelligentsia of the eighteenth century, trained at universities specializing in particular subjects, developed its self-expression, its own specific culture, in the arts and sciences. In France the bourgeoisie was already developed and prosperous to an entirely different degree. The rising intelligentsia had, besides the aristocracy, a broad bourgeois public, too. The intelligentsia itself, like certain other middle-class formations, was assimilated by the courtly circle. And so it came about that the German middle classes, with their very gradual rise to nationhood, increasingly perceived as the national character of their neighbor those modes of behavior which they had first observed predominantly at their own courts. And, having either judged this behavior second-rate or rejected it as incompatible with their own affect structure, so they also disapproved it to a greater or lesser degree in their neighbors.

2. It may seem paradoxical that in Germany, where the social walls between the middle class and the aristocracy were higher, social contacts fewer, and differences in manners more considerable, for a long time the discrepancies and tensions between the classes found no political expression; whereas in France, where the class barriers were lower and social contact between the classes incomparably more intimate, the political activity of the bourgeoisie developed earlier and the tension between the classes reached an early political resolution.

But the paradox is only apparent. The long denial of political functions to the French nobility by royal policy, the early involvement of bourgeois elements in government and administration, their access to even the highest governmental functions, their influence and advancement at the court—all this had two consequences: on the one hand, continuous close social contact between elements of differing social origin; on the other, the opportunity for bourgeois elements to engage in political activity when the social situation was ripe and, prior to this, a strongly political training, a tendency to think in political categories. In the German states, by and large, almost exactly the reverse was the case. The highest government posts were generally reserved for the nobility. At the least, unlike their French counterparts, the German nobility played a decisive role in higher state administration. Its strength as an autonomous class had never been so radically broken as in France. In contrast, the class strength of the bourgeoisie, in keeping with its economic power, was relatively low in Germany until well into the nineteenth century. The sharper social severance of German middle-class elements from the courtly aristocracy reflected their relative economic weakness and their exclusion from most key positions in the state.

3. The social structure of France made it possible for the moderate opposition, which had been slowly growing from about the mid-eighteenth century, to be represented with a certain success in the innermost court circles. Its representatives did not yet form a party. Other forms of political struggle fitted the institutional structure of the *ancien régime*. They formed a clique at the court without a definite organization, but were supported by people and groups within the broader court society and in the country itself. The variety of social interests found expression at court in the conflicts between such cliques, admittedly in a somewhat vague form and with a strong admixture of the most diverse personal interests; nevertheless, these conflicts were expressed and resolved.

The French concept of *civilisation*, exactly like the corresponding German concept of *Kultur*, was formed within this opposition movement in the second half of the eighteenth century. Its process of formation, its function, and its meaning are as different from those of the German concept as are the circumstances and manners of the middle classes in the two countries.

It is not uninteresting to observe how similar is the French concept of *civilisation*, as first encountered in literature, to the concept to which many years later Kant opposed his concept of *Kultur*. The first literary evidence of the evolution of the verb *civiliser* into the concept *civlisation* is to be found, according to present-day findings,[25] in the work of the elder Mirabeau in the 1760s.

"I marvel to see," he says, "how our learned views, false on all points, are wrong on what we take to be civilization. If they were asked what civilization is, most people would answer: softening of manners, urbanity, politeness, and a dissemination of knowledge such that propriety is established in place of laws of detail: all that only presents me with the mask of virtue and not its face, and civilization does nothing for society if it does not give it both the form and the substance of virtue."[26] This sounds very similar to what was also being said in Germany against courtly manners. Mirabeau, too, contrasts what most people, according to him, consider to be civilization (i.e., politeness and good manners) against the ideal in whose name everywhere in Europe the middle classes were aligning themselves against the courtly-aristocratic upper class, and through which they legitimized themselves—the ideal of virtue. He, too, exactly like Kant, links the concept of civilization to the specific characteristics of the courtly aristocracy, with reason: for the *homme civilisé* was nothing other than a somewhat extended version of that human type which represented the true ideal of court society, the *honnête homme*.

Civilisé was, like *cultivé, poli*, or *policé*, one of the many terms, often used almost as synonyms, by which the courtly people wished to designate, in a broad or narrow sense, the specific quality of their own behavior, and by which they contrasted the refinement of their own social manners, their "standard," to the manners of simpler and socially inferior people.

Concepts such as *politesse* or *civilité* had, before the concept *civilisation* was formed and established, practically the same function as the new concept: to express the self-image of the European upper class in relation to others whom its members considered simpler or more primitive, and at the same time to characterize the specific kind of behavior through which this upper class felt itself different to all simpler and more primitive people. Mirabeau's statement makes it quite clear to what extent the concept of civilization was at first a direct continuation of other incarnations of courtly self-consciousness: "If they were asked what 'civilization' is, people would answer: softening of manners, politeness, and suchlike." And Mirabeau, like Rousseau, if more moderately, inverts the existing valuations. You and your civilization, he says, all that you are so proud of, believing that it raises you above the simple people, is of very little value: "In all the languages . . . of all ages, the depiction of the love of shepherds for their flocks and their dogs finds its way into our soul, deadened as it is by the pursuit of luxury and a false civilization."[27]

A person's attitude toward the "simple man"—above all, toward the "simple man" in his most extreme form, the "savage"—is everywhere in the second half of the eighteenth century a symbol of his position in the internal, social debate. Rousseau launched the most radical attack on the dominant order of values of his time, and for this very reason his direct importance for the courtly/middle-class reform movement of the French intelligentsia was less than might be suggested by his resonance among the unpolitical yet intellectually more radical middle-class intelligentsia of Germany. But Rousseau, for all the radicalism of his social criticism, had not yet fashioned an inclusive, unified counterconcept against which to hurl the accumulated reproaches. Mirabeau creates it, or is at least the first to use it in his writings; perhaps it had previously existed in conversation. From the *homme civilisé* he derives a general characteristic of society: *civilisation*. But his social criticism, like that of the other Physiocrats, is moderate. It remains entirely within the framework of the existing social system. It is, indeed, the criticism of reformers. While members of the German middle-class intelligentsia, at least in the mind, in the daydreams of their books, forge concepts diverging absolutely from the models of the upper class, and thus fight on politically neutral ground all the battles which they are unable to fight on the political and social plane because the existing institutions and power relationships deny them instruments and even targets; while they, in their books, oppose to the human characteristics of the upper class their own new ideals and behavioral models; the courtly-reformist intelligentsia in France remains for a long time within the framework of courtly tradition. These Frenchmen desire to improve, modify, adapt. Apart from a few outsiders like Rousseau, they do not oppose radically different ideals and models to the dominant order, but reformed ideals and models of that order. In the words "false civilization" the whole difference from the German movement is contained. The French writers imply that the false civilization ought to be replaced by a genuine one. They do not oppose to the *homme civilisé* a radically different human model, as did the German bourgeois intelligentsia with the term *gebildeter Mensch* (educated man) and with the idea of the "personality"; instead, they pick up courtly models in order to develop and transform them. They address themselves to a critical intelligentsia which, directly or indirectly, is itself writing and struggling within the extensive network of court society.

II

Sociogenesis of Physiocratism and the French Reform Movement

4. Let us recall the situation of France after the middle of the eighteenth century.

The principles by which France was governed and on which, in particular, taxation and customs legislation was based were broadly the same as at Colbert's time. But the internal relationships of power and interest, the social structure of France itself, had shifted in crucial ways. Strict protectionism, the shielding of national manufacturing and commercial activity against foreign competition, had actually contributed decisively to the development of French economic life, and so to furthering what mattered more than anything else to the king and his representatives—the taxable capacity of the country. The barriers in the grain trade, monopolies, the granary system, and the customs walls between provinces had partly protected local interests but, above all, had from time to time preserved the district most important to the king's peace and perhaps to that of all France, Paris, from the extreme consequences of bad harvests and rising prices—starvation and revolt.

But in the meantime, the capital and the population of the country had increased. Compared to Colbert's time, the trade network had become denser and more extensive, industrial activity more vigorous, communications better, and the economic integration and inter-dependence of French territory closer. Sections of the bourgeoisie began to find the traditional taxation and customs systems, under whose protection they had grown up, irksome and absurd. Progressive country gentry and landowners like Mirabeau saw in the mercantilist restraints on the grain economy an impediment rather than an induce-ment to agricultural production; in this they profited not a little from the lessons of the freer English trading system. And most important of all, a section of the higher administrators themselves recognized the ill effects of the existing system; at their head was their most progressive type, the provincial intendants, the representatives of the single mod-ern form of bureaucracy which the *ancien régime* had produced, the only administrative function which was not, like the others, purchas-able and therefore hereditary. These progressive elements in the administration formed one of the most important bridges between the demand for reform making itself felt in the country, and the court. Directly or indirectly they played, in the struggle of court cliques for key political positions (primarily the ministries), a not inconsiderable part.

That these struggles were not yet the more impersonal, political conflicts they later became, when the various interests would be represented by parties within a parliamentary framework, has already been pointed out. But the courtly groups which, for the most diverse reasons, competed for influence and posts at the court were, at the same time, social nuclei through which the interests of broader groups and classes could find expression at the controlling center of the country. In this way reformist tendencies, too, were represented at court.

By the second half of the eighteenth century, the kings had long ceased to rule arbitrarily. Far more perceptibly than Louis XIV, for example, they were the prisoners of social processes and dependent on court cliques and factions, some of which extended far into the country and deep into middle-class circles.

Physiocratism is one of the theoretical expressions of these interfactional struggles. It is by no means confined to economics, being a large-scale system of political and social reform. It contains, in a pointed, abstract, and dogmatically hardened form, ideas which—expressed less theoretically, dogmatically, and rigorously, i.e., as practical demands for reform—characterize the whole movement of which Turgot, who was for a time in charge of finance, was an exponent. If this tendency (which had neither a name nor a unified organization) is to be given a name, it might be called the reformist bureaucracy. But these reformist administrators doubtless also had sections of the intelligentsia and of the commercial bourgeoisie behind them.

Among those desiring and demanding reform, moreover, there were considerable differences of opinion concerning the kind of reform that was needed. Some were wholly in favor of a reform of the taxation system and the state machinery, yet were far more protectionist than the Physiocrats, for example. Forbonnais is one of the leading representatives of this tendency, and it is to misunderstand him and like-minded people to include them, on account of their more strongly protectionist attitude, indiscriminately among the "mercantilists." The debate between Forbonnais and the Physiocrats was an early expression of a divergence within modern industrial society which was to lead to ever-recurring conflicts between the exponents of free trade and protectionism. Both sides are part of the middle-class reform movement.

On the other hand, it was by no means the case that the *whole* bourgeoisie desired reform while the aristocracy exclusively opposed it. There were a number of clearly definable middle-class groups which resisted to the utmost any serious attempt at reform, and whose existence was indeed bound up with the conservation of the *ancien régime* in its unreformed state. These groups included the majority of the higher administrators, the *noblesse de robe*, whose offices were family possessions in the same sense that a factory or business today is hereditary property. They also included the craft guilds and a good proportion of the financiers. And if reform failed in France, if the disproportions of society finally burst the institutional structure of the *ancien régime* violently asunder, the opposition of these middle-class groups to reform bears a large measure of responsibility.

This whole survey shows very clearly one thing which is important in this context: whereas the middle classes already played a political role in France at this time, in Germany they did not. In Germany the intellectual stratum is confined to the sphere of mind and ideas; in France, along with all the other human questions, social, economic, administrative, and political issues come within the range of interests of the courtly/middle-class intelligentsia. The German systems of thought, by contrast, are purely academic. Their social base is the university. The social base from which Physiocratism emerged is the court and court society, where intellectual effort has specific concrete aims, such as influencing the king or his mistress.

5. The basic ideas of Quesnay and the Physiocrats are well known. In his *Tableau économique* (1758), Quesnay depicts the economic life of society as a more or less autonomous process, a closed cycle of the production, circulation, and reproduction of commodities. He speaks of the natural laws of a social life in harmony with reason. Basing his argument on this idea, Quesnay opposes arbitrary intervention by rulers into the economic cycle. He wishes them to be aware of its laws in order to guide its processes, instead of issuing uninformed decrees at whim. He demands freedom of trade, particularly the grain trade, because self-regulation, the free play of forces, creates in his view a more beneficial order for consumers and producers than the traditional regulations from above and the countless trade barriers between province and province, country and country.

But he fully concedes that the self-regulating processes ought to be understood, and guided, by a wise and enlightened bureaucracy. Here, above all, lies the difference between the way in which the French reformers and the English reformers react to the discovery of self-regulation in economic life. Quesnay and his fellows remain wholly within the framework of the existing monarchic system. He leaves the basic elements of the *ancien régime* and its institutional structure untouched. And this applies all the more to the sections of the administration and intelligentsia whose position was close to his, and who, in a less abstract, less extreme, and more practically minded form, arrive at results similar to those of the central group of the Physiocrats. Fundamentally, the position common to all of them is extremely simple: roughly, it is not true that rulers are almighty and can regulate all human affairs as they think fit. Society and the economy have their own laws, which resist the irrational interference of rulers and force. Therefore an enlightened, rational administration must be created which governs in accordance with the "natural laws" of social processes, and thus in accordance with reason.

6. The term *civilisation* was, at the moment of its formation, a clear reflection of these reformist ideas. If in this term the idea of the *homme civilisé* leads to a concept designating the manners and condition of existing society as a whole, it is first and foremost an expression of insights derived from opposition, from social criticism. To this is added the realization that government cannot issue decrees at will, but is automatically resisted by anonymous social forces if its ordinances are not guided by an exact knowledge of these forces and laws; the realization that even the most absolute government is helpless in the face of the dynamisms of social development, and that disaster and chaos, misery and distress, are unleashed by arbitrary, "unnatural," "irrational" government. As already stated, this realization finds expression in the Physiocratic idea that social events, like natural phenomena, form part of an ordered process. This same realization manifests itself in the evolution of the earlier *civilisé* into the noun *civilisation*, helping to give it a meaning that transcends the individual.

The birth pangs of the industrial revolution, which could no longer be understood as the result of government, taught men, briefly and for the first time, to think of themselves and their social existence as a process. If we first pursue the use of the term *civilisation* in the work of Mirabeau, we see clearly how this discovery causes him to view the entire morality of his time in a new light. He comes to regard this morality, this "civilization" too as a cyclical manifestation, and wishes rulers to perceive its laws in order to use them. That is the meaning of the term *civilisation* at this early stage of its use.

In his *Ami des hommes*, Mirabeau argues in one place that a superfluity of money reduces population, so that consumption by each individual is increased. He considers that this excess of money, should it grow too large, "banishes industry and the arts, so casting states into poverty and depopulation." And he continues: "From this we perceive how the cycle from barbarism to decadence through civilization and wealth might be reversed by an alert and skillful minister, and the machine wound up again before it has run down."[28] This sentence really sums up all that was to become characteristic, in very general terms, of the fundamental standpoint of the Physiocrats: the conception of economy, population, and finally manners as an interrelated whole, developing cyclically; and the reformist political tendency which intends this knowledge finally for the rulers, to enable them, from an understanding of these laws, to guide social processes in a more enlightened and rational way than hitherto.

In Mirabeau's dedication of his *Théorie de l'impôt* to the king in 1760, in which he recommends to the monarch the Physiocratic plan for tax reform, exactly the same idea is still present: "The example of all the empires that have preceded yours, and which have run the circle of civilization, would be detailed evidence of what I have just advanced."

The critical attitude of Mirabeau, the landed nobleman, toward wealth, luxury, and the whole of prevailing manners gives his ideas a special tinge. Genuine civilization, he thinks, stands in a cycle between barbarism and a false, "decadent" civilization engendered by a superabundance of money. The task of enlightened government is to steer this automatism so that society can flourish on a middle course between barbarism and decadence. Here, the whole range of problems latent in "civilization" is already discernible at the moment of the concept's formation. Even at this stage it is connected to the idea of decadence or "decline," which has reemerged again and again, in an open or veiled form, to the rhythm of cyclical crises. But we can also see quite clearly that this desire for reform remains wholly within the framework of the existing social system manipulated from above, and that it does not oppose to what it criticizes in present manners an absolutely new image or concept, but instead takes its departure from the existing order, desiring to improve it: through skillful and enlightened measures by the government, "false civilization" shall again become a good and true civilization.

7. In this conception of civilization there may at first be many individual shades of meaning. But it contains elements corresponding to the general needs and experience of the reformist and progressive

circles of Parisian society. And the concept becomes all the more widely used in these circles the more the reform movement is accelerated by growing commercialization and industrialization.

The last period of Louis XV's reign is a time of visible debility and disorder in the old system. The internal and external tensions grow. The signals for social transformation multiply.

In 1773 tea chests are thrown into Boston harbor. In 1776 comes the Declaration of Independence by England's American colony: the government, it proclaims, is appointed to ensure the happiness of the people. Should it not succeed in this purpose, a majority of the people has the right to dismiss it.

The French middle-class circles sympathetic to reform observe what is happening across the sea with the utmost attention, and a sympathy in which their reformist social tendencies mingle with growing national hostility toward England, even though their leading minds are thinking of anything but an overthrow of the monarchy.

At the same time, from 1774 onward, there is a growing feeling that a confrontation with England is inevitable and that preparations must be made for war. In the same year, 1774, Louis XV dies. Under the new king the struggle for the reform of the administrative and taxation systems is immediately renewed with intensified force in both the narrower and the wider court circles. As a result of these conflicts, Turgot is welcomed in the same year as *contrôleur général des finances* by all the reformist and progressive elements in the country.

"At last the belated hour of justice has come," writes the Physiocrat Baudeau on Turgot's appointment. D'Alembert writes on the same occasion: "If good does not prevail now, it is because good is impossible." And Voltaire regrets being at the gates of death at the moment when he can observe "virtue and reason in their place."[29]

In the same years, *civilisation* appears for the first time as a widely used and more or less fixed concept. In the first edition of Raynal's *Histoire philosophique et politique des établissements et du commerce des Européens dans les deux Indes* (1770) the word does not occur once; in the second (1774) it is "used frequently and without any variation of meaning as an indispensable term that is obviously generally understood."[30]

Holbach's *Système de la nature* of 1770 does not yet contain the word *civilisation*. In his *Système sociale* of 1774, *civilisation* is used frequently. He says, for example, "There is nothing that places more obstacles in the way of public happiness, of the progress of human reason, of the entire civilization of men than the continual wars into which thoughtless princes are drawn at every moment."[31] Or, in another place: "Human reason is not yet sufficiently exercised; *the civilization of peoples is not yet complete*; obstacles without number have hitherto opposed the progress of useful knowledge, the advance of which can alone contribute to perfecting our government, our laws, our education, our institutions, and our morals."[32]

The concept underlying this enlightened, socially critical reform movement is always the same: that the improvement of institutions, education, and law will be brought about by the advance of knowledge. This does not mean "scholarship" in the eighteenth-century German sense, for the speakers are not university people but independent writers, officials, intellectuals, courtly citizens of the most diverse kind united through the medium of "good society," the *salons*. Progress will be achieved, therefore, first by the enlightenment of kings and rulers in conformity with "reason" or "nature," which come to the same thing, and then by placing in leading positions enlightened (i.e., reformist) men. A certain aspect of this whole progressive process of reform, came to be designated by a fixed concept: *civilisation*. What was visible in Mirabeau's individual version of the concept, which had not yet been polished by society, and what is characteristic of any reform movement is to be found here also: a half-affirmation and half-negation of the existing order. Society, from this point of view, has reached a particular stage on the road to civilization. But it is insufficient. Society cannot stand still there. The process continues and ought to be pushed further: "the civilization of peoples is not yet complete."

Two ideas are fused in the concept of civilization. On the one hand, it constitutes a general counterconcept to another stage of society, barbarism. This feeling had long pervaded courtly society. It had found its courtly-aristocratic expression in terms such as *politesse* or *civilité*.

But peoples are not yet civilized enough, say the men of the courtly/middle-class reform movement. Civilization is not only a state, it is a process which must be taken further. That is the new element expressed in the term *civilisation*. It absorbs much of what has always made court society believe itself, as compared to those living in a simpler, more uncivilized or more barbaric way, a higher kind of society: the idea of a standard of morals and manners, i.e., social tact, consideration for others, and many related complexes. But in the hands of the rising middle class, in the mouth of the reform movement, the idea of what is needed to make a society civilized is extended. The civilizing of the state, the constitution, education, and therefore of broader sections of the population, the liberation from all that was still barbaric or irrational in existing conditions, whether it be the legal penalties or the class restrictions on the bourgeoisie or the barriers impeding a freer development of trade—this civilizing must follow the refinement of manners and the internal pacification of the country by the kings.

"The king succeeded," Voltaire once said of the age of Louis XIV, "in making of a hitherto turbulent nation a peaceful people dangerous only to its enemies. . . . Manners were softened. . . ."[33] It will be seen in more detail later how important this internal pacification was for the civilizing process. Condorcet, however, who was by comparison to Voltaire a reformist of the younger generation and already far more inclined to opposition, comments as follows on this reflection of Voltaire's: "Despite the barbarity of some of the laws, despite the faults of the administrative principles, the increase in duties, their burdensome form, the harshness of fiscal laws, despite the pernicious maxims which direct the government's legislation on commerce and manufacture, and finally despite the persecution of the Protestants, one may observe that the peoples within the realm lived in peace under the protection of law."

This enumeration, itself not entirely without affirmation of the existing order, gives a picture of the many things thought in need of reform. Whether or not the term *civilisation* is here used explicitly, it relates to all this, everything which is still "barbaric."

This discussion makes very clear the divergence from developments in Germany and German concepts: it shows how members of the rising middle-class intelligentsia in France stand partly within the court circle, and so within the courtly-aristocratic tradition. They speak the language of this circle and develop it further. Their behavior and affects are, with certain modifications, modeled on the pattern of this tradition. Their concepts and ideas are by no means mere antitheses of those of the courtly aristocracy. Around courtly-aristocratic concepts such as the idea of "being civilized," they crystallize, in conformity with their social position within the court circle, further ideas from the area of their political and economic demands, ideas which, owing to the different social situation and range of experience of the German intelligentsia, were largely alien to it and at any rate far less relevant.

The French bourgeoisie—politically active, at least partly eager for reform, and even, for a short period, revolutionary—remained strongly bound to the courtly tradition in its behavior and its affect-molding even after the edifice of the old regime had been demolished. For through the close contact between aristocratic and middle-class circles, a great part of courtly manners had long before the revolution become middle-class manners. So it can be understood that the bourgeois revolution in France, though it destroyed the old political structure, did not disrupt the unity of traditional manners.

The German middle-class intelligentsia, politically entirely impotent but intellectually radical, forged a purely bourgeois tradition of its own, diverging widely from the courtly-aristocratic tradition and its models. The German national character which slowly emerged in the nineteenth century was not, to be sure, entirely lacking in aristocratic elements assimilated by the bourgeoisie. Nevertheless, for large areas of the German cultural tradition and German behavior, the specifically middle-class characteristics were predominant, particularly as the sharper social division between bourgeois and aristocratic circles, and with it a relative heterogeneity of German manners, survived long after the eighteenth century.

The French concept of *civilisation* reflects the specific social fortunes of the French bourgeoisie to exactly the same degree that the concept of *Kultur* reflects the German. The concept of *civilisation* is first, like *Kultur*, an instrument of middle-class circles—above all, the middle-class intelligentsia—in the internal social conflict. With the rise of the bourgeoisie, it too comes to epitomize the nation, to express the national self-image. In the revolution itself *civilisation* (which, of course, refers essentially to a gradual process, an evolution, and has not yet discarded its original meaning as a watchword of reform) does not play any considerable part among the revolutionary slogans. As the revolution grows more moderate, shortly before the turn of the century, it starts on its journey as a rallying cry throughout the world. Even as early as this, it has a level of meaning justifying French aspirations to national expansion and colonization. In 1798, as Napoleon sets off for Egypt, he shouts to his troops: ''Soldiers, you are undertaking a conquest with incalculable consequences for civilization." Unlike the situation when the concept was formed, from now on nations consider the *process* of civilization as completed within their own societies; they see themselves as bearers of an existing or finished civilization to others, as standard-bearers of expanding civilization. Of the whole preceding process of civilization nothing remains in their consciousness except a vague residue. Its outcome is taken simply as an expression of their own higher gifts; the fact that, and the question of how, in the course of many centuries, civilized behavior has been attained is of no interest. And the consciousness of their own superiority, the consciousness of this "civilization," from now on serves at least those nations which have become colonial conquerors, and therefore a kind of upper class to large sections of the non-European world, as a justification of their rule, to the same degree that earlier the ancestors of the concept of civilization, *politesse* and *civilité*, had served the courtly-aristocratic upper class as a justification of theirs.

Indeed, an essential phase of the civilizing process was concluded at exactly the time when the *consciousness* of civilization, the consciousness of the superiority of their own behavior and its embodiments in science, technology, or art began to spread over whole nations of the West.

This earlier phase of the civilizing process, the phase in which the consciousness of the process scarcely existed and the concept of civilization did not exist at all, will be discussed in the following chapter.

Chapter Two
Civilization as a Specific Transformation of Human Behavior

I

The Development of the Concept of Civilité

1. The decisive antithesis expressing the self-image of the West during the Middle Ages is that between Christianity and paganism or, more exactly, between correct, Roman-Latin Christianity, on the one hand, and paganism and heresy, including Greek and Eastern Christianity, on the other.[1]

In the name of the Cross, and later in that of civilization, Western society wages, during the Middle Ages, its wars of colonization and expansion. And for all its secularization, the watchword "civilization" always retains an echo of Latin Christendom and the knightly-feudal crusade. The memory that chivalry and the Roman-Latin faith bear witness to a particular stage of Western society, a stage which all the major Western peoples have passed through, has certainly not disappeared.

The concept of *civilité* acquired its meaning for Western society at a time when chivalrous society and the unity of the Catholic church were disintegrating. It is the incarnation of a society which, as a specific stage in the formation of Western manners or "civilization," was no less important than the feudal society before it. The concept of *civilité*, too, is an expression and symbol of a social formation embracing the most diverse nationalities, in which, as in the Church, a common language is spoken, first Italian and then increasingly French. These languages take over the function earlier performed by Latin. They manifest the unity of Europe, and at the same time the new social formation which forms its backbone, court society. The situation, the self-image, and the characteristics of this society find expression in the concept of *civilité*.

2. The concept of *civilité* received the specific stamp and function under discussion here in the second quarter of the sixteenth century. Its individual starting point can be exactly determined. It owes the specific meaning adopted by society to a short treatise by Erasmus of Rotterdam, *De civilitate morum puerilium* (On civility in children),

---

which appeared in 1530. This work clearly treated a theme that was ripe for discussion. It immediately achieved an enormous circulation, going through edition after edition. Even within Erasmus's lifetime—that is, in the first six years after its publication—it was reprinted more than thirty times.[2] In all, more than 130 editions may be counted, 13 of them as late as the eighteenth century. The multitude of translations, imitations, and sequels is almost without limit. Two years after the publication of the treatise the first English translation appeared. In 1534 it was published in catechism form, and at this time it was already being introduced as a schoolbook for the education of boys. German and Czech translations followed. In 1537, 1559, 1569, and 1613 it appeared in French, newly translated each time.

As early as the sixteenth century a particular French type face was given the name *civilité*, after a French work by Mathurin Cordier which combined doctrines from Erasmus's treatise with those of another humanist, Johannes Sulpicius. And a whole genre of books, directly or indirectly influenced by Erasmus's treatise, appeared under the title *Civilité* or *Civilité puérile*; these were printed up to the end of the eighteenth century in this *civilité* type.[3]

3. Here, as so often in the history of words, and as was to happen later in the evolution of the concept *civilité* into *civilisation*, an individual was the instigator. By his treatise, Erasmus gave new sharpness and impetus to the long-established and commonplace word *civilitas*. Wittingly or not, he obviously expressed in it something that met a social need of the time. The concept *civilitas* was henceforth fixed in the consciousness of people with the special sense it received from his treatise. And corresponding words were developed in the various popular languages: the French *civilité*, the English "civility," the Italian *civiltà*, and the German *Zivilität*, which, admittedly, was never so widely adopted as the corresponding words in the other great cultures.

The more or less sudden emergence of words within languages nearly always points to changes in the lives of people themselves, particularly when the new concepts are destined to become as central and long-lived as these.

Erasmus himself may not have attributed any particular importance to his short treatise *De civilitate morum puerilium* within his total *oeuvre*. He says in the introduction that the art of forming young people involves various disciplines, but that the *civilitas morum* is only one of them, and he does not deny that it is *crassissima philosophiae pars* (the grossest part of philosophy). This treatise has its special importance less as an individual phenomenon or work than as a symptom of change, an embodiment of social processes. Above all, it is the resonance, the elevation of the title word to a central expression of the self-interpretation of European society, which draws our attention to this treatise.

4. What is the treatise about? Its theme must explain to us for what purpose and in what sense the new concept was needed. It must contain indications of the social changes and processes which made the word fashionable.

Erasmus's book is about something very simple: the behavior of people in society—above all, but not solely, "outward bodily propriety." It is dedicated to a noble boy, a prince's son, and written for the instruction of boys. It contains simple thoughts delivered with great seriousness, yet at the same time with much mockery and irony, in clear, polished language and with enviable precision. It can be said that none of its successors ever equaled this treatise in force, clarity, and personal character. Looking more closely, one perceives beyond it a world and a pattern of life which in many respects, to be sure, are close to our own, yet in others still quite remote; the treatise points to attitudes that we have lost, that some among us would perhaps call "barbaric" or "uncivilized." It speaks of many things that have in the meantime become unspeakable, and of many others that are now taken for granted.[4]

Erasmus speaks, for example, of the way people look. Though his comments are meant as instruction, they also bear witness to the direct and lively observation of people of which he was capable. "Sint oculi placidi, verecundi, compositi," he says, "non torvi, quod est truculentiae . . . non vagi ac volubiles, quod est insaniae, non limi quod est suspiciosorum et insidias molentium. . . ." This can only with difficulty be translated without an appreciable alteration of tone: a wide-eyed look is a sign of stupidity, staring a sign of inertia; the looks of those prone to anger are too sharp; too lively and eloquent those of the immodest; if your look shows a calm mind and a respectful amiability, that is best. Not by chance do the ancients say: the seat of the soul is in the eyes. "Animi sedem esse in oculis."

Bodily carriage, gestures, dress, facial expressions—this "outward" behavior with which the treatise concerns itself is the expression of the inner, the whole man. Erasmus knows this and on occasion states it explicitly: "Although this outward bodily propriety proceeds from a well-composed mind, nevertheless we sometimes find that, for want of instruction, such grace is lacking in excellent and learned men."

There should be no snot on the nostrils, he says somewhat later. A peasant wipes his nose on his cap and coat, a sausage maker on his arm and elbow. It does not show much more propriety to use one's hand and then wipe it on one's clothing. It is more decent to take up the snot in a cloth, preferably while turning away. If when blowing the nose with two fingers somethings falls to the ground, it must be immediately trodden away with the foot. The same applies to spittle.

With the same infinite care and matter-of-factness with which these things are said—the mere mention of which shocks the "civilized" man of a later stage with a different affective molding—we are told how one ought to sit or greet. Gestures are described that have become strange to us, e.g., standing on one leg. And we might reflect that many of the bizarre movements of walkers and dancers that we see in medieval paintings or statues not only represent the "manner" of the painter or sculptor but also preserve actual gestures and movements that have grown strange to us, embodiments of a different mental and emotional structure.

The more one immerses oneself in the little treatise, the clearer becomes this picture of a society with modes of behavior in some respects related to ours, and in many ways remote. We see people seated at table: "A dextris sit poculum, et cultellus escarius rite purgatus, ad laevam panis," says Erasmus. The goblet and the well-cleaned knife on the right, on the left the bread. That is how the table is laid. Most people carry a knife, hence the precept to keep it clean. Forks scarcely exist, or at most for taking meat from the dish. Knives and spoons are very often used communally. There is not always a special implement for everyone: if you are offered something liquid, says Erasmus, taste it and return the spoon after you have wiped it.

When dishes of meat are brought in, usually everyone cuts himself a piece, takes it in his hand, and puts it on his plate if there are plates, otherwise on a thick slice of bread. The expression *quadra* used by Erasmus can clearly mean either a metal plate or a slice of bread.

"Quidam ubi vix bene considerint mox manus in epulas conjiciunt." Some put their hands into the dishes when they are scarcely seated, says Erasmus. Wolves or gluttons do that. Do not be the first to take from a dish that is brought in. Leave dipping your fingers into the broth to the peasants. Do not poke around in the dish but take the first piece that presents itself. And just as it shows a want of forbearance to search the whole dish with one's hand— "in omnes patinae plagas manum mittere"—neither is it very polite to turn the dish round so that a better piece comes to you. What you cannot take with your hands, take on your *quadra*. If someone passes you a piece of cake or pastry with a spoon, either take it with your *quadra* or take the spoon offered to you, put the food on the *quadra*, and return the spoon.

As has been mentioned, plates too are uncommon. Paintings of table scenes from this or earlier times always offer the same spectacle, unfamiliar to us, that is indicated by Erasmus's treatise. The table is sometimes covered with rich cloths, sometimes not, but always there is little on it: drinking vessels, saltcellar, knives, spoons, that is all. Sometimes we see the slices of bread, the *quadrae*, that in French are called *tranchoir* or *tailloir*. Everyone, from the king and queen to the peasant and his wife, eats with the hands. In the upper class there are more refined forms of this. One ought to wash one's hands before a meal, says Erasmus. But there is as yet no soap for this purpose. Usually the guest holds out his hands, and a page pours water over them. The water is sometimes slightly scented with chamomile or rosemary.[5] In good society one does not put both hands into the dish. It is most refined to use only three fingers of the hand. This is one of the marks of distinction between the upper and lower classes.

The fingers become greasy. "Digitos unctos vel ore praelingere vel ad tunicam extergere . . . incivile est," says Erasmus. It is not polite to lick them or wipe them on one's coat. Often you offer others your glass, or all drink from a communal tankard. Erasmus admonishes: "Wipe your mouth beforehand." You may want to offer someone you like some of the meat you are eating. "Refrain from that," says Erasmus, "it is not very decorous to offer something half-eaten to another." And he says further: "To dip bread you have bitten into the sauce is to behave like a peasant, and it shows little elegance to remove chewed food from the mouth and put it back on the *quadra*. If you cannot swallow a piece of food, turn round discreetly and throw it somewhere."

Then he says again: "It is good if conversation interrupts the meal from time to time. Some people eat and drink without stopping, not because they are hungry or thirsty, but because they can control their movements in no other way. They have to scratch their heads, poke their teeth, gesticulate with their hands, or play with a knife, or they can't help coughing, snorting, and spitting. All this really comes from a rustic embarrassment and looks like a form of madness."

But it is also necessary, and possible, for Erasmus to say: Do not expose without necessity "the parts to which Nature has attached modesty." Some prescribe, he says, that boys should "retain the wind by compressing the belly." But you can contract an illness that way. And in another place: "Reprimere sonitum, quem natura fert, ineptorum est, qui plus tribuunt civilitati, quam saluti" (Fools who value civility more than health repress natural sounds.) Do not be afraid of vomiting if you must; "for it is not vomiting but holding the vomit in your throat that is foul."

5. With great care Erasmus marks out in his treatise the whole range of human conduct, the chief situations of social and convivial life. He speaks with the same matter-of-factness of the most elementary as of the subtlest questions of human intercourse. In the first chapter he treats "the seemly and unseemly condition of the whole body," in the second "bodily culture," in the third "manners at holy places," in the fourth banquets, in the fifth meetings, in the sixth amusement, and in the seventh the bedchamber. This is the range of questions in the discussion of which Erasmus gave new impetus to the concept of *civilitas*.

Not always is our consciousness able to recall this other stage of our own history without hesitation. The unconcerned frankness with which Erasmus and his time could discuss all areas of human conduct is lost to us. Much of what he says oversteps our threshold of delicacy.

But precisely this is one of the problems to be considered here. In tracing the transformation of the concepts by which different societies have tried to express themselves, in following back the concept of civilization to its ancestor *civilité*, one finds oneself suddenly on the track of the civilizing process itself, of the actual change in behavior that took place in the West. That it is embarrassing for us to speak or even hear of much that Erasmus discusses is one of the symptoms of this civilizing process. The greater or lesser discomfort we feel toward people who discuss or mention their bodily functions more openly, who conceal and restrain these functions less than we do, is one of the dominant feelings expressed in the judgment "barbaric" or "uncivilized." Such, then, is the nature of "barbarism and its discontents" or, in more precise and less evaluative terms, the discontent with the different structure of affects, the different standard of repugnance which is still to be found today in many societies which we term "uncivilized," the standard of repugnance which preceded our own and is its precondition. The question arises as to how and why Western society actually moved from one standard to the other, how it was "civilized." In considering this process of civilization, we cannot avoid arousing feelings of discomfort and embarrassment. It is valuable to be aware of them. It is necessary, at least while considering this process, to attempt to suspend all the feelings of embarrassment and superiority, all the value judgments and criticism associated with the concepts "civilization" or "uncivilized." Our kind of behavior has grown out of that which we call uncivilized. But these concepts grasp the actual change too statically and coarsely. In reality, our terms "civilized" and "uncivilized" do not constitute an antithesis of the kind that exists between "good" and "bad," but represent stages in a development which, moreover, is still continuing. It might well happen that our stage of civilization, our behavior, will arouse in our descendants feelings of embarrassment similar to those we sometimes feel concerning the behavior of our ancestors. Social behavior and the expression of emotions passed from a form and a standard which was not a beginning, which could not in any absolute and undifferentiated sense be designated "uncivilized," to our own, which we denote by the word "civilized." And to understand the latter we must go back in time to that from which it emerged. The "civilization" which we are accustomed to regard as a possession that comes to us apparently ready-made, without our asking how we actually came to possess it, is a process or part of a process in which we are ourselves involved. Every particular characteristic that we attribute to it—machinery, scientific discovery, forms of state, or whatever else—bears witness to a particular structure of human relations, to a particular social structure, and to the corresponding forms of behavior. The question remains whether the change in behavior, in the social process of the "civilization" of man, can be understood, at least in isolated phases and in its elementary features, with any degree of precision.

II

On Medieval Manners

1. In Erasmus of Rotterdam's *De civilitate morum puerilium* a particular kind of social behavior is discernible. Even here, the simple antithesis of "civilized" and "uncivilized" hardly applies.

What came before Erasmus? Was he the first to concern himself with such matters?

By no means. Similar questions occupied the men of the Middle Ages, of Greco-Roman antiquity, and doubtless also of the related, preceding "civilizations."

This process that has no beginning cannot here be traced back indefinitely. Wherever we start, there is movement, something that went before. Limits must necessarily be set to a retrospective inquiry, preferably corresponding to the phases of the process itself. Here the medieval standard must suffice as a starting point, without itself being closely examined, so that the movement, the developmental curve joining it to the modern age may be pursued.

The Middle Ages have left us an abundance of information on what was considered socially acceptable behavior. Here, too, precepts on conduct while eating had a special importance. Eating and drinking then occupied a far more central position in social life than today, when they provide—frequently, not always—rather the framework and introduction for conversation and conviviality.

Learned ecclesiastics sometimes set down, in Latin, precepts for behavior that testify to the standard of their society. Hugh of St. Victor (d. 1141), in his *De institutione novitiarum*, is concerned with these questions among others. The baptized Spanish Jew Petrus Alphonsi deals with them in his *Disciplina clericalis* of the early twelfth century; Johannes von Garland devotes to manners, and particularly to table manners, a number of the 662 Latin verses bearing the title *Morale scolarium* of 1241.

Besides these precepts on behavior from the Latin-speaking clerical society, there are, from about the thirteenth century on, corresponding documents in the various lay languages—above all, at first, from the courts of the warrior nobility.

The earliest records of the manners prevalent in the secular upper class are doubtless those from Provence and neighboring, culturally related Italy. The earliest German work on *courtoisie* is also by an Italian, Thomasin von Zirklaria, and is called *The Italian Guest* (*Der wälsche Gast*, put into modern German by Rückert). Another such writing by Thomasin, in Italian, transmits to us in its German title an early form of the concept of "courtesy" (*Höflichkeit*). He refers to this book, which has been lost, as a "buoch von der hüfscheit."

Originating from the same knightly-courtly circles are the fifty *Courtesies* by Bonvicino da Riva and the *Hofzucht* (Courtly manners) attributed to Tannhäuser. Such precepts are also occasionally found in the great epic poems of chivalrous society, e.g., the *Roman de la rose*[6] of the fourteenth century. John Russell's *Book of Nurture*, written in English verse probably in the fifteenth century, already gives a complete compendium of behavior for the young nobleman in the service of a great lord, as does more briefly *The Babees Book*.[7]

In addition there is, primarily in fourteenth- or fifteenth-century versions but probably, in part, older in substance, a whole series of poems designed as mnemonics to inculcate table manners, *Tischzuchten* of varying length and in the most diverse languages. Learning by heart as a means of educating or conditioning played a far greater part in medieval society, where books were comparatively rare and expensive, than it does today, and these rhymed precepts were one of the means used to try to impress on people's memories what they should and should not do in society, above all at table.

2. These *Tischzuchten*, or table disciplines, like medieval writings on manners of known authorship, are not individual products in the modern sense, records of the personal ideas of particular people within an extensively individualized society. What has come down to us in writing are fragments of a great oral tradition, reflections of what actually was customary in that society; these fragments are significant precisely because they transmit not the great or the extraordinary but the typical aspects of society. Even poems handed down under a specific name, like Tannhäuser's *Hofzucht* or John Russell's *Book of Nurture*, are nothing other than individual versions of one of the many strands of tradition corresponding to the structure of this society. Those who wrote them down were not the legislators or creators of these precepts but collectors, arrangers of the commands and taboos customary in society; for this reason, whether or not there is a literary connection, similar precepts recur in almost all these writings. They

are reflections of the same customs, testimonies to a particular hand-book of behavior and emotions in the life of society itself.

It is perhaps possible on closer examination to discover certain differences of customs between individual national traditions, and variations in the social standards. Perhaps the material may also reveal certain changes within the same tradition. It appears, for example, that the tenor and perhaps also the customs of society underwent certain changes in the fourteenth or fifteenth century with the rise of guild and burgher elements, much as in modern times behavior-models originating in the court aristocracy here adopted in bourgeois circles.

A closer study of these modifications within medieval behavior remains to be carried out. It must suffice here to note them, bearing in mind that this medieval standard is not without inner movement and certainly is not a beginning or "bottom rung" of the process of civilization, nor does it represent, as has sometimes been asserted, the stage of "barbarism" or "primitiveness."

It was a different standard from our own—whether better or worse is not here at issue. And if, in our *recherche du temps perdu*, we have been led back step by step from the eighteenth to the sixteenth and from the sixteenth to the thirteenth and twelfth centuries, this does not imply that we are, as already stated, in anticipation of finding the "beginning" of the process of civilization. It is a sufficient task to present purposes, to take the short journey from the medieval to the early modern stage in an attempt to understand what actually happened to human beings in this transition.

3. The standard of "good behavior" in the Middle Ages is, like all later standards, represented by a quite definite concept. Through it the secular upper class of the Middle Ages, or at least some of its leading groups, gave expression to their self-image, to what, in their own estimation, made them exceptional. The concept epitomizing aristocratic self-consciousness and socially acceptable behavior appeared in French as *courtoisie*, in English "courtesy," in Italian *cortezia*, along with other related terms, often in divergent forms. In German it was, likewise in different versions, *hövescheit* or *hübescheit* and also *zuht*. All these concepts refer quite directly (and far more overtly than later ones with the same function) to a particular place in society. They say: That is how people behave at court. By these terms certain leading groups in the secular upper stratum, which does not mean the

knightly class as a whole, but primarily the courtly circles around the great feudal lords, designated what distinguished them in their own eyes, namely the specific code of behavior that has first formed at the great feudal courts, then spread to rather broader strata; this process of differentiation may, however, be disregarded here. Measured against later periods, the great uniformity in the good and bad manners referred to—what is called here a particular "standard"—is especially impressive.

What is this standard like? What emerges as typical behavior, as the pervasive character of its precepts?

Something, in the first place, that in comparison to later times might be called its simplicity, its naïveté. There are, as in all societies where the emotions are expressed more violently and directly, fewer psychological nuances and complexities in the general stock of ideas. There are friend and foe, desire and aversion, good and bad people.

> You should follow honorable men and vent your wrath on the wicked.

We read this in a German translation of the *Disticha Catonis*,[8] the code of behavior encountered throughout the Middle Ages under the name of Cato. Or in another place:

> When your companions anger you, my son, see that you are not so hot-tempered that you regret it afterward.[9]

In eating, too, everything is simpler, impulses and inclinations are less restrained:

> A man of refinement should not slurp with his spoon when in company; this is the way people at court behave who often indulge in unrefined conduct.

This is from Tannhäuser's *Hofzucht*.[10] *Hübsche Leute* (fine people) are the nobles, the courtly people. The precepts of the *Hofzucht* are meant expressly for the upper class, the knights who lived at court. Noble, courteous behavior is constantly contrasted to "coarse manners," the conduct of peasants.

> Some people bite a slice and then dunk it in the dish in a coarse way; refined people reject such bad manners.[11]

If you have taken a bite from the bread, do not dip it in the common dish again. Peasants may do that, not "fine people."

> A number of people gnaw a bone and then put it back in the dish—this is a serious offense.[12]

Do not throw gnawed bones back into the communal dish. From other accounts we know that it was customary to drop them on the floor. Another precept reads:

> A man who clears his throat when he eats and one who blows his nose in the tablecloth are both ill-bred, I assure you.[13]

Here is another:

> If a man wipes his nose on his hand at table because he knows no better, then he is a fool, believe me.[14]

To use the hand to wipe one's nose was a matter of course. Handkerchiefs did not yet exist. But at table a certain care should be exercised; and one should on no account blow one's nose into the tablecloth. Avoid lip-smacking and snorting, eaters are further instructed:

> If a man snorts like a seal when he eats, as some people do, and smacks his chops like a Bavarian yokel, he has given up all good breeding.[15]

If you have to scratch yourself, do not do so with your bare hand but use your coat:

> Do not scrape your throat with your bare hand while eating; but if you have to, do it politely with your coat.[16]

Everyone used his hands to take food from the common dish. For this reason one was not to touch one's ears, nose, or eyes:

> It is not decent to poke your fingers into your ears or eyes, as some people do, or to pick your nose while eating. These three habits are bad.[17]

Hands must be washed before meals:

I hear that some eat unwashed (if it is true, it is a bad sign). May their fingers be palsied![18]

And in *Ein spruch der ze tische kêrt* (A word to those at table)[19] another *Tischzucht* of which Tannhäuser's *Hofzucht* has many echoes, it is demanded that one eat with only one hand, and if one is eating from the same plate or slice of bread as another, as often happened, with the outside hand:

> You should always eat with the outside hand; if your companion sits on your right, eat with your left hand. Refrain from eating with both hands.[20]

If you have no towel, we read in the same work, do not wipe your hands on your coat but let the air dry them.[21] Or:

> Take care that, whatever your need, you do not flush with embarrassment.[22]

Nor is it good manners to loosen one's belt at table.[23]

All this is said to adults, not only to children. To our minds these are very elementary precepts to be given to upper-class people, more elementary in many respects than what, at the present stage of behavior, is generally accepted as the norm in rural-peasant strata. And the same standard emerges with certain variations from the *courtois* writings of other linguistic areas.

4. In the case of one of these different strands of tradition, which leads from certain Latin forms primarily to French, but perhaps also to Italian and to a Provençal code of table manners, a compilation has been made of the rules recurring in most or all of the variants.[24] They are by and large the same as in the German *Tischzuchten*. First there is the instruction to say grace, which is also found in Tannhäuser. Again and again we find the injunctions to take one's allotted place and not to touch nose and ears at table. Do not put your elbow on the table, they often say. Show a cheerful countenance. Do not talk too much. There are very frequent reminders not to scratch oneself or fall greedily on the food. Nor should one put a piece that one has had in one's mouth back into the communal dish; this, too, is often repeated. Not less frequent is the instruction to wash one's hands before eating, or not to dip food into the saltcellar. Then it is repeated over and over again: do not clean your teeth with your knife. Do not spit on or over the table.

Do not ask for more from a dish that has already been taken away. Do not let yourself go at table is a frequent command. Wipe your lips before you drink. Say nothing disparaging about the meal nor anything that might irritate others. If you have dipped bread into the wine, drink it up or pour the rest away. Do not clean your teeth with the tablecloth. Do not offer others the remainder of your soup or the bread you have already bitten into. Do not blow your nose too noisily. Do not fall asleep at table. And so on.

Indications of the same code of good and bad manners are also found in other collections of related mnemonic verses on etiquette, in traditions not directly related to the French one just mentioned. All bear witness to a certain standard of relationships between people, to the structure of medieval society and of the medieval psyche. The similarities between these collections are sociogenetic and psychogenetic; there may but need not be a literary relationship between all these French, English, Italian, German, and Latin precepts. The differences between them are less significant than the common features, which correspond to the unity of actual behavior in the medieval upper class, measured against the modern period.

For example, the *Courtesies* of Bonvicino da Riva, one of the most personal and—in keeping with Italian development—most "advanced" of table guides, contains, apart from the precepts mentioned from the French collection, the instructions to turn round when coughing and sneezing, and not to lick one's fingers. One should, he says, refrain from searching out the best pieces in the dish, and cut the bread decently. One should not touch the rim of the communal glass with one's fingers, and one should hold the glass with both hands. But here, too, the tenor of *courtoisie*, the standard, the customs are by and large the same. And it is not uninteresting that when Bonvicino da Riva's *Courtesies* were revised three centuries after him, of all the rules given by Da Riva only two not very important ones were altered: the editor advises not to touch the edge of the communal glass and to hold it with both hands, and if several are drinking from the same glass, one should refrain altogether from dipping bread into it (Da Riva only required that the wine thus used should be tipped away or drunk).[25]

A similar picture could be drawn from the German tradition. German *Tischzuchten*, of which we have copies from the fifteenth century, are perhaps somewhat coarser in tone than the *Italian Guest* of Thomasin von Zirklaria or Tannhäuser's *Hofzucht* from the thirteenth century. But the standard of good and bad manners seems scarcely to have altered to any considerable extent. It has been pointed out that in one of the later codes which has much in common with the earlier ones already mentioned, the new injunction appears that one should spit not on the table but only under it or against the wall. And this has been interpreted as a symptom of a coarsening of manners. But it is more than questionable whether things were done very differently in the preceding centuries, particularly as similar precepts from earlier periods are transmitted by the French tradition, for example. And what is to be derived from literature in the broadest sense is confirmed by paintings. Here, too, more detailed studies are needed; but compared to the later age, pictures of people at table show, until well into the fifteenth century, very sparse table utensils, even if, in some details, certain changes are undoubtedly present. In the houses of the more wealthy, the platters are usually taken from the sideboard, frequently in no particular order. Everyone takes—or sends for—what he fancies at the moment. People help themselves from communal dishes. Solids (above all, meat) are taken by hand, liquids with ladles or spoons. But soups and sauces are still very frequently drunk. Plates and dishes are lifted to the mouth. For a long period, too, there are no special implements for different foods. The same knife or spoon is used. The same glasses are drunk from. Frequently two diners eat from the same board.

This is, if it may so be called, the standard eating technique during the Middle Ages, which corresponds to a very particular standard of human relationships and structure of feeling. Within this standard there is, as has been said, an abundance of modifications and nuances. If people of different rank are eating at the same time, the person of higher rank is given precedence when washing hands, for example, or when taking from the dish. The forms of utensils vary considerably in the course of centuries. There are fashions, but also a very definite trend that persists through the fluctuations of fashion. The secular upper class, for example, indulges in extraordinary luxury at table. It is not a poverty of utensils that maintains the standard, it is quite simply that nothing else is needed. To eat in this fashion is taken for granted. It suits these people. But it also suits them to make visible their wealth and rank by the opulence of their utensils and table decoration. At the rich tables of the thirteenth century the spoons are of gold, crystal, coral, ophite. It is occasionally mentioned that during

Lent knives with ebony handles are used, at Easter knives with ivory handles, and inlaid knives at Whitsun. The soupspoons are round and rather flat to begin with, so that one is forced when using them to open one's mouth wide. From the fourteenth century onward, soupspoons take on an oval form.

At the end of the Middle Ages the fork appears as an instrument for taking food from the common dish. A whole dozen forks are to be found among the valuables of Charles V. The inventory of Charles of Savoyen, which is very rich in opulent table utensils, counts only a single fork.[26]

5. It is sometimes said, "How far we have progressed beyond this standard," although it is not usually quite clear who is the "we" with whom the speaker identifies himself on such occasions, as if he deserved part of the credit.

The opposite judgment is also possible: "What has really changed? A few customs, no more." And some observers seem inclined to judge these customs in much the same way as one would today judge children: "If a man of sense had come and told these people that their practices were unappetizing and unhygienic, if they had been taught to eat with knives and forks, these bad manners would rapidly have disappeared."

But conduct while eating cannot be isolated. It is a segment—a very characteristic one—of the totality of socially instilled forms of conduct. Its standard corresponds to a quite definite social structure. It remains to be ascertained what this structure is. The behavior of medieval people was no less tightly bound to their total way of life, to the whole structure of their existence, than our own behavior and social code are bound to ours.

At times, some minor statement shows how firmly rooted these customs were, and makes it apparent that they must be understood not merely as something "negative," as a "lack of civilization" or of "knowledge" (as it is easy to suppose from our standpoint), but as something that fitted the needs of these people and that seemed meaningful and necessary to them in exactly this form.

In the eleventh century a Venetian doge married a Greek princess. In her Byzantine circle the fork was clearly in use. At any rate, we hear that she lifted food to her mouth "by means of little golden forks with two prongs."[27]

This gave rise in Venice to a dreadful scandal: "This novelty was regarded as so excessive a sign of refinement that the dogaressa was severely rebuked by the ecclesiastics who called down divine wrath upon her. Shortly afterward she was afflicted by a repulsive illness and St. Bonaventure did not hesitate to declare that this was a punishment of God.''

Five more centuries were to pass before the structure of human relations had so changed that the use of this instrument met a more general need. From the sixteenth century on, at least among the upper classes, the fork comes into use as an eating instrument, arriving by way of Italy first in France and then in England and Germany, after having served for a time only for taking solid foods from the dish. Henri III brought it to France, probably from Venice. His courtiers were not a little derided for this "affected" manner of eating, and at first they were not very adept in the use of the instrument: at least it was said that half the food fell off the fork as it traveled from plate to mouth. As late as the seventeenth century the fork was still essentially a luxury article of the upper class, usually made of gold or silver. What we take entirely for granted, because we have been adapted and conditioned to this social standard from earliest childhood, had first to be slowly and laboriously acquired and developed by society as a whole. This applies to such a small and seemingly insignificant thing as a fork no less than to forms of behavior that appear to us larger and more important.[28]

However, the attitude that has just been described toward the "innovation" of the fork shows one thing with special clarity. People who ate together in the way customary in the Middle Ages, taking meat with their fingers from the same dish, wine from the same goblet, soup from the same pot or the same plate, with all the other peculiarities of which examples have been and will further be given— such people stood in a different relationship to one another than we do. And this involves not only the level of clear, rational consciousness; their emotional life also had a different structure and character. Their affects were conditioned to forms of relationship and conduct which, by today's standard of conditioning, are embarrassing or at least unattractive. What was lacking in this *courtois* world, or at least had not been developed to the same degree, was the invisible wall of affects which seems now to rise between one human body and another, repelling and separating, the hall which is often perceptible today at the mere approach of something that has been in contact with

---

the mouth or hands of someone else, and which manifests itself as embarrassment at the mere sight of many bodily functions of others, and often at their mere mention, or as a feeling of shame when one's own functions are exposed to the gaze of others, and by no means only then.

III

The Problem of the Change in Behavior during the Renaissance

1. Were the thresholds of embarrassment and shame raised at the time of Erasmus? Does his treatise contain indications that the frontiers of sensibility and the reserve which they expected of each other were increasing? There are good reasons for supposing so. The humanists' works on manners form a kind of bridge between those of the Middle Ages and modern times. Erasmus's treatise, the high point in the succession of humanist writings on manners, also has this double face. In many respects it stands entirely within medieval tradition. A good part of the rules and precepts from the *courtois* writings recur in his treatise. But at the same time, it clearly contains the beginnings of something new. In it a concept is gradually developing which was to force the knightly-feudal concept of courtesy into the background. In the course of the sixteenth century the use of the concept of *courtoisie* slowly recedes in the upper class, while *civilité* grows more common and finally gains the upper hand, at least in France, in the seventeenth century.

This is a sign of a behavioral change of considerable proportions. It did not take place, of course, in such a way that one ideal of good behavior was suddenly opposed by another radically different to it. The *De civilitate morum puerilium* of Erasmus—to confine the discussion to this work for the time being—stands in many respects, as we have said, entirely within medieval tradition. Almost all the rules of *courtois* society reappear in it. Meat is still eaten with the hand, even if Erasmus stresses that it should be picked up with three fingers, not the whole hand. The precept not to fall upon the meal like a glutton is also repeated, as are the direction to wash one's hands before dining and the strictures on spitting, blowing the nose, the use of the knife, and many others. It may be that Erasmus knew one or another of the rhymed *Tischzuchten* or the clerical writings in which such questions were treated. Many of these writings were no doubt in wide circulation; it is unlikely that they escaped Erasmus. More precisely demonstrable is his relation to the heritage of antiquity. In the case of this treatise, it was partly shown by the commentaries of his contemporaries. Its place in the rich humanist discussion of these problems of education and propriety remains to be examined in more detail.[29] But whatever the literary interconnections may be, of primary interest in this context are the sociogenetic ones. Erasmus certainly did not merely compile this treatise from other books; like anyone who reflects on such questions, he had a particular social code, a particular standard of manners directly before his eyes. This treatise on manners is a collection of observations from the life of his society. It is, as someone said later, "a little the work of everyone." And if nothing else, its success, its rapid dissemination, and its use as an educational manual for boys show how much it met a social need, and how it recorded the models of behavior for which the time was ripe, which society—or, more exactly, the upper class first of all—demanded.

2. Society was "in transition." So, too, were works on manners. Even in the tone, the manner of seeing, we feel that despite all their attachment to the Middle Ages something new is on the way. "Simplicity" as we experience it, the simple opposition of "good" and "bad," "pious" and "wicked," has been lost. People see things with more differentiation, i.e., with a stronger restraint of their emotions.

It is not so much, or at least not exclusively, the rules themselves or the manners to which they refer that distinguish a part of the humanistic writings—above all, the treatise of Erasmus—from the *courtois* codes. It is first of all their tone, their way of seeing. The same social rules which in the Middle Ages were passed impersonally from mouth to mouth are now spoken in the manner and with the emphasis of someone who is not merely passing on tradition, no matter how many medieval and, above all, ancient writings he may have absorbed, but who has observed all this personally, who is recording experience.

Even if this were not seen in *De civilitate morum puerilium* itself, we should know it from Erasmus's earlier writings, in which the permeation of medieval and ancient tradition with his own experience is expressed perhaps more clearly and directly. In his *Colloquies*, which in part certainly draw on ancient models (above all, Lucian), and particularly in the dialogue *Diversoria* (Basel, 1523), Erasmus describes directly experiences elaborated in the later treatise.

The *Diversoria* is concerned with the difference between manners at German and French inns. He describes, for example, the interior of a German inn: some eighty or ninety people are sitting together, and it is stressed that they are not only common people but also rich men and nobles, men, women, and children, all mixed together. And each is doing what he considers necessary. One washes his clothes and hangs the soaking articles on the stove. Another washes his hands. But the bowl is so clean, says the speaker, that one needs a second one to cleanse oneself of the water. Garlic smells and other bad odors rise. People spit everywhere. Someone is cleaning his boots on the table. Then the meal is brought in. Everyone dips his bread into the general dish, bites the bread, and dips it in again. The place is dirty, the wine bad. And if one asks for a better wine the innkeeper replies: I have put up enough nobles and counts. If it does not suit you, look for other quarters.

The stranger to the country has a particularly difficult time. The others stare at him fixedly as if he were a fabulous animal from Africa. Moreover, these people acknowledge as human beings only the nobles of their own country.

The room is overheated; everyone is sweating and steaming and wiping himself. There are doubtless many among them who have some hidden disease. "Probably," says the speaker, "most of them have the Spanish disease, and are thus no less to be feared than lepers."

"Brave people," says the other, "they jest and care nothing for it."

"But this bravery has already cost many lives."

"What are they to do? They are used to it, and a stouthearted man does not break with his habits."

3. It can be seen that Erasmus, like others who wrote before or after him about conduct, is in the first place a collector of good and bad manners that he finds present in social life itself. It is primarily this that explains both the agreement and the differences between such writers. That their writings do not contain as much as others to which we habitually give more attention, the extraordinary ideas of an outstanding individual, that they are forced by their subject itself to adhere closely to social reality, gives them their special significance as a source of information on social processes.

But the observations of Erasmus on this subject are nevertheless to be numbered, along with a few by other authors from the same phase, among the exceptions in the tradition of writing on manners. For in them the presentation of partly very ancient precepts and commands is permeated by a very individual temperament. And precisely that is, in its turn, a "sign of the times," an expression of a transformation of society, a symptom of what is somewhat misleadingly called "individualization." It also points to something else: the problem of behavior in society had obviously taken on such importance in this period that even people of extraordinary talent and renown did not disdain to concern themselves with it. Later this task falls back in general to minds of the second and third rank, who imitate, continue, extend, thus giving rise once more, even if not so strongly as in the Middle Ages, to a more impersonal tradition of books on manners.

The social transitions connected with the changes in conduct, manners, and feelings of embarrassment will be studied separately later. However, an indication of them is needed here for an understanding of Erasmus's own position, and therefore of his way of speaking about manners.

Erasmus's treatise comes at a time of social regrouping. It is the expression of the fruitful transitional period after the loosening of the medieval social hierarchy and before the stabilizing of the modern one. It belongs to the phase in which the old, feudal knights nobility was still in decline, while the new aristocracy of the absolutist courts was still in the process of formation. This situation gave, among others, the representatives of a small, secular-bourgeois intellectual class, the humanists, and thus Erasmus, not only an opportunity to rise in social station, to gain renown and authority, but also a possibility of candor and detachment that was not present to the same degree either before or afterward. This chance of distancing themselves, which permitted individual representatives of the intellectual class to identify totally and unconditionally with none of the social groups of their world—though, of course, they always stood closer to one of them, that of the princes and of the courts, than to the others—also finds expression in *De civilitate morum puerilium*. Erasmus in no way overlooks or conceals social differences. He sees very exactly that the real nurseries of what is regarded as good manners in his time are the princely courts. He says, for example, to the young prince to whom he dedicates his treatise: "I shall address your youth on the manners fitting to a boy not because you are so greatly in need of these precepts; from childhood you have been educated among courtly people and you early had an excellent instructor . . . or because all that is said in this treatise applies to you; for you are of princely blood and are born to rule.''

But Erasmus also manifests, in a particularly pronounced form, the characteristic self-confidence of the intellectual who has ascended through knowledge and writing, who is legitimized by books, the self-assurance of a member of the humanistic intellectual class who is able to keep his distance even from ruling strata and their opinions, however bound to them he may be. "Modesty, above all, befits a boy," he says at the close of the dedication to the young prince, "and particularly a noble boy.'' And he also says: "Let others paint lions, eagles, and other creatures on their coats of arms. More true nobility is possessed by those who can inscribe on their shields all that they have achieved through the cultivation of the arts and sciences.''

This is the language, the typical self-image of the intellectual in this phase of social development. The sociogenetic and psychogenetic kinship of such ideas with those of the German intellectual class of the eighteenth century, who were epitomized to themselves by concepts such as *Kultur* and *Bildung*, is immediately visible. But in the period immediately after Erasmus's time, few people would have had the assurance or even the social opportunity to express such thoughts openly in a dedication to a noble. With the increasing stabilization of the social hierarchy, such an utterance would have been increasingly seen as an error of tact, perhaps even as an attack. The most exact observance of differences of rank in behavior becomes from now on the essence of courtesy, the basic requirement of *civilité*, at least in France. The aristocracy and the bourgeois intelligentsia mix socially, but it is an imperative of tact to observe social differences and to give them unambiguous expression in social conduct. In Germany, by contrast, there is always, from the time of the humanists onward, a bourgeois intelligentsia whose members, with few exceptions, live more or less in isolation from aristocratic court society, an intellectual class of specifically middle-class character.

4. The development of German writings on manners and the way these writings differ from the French give numerous clear illustrations of this. It would lead too far to pursue this in detail, but one need only think of a work like Dedekind's *Grobianus*[30] and its widely dis-

seminated and influential German translation by Kaspar Scheidt to be aware of the difference. The whole German *grobianisch* (boorish) literature in which, spiced with mockery and scorn, a very serious need for a "softening of manners" finds expression, shows unambiguously and more purely than any of the corresponding traditions of other nationalities the specifically middle-class character of its writers, who include Protestant clergymen and teachers. And the case is similar with most of what was written in the ensuing period about manners and etiquette in Germany. Certainly, manners here too are stamped primarily at the courts; but since the social walls between the bourgeoisie and court nobility are relatively high, the later bourgeois authors of books on manners usually speak of them as something alien that has to be learned because that is the way things are done at court. However familiar with the subject these authors may be, they speak of it as outsiders, very often with noticeable clumsiness. It is a relatively constricted, regional, and penurious intellectual stratum which writes in Germany in the following period, and particularly after the Thirty Years War. And only in the second half of the eighteenth century, when the German bourgeois intelligentsia, as a kind of vanguard of the commercial bourgeoisie, attains new opportunities for social advance and rather more freedom of movement, do we again hear the language and expression of a self-image related to that of the humanists, especially Erasmus. Even now, however, the nobles are hardly ever told so openly that all their coats of arms are worth less than the cultivation of the *artes liberales*, even if this is often enough what is really meant.

What has been shown in the introductory chapter on the movement of the late eighteenth century goes back to a far older tradition, to a pervasive structural characteristic of German society following the particularly vigorous development of the German cities and burgher class toward the end of the Middle Ages. In France, and periodically in England and Italy also, a proportion of the bourgeois writers feel themselves to belong to the circles of the court aristocracies; in Germany this is far less the case. In the other countries, bourgeois writers not only write largely for circles of the court aristocracies but also identify extensively with their manners, customs, and views. In Germany this identification of members of the intelligentsia with the courtly upper class is much weaker, less taken for granted and far more rare. Their dubious position (along with a certain mistrust of those who legitimize themselves primarily by their manners, courtesy, and ease of behavior) is part of a long tradition, particularly as the values of the German court aristocracy—which is split up into numerous greater or lesser circles, not unified in a large, central "society," and moreover is bureaucratized at an early stage—cannot be developed as fully as in the Western countries. Instead, there emerges here more sharply than in the Western countries a split between the university-based cultural-bureaucratic tradition of "Kultur" of the middle-class, on the one hand, and the no less bureaucratic-military tradition of the nobility, on the other.

5. Erasmus's treatise on manners has an influence both on Germany and on England, France, and Italy. What links his attitude with that of the later German intelligentsia is the lack of identification with the courtly upper class; and his observation that the treatment of "civility" is without doubt *crassissima philosophiae pars* points to a scale of values which was not without a certain kinship to the later evaluation of *Zivilisation* and *Kultur* in the German tradition.

Accordingly, Erasmus does not see his precepts as intended for a particular class. He places no particular emphasis on social distinctions, if we disregard occasional criticism of peasants and small tradesmen. It is precisely this lack of a specific social orientation in the precepts, their presentation as general human rules, that distinguishes his treatise from its successors in the Italian and especially the French traditions.

Erasmus simply says, for example, "Incessus nec fractus sit, nec praeceps" (The step should be neither too slow nor too quick). Shortly afterward, in his *Galateo*, the Italian Giovanni della Casa says the same thing (ch. VI, 5, pt. III). But for him the same precept has a direct and obvious function as a means of social distinction: "Non dee l'huomo nobile correre per via, ne troppo affrettarsi, che cio conviene a palafreniere e non a gentilhuomo. Ne percio si dee andare sì lento, ne sì conregnoso come femmina o come sposa." (The noblemen ought not to run like a lackey, or walk as slowly as women or brides.) It is characteristic, and in agreement with all our other observations, that a German translation of *Galateo*—in a five-language edition of 1609 (Geneva)—regularly seeks, like the Latin translation and unlike all the others, to efface the social differentiations in the original. The passage quoted, for example, is translated as follows: "Therefore a noble, or any other *honorable man*, should not run in the street or hurry too much, since this befits a lackey and not a gentleman. . . . Nor should one walk unduly slowly like a stately matron or a young bride" (p. 562).

The words "honorable man" are inserted here, possibly referring to burgher councillors, and similar changes are found in many other places; when the Italian says simply *gentilhuomo* and the French *gentilhomme*, the German speaks of the "virtuous, honorable man" and the Latin of "homo honestus et bene moratus." These examples could be multiplied.

Erasmus proceeds similarly. As a result, the precepts that he gives without any social characteristics appear again and again in the Italian and French traditions with a sharper limitation to the upper class, while in Germany the tendency to obliterate the social characteristics remains, even if for a long period hardly a single writer achieves the degree of social detachment possessed by Erasmus. In this respect he occupies a unique position among all those who write on the subject. It stems from his personal character. But at the same time, it points beyond his personal character to this relatively brief phase of relaxation between two great epochs characterized by more inflexible social hierarchies.

The fertility of this loosening transitional situation is perceptible again and again in Erasmus's way of observing people. It enables him to criticize "rustic," "vulgar," or "coarse" qualities without accepting unconditionally (as did most who came later) the behavior of the great courtly lords, whose circle was finally, as he himself puts it, the nursery of refined conduct. He sees very exactly the exaggerated, forced nature of many courtly practices, and is not afraid to say so. Speaking of how to hold the lips, for example, he says: "It is still less becoming to purse the lips from time to time as if whistling to oneself. This can be left to the great lords when they stroll among the crowd." Or he says: "You should leave to a few courtiers the pleasure of squeezing bread in the hand and then breaking it off with the fingertips. You should cut it decently with a knife."

6. But here again we see very clearly the difference between this and the medieval manner of giving directions on behavior. Earlier, people were simply told, to give one example, "The bread cut fayre and do not breake."[31] Such rules are embedded by Erasmus directly in his experience and observation of people. The traditional precepts, mirrors of ever-recurring customs, awaken in his observation from a

---

kind of petrifaction. An old rule ran: "Do not fall greedily upon the food."

Do not eat bread before the meat is served, for this would appear greedy.

Remember to empty and wipe your mouth before drinking.[32]

Erasmus gives the same advice, but in so doing he sees people directly before him: some, he says, devour rather than eat, as if they were about to be carried off to prison, or were thieves wolfing down their booty. Others push so much into their mouths that their cheeks bulge like bellows. Others pull their lips apart while eating, so that they make a noise like pigs. And then follows the general rule that was, and obviously had to be, repeated over and again: "Ore pleno vel bibere vel loqui, nec honestum, nec tutum." (To eat or drink with a full mouth is neither becoming nor safe.)

In all this, besides the medieval tradition, there is certainly much from antiquity. But reading has sharpened seeing, and seeing has enriched reading and writing.

Clothing, he says in one place, is in a sense the body of the body. From it we can deduce the attitude of the soul. And then Erasmus gives examples of what manner of dress corresponds to this or that spiritual condition. This is the beginning of the mode of observation that will at a later stage be termed "psychological." The new stage of courtesy and its representation, summed up in the concept of *civilité*, is very closely bound up with this manner of seeing, and gradually becomes more so. In order to be really "courteous" by the standards of *civilité*, one is to some extent obliged to observe, to look about oneself and pay attention to people and their motives. In this, too, a new relationship of man to man, a new form of integration is announced.

Not quite 150 years later, when *civilité* has become a firm and stable form of behavior in the courtly upper class of France, in the *monde*, one of its members begins his exposition of the *science du monde* with these words: "It seems to me that to acquire what is called the science of the world one must first apply oneself to knowing men as they are in general, and then gain particular knowledge of those with whom we have to live, that is to say, knowledge of their inclinations and their good and bad opinions, of their virtues and their faults."[33]

THE CIVILIZING PROCESS

What is here said with great precision and lucidity was anticipated by Erasmus. But this increased tendency of society and therefore of writers to observe, to connect the particular with the general, seeing with reading, is found not only in Erasmus but also in the other Renaissance books on manners, and certainly not only in these.

7. If one is asked, therefore, about the new tendencies[34] that make their appearance in Erasmus's way of observing the behavior of people—this is one of them. In the process of transformation and innovation that we designate by the term "Renaissance," what was regarded as "fitting" and "unfitting" in human intercourse no doubt changed to a certain degree. But the rupture is not marked by a sudden demand for new modes of behavior opposed to the old. The tradition of *courtoisie* is continued in many respects by the society which adopts the concept of *civilitas*, as in *Civilitas morum puerilium*, to designate social "good behavior."

The increased tendency of people to observe themselves and others is one sign of how the whole question of behavior is now taking on a different character: people mold themselves and others more deliberately than in the Middle Ages.

Then they were told, do this and not that; but by and large a great deal was let pass. For centuries roughly the same rules, elementary by our standards, were repeated, obviously without producing fiɪ ɪly established habits. This now changes. The coercion exerted by people on one another increases, the demand for "good behavior" is raised more emphatically. All problems concerned with behavior take on new importance. The fact that Erasmus brought together in a prose work rules of conduct that had previously been uttered chiefly in mnemonic verses or scattered in treatises on other subjects, and for the first time devoted a separate book to the whole question of behavior in society, not only at table, is a clear sign of the growing importance of the question, as is the book's success.[35] And the emergence of related writings, like the *Courtier* of Castiglione or the *Galateo* of Della Casa, to name only the most well-known, points in the same direction. The underlying social processes have already been indicated and will be discussed in more detail later: the old social ties are, if not broken, extensively loosened and are in a process of transformation. Individuals of different social origins are thrown together. The social circulation of ascending and descending groups and individuals speeds up.

Then, slowly, in the course of the sixteenth century, earlier here and later there and almost everywhere with numerous reverses until well into the seventeenth century, a more rigid social hierarchy begins to establish itself once more, and from elements of diverse social origins a new upper class, a new aristocracy forms. For this very reason the question of uniform good behavior becomes increasingly acute, particularly as the changed structure of the new upper class exposes each individual member to an unprecedented extent to the pressure of others and of social control. It is in this context that the writings on manners of Erasmus, Castiglione, Della Casa, and others are produced. People, forced to live with one another in a new way, become more sensitive to the impulses of others. Not abruptly but very gradually the code of behavior becomes stricter and the degree of consideration expected of others becomes greater. The sense of what to do and what not to do in order not to offend or shock others becomes subtler, and in conjunction with the new power relationships the social imperative not to offend others becomes more binding, as compared to the preceding phase.

The rules of *courtoisie* also prescribed, "Say nothing that can arouse conflict, or anger others":

> Non dicas verbum
> cuiquam quod ei sit acerbum.[36]

"Be a good table companion":

> Awayte my chylde, ye be have you manerly
> When at your mete ye sitte at the table
> In every prees and in every company
> Dispose you to be so compenable
> That men may of you reporte for commendable
> For thrusteth wel upon your berynge
> Men wil you blame or gyue preysynge. . . .

So we read in an English *Book of Curtesye*.[37] In purely factual terms, much of what Erasmus says has a similar tendency. But the change of tone, the increased sensitivity, the heightened human observation, and the sharper understanding of what is going on in others are unmistakable. They are particularly clear in a remark at the end of his treatise. There he breaks through the fixed pattern of "good behavior," together with the arrogance that usually accompanies it, and relates conduct back to a more comprehensive humanity: "Be lenient toward the offenses of others. This is the chief virtue of *civilitas*, of courtesy. A companion ought not to be less dear to you because he has worse manners. There are people who make up for the awkwardness of their behavior by other gifts." And further on he says: "If one of your comrades unknowingly gives offense . . . tell him so alone and say it kindly. That is civility."

But this attitude only expresses again how little Erasmus, for all his closeness to the courtly upper class of his time, identifies with it, keeping his distance from its code, too.

Galateo takes its name from an account in which Erasmus's precept "Tell him alone and say it kindly" applies in reality; an offense is corrected in that very way. But here the courtly character of such customs is emphasized as far more self-evident than in Erasmus.

The Bishop of Verona, the Italian work relates,[38] one day receives a visit from a Duke Richard. He appears to the Bishop and his court as "gentilissime cavaliere e di bellissime maniere." The host notes in his guest a single fault. But he says nothing. On the Duke's departure the Bishop sends a man of his court, Galateo, to accompany him. Galateo has particularly good manners, acquired at the courts of the great: "molto havea de' suoi dì usato alle corti de' gran Signori." This is explicitly emphasized.

This Galateo therefore accompanies Duke Richard part of the way, and says the following to him before taking his leave: His master, the Bishop, would like to make the Duke a parting gift. The Bishop has never in his life seen a nobleman with better manners than the Duke. He has discovered in him only a single fault—he smacks his lips too loudly while eating, so making a noise that is unpleasant for others to hear. To inform him of this is the Bishop's parting gift, which he begs will not be ill-received.

The precept not to smack the lips while eating is also found frequently in medieval instructions. But its occurrence at the beginning of *Galateo* shows clearly what has changed. It not only demonstrates how much importance is now attached to "good behavior." It shows, above all, how the pressure people now exert on one another in this direction has increased. It is immediately apparent that this polite, extremely gentle, and comparatively considerate way of correcting is, particularly when exercised by a social superior, much more compelling as a means of social control, much more effective in inculcating lasting habits, than insults, mockery, or any threat of outward physical violence.

Within countries, pacified societies are formed. The old code of behavior is transformed only step by step. But social control becomes more binding. And above all, the nature and mechanism of affect-molding by society are slowly changed. In the course of the Middle Ages the standard of good and bad manners, for all the regional and social differences, clearly did not undergo any decisive change. Over and again, down the centuries, the same good and bad manners are mentioned. The social code hardened into lasting habits only to a limited extent in people themselves. Now, with the structural transformation of society, with the new pattern of human relationships, a change slowly comes about: the compulsion to check one's own behavior increases. In conjunction with this the standard of behavior is set in motion.

Caxton's *Book of Curtesye*, probably of the late fifteenth century, already gives unambiguous expression to this feeling that habits, customs, and rules of conduct are in flux:[39]

> Thingis whilom used ben now leyd a syde
> And newe feetis, dayly ben contreuide
> Mennys actes can in no plyte abyde
> They be changeable ande ofte meuide
> Thingis somtyme alowed is now repreuid
> And after this shal thines up aryse
> That men set now but at lytyl pryse.

This sounds, indeed, like a motto for the whole movement that is now coming: "Thingis somtyme alowed is now repreuid." The sixteenth century is still wholly within the transition. Erasmus and his contemporaries are still permitted to speak about things, functions, and ways of behaving that one or two centuries later are overlaid with feelings of shame and embarrassment, and whose public exposure or mention are proscribed in society. With the same simplicity and clarity with which he and Della Casa discuss questions of the greatest tact and propriety, Erasmus also says: Do not move back and forth on your chair. Whoever does that "speciem habet subinde ventris flatum emittentis ant emittere conantis" (gives the impression of constantly breaking or trying to break wind). This still shows the old unconcern in referring to bodily functions that was characteristic of medieval people, but enriched by observation, by consideration of "what others *might* think." Comments of this kind occur frequently.

Consideration of the behavior of people in the sixteenth century, and of their code of behavior, casts the observer back and forth between the impressions "That's still utterly medieval" and "That's exactly the way we feel today." And precisely this apparent contradiction clearly corresponds to reality. The people of this time have a double face. They stand on a bridge. Behavior and the code of behavior are in motion, but the movement is quite slow. And above all, in observing a single stage, we lack a sure measure. What is accidental fluctuation? When and where is something advancing? When is something falling behind? Are we really concerned with a change in a definite direction? Is European society really, under the watchword *civilité*, slowly moving toward that kind of refined behavior, that standard of conduct, habits, and affect formation, which is characteristic in our minds of "civilized" society, of Western "civilization"?

8. It is not very easy to make this movement clearly visible precisely because it takes place so slowly—in very small steps, as it were—and because it also shows manifold fluctuations, following smaller and larger curves. It clearly does not suffice to consider in isolation each single stage to which this or that statement on customs and manners bears witness. We must attempt to see the movement itself, or at least a large segment of it, as a whole, as if speeded up. Images must be placed together in a series to give an overall view, from one particular aspect, of the process: the gradual transformation of behavior and the emotions, the expanding threshold of aversion.

The books on manners offer an opportunity for this. On individual aspects of human behavior, particularly eating habits, they give us detailed information—always on the same feature of social life—which extends relatively unbroken, even if at rather fortuitous intervals, from at least the thirteenth to the nineteenth and twentieth centuries. Here images can be seen in a series, and segments of the total process can be made visible. And it is perhaps an advantage, rather than a disadvantage, that modes of behavior of a relatively simple and elementary kind are observed, in which scope for individual variation within the social standard is relatively small.

These *Tischzuchten* and books on manners are a literary genre in their own right. If the written heritage of the past is examined primarily from the point of view of what we are accustomed to call "literary significance," then most of them have no great value. But if we examine the modes of behavior which in every age a particular society has expected of its members, attempting to condition individuals to them; if we wish to observe changes in habits, social rules and taboos; then these instructions on correct behavior, though perhaps worthless as literature, take on a special significance. They throw some light on elements in the social process on which we possess, at least from the past, very little direct information. They show precisely what we are seeking—namely, the standard of habits and behavior to which society at a given time sought to accustom the individual. These poems and treatises are themselves direct instruments of "conditioning" or "fashioning,"[40] of the adaptation of the individual to those modes of behavior which the structure and situation of his society make necessary. And they show at the same time, through what they censure and what they praise, the divergence between what was regarded at different times as good and bad manners.

IV

On Behavior at Table

Part One

Examples

(a) Examples representing upper-class behavior in a fairly pure form:

A

Thirteenth century
This is Tannhäuser's poem of courtly good manners:[41]

1 I consider a well-bred man to be one who always recognizes good manners and is never ill-mannered.

2 There are many forms of good manners, and they serve many good purposes. The man who adopts them will never err.

THE CIVILIZING PROCESS

25 When you eat do not forget the poor.　God will reward you if you treat them kindly.

33 A man of refinement should not slurp with his spoon when in company; that is the way people at court behave who often indulge in unrefined conduct.

37 It is not polite to drink from the dish, although some who approve of this rude habit insolently pick up the dish and pour it down as if they were mad.

41 Those who fall upon the dishes like swine while eating, snorting disgustingly and smacking their lips . . .

45 Some people bite a slice and then dunk it in the dish in a coarse way; refined people reject such bad manners.

49 A number of people gnaw a bone and then put it back in the dish—this is a serious offense.

On v. 25, cf. the first rule of Bonvicino da Riva·

The first is this: when at table, think first of the poor and needy.

From *Ein spruch der ze tische kêrt* (A word to those at table):[42]

313 You should not drink from the dish, but with a spoon as is proper.

315 Those who stand up and snort disgustingly over the dishes like swine belong with other farmyard beasts.

319 To snort like a salmon, gobble like a badger, and complain while eating—these three things are quite improper.

or

In the *Courtesies* of Bonvicino da Riva:

Do not slurp with your mouth when eating from a spoon. This is a bestial habit.

or

In *The Book of Nurture and School of Good Manners*:[43]

201 And suppe not lowde of thy Pottage
　　　no tyme in all thy lyfe.

---

53 Those who like mustard and salt should take care to avoid the filthy habit of putting their fingers into them.

57 A man who clears his throat when he eats and one who blows his nose in the tablecloth are both ill-bred, I assure you.

65 A man who wants to talk and eat at the same time, and talks in his sleep, will never rest peacefully.

69 Do not be noisy at table, as some people are. Remember, my friends, that nothing is so ill-mannered.

81 I find it very bad manners whenever I see someone with food in his mouth and drinking at the same time, like an animal.

On v. 45, cf. *Ein spruch der ze tische kêrt*:

346 May refined people be preserved from those who gnaw their bones and put them back in the dish.

or

From *Quisquis es in mensa* (For those at table):[44]

A morsel that has been tasted should not be returned to the dish.

On v. 65, cf. from *Stans puer in mensam* (The boy at table):[45]

22 Numquam ridebis nec faberis
ore repleto.
   Never laugh or talk with a full
mouth.

On v. 81, cf. from *Quisquis es in mensa*:

15 Qui vult potare debet prius
os vacuare.
   If you wish to drink, first empty
your mouth.

or

From *The Babees Book*:

149 And withe fulle mouthe drinke in no wyse.

---

85 You should not blow into your drink, as some are fond of doing; this is an ill-mannered habit that should be avoided.

94 Before drinking, wipe your mouth so that you do not dirty the drink; this act of courtesy should be observed at all times.

105 It is bad manners to lean against the table while eating, as it is to keep your helmet on when serving the ladies.

109 Do not scrape your throat with your bare hand while eating; but if you have to, do it politely with your coat.

113 And it is more fitting to scratch with that than to soil your hand; onlookers notice people who behave like this.

117 You should not poke your teeth with your knife, as some do; it is a bad habit.

On v. 85, cf. *The Book of Curtesye*:[46]

111 Ne blow not on thy drinke ne mete,
Nether for colde, nether for hete.

On v. 94, cf. *The Babees Book*:

155 Whanne ye shalle drynke,
your mouthe clence withe a clothe.

or

From a *Contenance de table* (Guide to behavior at table):[47]

Do not slobber while you drink, for this is a shameful habit.

On v. 105, cf. *The Babees Book*:

Nor on the borde lenynge be yee nat sene.

On v. 117, cf. *Stans puer in mensam*:[48]

30 Mensa cultello, dentes mundare
caveto.
    Avoid cleaning your teeth with a
knife at table.

---

125 If anyone is accustomed to loosening his belt at table, take it from me that he is not a true courtier.

129 If a man wipes his nose on his hand at table because he knows no better, then he is a fool, believe me.

141 I hear that some eat unwashed (if it is true, it is a bad sign). May their fingers be palsied!

157 It is not decent to poke your fingers into your ears or eyes, as some people do, or to pick your nose while eating. These three habits are bad.

B

Fifteenth century?
From *S'ensuivent les contenances de la table* (These are good table manners):[49]

I
Learn these rules.

II
Take care to cut and clean your nails; dirt under the nails is dangerous when scratching.

III
Wash your hands when you get up and before every meal.

On v. 141, cf. *Stans puer in mensam*:

11 Illotis manibus escas ne sumpseris
unquam.
    Never pick up food with unwashed
hands.

On v. 157, cf. *Quisquis es in mensa*:

9 Non tangas aures nudis digitis
neque nares.
    Touch neither your ears nor your nostrils
with your bare fingers.

This small selection of passages was compiled from a brief perusal of various guides to behavior at table and court. It is very far from exhaustive. It is intended only to give an impression of how similar in tone and content were the rules in different traditions and in different centuries of the Middle Ages. Originals may be found in Appendix II.

THE CIVILIZING PROCESS

XII

Do not be the first to take from the dish.

XIII

Do not put back on your plate what has been in your mouth.

XIV

Do not offer anyone a piece of food you have bitten into.

XV

Do not chew anything you have to spit out again.

XVII

It is bad manners to dip food into the saltcellar.

XXIV

Be peaceable, quiet, and courteous at table.

XXVI

If you have crumbled bread into your wineglass, drink up the wine or throw it away.

XXXI

Do not stuff too much into yourself, or you will be obliged to commit a breach of good manners.

XXXIV

Do not scratch at table, with your hands or with the tablecloth.

C

1530

From *De civilitate morum puerilium* (On civility in boys), by Erasmus of Rotterdam, ch. 4:

If a serviette is given, lay it on your left shoulder or arm.

If you are seated with people of rank, take off your hat and see that your hair is well combed.

Your goblet and knife, duly cleansed, should be on the right, your bread on the left.

Some people put their hands in the dishes the moment they have sat down. Wolves do that. . . .

Do not be the first to touch the dish that has been brought in, not only because this shows you greedy, but also because it is dangerous. For someone who puts something hot into his mouth unawares must either spit it out or, if he swallows it, burn his throat. In either case he is as ridiculous as he is pitiable.

It is a good thing to wait a short while before eating, so that the boy grows accustomed to tempering his affects.

To dip the fingers in the sauce is rustic. You should take what you want with your knife and fork; you should not search through the whole dish as epicures are wont to do, but take what happens to be in front of you.

What you cannot take with your fingers should be taken with the *quadra*.

If you are offered a piece of cake or pie on a spoon, hold out your plate or take the spoon that is held out to you, put the food on your plate, and return the spoon.

If you are offered something liquid, taste it and return the spoon, but first wipe it on your serviette.

To lick greasy fingers or to wipe them on your coat is impolite. It is better to use the tablecloth or the serviette.

D

1558

From *Galateo*, by Giovanni della Casa, Archbishop of Benevento, quoted from the five-language edition (Geneva, 1609), p. 68:

What do you think this Bishop and his noble company (*il Vescove e la sua nobile brigata*) would have said to those whom we sometimes see lying like swine with their snouts in the soup, not once lifting their heads and turning their eyes, still less their hands, from the food, puffing out both cheeks as if they were blowing a trumpet or trying to fan a fire, not eating but gorging themselves, dirtying their arms almost to the elbows and then reducing their serviettes to a state that would make a kitchen rag look clean.

Nonetheless, these hogs are not ashamed to use the serviettes thus sullied to wipe away their sweat (which, owing to their hasty and excessive feeding, often runs down their foreheads and faces to their necks), and even to blow their noses into them as often as they please.

E

1560

From a *Civilité* by C. Calviac[50] (based heavily on Erasmus, but with some independent comments):

When the child is seated, if there is a serviette on the plate in front of him, he shall take it and place it on his left arm or shoulder; then he shall place his bread on the left and the knife on the right, like the glass, if he wishes to leave it on the table, and if it can be conveniently left there without annoying anyone. For it might happen that the glass could not be left on the table or on his right without being in someone's way.

The child must have the discretion to understand the needs of the situation he is in.

When eating . . . he should take the first piece that comes to his hand on his cutting board.

If there are sauces, the child may dip into them decently, without turning his food over after having dipped one side. . . .

It is very necessary for a child to learn at an early age how to carve a leg of mutton, a partridge, a rabbit, and such things.

It is a far too dirty thing for a child to offer others something he has gnawed, or something he disdains to eat himself, *unless it be to his servant.* [Author's emphasis]

Nor is it decent to take from the mouth something he has already chewed, and put it on the cutting board, unless it be a small bone from which he has sucked the marrow to pass time while awaiting the dessert; for after sucking it he should put it on his plate, where he should also place the stones of cherries, plums, and suchlike, as it is not good either to swallow them or to drop them on the floor.

The child should not gnaw bones indecently, as dogs do.

When the child would like salt, he shall take it with the point of his knife and not with three fingers.

The child must cut his meat into very small pieces on his cutting board . . . and he must not lift the meat to his mouth now with one hand and now with the other, like little children who are learning to eat; he should always do so with his right hand, taking the bread or meat decently with three fingers only.

As for the manner of chewing, it varies according to the country. The Germans chew with the mouth closed, and find it ugly to do otherwise. The French, on the other hand, half open the mouth, and find the procedure of the Germans rather dirty. The Italians proceed in a very slack manner and the French more roundly, finding the Italian way too delicate and precious.

And so each nation has something of its own, different to the others. So that the child will proceed in accordance with the customs of the place where he is.

Further, the Germans use spoons when eating soup and everything liquid, and the Italians forks. The French use either, as they think fit and as is most convenient. The Italians generally prefer to have a knife for each person. But the Germans place special importance on this, to the extent that they are greatly displeased if one asks for or takes the knife in front of them. The French way is quite different: a whole table full of people will use two or three knives, without making difficulties in asking for or taking a knife, or passing it if they have it. So that if someone asks the child for his knife, he should pass it after wiping it with his serviette, holding it by the point and offering the handle to the person requesting it: for it would not be polite to do otherwise.

F

Between 1640 and 1680
From a song by the Marquis de Coulanges:[51]

In times past, people ate from the common dish and dipped their bread and fingers in the sauce.

Today everyone eats with spoon and fork from his own plate, and a valet washes the cutlery from time to time at the buffet.

G

1672
From Antoine de Courtin, *Nouveau traité de civilité*, pp. 127, 273:

If everyone is eating from the same dish, you should take care not to put your hand into it *before those of higher rank have done so*, and to take food only from the part of the dish opposite you. Still less should you take the best pieces, even though you might be the last to help yourself.

It must also be pointed out that you should always wipe your spoon when, after using it, you want to take something from another dish, *there being people so delicate that they would not wish to eat soup into which you had dipped it after putting it into your mouth*. [Author's emphasis]

And even, if you are at the table of very refined people, it is not enough to wipe your spoon; you should not use it but ask for another. Also, in many places, spoons are brought in with the dishes, *and these serve only for taking soup and sauce*. [Author's emphasis]

You should not eat soup from the dish, but put it neatly on your plate; if it is too hot, it is impolite to blow on each spoonful; you should wait until it has cooled.

If you have the misfortune to burn your mouth, you should endure it patiently if you can, without showing it; but if the burn is unbearable, as sometimes happens, you should, before the others have noticed, take your plate promptly in one hand and lift it to your mouth and, while covering your mouth with the other hand, return to the plate what you have in your mouth, and quickly pass it to a footman behind you. Civility requires you to be polite, but it does not expect you to be homicidal toward yourself. It is very impolite to touch anything greasy, a sauce or syrup, etc., with your fingers, apart from the fact that it obliges you to commit two or three more improper acts. One is to wipe your hand frequently on your serviette and to soil it like a kitchen cloth, so that those who see you wipe your mouth with it feel nauseated. Another is to wipe your fingers on your bread, which again is very improper. The third is to lick them, which is the height of impropriety.

. . . As there are many [customs] which have already changed, I do not doubt that several of these will likewise change in the future.

Formerly one was permitted . . . to dip one's bread into the sauce, provided only that one had not already bitten it. Nowadays that would be a kind of rusticity.

Formerly one was allowed to take from one's mouth what one could not eat and drop it on the floor, provided it was done skillfully. Now that would be very disgusting. . . .

H

1717

From François de Callières, *De la science du monde et des connois-sances utiles à la conduite de la vie*, pp. 97, 101:

In Germany and the Northern Kingdoms it is civil and decent for a prince to drink first to the health of those he is entertaining, and then to offer them the same glass or goblet usually filled with the same wine; nor is it a lack of politeness in them to drink from the same glass, but a mark of candor and friendship. The women also drink first and then give their glass, or have it taken, to the person they are addressing, with the same wine from which they have drunk his health, *without this being taken as a special favor, as it is among us. . . .* [Author's emphasis]

"I cannot approve," a lady answers "—without offense to the gentlemen from the north—this manner of drinking from the same glass, and still less of drinking what the ladies have left; it has an air of impropriety that makes me wish they might show other marks of their candor."

(b) Examples from books which either, like La Salle's *Les Règles de la bienséance et de la civilité chrétienne*, represent the spreading of courtly manners and models to broader bourgeois strata, or, like Example I, reflect fairly purely the bourgeois and probably the provincial standard of their time.

In Example I, from about 1714, people still eat from a communal dish. Nothing is said against touching the meat on one's own plate with the hands. And the "bad manners" that are mentioned have largely disappeared from the upper class.

The *Civilité* of 1780 (Example L) is a little book of forty-eight pages in bad *civilité* type, printed in Caen but undated. The British Museum catalogue has a question mark after the date. In any case, this book is an example of the multitude of cheap books or pamphlets on *civilité* that were disseminated throughout France in the eighteenth century. This one, to judge from its general attitude, was clearly intended for provincial town-dwellers. In no other eighteenth-century work on *civilité* quoted here are bodily functions discussed so openly. The standard the book points to recalls in many respects the one that Erasmus's *De civilitate* had marked for the upper class. It is still a matter of course to take food in the hands. This example seemed useful here to complement the other quotations, and particularly to remind the reader that the movement ought to be seen in its full multilayered polyphony, not as a line but as a kind of fugue with a succession of related movement-motifs on different levels.

Example M from 1786 shows the dissemination from above to below very directly. It is particularly characteristic because it contains a large number of customs that have subsequently been adopted by "civilized society" as a whole, but are here clearly visible as specific customs of the courtly upper class which still seem relatively alien to the bourgeoisie. Many customs have been arrested, as "civilized customs," in exactly the form they have here as courtly manners.

The quotation from 1859 (Example N) is meant to remind the reader that in the nineteenth century, as today, the whole movement had already been entirely forgotten, that the standard of "civilization" which in reality had been attained only quite recently was taken for granted, what preceded it being seen as "barbaric."

I

1714

From an anonymous *Civilité française* (Liège, 1714?), p. 48:

> It is not . . . polite to drink your soup from the bowl unless you are in your own family, and only then if you have drunk the most part with your spoon.
> If the soup is in a communal dish, take some with your spoon in your turn, without precipitation.
> Do not keep your knife always in your hand, as village people do, but take it only when you need it.

When you are being served meat, it is not seemly to take it in your hand. You should hold out your plate in your left hand while holding your fork or knife in your right.

It is against propriety to give people meat to smell, and you should under no circumstances put meat back into the common dish if you have smelled it yourself. If you take meat from a common dish, do not choose the best pieces. Cut with the knife, holding still the piece of meat in the dish with the fork, which you will use to put on your plate the piece you have cut off; do not, therefore, take the meat with your hand [nothing is said here against touching the meat on one's own plate with the hand].

You should not throw bones or eggshells or the skin of any fruit onto the floor.

The same is true of fruit stones. It is more polite to remove them from the mouth with two fingers than to spit them into one's hand.

J

1729

From La Salle, *Les Règles de la bienséance et de la civilité chrétienne* (Rouen, 1729), p. 87:

On Things to Be Used at Table

At table you should use a serviette, a plate, a knife, a spoon, and a fork. It would be entirely contrary to propriety to be without any of these things while eating.

It is for the person of highest rank in the company to unfold his serviette first, and the others should wait until he has done so before unfolding theirs. When the people are approximately equal, all should unfold it together without ceremony. [N.B. With the "democratization" of society and the family, this becomes the rule. The social structure, here still of the hierarchical-aristocratic type, is mirrored in the most elementary human relationships.]

It is improper to use the serviette to wipe your face; it is far more so to rub your teeth with it, and it would be one of the grossest offenses against civility to use it to blow your nose. . . . The use you may and must make of the serviette when at table is for wiping your mouth, lips, and fingers when they are greasy, wiping the knife before cutting bread, and cleaning the spoon and fork after using them. [N.B. This is one of many examples of the extraordinary control of behavior embedded in our eating habits. The use of each utensil is limited and defined by a multiplicity of very precise rules. None of them is simply self-evident, as they appear to later generations. Their use is formed very gradually in conjunction with the structure and changes of human relationships.]

When the fingers are very greasy, wipe them first on a piece of bread, which should then be left on the plate, before cleaning them on the serviette, in order not to soil it too much.

When the spoon, fork, and knife are dirty or greasy, it is very improper to lick them, and it is not at all decent to wipe them, or anything else, on the tablecloth. On these and similar occasions you should use the serviette, and regarding the tablecloth you should take care to keep it always very clean, and not to drop on it water, wine, or anything that might soil it.

When the plate is dirty, you should be sure not to scrape it with the spoon or fork to clean it, or to clean your plate or the bottom of any dish with your fingers: that is very impolite. Either they should not be touched or, if you have the opportunity of exchanging them, you should ask for another.

When at table you should not keep the knife always in your hand; it is sufficient to pick it up when you wish to use it.

It is also very impolite to put a piece of bread into your mouth while holding the knife in your hand; it is even more so to do this with the point of the knife. The same thing must be observed in eating apples, pears, or some other fruits. [N.B. Examples of taboos relating to knives.]

It is against propriety to hold the fork or spoon with the whole hand, like a stick; you should always hold them between your fingers.

You should not use your fork to lift liquids to the mouth . . . it is the spoon that is intended for such uses.

It is polite always to use the fork to put meat into your mouth, for *propriety does not permit the touching of anything greasy with the fingers* [Author's emphasis], neither sauces nor syrups; and if anyone did so, he could not escape subsequently commiting several further incivilities, such as frequently wiping his fingers on his serviette, which would make it very dirty, or on his bread, which would be very impolite, or licking his fingers, which is not permitted to well-born, refined people.

This whole passage, like several others, is taken from A. de Courtin's *Nouveau traité* of 1672; cf. Example G, p. 00. It also reappears in other eighteenth-century works on *civilité*. The reason given for the prohibition on eating with the fingers is particularly instructive. In Courtin, too, it applies in the first place only to greasy foods, especially those in sauces, since this gives rise to actions that are "distasteful" to behold. In La Salle this is not entirely consistent with what he says in another place: "If your fingers are greasy . . ." etc. The prohibition is not remotely so self-evident as today. We see how gradually it becomes an internalized habit, a piece of "self-control."

In the critical period at the end of the reign of Louis XV—in which, as shown earlier, the urge for reform is intensified as an outward sign of social changes, and in which the concept of "civilization" comes to the fore—La Salle's *Civilité*, which had previously passed through several editions largely unchanged, was revised. The changes in the standard are very instructive (Example K, below). They are in some respects very considerable. The difference is partly discernible in what no longer needs to be said. Many chapters are shorter. Many "bad manners" earlier discussed in detail are mentioned only briefly in passing. The same applies to many bodily functions originally dealt with at length and in great detail. The tone is generally less mild, and often incomparably harsher than in the first version.

K

1774

From La Salle, *Les Règles de la bienséance et de la civilité chrétienne* (1774 ed.), pp. 45ff.:

The serviette which is placed on the plate, being intended to preserve clothing from spots and other soiling inseparable from meals, should be spread over you so far that it covers the front of your body to the knees, going under the collar and not being passed inside it. The spoon, fork, and knife should always be placed on the right.

The spoon is intended for liquids, and the fork for solid meats.

When one or the other is dirty, they can be cleaned with the serviette, if another service cannot be procured. You should avoid wiping them with the tablecloth, which is an unpardonable impropriety.

When the plate is dirty you should ask for another; it would be revoltingly gross to clean spoon, fork, or knife with the fingers.

At good tables, attentive servants change plates without being called upon.

Nothing is more improper than to lick your fingers, to touch the meats and put them into your mouth with your hand, to stir sauce with your fingers, or to dip bread into it with your fork and then suck it.

You should never take salt with your fingers. It is very common for children to pile pieces one on top of the other, and even to take out of their mouths something they have chewed, and flick pieces with their fingers. [All these were mentioned earlier as general misdemeanors, but are here mentioned only as the "bad" manners of children. Grown-ups no longer do such things.] Nothing is more impolite [than] to lift meat to your nose to smell it; to let others smell it is a further impoliteness toward the master of the table; if you should happen to find dirt in the food, you should get rid of the food without showing it.

L

1780?

From an anonymous work, *La Civilité honete pour les enfants* (Caen, n.d.), p. 35:

Afterward, he shall place his serviette on him, his bread on the left and his knife on the right, to cut the meat without breaking it. [The sequence described here is found in many other documents. The most elementary procedure, earlier usual among the upper class as well, is to break up the meat with the hands. Here the next stage is described, when the meat is cut with the knife. The use of the fork is not mentioned. To break off pieces of meat is regarded here as a mark of the peasant, cutting it as clearly the manners of the town.] He will also take care not to put his knife into his mouth. He should not leave his hands on his plate . . . nor rest his elbow on it, for this is done only by the aged and infirm.

The well-behaved child will be the last to help himself if he is with his superiors.

. . . next, if it is meat, he will cut it politely with his knife and eat it with his bread.

It is a rustic, dirty habit to take chewed meat from your mouth and put it on your plate. Nor should you ever put back into the dish something you have taken from it.

M

1786

From a conversation between the poet Delille and Abbé Cosson:[52]

A short while ago Abbé Cosson, Professor of Belles Lettres at the Collège Mazarin, told me about a dinner he had attended a few days previously with some *court people* . . . at Versailles.

"I'll wager," I told him, "that you perpetrated a hundred incongruities."

"What do you mean?" Abbé Cosson asked quickly, greatly perturbed. "I believe I did everything in the same way as everyone else."

"What presumption! I'll bet you did nothing in the same way as anyone else. But I'll limit myself to the dinner. First, what did you do with your serviette when you sat down?"

"With my serviette? I did the same as everyone else. I unfolded it, spread it out, and fixed it by a corner to my buttonhole."

"Well, my dear fellow, you are the only one who did that. One does not spread out one's serviette, one keeps it on one's knees. And how did you eat your soup?"

"Like everyone else, I think. I took my spoon in one hand and my fork in the other. . . ."

"Your fork? Good heavens! No one uses his fork to eat soup. . . . But tell me how you ate your bread."

"Certainly, like everyone else: I cut it neatly with my knife."

"Oh dear, you break bread, you do not cut it. . . . Let's go on. The coffee—how did you drink it?"

"Like everyone, to be sure. It was boiling hot, so I poured it little by little from my cup into my saucer."

"Well, you certainly did not drink it like anyone else. Everyone drinks coffee from the cup, never from the saucer. . . ."

N

1859

From *The Habits of Good Society* (London, 1859; 2d ed., verbatim, 1889), p. 257:

Forks were undoubtedly a later invention than fingers, but as we are not *cannibals* I am inclined to think they were a good one.

Part Two

Comments on the Quotations on Table Manners

Group 1:

A Brief Survey of the Societies to which the Texts were Addressed

1. The quotations have been assembled to illustrate a real process, a change in the behavior of people. In general, the examples have been so selected that they may stand as typical of at least certain social groups or strata. No single person, not even so pronounced an individual as Erasmus, invented the *savoir-vivre* of his time.

We hear people of different ages speaking on roughly the same subject. In this way, the changes become more distinct than if we had described them in our own words. From at least the sixteenth century

---

onward, the commands and prohibitions by which the individual is shaped (in conformity with the standard of society) are in continuous movement. This movement, certainly, is not perfectly rectilinear, but through all its fluctuations and individual curves a definite overall trend is nevertheless perceptible if these voices from past centuries are heard together in context.

Sixteenth-century writings on manners are embodiments of the new court aristocracy that is slowly coalescing from elements of diverse social origin. With it grows a different code of behavior.

De Courtin, in the second half of the seventeenth century, speaks from a court society which is consolidated to the highest degree—the court society of Louis XIV. And he speaks primarily to people of rank, people who do not live directly at court but who wish to familiarize themselves with the manners and customs of the court.

He says in his foreword: "This treatise is not intended for printing but only to satisfy a provincial gentleman who had requested the author, as a particular friend, to give some precepts on civility to his son, whom he intended to send to the court on completing his studies. . . . He [the author] undertook this work only for well-bred people; *it is only to them that it is addressed*; and particularly to youth, which might derive some utility from these small pieces of advice, as not everyone has the opportunity nor the means of coming to the court at Paris to learn the fine points of politeness."

People living in the example-setting circle do not need books in order to know how "one" behaves. This is obvious; it is therefore important to ascertain with what intentions and for which public these precepts are written and printed-precepts which are originally the distinguishing secret of the narrow circles of the court aristocracy.

The intended public is quite clear. It is stressed that the advice is only for *honnêtes gens*, i.e., by and large for upper-class people. Primarily the book meets the need of the provincial nobility to know about behavior at court, and in addition that of distinguished foreigners. But it may be assumed that the not inconsiderable success of this book resulted, among other things, from the interest of leading bourgeois strata. There is ample evidence to show that at this period customs, behavior, and fashions from the court are continuously penetrating the upper middle classes, where they are imitated and more or less altered in accordance with the different social situation. They thereby lose, to some extent, their character as means of distinguishing the upper class. They are somewhat devalued. This compels those above to further refinement and development of behavior. And from this mechanism—the development of courtly customs, their dissemination downward, their slight social deformation, their devaluation as marks of distinction—the constant movement in behavior patterns through the upper class receives part of its motivation. What is important is that in this change, in the inventions and fashions of courtly behavior, which are at first sight perhaps chaotic and accidental, over extended time spans certain directions or lines of development emerge. These include, for example, what may be described as an advance of the threshold of embarrassment and shame, as "refinement," or as "civilization." A particular social dynamism triggers a particular psychological one, which has its own regularities.

2. In the eighteenth century wealth increases, and with it the advance of the bourgeois classes. The court circle now includes, directly alongside aristocratic elements, a larger number of bourgeois elements than in the preceding century, without the differences in social rank ever being lost. Shortly before the French Revolution the tendency toward self-encapsulation of the socially weakening aristocracy is intensified once more.

Nevertheless, this extended court society, in which aristocratic and bourgeois elements intermingle, and which has no distinct boundaries barring entry from below must be envisaged as a whole. It comprises the hierarchically structured elite of the country. The compulsion to penetrate or at least imitate it constantly increases with the growing interdependence and prosperity of broad strata. Clerical circles, above all, become popularizers of the courtly customs. The moderated restraint of the emotions and the disciplined shaping of behavior as a whole, which under the name of *civilité* have been developed in the upper class as a purely secular and social phenomenon, a consequence of certain forms of social life, have affinities to particular tendencies in traditional ecclesiastical behavior. *Civilité* is given a new Christian religious foundation. The Church proves, as so often, one of the most important organs of the downward diffusion of behavioral models.

"It is a surprising thing," says the venerable Father La Salle at the beginning of the preface to his rules of Christian *civilité*, "that the majority of Christians regard decency and civility only as a *purely human and worldly quality* and, not thinking to elevate their minds more highly, do not consider it a virtue related to God, our neighbor, and ourselves. This well shows how little Christianity there is in the world.'' And as a good deal of the education in France lay in the hands of ecclesiastical bodies, it was above all, if not exclusively, through their mediation that a growing flood of *civilité* tracts now inundated the country. They were used as manuals in the elementary education of children, and were often printed and distributed together with the first instructions on reading and writing.

Precisely thereby the concept of *civilité* is increasingly devalued for the social elite. It begins to undergo a process similar to that which earlier overtook the concept of *courtoisie*.

Excursus on the Rise and Decline of the
Concepts of Courtoisie and Civilité

3. *Courtoisie* originally referred to the forms of behavior that developed at the courts of the great feudal lords. Even during the Middle Ages the meaning of the word clearly lost much of its original social restriction to the "court," coming into use in bourgeois circles as well. With the slow extinction of the knightly-feudal warrior nobility and the formation of a new absolute court aristocracy in the course of the sixteenth and seventeenth centuries, the concept of *civilité* is slowly elevated as the expression of socially acceptable behavior. *Courtoisie* and *civilité* exist side by side during the French transitional society of the sixteenth century, with its half knightly-feudal, half absolute court character. In the course of the seventeenth century, however, the concept *courtoisie* gradually goes out of fashion in France.

"The words *courtois* and *courtoisie*," says a French writer in 1675,[33] "are beginning to age and are no longer good usage. We say *civil*, *honneste*; *civilité*, *honnesteté*."

Indeed, the word *courtoisie* now actually appears as a bourgeois concept. "My neighbor, the bourgeois, . . . says in accordance with the language of the bourgeoisie of Paris 'affable' and 'courteous' (*courtois*) . . . he does not express himself politely because the words 'courteous' and 'affable' are scarcely in use among people of the world, and the words 'civil' and 'decent' (*honnête*) have taken their place, just as 'civility' and 'decency' have taken the place of 'courtesy' and 'affability.'" So we read in a conversation with the title *On*

Good and Bad Usage in Expressing Oneself: On Bourgeois Manners of Speaking, by F. de Callières (1694, pp. 110ff.).

In a very similar way, in the course of the eighteenth century, the concept of *civilité* slowly loses its hold among the upper class of court society. This class is now in its turn undergoing a very slow process of transformation, of bourgeoisification, which, at least up to 1750, is always combined with an inverse process assimilating bourgeois elements to the court. Something of the resultant problem is perceptible, for example, when in 1745 Abbé Gedoyn, in an essay "De l'urbanité romaine" (*Oeuvres diverses*, p. 173), discusses the question of why, in his own society, the expression *urbanité*, though it refers to something very fine, has never come into use as much as *civilité, humanité, politesse*, or *galanterie*, and he replies: "*Urbanitas* signified that *politesse* of language, mind, and manners attached singularly to the city of Rome, which was called par excellence *Urbs*, the city, whereas among us, where this politeness is not the privilege of any city in particular, not even of the capital, but solely of the court, the term urbanity becomes a term . . . with which we may dispense."

If one realizes that "city" at this time refers more or less to "bourgeois good society" as against the narrower court society, one readily perceives the topical importance of the question raised here.

In most of the statements from this period, the use of *civilité* has receded, as here, in the face of *politesse*, and the identification of this whole complex of ideas with *humanité* emerges more sharply.

As early as 1733, Voltaire, in the dedication of his *Zaïre* to a bourgeois, A. M. Faulkner, an English merchant, expressed these tendencies very clearly: "Since the regency of Anne of Austria the French have been the most sociable and the most polite people in the world . . . and *this politeness is not in the least an arbitrary matter, like that which is called* civilité, *but is a law of nature* which they have happily cultivated more than other peoples."

Like the concept of *courtoisie* earlier, *civilité* now is slowly beginning to sink. Shortly afterward, the content of this and related terms is taken up and extended in a new concept, the expression of a new form of self-consciousness, the concept of *civilisation. Courtoisie, civilité*, and *civilisation* mark three stages of a social development. They indicate which society is speaking and being addressed at a given time. However, the actual change in the behavior of the upper classes, the development of the models of behavior which will henceforth be called "civilized," takes place—at least so far as it is visible in the areas discussed here—in the middle phase. The concept of *civilisation* indicates quite clearly in its nineteenth-century usage that the *process* of civilization—or, more strictly speaking, a phase of this process—has been completed and forgotten. People only want to accomplish this process for other nations, and also, for a period, for the lower classes of their own society. To the upper and middle classes of their own society, civilization appears as a firm possession. They wish above all to disseminate it, and at most to develop it within the framework of the standard already reached.

The examples quoted clearly express the movement toward this standard in the preceding stage of the absolute courts.

A Review of the Curve Marking the "Civilization" of Eating Habits

4. At the end of the eighteenth century, shortly before the revolution, the French upper class attained approximately the standard of eating manners, and certainly not only of eating manners, that was gradually to be taken for granted in the whole of civilized society. Example M from the year 1786 is instructive enough: it shows as still a decidedly courtly custom exactly the same use of the serviette which in the meantime has become customary in the whole of civilized bourgeois society. It shows the exclusion of the fork from the eating of soup, the necessity of which, to be sure, is only understood if we recall that soup often used to contain, and still contains in France, more solid content than it does now. It further shows the requirement not to cut but to break one's bread at table, a requirement that has in the meantime been democratized, as a courtly demand. And the same applies to the way in which one drinks coffee.

These are a few examples of how our everyday ritual was formed. If this series were continued up to the present day, further changes of detail would be seen: new imperatives are added, old ones are relaxed; a wealth of national and social variations on table manners emerges; the penetration of the middle classes, the working class, the peasantry by the uniform ritual of civilization, and by the regulation of drives that its acquisition requires, is of varying strength. But the essential basis of what is required and what is forbidden in civilized society— the standard eating technique, the manner of using knife, fork, spoon, plate, serviette, and other eating utensils—these remain in their essential features unchanged. Even the development of technology in all areas—even that of cooking—by the introduction of new sources of energy has left the techniques of eating and other forms of behavior essentially unchanged. Only on very close inspection does one observe traces of a trend that is continuing to develop.

What is still changing now is, above all, the technology of production. The technology of consumption was developed and kept in motion by social formations which were, to a degree never since equaled, consumption classes. With their social decline, the rapid and intensive elaboration of consumption techniques ceases and is delegated into what now becomes the private (in contrast to the occupational) sphere of life. Correspondingly, the tempo of movement and change in these spheres which during the stage of the absolute courts was relatively fast, slows down once again.

Even the shapes of eating utensils—plates, dishes, knives, forks, and spoons—are from now on no more than variations on themes of the *dix-huitième* and preceding centuries. Certainly there are still very many changes of detail. One example is the differentiation of utensils. On many occasions, not only the plates are changed after each course but the eating utensils, too. It does not suffice to eat simply with knife, fork, and spoon instead of with one's hands. More and more in the upper class a special implement is used for each kind of food. Soup-spoons, fish knives, and meat knives are on one side of the plate. Forks for the hors d'oeuvre, fish, and meat on the other. Above the plate are fork, spoon, or knife—according to the custom of the country—for sweet foods. And for the dessert and fruit yet another implement is brought in. All these utensils are differently shaped and equipped. They are now larger, now smaller, now more round, now more pointed. But on closer consideration they do not represent anything actually new. They, too, are variations on the same theme, differentiations within the same standard. And only on a few points— above all, in the use of the knife—do slow movements begin to show themselves that lead beyond the standard already attained. Later there will be more to say on this.

5. In a sense, something similar is true of the period up to the fifteenth century. Up to then—for very different reasons—the standard eating technique, the basic stock of what is socially prohibited and permitted, like the behavior of people toward one another and

toward themselves (of which these prohibitions and commands are expressions), remains fairly constant in its essential features, even if here too fashions, fluctuations, regional and social variations, and a slow movement in a particular direction are by no means entirely absent.

Nor are the transitions from one phase to another to be ascertained with complete exactness. The more rapid movement begins later here, earlier there, and everywhere one finds slight preparatory shifts. Nevertheless, the overall shape of the curve is everywhere broadly the same: first the medieval phase, with a certain climax in the flowering of knightly-courtly society, marked by eating with the hands. Then a phase of relatively rapid movement and change, embracing roughly the sixteenth, seventeenth, and eighteenth centuries, in which the compulsions to elaborate eating behavior press constantly in one direction, toward a new standard of table manners.

From then on, one again observes a phase which remains within the framework of the standard already reached, though with a very slow movement in a certain direction. The elaboration of everyday conduct never entirely loses, in this period either, its importance as an instrument of social distinction. But from now on, it no longer plays the same role as in the preceding phase. More exclusively than before, money becomes the basis of social differences. And what people actually achieve and produce becomes more important than their manners.

6. Taken together, the examples show very clearly how this movement progresses. The prohibitions of medieval society, even at the feudal courts do not yet impose any very great restraint on the play of emotions. Compared to later eras, social control is mild. Manners, measured against later ones, are relaxed in all senses of the word. One ought not to snort or smack one's lips while eating. One ought not to spit across the table or blow one's nose on the tablecloth (for this is used for wiping greasy fingers) or into the fingers (with which one holds the common dish). Eating from the same dish or plate as others is taken for granted. One must only refrain from falling on the dish like a pig, and from dipping bitten food into the communal sauce.

Many of these customs are still mentioned in Erasmus's treatise and in its adaptation by Calviac. More clearly than by inspecting particular accounts of contemporary manners, by surveying the whole movement one sees how it progresses. Table utensils are still limited; on the left the bread, on the right the glass and knife. That is all. The fork is already mentioned, although with a limited function as an instrument for lifting food from the common dish. And, like the handkerchief, the napkin also appears already, both still—a symbol of transition—as optional rather than necessary implements: if you have a handkerchief, the precepts say, use it rather than your fingers. If a napkin is provided, lay it over your left shoulder. One hundred and fifty years later both napkin and handkerchief are, like the fork, more or less indispensable utensils in the courtly class.

The curve followed by other habits and customs is similar. First the soup is often drunk, whether from the common dish or from ladles used by several people. In the *courtois* writings the use of the spoon is prescribed. It, too, will first of all serve several together. A further step is shown by the quotation from Calviac of 1560. He mentions that it was customary among Germans to allow each guest his own spoon. The next step is shown by Courtin's text from the year 1672. Now one no longer eats the soup directly from the common dish, but pours some into one's own plate, first of all using one's own spoon; but there are even people, we read here, who are so *delicate* that they do not wish to eat from a dish into which others have dipped a spoon already used. It is therefore necessary to wipe one's spoon with the serviette before dipping it into the dish. And some people are not satisfied even with this. For them, one is not allowed to dip a used spoon back into the common dish at all; instead, one must ask for a clean one for this purpose.

Statements like these show not only how the whole ritual of living together is in flux, but also how people themselves are aware of this change.

Here, step by step, the now accepted way of taking soup is being established: everyone has his own plate and his own spoon, and the soup is distributed with a specialized implement. Eating has acquired a new style corresponding to the new necessities of social life.

Nothing in table manners is self-evident or the product, as it were, of a "natural" feeling of delicacy. The spoon, fork, and napkin are not invented by individuals as technical implements with obvious purposes and clear directions for use. Over centuries, in direct social intercourse and use, their functions are gradually defined, their forms sought and consolidated. Each custom in the changing ritual, however minute, establishes itself infinitely slowly, even forms of behavior that to us seem quite elementary or simply "reasonable," such as the custom of taking liquid only with the spoon. Every movement of the hand—for example, the way in which one holds and moves knife, spoon, or fork—is standardized only step by step. And the social mechanism of standardization is itself seen in outline if the series of images is surveyed as a whole. There is a more or less limited courtly circle which first stamps the models only for the needs of its own social situation and in conformity with the psychological condition corresponding to it. But clearly the structure and development of French society as a whole gradually makes ever broader strata willing and anxious to adopt the models developed above them: they spread, also very gradually, throughout the whole of society, certainly not without undergoing some modification in the process.

The passage of models from one social unit to another, now from the centers of a society to its outposts (e.g., from the Parisian court to other courts), now within the same political-social unit (e.g., within France or Saxony, from above to below or from below to above), is to be counted, in the whole civilizing process, among the most important individual movements. What the examples show is only a limited segment of these. Not only the eating manners but also forms of thinking or speaking, in short, of behavior in general, are molded in a similar way throughout France, even if there are significant differences in the timing and structure of their patterns of development. The elaboration of a particular ritual of human relations in the course of social and psychological development cannot be isolated, even if here, as a first attempt, it has only been possible to follow a single strand. A short example from the process of the "civilization" of speech may serve as a reminder that the observation of manners and their transformation exposes to view only a very simple and easily accessible segment of a much more far-reaching process of social change.

Excursus on the Modeling of Speech at Court

7. For speech, too, a limited circle first develops certain standards.

As in Germany, though to a far lesser extent, the language spoken in court society was different from the language spoken by the bourgeoisie.

"You know," we read in a little work which in its time was much read, *Mots à la mode* by Callières, in the edition of 1693 (p. 46), "that the bourgeois speak very differently from us."

If we examine more closely what is termed "bourgeois" speech, and what is referred to as the expression of the courtly upper class, we encounter the same phenomenon that can be observed in eating-customs and manners in general: much of what in the seventeenth and to some extent the eighteenth century was the distinguishing form of expression and language of court society gradually becomes the French national language.

The young son of bourgeois parents, M. Thibault, is presented to us visiting a small aristocratic society. The lady of the house asks after his father. "He is your very humble servant, Madame," Thibault answers, "and he is still poorly, as you well know, since you have graciously sent oftentimes to inquire about the state of his health."

The situation is clear. A certain social contact exists between the aristocratic circle and the bourgeois family. The lady of the house has mentioned it previously. She also says that the elder Thibault is a very nice man, not without adding that such acquaintances are sometimes quite useful to the aristocracy because these people, after all, have money.[54] And at this point one recalls the very different structure of German society.

But social contacts at this time are clearly not close enough, leaving aside the bourgeois intelligentsia, to have effaced the linguistic differences between the classes. Every other word the young Thibault says is, by the standards of court society, awkward and gross, smelling bourgeois—as the courtiers put it, "from the mouth." In court society one does not say "as you well know" or "oftentimes" or "poorly" (*comme bien sçavez, souventes fois, maladif*).

One does not say, like M. Thibault in the ensuing conversation, "Je vous demande excuse" (I beg to be excused). In courtly society one says, as today in bourgeois society, "Je vous demande pardon" (I beg your pardon).

M. Thibault says: "Un mien ami, un mien parent, un mien cousin" (A friend of mine, etc.), instead of the courtly "un de mes amis, un de mes parents" (p. 20). He says "deffunct mon père, le pauvre deffunct" (deceased). And he is instructed that that too is not one of the expressions "which civility has introduced among well-spoken people. People of the world do not say that a man is deceased when they mean that he is dead" (p. 22). The word can be used at most when saying "we must pray to God for the soul of the deceased . . . but those who speak well say rather: my late father, the late Duke, etc." (*feu mon père*, etc.). And it is pointed out that "for the poor deceased" is "a very bourgeois turn of phrase."

8. Here, too, as with manners, there is a kind of double movement: the bourgeois are, as it were, "courtified," and the aristocracy, "bourgeoisified." Or, more precisely: bourgeois people are influenced by the behavior of courtly people, and vice versa. The influence from below to above is certainly very much weaker in the seventeenth century in France than in the eighteenth. But it is not entirely absent: the château Vaux-le Vicomte of the bourgeois intendant of finances, Nicolas Fouquet, antedates the royal Versailles, and is in many ways its model. That is a clear example. The wealth of leading bourgeois strata compels those above to compete. And the incessant influx of bourgeois people to the circle of the court also produces a specific movement in speech: with the new human substance it brings new linguistic substance, the slang of the bourgeoisie, into the circle of the court. Elements of it are constantly being assimilated into courtly language, polished, refined, transformed; they are made, in a word, "courtly," i.e., adapted to the standard of sensibility of the court circles. They are thereby turned into means of distinguishing the *gens de la cour* from the bourgeoisie, and then perhaps, after some time, penetrate the bourgeoisie once more, thus refined and modified, to become "specifically bourgeois."

There is, says the Duke in one of the conversations quoted from Callières (*Du bon et du mauvais usage*, p. 98), a manner of speaking "most common among the bourgeois of Paris and even among some courtiers raised among the bourgeoisie. It is to say 'Let us go and see' (*voyons voir*), instead of saying 'Let us see' (*voyons*), and avoiding the word 'go,' which is perfectly useless and disagreeable in this place."

But there has recently come into use, the Duke continues, "another bad turn of phrase, which began among the lowest people and made its fortune at the court, like those favorites without merit who got themselves elevated there in the old days. It is 'il en sçait bien long,' meaning that someone is subtle and clever. The ladies of the court are beginning to use it, too."

So it goes on. The bourgeois and even some court people say "il faut que nous faisions cela" instead of "il faut que nous fassions cela." Some say "l'on za" and "l'on zest" instead of the courtly "l'on a" and "l'on est." They say "Je le l'ai" instead of "Je l'ai."

In almost all these cases the linguistic form which here appears as courtly has indeed become the national usage. But there are also examples of courtly linguistic formations being gradually discarded as "too refined," "too affected."

9. All this elucidates at the same time what was said earlier about the sociogenetic differences between the German and French national characters. Language is one of the most accessible manifestations of what we perceive as national character. Here it can be seen from a single concrete example how this peculiar and typical character is elaborated in conjunction with certain social formations. The French language was decisively stamped by the court and court society. For the German language the Imperial Chamber and Chancellery for a time played a similar role, even if they did not have remotely the same influence as the French court. As late as 1643, someone claims his language to be exemplary "because it is modeled on writings from the Chamber at Speyer."[55] Then it was the universities that attained almost the same importance for German culture and language as the court in France. But these two socially closely related entities, Chancellery and university, influenced speech less than writing; they formed the German written language not through conversation but through documents, letters, and books. And if Nietzsche observes that even the German drinking song is erudite, or if he contrasts the elimination of specialist terms by the courtly Voltaire to the practice of the Germans, he sees very clearly the results of these different historical developments.

10. If in France the *gens de la cour* say "This is spoken well and this badly," a large question is raised that must be at least touched on in passing: "By what standards are they actually judging what is good and bad in language? What are their criteria for selecting, polishing, and modifying expressions?"

Sometimes they reflect on this themselves. What they say on the subject is at first sight rather surprising, and at any rate significant beyond the area of language. Phrases, words, and nuances are good *because* they, the members of the social elite, use them; and they are bad *because* social inferiors speak in this way.

M. Thibault sometimes defends himself when he is told that this or that turn of phrase is bad. "I am much obliged to you, Madame," he says (*Du bon et du mauvais usage*, p. 23), "for the trouble you are taking to instruct me, yet it seems to me that the term 'deceased' is a well-established word used by a great many well-bred people (*honnêtes gens*)."

"It is very possible," the lady answers, "that there are many well-bred people who are insufficiently familiar with the delicacy of our language . . . a delicacy which is known to only a small number of well-spoken people and causes them not to say that a man is deceased in order to say that he is dead."

A small circle of people is versed in this delicacy of language; to speak as they do is to speak correctly. What the others say does not count. The judgments are apodictic. A reason other than that "We, the elite, speak thus, and only we have sensitivity to language" is neither needed nor known. "With regard to errors committed against good usage," it is expressly stated in another place, "as there are no definite rules it depends only on the consent of a certain number of polite people whose ears are accustomed to certain ways of speaking and to preferring them to others" (p. 98). And then the words are listed that should be avoided.

Antiquated words are unsuited to ordinary, serious speech. Very new words must arouse suspicion of affectation—we might perhaps say, of snobbery. Learned words that smack of Latin and Greek must be suspect to all *gens du monde*. They surround anyone using them with an atmosphere of pedantry, if other words are known that express the same thing simply.

Low words used by the common people must be carefully avoided, for those who use them show that they have had a "low education." "And it is of these words, that is, low words," says the courtly speaker, "that we speak in this connection"—he means in the contraposition of courtly and bourgeois language.

The reason given for the expurgation of "bad" words from language is the refinement of feeling that plays no small role in the whole civilizing process. But this refinement is the possession of a relatively small group. Either one has this sensitivity or one has not—that, roughly, is the speaker's attitude. The people who possess this delicacy, a small circle, determine by their consensus what is held to be good or bad.

In other words, of all the rational arguments that might be put forward for the selection of expressions, the social argument, that something is better because it is the usage of the upper class, or even of only an elite within the upper class, is by far the most prominent.

"Antiquated words," words that have gone out of fashion, are used by the older generation or by those who are not permanently involved directly in court life, the déclassé. "Too new words" are used by the clique of young people who have yet to be accepted, who speak their special "slang," a part of which will perhaps be tomorrow's fashion. "Learned words" are used, as in Germany, by those educated at the universities, especially lawyers and the higher administrators, i.e., in France, the *noblesse de robe*. "Low expressions" are all the words used by the bourgeoisie down to the populace. The linguistic polemic corresponds to a quite definite, very characteristic social stratification. It shows and delimits the group which at a given moment exerts control over language: in a broader sense the *gens de la cour*, but in a narrower sense a smaller, particularly aristocratic circle of people who temporarily have influence at court, and who carefully distinguish themselves from the social climbers, the courtiers from bourgeois nurseries, from the "antiquated," from the "young people," the "snobbish" competitors of the rising generation, and last but not least, from the specialized officials emanating from the university. This circle is the predominant influence on language formation at this time. How the members of these narrower and broader court circles speak is "how to speak," to speak *comme il faut*. Here the models of speech are formed that subsequently spread out in longer or shorter waves. The manner in which language develops and is stamped corresponds to a certain social structure. Accordingly, from the mid-eighteenth century onward, bourgeois influence on the French language slowly gains in strength. But this long passage through a stage dominated by the court aristocracy remains perceptible in the French language today, as does the passage of German through a stage of dominance by a learned middle-class intelligentsia. And wherever elites or pseudo-elites form within French bourgeois society, they attach themselves to these older, distinguishing tendencies in their language.

11. Language is one of the embodiments of social or mental life. Much that can be observed in the way language is molded is also evident in other embodiments of society. For example, the way people argue that this behavior or this custom at table is better than that, is scarcely distinguishable from the way they claim one linguistic expression to be preferable to another.

This does not entirely correspond to the expectation that a twentieth-century observer may have. For example, he expects to find the elimination of "eating with the hands," the introduction of the fork, individual cutlery and crockery, and all the other rituals of his own standard explained by "hygienic reasons." For that is the way in which he himself in general explains these customs. But as late as the second half of the eighteenth century, hardly anything of this kind is found to motivate the greater restraint that people impose upon themselves. At any rate, the so-called "rational explanations" are very far in the background compared to others.

In the earliest stages the need for restraint was usually explained by saying: Do this and not that, for it is not *courtois*, not "courtly"; a "noble" man does not do such things. At most, the reason given is consideration for the embarrassment of others, as in Tannhäuser's *Hofzucht*, where he says, in effect, "Do not scratch yourself with your hand, with which you also hold the common dish; your table companions might notice it, so use your coat to scratch yourself" (Example A, v. 109ff.). And clearly here the threshold of embarrassment differs from that of the following period.

Later on, a similar argument is used for everything: Do not do that, for it is not *civil* or *bienséant*. Or such an argument is used to explain the respect due to those of higher social rank.

As in the molding of speech, so too in the molding of other aspects of behavior in society, social motivations, adaptations of behavior to the models of influential circles, are by far the most important. Even the expressions used in motivating "good behavior" at table are very frequently exactly the same as those used in motivating "good speech."

In Callières's *Du bon et du mauvais usage dans les manières de s'exprimer*, reference is made, for example, to this or that expression "which civility has introduced among people who speak well" (p. 22).

Exactly the same concept of *civilité* is also used again and again by Courtin and La Salle to express what is good and bad in manners. And exactly as Callières here speaks simply of the people *qui parlent bien*, Courtin (at the end of Example G) says, in effect, "Formerly one was allowed to do this or that, but today one is no longer allowed to." Callières says in 1694 that there are a great many people who are not sufficiently conversant with the *délicatesse* of the language: "C'est cette délicatesse qui n'est connu que d'une petite nombre de gens." Courtin uses the same expression in 1672 when he says that it is necessary always to wipe one's spoon before dipping it into the common dish if one has already used it, "there being people so *delicate* that they would not wish to eat soup in which you had dipped it after putting it into your mouth" (Example G).

This *délicatesse*, this sensibility and a highly developed feeling for the "embarrassing," is at first all a distinguishing feature of small courtly circles, then of court society as a whole. This applies to language in exactly the same way as to eating habits. On what this delicacy is based, and why it demands that this be done and not that, is not said and not asked. What is observed is simply that "delicacy"— or, rather, the embarrassment threshold—is advancing. In conjunction with a very specific social situation, the feelings and affects are first transformed in the upper class, and the structure of society as a whole permits this changed affect standard to spread slowly throughout society. Nothing indicates that the affective condition, the degree of sensitivity, is changed for reasons that we describe as "clearly rational" from a demonstrable understanding of particular causal connections. Courtin does not say, as would be said later, that some people feel it to be "unhygienic" or "detrimental to health" to take soup from the same dish as others. Certainly, delicacy of feeling is heightened under the pressure of the courtly situation in a way which is later justified partly by scientific investigations, even though a major part of the taboos that people gradually impose on themselves in their dealings with each other, a far larger part than is usually thought, has not the slightest connection with "hygiene" but is concerned even today merely with "delicacy of feeling." At any rate, the process moves in some respects in a way that is exactly opposite to what is commonly assumed today. First, over a long period and in conjunction with a specific change in human relationships, that is in society, the embarrassment threshold is raised. The structure of emotions, the sensitivity, and the behavior of people change, despite fluctuations, in a quite definite direction. Then, at a certain point, this behavior is recognized as "hygienically correct," i.e., it is justified by clear insight into causal connections and taken further in the same direction or consolidated. The expansion of the threshold of embarrassment may be connected at some points with more or less indefinite and, at first, rationally inexplicable experiences of the way in which certain diseases are passed on or, more precisely, with indefinite and therefore rationally undefined fears and anxieties which point vaguely in the direction subsequently confirmed by clear understanding. But "rational understanding" is not the motor of the "civilizing" of eating or of other behavior.

The close parallel between the "civilizing" of eating and that of speech is highly instructive in this context. It makes clear that the change in behavior at table is part of a very extensive transformation of human feelings and attitudes. It also illustrates to what degree the motive forces of this development come from the social structure, from the way in which people are connected to each other. We see more clearly how relatively small circles first form the center of the movement and how the process then gradually passes to broader sections. But this diffusion presupposes very specific contacts, and therefore a quite definite structure of society. Moreover, it could certainly not have taken place had there not been established for larger classes, as well as for the model-forming circles, conditions of life—or, in other words, a social situation—that made both possible and necessary a gradual transformation of the emotions and behavior, an advance in the threshold of embarrassment.

The process that emerges resembles in form—though not in substance—chemical processes in which a liquid, the whole of which is subjected to conditions of chemical change (e.g., crystallization), first takes on crystalline form at a small nucleus, while the rest then gradually crystallizes around this core. Nothing would be more erroneous than to take the core of crystallization for the cause of the transformation.

The fact that a particular class in one or another phase of social development forms the center of a process and thus supplies models for other classes, and that these models are diffused to other classes and received by them, itself presupposes a social situation and a special structure of society as a whole, by virtue of which one circle is allotted the function of creating models and the other that of spreading and assimilating them. What kinds of change in the integration of society set these behavioral changes in motion will be discussed in detail later.

Group 2:

On the Eating of Meat

1. Although human phenomena—whether attitudes, wishes, or products of human action may be looked at on their own, independently of their connections with the social life of men, they are by nature nothing but substantializations of human relations and of human behavior, embodiments of social and mental life. This is true of speech, which is nothing other than human relations turned into sound; it is true of art, science, economics, and politics; it is true both of phenomena which rank high on our scale of values and of others which seem trivial or worthless. Often it is precisely these latter, trivial phenomena that give us clear and simple insights into the structure and development of the psyche and its relations which are denied us by the former. The attitudes of men to meat-eating, for example, is highly illuminating with regard to the dynamics of human relationships and personality structures.

In the Middle Ages, people move between at least three different sets of behavior toward meat. Here, as with a hundred other phenomena, we see the extreme diversity of behavior characteristic of medieval society as compared with its modern counterpart. The medieval social structure is far less conducive to the permeation of models developed in a specific social center through the society as a whole. Certain modes of behavior often predominate in a particular social class throughout the Western world, while in a different class or estate behavior is very different. For this reason, the behavioral differences between different classes in the same region are often greater than those between regionally separate representatives of the same social class. And if modes of behavior pass from one class to another, which certainly happens, they change their face more radically in accordance with the greater isolation of the classes.

The relation to meat-eating moves in the medieval world between the following poles. On the one hand, in the secular upper class the consumption of meat is extraordinarily high, compared to the standard of our own times. A tendency prevails to devour quantities of meat that to us seem fantastic. On the other hand, in the monasteries an ascetic abstention from all meat-eating largely prevails, an absention resulting from self-denial, not from shortage, and often accompanied by a radical depreciation or restriction of eating. From these circles come expressions of strong aversion to the "gluttony" among the upper-class laymen.

The meat consumption of the lowest class, the peasants, is also frequently extremely limited—not from a spiritual need, a voluntary renunciation with regard to God and the next world, but from shortage. Cattle are expensive and therefore destined, for a long period, essentially for the rulers' tables. "If the peasant reared cattle," it has been said,[56] "it was largely for the privileged, the nobility, and the burghers," not forgetting the clerics, who ranged in varying degrees from asceticism to approximately the behavior of the secular upper class. Exact data on the meat consumption of the upper classes in the Middle Ages and at the beginning of the modern age are sparse. There were, no doubt, considerable differences between the lesser, poorer knights and the great feudal lords. The standards of the knights will frequently have been scarcely removed from those of the peasants.

A calculation of the meat consumption of a north German court from relatively recent times, the seventeenth century, indicates a consumption of two pounds per head per day, in addition to large quantities of venison, birds, and fish.[57] Spices play a major, vegetables a relatively minor role. Other information points fairly unanimously in the same direction. The subject remains to be investigated in detail.

2. Another change can be documented more exactly. The manner in which meat is served changes considerably from the Middle Ages to modern times. The curve of this change is very instructive. In the upper class of medieval society, the dead animal or large parts of it are often brought whole to the table. Not only whole fish and whole birds (sometimes with their feathers) but also whole rabbits, lambs, and quarters of veal appear on the table, not to mention the larger venison or the pigs and oxen roasted on the spit.[58]

The animal is carved on the table. This is why the books on manners repeat, up to the seventeenth and sometimes even the eighteenth century, how important it is for a well-bred man to be good at carving meat. "Discenda a primis statim annis secandi ratio . . ." (The correct way to carve should be taught from the first years) says Erasmus in 1530.

"When serving," says Courtin in 1672,

> one must always give away the best portion and keep the smallest, and touch nothing except with the fork; this is why, if a person of rank asks you for something that is in front of you, it is important to know how to cut meat with propriety and method, and to know the best portions, in order to be able to serve them with civility. The way to cut them is not prescribed here, because it is a subject on which special books have been written, in which all the pieces are illustrated to show where the meat must first be held with a fork to cut it, for as we have just said, *the meat must never be touched . . . by hand, not even while eating;* then where the knife must be placed to cut it; what must be lifted first . . . what is the best piece, and the piece of honor that must be served to the person of highest rank. It is easy to learn how to carve when one has eaten three or four times at a good table, and for the same reason it is no disgrace to excuse oneself and leave to another what one cannot do oneself.

And the German parallel, the *New vermehrtes Trincier-Büchlein* (New, enlarged carving manual), printed in Rintelen in 1650, says:

> Because the office of carver at princely courts is not reckoned as the lowest but among the most honorable, the same must therefore be either of the nobility or other good origin, of straight and well-proportioned body, good straight arms and nimble hands. In all public cutting he should . . . abstain from large movements and useless and foolish ceremonies . . . and make quite sure that he is not nervous, *so that he does not bring dishonor through trembling of the body and hands* and because in any case this does not befit those at princely tables.

Both carving and distributing the meat are particular honors. It usually falls to the master of the house or to distinguished guests whom he requests to perform the office. "The young and those of lower rank should not interfere in serving, but only take for themselves in their turn," says the anonymous *Civilité française* of 1714.

In the seventeenth century the carving of meat at table gradually ceases, in the French upper class, to be an indispensable accomplishment of the man of the world, like hunting, fencing, and dancing. The passage quoted from Courtin points to this.

3. That the serving of large parts of the animal to be carved at table slowly goes out of use is connected with many factors. One of the most important may be the gradual reduction in the size of the household[59] as part of the movement from larger to smaller family units; then comes the removal of production and processing activities like weaving, spinning, and slaughtering from the household, and their gradual transference to specialists, craftsmen, merchants, and manufacturers, who practice them professionally while the household becomes essentially a consumption unit.

Here, too, the psychological tendency matches the large social process: today it would arouse rather uneasy feelings in many people if they or others had to carve half a calf or pig at table or cut meat from a pheasant still adorned with its feathers.

There are even *des gens si délicats*—to repeat the phrase of Courtin, which refers to a related process—to whom the sight of butchers' shops with the bodies of dead animals is distasteful, and others who from more or less rationally disguised feelings of disgust refuse to eat meat altogether. But these are forward thrusts in the threshold of repugnance that go beyond the standard of civilized society in the twentieth century, and are therefore considered "abnormal." Nevertheless, it cannot be ignored that it was advances of this kind (if they coincided with the direction of social development in general) that led in the past to changes of standards, and that this particular advance in the threshold of repugnance is proceeding in the same direction that has been followed thus far.

This direction is quite clear. From a standard of feeling by which the sight and carving of a dead animal on the table are actually pleasurable, or at least not at all unpleasant, the development leads to another standard by which reminders that the meat dish has something to do with the killing of an animal are avoided to the utmost. In many of our meat dishes the animal form is so concealed and changed by the art of its preparation and carving that while eating one is scarcely reminded of its origin.

It will be shown how people, in the course of the civilizing process, seek to suppress in themselves every characteristic that they feel to be "animal." They likewise suppress such characteristics in their food.

In this area, too, the development is certainly not uniform everywhere. In England, for example, where in many aspects of life older forms are more prominently preserved than on the Continent, the serving of large portions of meat (and with it the task, which falls to the master of the house, of carving and distributing it) survives in the form of the "joint" to a greater extent than in the urban society of Germany and France. However, quite apart from the fact that the present-day joint is itself a very reduced form of the serving of large pieces of meat, there has been no lack of reactions to it that mark the advance in the threshold of repugnance. The adoption of the "Russian system" of table manners in society about the middle of the last century acted in this direction. "Our chief thanks to the new system," says an English book on manners, *The Habits of Good Society* (1859), "are due for its ostracising that unwieldy barbarism—the joint. Nothing can make a joint look elegant, while it hides the master of the house, and condemns him to the misery of carving. . . . The truth is, *that unless our appetites are very keen, the sight of much meat reeking in its gravy is sufficient to destroy them entirely*, and a huge joint especially is calculated to disgust the epicure. If joints are eaten at all, they should be placed on the side-table, *where they will be out of sight*" (p. 314).

The increasingly strong tendency to remove the distasteful from the sight of society clearly applies, with few exceptions, to the carving of the whole animal.

This carving, as the examples show, was formerly a direct part of social life in the upper class. Then the spectacle is felt more and more to be distasteful. Carving itself does not disappear, since the animal must, of course, be cut when being eaten. But the distasteful is *removed behind the scenes of social life*. Specialists take care of it in the shop or the kitchen. It will be seen again and again how characteristic of the whole process that we call civilization is this movement of segregation, this hiding "behind the scenes" of what has become distasteful. The curve running from the carving of a large part of the animal or even the whole animal at table, through the advance in the threshold of repugnance at the sight of dead animals, to the removal of carving to specialized enclaves behind the scenes is a typical civilization-curve.

It remains to be investigated how far similar processes underlie similar phenomena in other societies. In earlier Chinese civilisation, above all, the concealment of carving behind the scenes was effected much earlier and more radically than in the West. There the process is taken so far that the meat is carved and cut up entirely behind the scenes, and the knife is banished altogether from use at table.

Use of the Knife at Table

4. The knife, too, by the nature of its social use, reflects changes in the human personality with its changing drives and wishes. It is an embodiment of historical situations and structural regularities of society.

One thing above all is characteristic of its use as an eating implement in present-day Western society: the innumerable prohibitions and taboos surrounding it.

Certainly the knife is a dangerous instrument in what may be called a rational sense. It is a weapon of attack. It inflicts wounds and cuts up animals that have been killed.

But this obviously dangerous quality is beset with emotions. The knife becomes a symbol of the most diverse feelings, which are connected to its function and shape but are not deduced "logically" from its purpose. The fear it awakens goes beyond what is rational and is greater than the "calculable," probable danger. And the same is true of the pleasure its use and appearance arouse, even if this aspect is less evident today. In keeping with the structure of our society, the everyday ritual of its use is today determined more by the displeasure and fear than by the pleasure surrounding it. Therefore its use even while eating is restricted by a multitude of prohibitions. These, we have said, extend far beyond the "purely functional"; but for every one of them a rational explanation, usually vague and not easily proved, is in everyone's mouth. Only when these taboos are considered together does the supposition arise that the social attitude toward the knife and the rules governing its use while eating—and, above all, the taboos surrounding it—are primarily emotional in nature. Fear, distaste, guilt, associations and emotions of the most disparate kinds exaggerate the real danger. It is precisely this which anchors such prohibitions so firmly and deeply in the personality and which gives them their taboo character.

5. In the Middle Ages, with their upper class of warriors and the constant readiness of people to fight, and in keeping with the stage of

affect control and the relatively lenient regulations imposed on drives, the prohibitions concerning knives are quite few. "Do not clean your teeth with your knife" is a frequent demand. This is the chief prohibition, but it does indicate the direction of future restrictions on the implement. Moreover, the knife is by far the most important eating utensil. That it is lifted to the mouth is taken for granted.

But there are indications in the late Middle Ages, even more direct ones than in any later period, that the caution required in using a knife results not only from the rational consideration that one might cut or harm oneself, but above all from the emotion aroused by the sight or the idea of a knife pointed at one's own face.

> Bere not your knyf to warde your visage
> For therein is parelle and mykyl drede

we read in Caxton's *Book of Curtesye* (v. 28). Here, as everywhere later, an element of rationally calculable danger is indeed present, and the warning refers to this. But it is the general memory of and association with death and danger, it is the *symbolic* meaning of the instrument that leads, with the advancing internal pacification of society, to the preponderance of feelings of displeasure at the sight of it, and to the limitation and final exclusion of its use in society. The mere sight of a knife pointed at the face arouses fear: "Bear not your knife toward your face, for therein lies much dread." This is the emotional basis of the powerful taboo of a later phase, which forbids the lifting of the knife to the mouth.

The case is similar with the prohibition which in our series of examples was mentioned first by Calviac in 1560 (at the end of Example E): If you pass someone a knife, take the point in your hand and offer him the handle, "for it would not be polite to do otherwise."

Here, as so often until the later stage when the child is given a "rational" explanation for every prohibition, no reason is given for the social ritual except that "it would not be polite to do otherwise." But it is not difficult to see the emotional meaning of this command: one should not move the point of the knife toward someone as in an attack. The mere symbolic meaning of this act, the memory of the warlike threat, is unpleasant. Here, too, the knife ritual contains a rational element. Someone might use the passing of the knife in order suddenly to stab someone. But a social ritual is formed from this danger because the dangerous gesture establishes itself on an emotional level as a general source of displeasure, a symbol of death and danger. Society, which is beginning at this time more and more to limit the real dangers threatening men, and consequently to remodel the affective life of the individual, increasingly places a barrier around the symbols as well, the gestures and instruments of danger. Thus the restrictions and prohibitions on the use of the knife increase, along with the restraints imposed on the individual.

6. If we leave aside the details of this development and only consider the result, the present form of the knife ritual, we find an astonishing abundance of taboos of varying severity. The imperative never to put a knife to one's mouth is one of the gravest and best known. That it greatly exaggerates the actual, probable danger scarcely needs to be said; for social groups accustomed to using knives and eating with them hardly ever injure their mouths with them. The prohibition has become a means of social distinction. In the uneasy feeling that comes over us at the mere sight of someone putting his knife into his mouth, all this is present at once: the general fear that the dangerous symbol arouses, and the more specific fear of social degradation which parents and educators have from early on linked to this practice with their admonitions that "it is not done."

But there are other prohibitions surrounding the knife that have little or nothing to do with a direct danger to the body, and which seem to point to symbolic meanings of the knife other than the association with war. The fairly strict prohibition on eating fish with a knife—circumvented and modified today by the introduction of a special fish knife—seems at first sight rather obscure in its emotional meaning, though psychoanalytical theory points at least in the direction of an explanation. There is a well-known prohibition on holding cutlery, particularly knives, with the whole hand, "like a stick," as La Salle put it, though he was only at that time referring to fork and spoon (Example J). Then there is obviously a general tendency to eliminate or at least restrict the contact of the knife with round or egg-shaped objects. The best-known and one of the gravest of such prohibitions is on cutting potatoes with a knife. But the rather less strict prohibition on cutting dumplings with a knife or opening boiled eggs with one also point in the same direction, and occasionally, in especially sensitive circles, one finds a tendency to avoid cutting apples or even oranges with a knife. "I may hint that no epicure ever yet put knife to apple, and that an orange should be peeled with a spoon," says *The Habits of Good Society* of 1859 and 1889.

7. But these more or less strict particular prohibitions, the list of which could certainly be extended, are in a sense only examples of a general line of development in the use of the knife that is fairly distinct. There is a tendency that slowly permeates civilized society, from the top to the bottom, to restrict the use of the knife (within the framework of existing eating techniques) and wherever possible not to use the instrument at all.

This tendency makes its first appearance in a precept as apparently trivial and obvious as that quoted in Example I: "Do not keep your knife always in your hand, as village people do, but take it only when you need it." It is clearly very strong in the middle of the last century, when the English book on manners just quoted, *The Habits of Good Society*, says: "Let me give you a rule—everything that can be cut without a knife, should be cut with fork alone." And one need only observe present-day usage to find this tendency confirmed. This is one of the few distinct cases of a development which is beginning to go beyond the standard of eating technique and ritual attained by court society. But this is not, of course, to say that the "civilization" of the West will actually continue in this direction. It is a beginning, a possibility like many others that exist in any society. All the same, it is not inconceivable that the preparation of food in the kitchen will develop in a direction that restricts the use of the knife at table still further, displacing it even more than hitherto to specialized enclaves behind the scenes.

Strong retroactive movements are certainly not inconceivable. It is sufficiently known that the conditions of life in the World War I automatically enforced a breakdown of some of the taboos of peacetime civilization. In the trenches, officers and soldiers again ate when necessary with knives and hands. The threshold of delicacy shrank rather rapidly under the pressure of the inescapable situation.

Apart from such breaches, which are always possible and can also lead to new consolidations, the line of development in the use of the knife is quite clear.[60] The regulation and control of emotions intensifies. The commands and prohibitions surrounding the menacing instrument become ever more numerous and differentiated. Finally, the use of the threatening symbol is limited as far as possible.

One cannot avoid comparing the direction of this civilization-curve with the custom long practiced in China. There, as has been said, the knife disappeared many centuries ago from use at table. To many Chinese the manner in which Europeans eat is quite uncivilized. "The Europeans are barbarians," people say there, "they eat with swords." One may surmise that this custom is connected with the fact that for a long time in China the model-making upper class has not been a warrior class but a class pacified to a particularly high degree, a society of scholarly officials.

On the Use of the Fork at Table

8. What is the real use of the fork? It serves to lift food that has been cut up to the mouth. Why do we need a fork for this? Why do we not use our fingers? Because it is "cannibal," as the "Man in the Club-Window," the anonymous author of *The Habits of Good Society* said in 1859. Why is it "cannibal" to eat with one's fingers? That is not a question; it is self-evidently cannibal, barbaric, uncivilized, or whatever else it is called.

But that is precisely the question. Why is it more civilized to eat with a fork?

"Because it is unhygienic to eat with one's fingers." That sounds convincing. To our sensibility it is unhygienic if different people put their fingers into the same dish, because there is a danger of contracting disease through contact with others. Each of us seems to fear that the others are diseased.

But this explanation is not entirely satisfactory. Nowadays we do not eat from common dishes. Everyone puts food into his mouth from his own plate. To pick it up from one's own plate with one's fingers cannot be more "unhygienic" than to put cake, bread, chocolate, or anything else into one's mouth with one's own fingers.

So why does one really need a fork? Why is it "barbaric" and "uncivilized" to put food into one's mouth by hand from one's own plate? Because it is distasteful to dirty one's fingers, or at least to be seen in society with dirty fingers. The suppression of eating by hand from one's own plate has very little to do with the danger of illness, the so-called "rational" explanation. In observing our feelings toward the fork ritual, we can see with particular clarity that the first authority in our decision between "civilized" and "uncivilized" behavior at table is our feeling of distaste. The fork is nothing other than the embodiment of a specific standard of emotions and a specific level of revulsion. Behind the change in eating techniques between the Middle Ages and modern times appears the same process that emerged in the analysis of other incarnations of this kind: a change in the structure of drives and emotions.

Modes of behavior which in the Middle Ages were not felt to be in the least distasteful are increasingly surrounded by unpleasurable feelings. The standard of delicacy finds expression in corresponding social prohibitions. These taboos, so far as one can be ascertained, are nothing other than ritualized or institutionalized feelings of displeasure, distaste, disgust, fear, or shame, feelings which have been socially nurtured under quite specific conditions and which are constantly reproduced, not solely but mainly because they have become institutionally embedded in a particular ritual, in particular forms of conduct.

The examples show—certainly only in a narrow cross-section and in the relatively randomly selected statements of individuals—how, in a phase of development in which the use of the fork was not yet taken for granted, the feeling of distaste that first formed within a narrow circle is slowly extended. "It is very impolite," says Courtin in 1672 (Example G), "to touch anything greasy, a sauce or syrup, etc., with your fingers, apart from the fact that it obliges you to commit two or three more improper acts. One is to wipe your hand frequently on your serviette and to soil it like a kitchen cloth, so that those who see you wipe your mouth with it feel nauseated. Another is to wipe your fingers on your bread, which again is very improper. [N.B. The French terms *propre* and *malpropre* used by Courtin and explained in one of his chapters coincide less with the German terms for clean and unclean (*sauber* and *unsauber*) than with the word frequently used earlier, *proper*.] The third is to lick them, which is the height of impropriety."

The *Civilité* of 1729 by La Salle (Example J), which transmits the behavior of the upper class to broader circles, says on one page: "When the fingers are very greasy, wipe them first on a piece of bread." This shows how far from general acceptance, even at this time, was the standard of delicacy that Courtin had already represented decades earlier. On the other hand, La Salle takes over fairly literally Courtin's precept that "*Bienséance* does not permit anything greasy, a sauce or a syrup, to be touched with the fingers." And, exactly like Courtin, he mentions among the ensuing *incivilités* wiping the hands on bread and licking the fingers, as well as soiling the napkin.

It can be seen that manners are here still in the process of formation. The new standard does not appear suddenly. Certain forms of behavior are placed under prohibition, not because they are unhealthy but because they lead to an offensive sight and disagreeable associations; shame at offering such a spectacle, originally absent, and fear of arousing such associations are gradually spread from the standard setting circles to larger circles by numerous authorities and institutions. However, once such feelings are aroused and firmly established in society by means of certain rituals like that involving the fork, they are constantly reproduced so long as the structure of human relations is not fundamentally altered. The older generation, for whom such a standard of conduct is accepted as a matter of course, urges the children, who do not come into the world already equipped with these feelings and this standard, to control themselves more or less rigorously in accordance with it, and to restrain their drives and inclinations. If a child tries to touch something sticky, wet, or greasy with his fingers, he is told, "You must not do that, people do not do things like that." And the displeasure toward such conduct which is thus aroused by the adult finally arises through habit, without being induced by another person.

To a large extent, however, the conduct and instinctual life of the child are forced even without words into the same mold and in the same direction by the fact that a particular use of knife and fork, for example, is completely established in the adult world—that is, by the example of the environment. Since the pressure or coercion of individual adults is allied to the pressure and example of the whole surrounding world, most children, as they grow up, forget or repress relatively early the fact that their feelings of shame and embarrassment, of pleasure and displeasure, are molded into conformity with a certain standard by external pressure and compulsion. All this appears to them as highly personal, something "inward," implanted in them by nature. While it is still directly visible in the writings of Courtin and La Salle that adults, too, were at first dissuaded from eating with their fingers by consideration for each other, by "politeness," to spare others a distasteful spectacle and themselves the shame of being seen

THE CIVILIZING PROCESS

with soiled hands, later it becomes more and more an inner automatism, the imprint of society on the inner self, the superego, that forbids the individual to eat in any other way than with a fork. The social standard to which the individual was first made to conform by external restraint is finally reproduced more or less smoothly within him, through a self-restraint which may operate even against his conscious wishes.

Thus the sociohistorical process of centuries, in the course of which the standard of what is felt to be shameful and offensive is slowly raised, is reenacted in abbreviated form in the life of the individual human being. If one wished to express recurrent processes of this kind in the form of laws, one could speak, as a parallel to the laws of biogenesis, of a fundamental law of sociogenesis and psychogenesis.

V

Changes in Attitude Toward
the Natural Functions

Examples

Fifteenth century?

A

From *S'ensuivent les contenances de la table*:

VIII

Before you sit down, make sure your seat has not been fouled.

B

From *Ein spruch der ze tische kêrt*:[61]

329 Do not touch yourself under your clothes with your bare hands.

C

1530

From *De civilitate morum puerilium*, by Erasmus. The glosses are taken from a Cologne edition of 1530 which was probably already intended for educational purposes. Under the title is the following note: "Recognized by the author, and elucidated with new scholia by Gisbertus Longolius Ultratraiectinus, Cologne, in the year XXX." The fact that these questions were discussed in such a way in schoolbooks makes the difference from later attitudes particularly clear:

It is impolite to greet someone who is urinating or defecating. . . .

A well-bred person should always avoid exposing without necessity the parts to which nature has attached modesty. If necessity compels this, it should be done with decency and reserve, even if no witness is present. For angels are always present, and nothing is more welcome to them in a boy than modesty, the companion and guardian of decency. If it arouses shame to show them to the eyes of others, still less should they be exposed to their touch.

To hold back urine is harmful to health, to pass it in secret betokens modesty. There are those who teach that the boy should retain wind by compressing the belly. Yet it is not pleasing, while striving to appear urbane, to contract an illness. If it is possible to withdraw, it should be done alone. But if not, in accordance with the ancient proverb, let a cough hide the sound. Moreover, why do not the same works teach that boys should not defecate, since it is more dangerous to hold back wind than to constrict the bowel?

[This is glossed as follows in the scholia, p. 33:]

To contract an illness: Listen to the old maxim about the sound of wind. If it can be purged without a noise that is best. But it is better that it be emitted with a noise than that it be held back.

At this point, however, it would have been useful to suppress the feeling of embarrassment so as to either calm your body or, following the advice of all doctors, to press your buttocks together and to act according to the suggestions in Aethon's epigrams: Even though he had to be careful not to fart explosively in the holy place, he nevertheless prayed to Zeus, though with compressed buttocks. The sound of farting, especially of those who stand on elevated ground, is horrible. One should make sacrifices with the buttocks firmly pressed together.

To let a cough hide the explosive sound: Those who, because they are embarrassed, want the explosive wind to be heard, simulate a cough. Follow the law of Chiliades: Replace farts with coughs.

Regarding the unhealthiness of retaining the wind: There are some verses in volume two of Nicharchos' epigrams where he describes the illness-bearing power of the retained fart, but since these lines are quoted by everybody I will not comment on them here.

The unabashed care and seriousness with which questions are publicly discussed here that have subsequently become highly private and strictly prohibited in society emphasizes the shift of the frontier of embarrassment. That feelings of shame are frequently mentioned explicitly in the discussion underlines the difference in the shame standard.

D

1558

From *Galateo*, by Della Casa, quoted from the five-language edition (Geneva, 1609), p. 32:

> Moreover, it does not befit a modest, honorable man to prepare to relieve nature in the presence of other people, nor to do up his clothes afterward in their presence. Similarly, he will not wash his hands on returning to decent society from private places, as the reason for his washing will arouse disagreeable thoughts in people. For the same reason it is not a refined habit, when coming across something disgusting in the street, as sometimes happens, to turn at once to one's companion and point it out to him.
>
> It is far less proper to hold out the stinking thing for the other to smell, as some are wont, who even urge the other to do so, lifting the foul-smelling thing to his nostrils and saying, "I should like to know how much that stinks," when it would be better to say, "Because it stinks do not smell it."

E

1570

From the Wernigerode Court Regulations of 1570:[62]

> One should not, like rustics who have not been to court or lived among refined and honorable people, relieve oneself without shame or reserve in front of ladies, or before the doors or windows of court chambers or other rooms. Rather, everyone ought at all times and in all places to show himself reasonable, courteous, and respectful in word and gesture.

F

1589

From the Brunswick Court Regulations of 1589:[63]

> Let no one, whoever he may be, before, at, or after meals, early or late, foul the staircases, corridors, or closets with urine or other filth, but go to suitable, prescribed places for such relief.

G

c. 1619

Richard Weste, *The Booke of Demeanor and the Allowance and Disallowance of Certaine Misdemeanors in Companie*:[64]

> 143 Let not thy privy members be
>   layd open to be view'd,

---

it is most shameful and abhord,
detestable and rude.
Retaine not urine nor the winde
which doth thy body vex
so it be done with secresie
let that not thee perplex.

H

1694

From the correspondence of the Duchess of Orléans (October 9, 1694; date also given as August 25, 1718):

The smell of the mire is horrible. Paris is a dreadful place. The streets smell so badly that you cannot go out. The extreme heat is causing large quantities of meat and fish to rot in them, and this, coupled to the multitude of people who . . . in the street, produces a smell so detestable that it cannot be endured.

I

1729

From La Salle, *Les Règles de la bienséance et de la civilité chrétienne* (Rouen, 1729), pp. 45ff.:

It is a part of decency and modesty to cover all parts of the body except the head and hands. You should take care, so far as you can, not to touch with your bare hand any part of the body that is not normally uncovered. And if you are obliged to do so, it should be done with great precaution. You should get used to suffering small discomforts without twisting, rubbing, or scratching. . . .

It is far more contrary to decency and propriety to touch or see in another person, particularly of the other sex, that which Heaven forbids you to look at in yourself. When you need to pass water, you should always withdraw to some unfrequented place. And it is proper (even for children) to perform other natural functions where you cannot be seen.

It is very impolite to emit wind from your body when in company, either from above or from below, even if it is done without noise [This rule, in line with more recent custom, is the exact opposite of what is prescribed in Examples C and G]; and it is shameful and indecent to do it in a way that can be heard by others.

It is never proper to speak of the parts of the body that should be hidden, nor of certain bodily necessities to which Nature has subjected us, nor even to mention them.

German developments were somewhat slower than French. As the following selection shows, as late as the first half of the eighteenth century a precept is given which represents the same standard of manners as that found in the passage by Erasmus quoted above: "It is impolite to greet someone who is urinating or defacating."

J

1731

From Johann Christian Barth, *The Gallant Ethic, in which it is shown how a young man should commend himself to polite society through refined acts and complaisant words. Prepared for the special advantage and pleasure of all amateurs of present-day good manners*, 4th ed. (Dresden and Leipzig, 1731), p. 288:

> If you pass a person who is relieving himself you should act as if you had not seen him, and so it is impolite to greet him.

K

1774

From La Salle, *Les Règles de la bienséance et de la civilité chrétienne* (1774 ed.), p. 24. The chapter "On the Parts of the Body That Should Be Hidden, and on Natural Necessities" covers a good two and one-half pages in the earlier edition and scarcely one and one-half in that of 1774. The passage "You should take care . . . not to touch, etc." is missing. Much that could be and had to be expressed earlier is no longer spoken of:

> It is a part of decency and modesty to cover all parts of the body except the head and hands.
> As far as natural needs are concerned, it is proper (even for children) to satisfy them only where one cannot be seen.
> It is never proper to speak of the parts of the body that should always be hidden, or of certain bodily necessities to which nature has subjected us, or even to mention them.

L

1768

Letter from Madame du Deffand to Madame de Choiseul, May 9, 1768;[65] quoted as an example of the prestige value of the utensil

I should like to tell you, dear Grandmother, as I told the Grand-Abbé, how great was my surprise when a large bag from you was brought to me at my bed yesterday morning. I hasten to open it, put in my hand, and find some green peas . . . and then a vase . . . that I quickly pull out: it is a chamber pot. But of such beauty and magnificence that my people say in unison *that it ought to be used as a sauce boat. The chamber pot was on display the whole of yesterday evening and was admired by everyone.* The peas . . . were eaten till not one was left.

Some Remarks on the Examples and on These Changes in General

1. The *courtois* verses say little on this subject. The social commands and prohibitions surrounding this area of life are relatively few. In this respect, too, at least in secular society, everything is far more lax. Neither the functions themselves, nor speaking about them or associations with them, are so intimate and private, so invested with feelings of shame and embarrassment, as they later become.

Erasmus's treatise marks, for these areas too, a point on the curve of civilization which represents, on the one hand, a notable rise of the shame threshold, compared to the preceding epoch; and on the other, compared to more recent times, a freedom in speaking of natural functions, a "lack of shame," which to most people adhering to the present-day standard may at first appear incomprehensible and often "embarrassing."

But at the same time, it is quite clear that this treatise has precisely the function of cultivating feelings of shame. Reference to the omnipresence of angels, used to justify the restraint on impulses to which the child is to be accustomed, is very characteristic. The manner in which anxiety is aroused in young people, in order to force them to repress display of pleasure in accordance with the standard of social conduct, changes in the course of centuries. Here, the anxiety aroused in connection with the renunciation of instinctual gratification is explained to oneself and others in terms of external spirits. Somewhat later, the restraint imposed on oneself, along with the fear, shame, and distaste toward any infringement, often appears, at least in the upper class, in courtly-aristocratic society, as social restraint, as shame and fear of men. In wider circles, admittedly, reference to the guardian angel clearly remains very long in use as an instrument for conditioning children. It recedes somewhat when health and "hygienic reasons" are given more emphasis in bringing about a certain degree of restraint of impulses and emotions. These hygienic reasons then play an important role in adult ideas on civilization, usually without their relation to the arsenal of childhood conditioning being realized. It is only from such a realization, however, that what is rational in them can be distinguished from what is only seemingly rational, i.e., founded primarily on the disgust and shame feelings of adults.

2. As already mentioned, Erasmus in his treatise acts as a cursor of a new standard of shame and repugnance which first begins to form slowly in the secular upper class. Yet he also speaks as a matter of course about things which it has since become embarrassing to mention. He, whose delicacy of feeling is demonstrated again and again by this very treatise, finds nothing amiss in calling by their names bodily functions which, by our present standards, may not be even mentioned in company, and still less in books on etiquette. But between this delicacy and this unconcern there is no contradiction. He speaks from another stage of control and restraint of emotions.

The different standard of society at Erasmus's time becomes clear if one reads how commonplace it is to meet someone "qui urinam reddit aut alvum exonerat" (urinating or defecating). And the greater freedom with which people were able at this time to perform and speak about their bodily functions before others recalls the behavior that can still be encountered throughout the Orient today. But delicacy forbids that one greet anyone encountered in this position.

The different standard is also visible when Erasmus says it is not civil to require that the young man "ventris flatum retineat" (hold back his wind), for in doing so he might, under the appearance of urbanity, contract an illness; and Erasmus comments similarly on sneezing and related acts.

Medical arguments are not found very frequently in this treatise. When they occur it is almost always, as here, to oppose demands for the restraint of natural functions; whereas later, above all in the nineteenth century, they nearly always serve as instruments to compel restraint and renunciation of instinctual gratification. It is only in the twentieth century that a slight relaxation appears.

3. The examples from La Salle must suffice to indicate how the feeling of delicacy is advancing. Again the difference between the editions of 1729 and 1774 is very instructive. Certainly, even the

---

earlier edition already embodies a quite different standard of delicacy than Erasmus's treatise. The demand that all natural functions be removed from the view of other people is raised quite unequivocally, even if the uttering of this demand indicates that the actual behavior of people—both adults and children—did not yet conform to it. Although La Salle says that it is not very polite even to speak of such functions or the parts of the body concerned, he himself still speaks of them with a minuteness of detail astonishing to us; he calls things by their names, whereas the corresponding terms are missing in Courtin's *Civilité* of 1672, which was intended for the upper classes.

In the later edition of La Salle, too, all detailed references are avoided. More and more these necessities are "passed over in silence." The mere reminder of them becomes embarrassing to people in the presence of others who are not close acquaintances, and in society everything that might even remotely or associatively recall such necessities is avoided.

At the same time, the examples make it apparent how slowly the real process of suppressing these functions from social life took place. Sufficient material[66] has been passed down to us precisely because the silence on these subjects did not exist earlier, or was less strictly observed. What is usually lacking is the idea that information of this kind has more than curiosity value, so that it is seldom synthesised into a picture of the overall line of development. However, if one takes a comprehensive view, a pattern emerges that is typical of the civilizing process.

4. At first these functions and their exhibition are invested only slightly with feelings of shame and repugnance, and are therefore subjected only mildly to isolation and restraint. They are taken as much for granted as combing one's hair or putting on one's shoes. Children are conditioned accordingly.

"Tell me in exact sequence," says the teacher to a pupil in a schoolbook of 1568, Mathurin Cordier's dialogues for schoolboys,[67] "what you did between getting up and having your breakfast. Listen carefully, boys, so that you learn to imitate your fellow pupil." "I woke up," says the pupil, "got out of bed, put on my shirt, stockings, and shoes, buckled my belt, urinated against the courtyard wall, took fresh water from the bucket, washed my hands and face and dried them on the cloth, etc."

In later times the action in the courtyard, at least in a book written like this one expressly as a manual of instruction and example, would have been simply passed over as "unimportant." Here it is neither particularly "unimportant" nor particularly "important." It is taken for granted as much as anything else.

The pupil who wished to report on this necessity today would do so either as a kind of joke, taking the invitation of the teacher "too literally," or would speak of it in circumlocutions. But most probably he would conceal his embarrassment with a smile, and an "understanding" smile of the others, the expression of minor infringement of a taboo, would be the response.

The conduct of adults corresponds to these different kinds of conditioning. For a long period the street, and almost any place one happened to be, served the same and related purposes as the courtyard wall above. It is not even unusual to turn to the staircase, the corners of rooms, or the hangings on the walls of a castle if one is overtaken by a need. Examples E and F make this clear. But they also show how, given the specific and permanent interdependence of many people living together at the courts, the pressure exerted from above toward a stricter regulation of impulses, and therefore toward greater restraint.

Stricter control of impulses and emotions is first imposed by those of high social rank on their social inferiors or, at most, their social equals. It is only comparatively late, when bourgeois classes comprising a large number of social equals have become the upper, ruling class, that the family becomes the only—or, more exactly, the primary and dominant—institution with the function of installing drive control. Only then does the social dependence of the child on its parents become particularly important as a leverage for the socially required regulation and molding of impulses and emotions.

In the stage of the feudal courts, and still more in that of the absolute courts, the courts themselves largely fulfilled this function for the upper class. In the latter stage, much of what has been made "second nature" to us has not yet been inculcated in this form, as an automatic self-restraint, a habit that, within certain limits, also functions when a person is alone. Rather, restraint on the instincts is at first imposed only in the company of others, i.e., more consciously for social reasons. And both the kind and the degree of restraint correspond to the social position of the person imposing them, relative to the position of those in whose company he is. This slowly changes as people move closer together socially and as the hierarchical character of society becomes less rigid. As the interdependence of men increases with the increasing division of labor, everyone becomes increasingly dependent on everyone else, those of high social rank on those socially inferior and weaker. The latter become so much the equals of the former that they, the socially superior, feel shame even before their inferiors. It is only now that the armor of restraints is fastened to the degree which is gradually taken for granted by people in democratic industrial societies.

To take from the wealth of examples one instance which shows the contrast particularly clearly and which, correctly understood, throws light on the whole development, Della Casa gives in his *Galateo* a list of malpractices to be avoided. One should not fall asleep in society, he says; one should not take out letters and read them; one should not pare or clean one's fingernails. "Furthermore," he continues (p. 92), "one should not sit with one's back or posterior turned toward another, nor raise a thigh so high that the members of the human body, which should properly be covered with clothing at all times, might be exposed to view. *For this and similar things are not done, except among people before whom one is not ashamed* (se non tra quelle persone, che l'huom non riverisce). *It is true that a great lord might do so before one of his servants or in the presence of a friend of lower rank; for in this he would not show him arrogance but rather a particular affection and friendship.*"

There are people before whom one is ashamed, and others before whom one is not. The feeling of shame is clearly a social function molded according to the social structure. This is perhaps not often *expressed* so clearly. But the corresponding *behavior* is amply documented. In France,[68] as late as the seventeenth century, kings and great lords receive specially favored inferiors on occasions on which, a German saying was later to run, even the emperor should be alone. To receive inferiors when getting up and being dressed, or on going to bed, was for a whole period a matter of course. And it shows exactly the same stage of the shame-feeling when Voltaire's mistress, the Marquise de Châtelet, shows herself naked to her servant while bathing in a way that casts him into confusion, and then with total unconcern scolds him because he is not pouring in the hot water properly.[69]

Behavior which in more democratized industrial societies is surrounded on all sides with taboos, with trained feelings of shame or embarrassment of varying degrees, is here only partially affected. It is omitted in the company of those of higher or equal rank. In this area, too, coercion and restraint are self-imposed on the same pattern as was visible earlier in table manners. "Nor do I believe," we read in *Galateo* (p. 580), "that it is fitting to serve from the common dish intended for all guests, unless the server is of higher rank so that the other, who is served, is thereby especially honored. For when this is done among equals, it appears as if the server is partly placing himself above the others."

In this hierarchically structured society, every act performed in the presence of many people took on prestige value. For this reason the restraint of the emotions, that we call "politeness," also had a different form than later, when outward differences of rank had been partly leveled. What is mentioned here as a special case in intercourse between equals, that one should not serve another, later becomes a general practice. In society everyone helps himself, and everyone begins eating at the same time.

The situation is similar with the exposure of the body. First it becomes a distasteful offense to show oneself exposed in any way before those of higher or equal rank; with inferiors it can even be a sign of benevolence. Then, as all become socially more equal, it slowly becomes a general offense. The social reference of shame and embarrassment recedes more and more from consciousness. Precisely because the social command not to show oneself exposed or performing natural functions now operates with regard to everyone and is imprinted in this form on the child, it seems to the adult a command of his own inner self and takes on the form of a more or less total and automatic self-restraint.

5. But this isolation of the natural functions from public life, and the corresponding regulation or molding of instinctual urges, was only possible because, together with growing sensitivity, a technical apparatus was developed which solved fairly satisfactorily the problem of eliminating these functions from social life and displacing them behind the scenes. The situation was not unlike that regarding table manners. The process of social change, the advance in the frontiers of shame and the threshold of repugnance, cannot be explained by any one thing, and certainly not by the development of technology or by scientific discoveries. On the contrary, it would not be difficult to

demonstrate the sociogenetic and psychogenetic bases of these inventions and discoveries.

After a reshaping of human needs had once been set in motion with the general transformation of human relations, the development of a technical apparatus corresponding to the changed standard consolidated the changed habits to an extraordinary degree. This apparatus served both the constant reproduction of the standard and its dissemination.

It is not uninteresting to observe that today [in the 1930s, the translator], when this standard of conduct has been so heavily consolidated that it is taken for granted, a certain relaxation is setting in, particularly in comparison to the nineteenth century, at least with regard' to speech about the natural functions. The freedom and unconcern with which people say what has to be said without embarrassment, without the forced smile and laughter of a taboo infringement, has clearly increased in the postwar period. But this, like modern bathing and dancing practices, is only possible because the level of habitual, technically and institutionally consolidated self-control, the individual capacity to restrain one's urges and behavior in correspondence with the more advanced feelings for what is offensive, has been on the whole secured. It is a relaxation within the framework of an already established standard.

6. The standard which is emerging in our phase of civilization is characterized by a profound discrepancy between the behavior of so-called "adults" and children. The children have in the space of a few years to attain the advanced level of shame and revulsion that has developed over many centuries. Their instinctual life must be rapidly subjected to the strict control and specific molding that gives our societies their stamp, and which developed very slowly over centuries. In this the parents are only the (often inadequate) instruments, the primary agents of conditioning; through them and thousands of other instruments it is always society as a whole, the entire figuration of human beings, that exerts its pressure on the new generation, bending them more or less perfectly to its purpose.

In the Middle Ages, too, it was society as a whole that exerted this formative pressure, even if—as will be shown in more detail—the mechanisms and organs of conditioning, particularly in the upper class, were largely different from those of today. But above all, the control and restraint to which the instinctual life of adults was subjected was considerably less than in the following phase of civilization, as consequently was the difference in behavior between adults and children.

The individual inclinations and tendencies which medieval writings on etiquette were concerned to control were often the same as can be frequently observed in children today. However, they are now dealt with so early that certain kinds of "misbehavior" which were quite commonplace in the medieval world scarcely manifest themselves in present-day social life.

Children today are admonished not to snatch whatever they want from the table, and not to scratch themselves or touch their noses, ears, eyes, or other parts of their bodies at table. The child is instructed not to speak or drink with a full mouth, or to sprawl on the table, and so on. Many of these precepts are also to be found in Tannhäuser's *Hofzucht*, for example, but there they are addressed not to children but unequivocally to adults. This becomes still more apparent if one considers the way in which adults earlier satisfied their natural needs. This very often happened—as the examples show—in a manner that would be just tolerated in children today. Often enough, needs were satisfied where and when they happened to be felt. The degree of instinctual restraint and control expected by adults of each other was not much greater than that imposed on children. The distance between adults and children, measured by that of today, was slight.

Today the circle of precepts and regulations is drawn so tightly about people, the censorship and pressure of social life forming their habits are so strong, that young people have only two alternatives: to submit to the pattern of behavior demanded by society, or to be excluded from life in "decent society." A child that does not attain the level of control of emotions demanded by society is regarded in varying gradations as "ill," "abnormal," "criminal," or just "impossible" from the point of view of a particular caste or class, and is accordingly excluded from the life of that class. Indeed, from the psychological point of view, the terms "sick," "abnormal," "criminal," and "impossible" have, within certain limits, no other meaning; how they are understood varies with the historically mutable models of affect formation.

Very instructive in this regard is the conclusion of Example D: "It is far less proper to hold out the stinking thing for the other to smell, etc." Instinctual tendencies and behavior of this kind would, by today's standard of shame and revulsion, simply exclude a person as "sick," "pathological," or "perverse" from mixing with others. If the inclination to such behavior were manifested publicly, he would, depending on his social position, be confined indoors or in an institution. At best, if this tendency were only manifested behind the scenes, a specialist in nervous disorders would be assigned the task of correcting this person's unsuccessful conditioning. In general, impulses of this kind have disappeared from the waking consciousness of adults under the pressure of conditioning. Only psychoanalysis uncovers them in the form of unsatisfied and unsatisfiable desires which can be described as the unconscious or the dream level of the mind. And these desires have indeed in our society the character of an "infantile" residue, because the social standard of adults makes a complete suppression and transformation of such tendencies necessary, so that they appear, when occurring in adults, as a "remnant" from childhood.

The standard of delicacy represented by *Galateo* also demands a detachment from these instinctual tendencies. But the pressure to transform such inclinations exerted on the individual by society is minimal compared to that of today. The feeling of revulsion, distaste, or disgust aroused by such behavior is, in keeping with the earlier standard, incomparably weaker than ours. Consequently, the social prohibition on the expression of such feelings is much less grave. This behavior is not regarded as a "pathological anomaly" or a "perversion," but rather as an offense against tact, politeness, or good form.

Della Casa speaks of this "misdemeanor" with scarcely more emphasis than we might today speak of someone biting his nails in society. The very fact that he speaks of "such things" at all shows how harmless this practice then appeared.

Nevertheless, in one way this example marks a turning point. It may be supposed that the expression of these feelings was not lacking in the preceding period. But only now does it begin to attract attention. Society is gradually beginning to suppress the positive pleasure component in certain functions more and more strongly by the arousal of anxiety; or, more exactly, it is rendering this pleasure "private" and "secret" (i.e., suppressing it within the individual), while fostering the negatively charged affects—displeasure, revulsion, distaste—as the only feelings customary in society. But precisely by this increased social proscription of many impulses, by their "repression" from the surface both of social life and of consciousness, the distance between the personality structure and behavior of adults and children is necessarily increased.

VI

On Blowing One's Nose

Examples

A

Thirteenth century

From Bonvesin de la Riva (Bonvicino da Riva), *De la zinquanta cortexie da tavola* (Fifty table courtesies):

(a) Precept for gentlemen:

> When you blow your nose or cough, turn round so that nothing falls on the table.

(b) Precept for pages or servants:

> Pox la trentena è questa:
>   zaschun cortese donzello
> Che se vore mondà lo naxo,
>   con li drapi se faza bello;
> Chi mangia, over chi menestra,
>   no de'sofià con le die;
> Con li drapi da pey se monda
>   vostra cortexia.*

B

Fifteenth century

From *Ein spruch der ze tische kêrt*:

---

*The meaning of passage (b) is not entirely clear. What is apparent is that it is addressed especially to people who serve at table. A commentator, Uguccione Pisano, says: "Those are called *donizelli* who are handsome, young, and the servants of great lords. . . ." These *donizelli* were not allowed to sit at the same table as the knights; or, if this was permitted, they had to sit on a lower chair. They, pages of a kind and at any rate social inferiors, are told: The thirty-first courtesy is this— every *courtois* "donzel" who wishes to blow his nose should beautify himself with a cloth. When he is eating or serving he should not blow (his nose?) through his fingers. It is *courtois* to use the foot bandage.

It is unseemly to blow your nose into the tablecloth.

C

From *S'ensuivent les contenances de la table*:

XXXIII

Do not blow your nose with the same hand that you use to hold the meat.*

*According to an editor's note (*The Babees Book*, vol. 2, p. 14), courtesy consisted in blowing the nose with the fingers of the left hand if one ate and took meat from the common dish with the right.

D

From A. Cabanès, *Moeurs intimes du temps passé* (Paris, 1910), 1st series, p. 101:

In the fifteenth century people blew their noses into their fingers, and the sculptors of the age were not afraid to reproduce the gesture, in a passably realistic form, in their monuments.

Among the knights, the *plourans*, at the grave of Philip the Bold at Dijon, one is seen blowing his nose into his coat, another into his fingers.

E

Sixteenth century

From *De civilitate morum puerilium*, by Erasmus, ch. 1:

To blow your nose on your hat or clothing is rustic, and to do so with the arm or elbow befits a tradesman; nor is it much more polite to use the hand, if you immediately smear the snot on your garment. It is proper to wipe the nostrils with a handkerchief, and to do this while turning away, *if more honorable people are present*.

If anything falls to the ground when blowing the nose with two fingers, it should immediately be trodden away.

[From the scholia on this passage:]

Between snot and spit there is little difference, except that the former fluid is to be interpreted as coarser and the latter more unclean. The Latin writers constantly confuse a breastband, a napkin, or any piece of linen with a handkerchief.

F

1558

From *Galateo*, by Della Casa, quoted from the five-language edition (Geneva, 1609), pp. 72, 44, 618:

> You should not offer your handkerchief to anyone unless it has been freshly washed. . . .
> Nor is it seemly, after wiping your nose, to spread out your handkerchief and peer into it as if pearls and rubies might have fallen out of your head.
> . . . What, then, shall I say of those . . . who carry their handkerchiefs about in their mouths? . . .

G

From Cabanès, *Moeurs intimes*, pp. 103, 168, 102:

> [From Martial d'Auvergue, "Love decrees"] . . . in order that she might remember him, he decided to have one of the most beautiful and sumptuous handkerchiefs made for her, in which his name was in letters entwined in the prettiest fashion, for it was joined to a fine golden heart bordered with tiny heart's eases.*

*This cloth was intended to be hung from the lady's girdle, with her keys. Like the fork, night-commode, etc., the handerkerchief is first an expensive luxury article.

> [From Lestoil, *Journal d'Henri IV*] In 1594, Henri IV asked his valet how many shirts he had, and the latter replied: "A dozen, sire, and some torn ones." "And how many handkerchiefs?" asked the king. "Have I not eight?" "For the moment there are only five," he said.

> In 1599, after her death, the inventory of Henri IV's mistress is found to contain "five handkerchiefs worked in gold, silver and silk, worth 100 crowns."

> In the sixteenth century, Monteil tells us, in France as everywhere else, the common people blow their noses without a handkerchief, but among the bourgeoisie it is accepted practice to use the sleeve. As for the rich, they carry a handkerchief in their pockets; therefore, to say that a man has wealth, one says that he does not blow his nose on his sleeve.

H

Late seventeenth century
The Peak of Refinement
First Highpoint of Modeling and Restrictions

1672

From Courtin, *Nouveau traité de civilité*:

> [At table] to blow your nose openly into your handkerchief, without concealing yourself with your serviette, and to wipe away your sweat with it . . . are filthy habits fit to make everyone's gorge rise. . . .
>
> You should avoid yawning, blowing your nose, and spitting. If you are obliged to do so in places that are kept clean, do it in your handkerchief, while turning your face away and shielding yourself with your left hand, and do not look into your handkerchief afterward.

I

1694

From Ménage, *Dictionnaire étymologique de la langue française*:

Handkerchief for blowing the nose.
As this expression "blowing the nose" gives a very disagreeable impression, ladies ought to call this a pocket handkerchief, as one says neckerchief, rather than a handkerchief for blowing the nose. [N.B. *Mouchoir de poche*, *Taschentuch*, handkerchief as more polite expressions; the word for functions that have become distasteful is repressed.]

Eighteenth century
Note the increasing distance between adults and children. Only children are still allowed, at least in the middle classes, to behave as adults did in the Middle Ages.

J

1714

From an anonymous *Civilité française* (Liège, 1714), p. 141:

> Take good care not to blow your nose with your fingers or on your sleeve *like children*; use your handkerchief and do not look into it afterward.

K

1729

From La Salle, *Les Règles de la bienséance et de la civilité chrétienne* (Rouen, 1729), in a chapter called "On the Nose, and the Manner of Blowing the Nose and Sneezing," p. 23:

It is very impolite to keep poking your finger into your nostrils, and still more insupportable to put what you have pulled from your nose into your mouth. . . .

It is vile to wipe your nose with your bare hand, or to blow it on your sleeve or your clothes. It is very contrary to decency to blow your nose with two fingers and then to throw the filth onto the ground and wipe your fingers on your clothes. It is well known how improper it is to see such uncleanliness on clothes, which should always be very clean, no matter how poor they may be.

There are some who put a finger on one nostril and by blowing through their nose cast onto the ground the filth inside; those who act thus are people who do not know what decency is.

You should always use your handkerchief to blow your nose, and never anything else, and in doing so usually hide your face with your hat. [A particularly clear example of the dissemination of courtly customs through this work.]

You should avoid making a noise when blowing your nose. . . . Before blowing it, it is impolite to spend a long time taking out your handkerchief. *It shows a lack of respect toward the people you are with* to unfold it in different places to see where you are to use it. You should take your handkerchief from your pocket and use it quickly in such a way that you are scarcely noticed by others.

After blowing your nose you should take care not to look into your handkerchief. It is correct to fold it immediately and replace it in your pocket.

L

1774

From La Salle, *Les Règles de la bienséance et de la civilité chrétienne* (1774 ed.), pp. 14f. The chapter is now called only "On the Nose" and is shortened:

Every voluntary movement of the nose, whether caused by the hand or otherwise, is impolite and puerile. To put your fingers into your nose is a revolting impropriety, and from touching it too often *discomforts may*

---

arise which are felt for a long time.* Children are sufficiently in the habit of committing this lapse; *parents should correct them carefully.*

> You should observe, in blowing your nose, all the rules of propriety and cleanliness.

All details are avoided. The "conspiracy of silence" is spreading. It is based on the presupposition—which evidently could not be made at the time of the earlier edition—that all the details are known to adults and can be controlled within the family.

M

1797

From La Mésangère, *Le voyageur de Paris* (1797), vol. 2, p. 95. This is probably seen, to a greater extent than the preceding eighteenth-century examples, from the point of view of the younger members of "good society":

> Some years ago people made an art of blowing the nose. One imitated the sound of the trumpet, another the screech of a cat. Perfection lay in making neither too much noise nor too little.

Comments on the Quotations on Nose-Blowing

1. In medieval society people generally blew their noses into their hands, just as they ate with their hands. That necessitated special precepts for nose-cleaning at table. Politeness, *courtoisie*, required that one blow one's nose with the left hand if one took meat with the right. But this precept was in fact restricted to the table. It arose solely out of consideration for others. The distasteful feeling frequently aroused today by the mere thought of soiling the fingers in this way was at first entirely absent.

Again the examples show very clearly how slowly the seemingly simplest instruments of civilization have developed. They also illustrate to a certain degree the particular social and psychological preconditions that were required to make the need for and use of so simple an

---

*This argument, absent in the earlier edition, shows clearly how the reference to damage to health is gradually beginning to emerge as an instrument of conditioning, often in place of the remainder about the respect due to social superiors.

instrument general. The use of the handkerchief—like that of the fork—first established itself in Italy, and was diffused on account of its prestige value. The ladies hang the precious, richly embroidered cloth from their girdles. The young "snobs" of the Renaissance offer it to others or carry it about in their mouths. And since it is precious and relatively expensive, at first there are not many of them even among the upper class. Henri IV, at the end of the sixteenth century, possessed (as we hear in Example G) five handkerchiefs. And it is generally taken as a sign of wealth not to blow one's nose into one's hand or sleeve but into a handkerchief. Louis XIV is the first to have an abundant supply of handkerchiefs, and under him the use of them becomes general, at least in courtly circles.

2. Here, as so often, the transitional situation is clearly visible in Erasmus. It is proper to use a handkerchief, he says, and if people of a higher social position are present, turn away when blowing your nose. But he also says: If you blow your nose with two fingers and something falls to the ground, tread on it. The use of the handkerchief is known but not yet widely disseminated, even in the upper class for which Erasmus primarily writes.

Two centuries later, the situation is almost reversed. The use of the handkerchief has become general, at least among people who lay claim to "good behavior." But the use of the hands has by no means disappeared. Seen from above, it has become "ill-mannered," or at any rate common and vulgar. One reads with amusement La Salle's gradations between *vilain*, for certain very coarse ways of blowing the nose with the hand, and *très contraire à la bienséance*, for the better manner of doing so with two fingers (Examples H, J, K, L).

Once the handkerchief begins to come into use, there constantly recurs a prohibition on a new form of "bad manners" that emerges at the same time as the new practice—the prohibition on looking into one's handkerchief when one has used it (Examples F, H, J, K, L). It almost seems as if inclinations which have been subjected to a certain control and restraint by the introduction of the handkerchief are seeking a new outlet in this way. At any rate, an instinctual tendency which today appears at most in the unconscious, in dreams, in the sphere of secrecy, or more consciously only behind the scenes, the interest in bodily secretions, here shows itself at an earlier stage of the historical process more clearly and openly, and so in a form in which today it is only "normally" visible in children.

In the later edition of La Salle, as in other cases, the major part of the very detailed precepts from the earlier one are omitted. The use of the handkerchief has become more general and self-evident. It is no longer necessary to be so explicit. Moreover, there is less and less inclination to speak about these details that La Salle originally discussed straightforwardly and at length without embarrassment. More stress, on the other hand, is laid on children's bad habit of putting the fingers in the nose. And, as with other childish habits, the medical warning now appears alongside or in place of the social one as an instrument of conditioning, in the reference to the injury that can be done by doing "such a thing" too often. This is an expression of a change in the manner of conditioning that has already been considered from other aspects. Up to this time, habits are almost always judged expressly in their relation to other people, and they are forbidden, at least in the secular upper class, because they may be troublesome or embarrassing to others, or because they betray a "lack of respect." Now habits are condemned more and more as such, not in regard to others. In this way, socially undesirable impulses or inclinations are more radically repressed. They are associated with embarrassment, fear, shame, or guilt, even when one is alone. Much of what we call "morality" or "moral" reasons has the same function as "hygiene" or "hygienic" reasons: to condition children to a certain social standard. Molding by such means aims at making socially desirable behavior automatic, a matter of self-control, causing it to appear in the consciousness of the individual as the result of his own free will, and in the interests of his own health or human dignity. And it is only with the advent of this way of consolidating habits, or conditioning, which gains predominance with the rise of the middle classes, that conflict between the socially inadmissible impulses and tendencies, on the one hand, and the pattern of social demands anchored in the individual, on the other, takes on the sharply defined form central to the psychological theories of modern times—above all, to psychoanalysis. It may be that there have always been "neuroses." But the "neuroses" we see about us today are a specific historical form of psychic conflict which needs psychogenetic and sociogenetic elucidation.

3. An indication of the mechanisms of repression may already be contained in the two verses quoted from Bonvicino da Riva (Example A). The difference between what is expected of knights and lords, on ^he one hand, and of the *donizelli*, pages, or servants, on the other,

calls to mind a much-documented social phenomenon. The masters find the sight of the bodily functions of their servants distasteful; they compel them, the social inferiors in their immediate surroundings, to control and restrain these functions in a way that they do not at first impose on themselves. The verse addressed to the masters says simply: If you blow your nose, turn round so that nothing falls on the table. There is no mention of using a cloth. Should we believe that the use of cloths for cleaning the nose was already taken so much for granted in this society that it was no longer thought necessary to mention it in a book on manners? That is highly improbable. The servants, on the other hand, are expressly instructed to use not their fingers but their foot bandages if they have to blow their noses. To be sure, this interpretation of the two verses cannot be considered absolutely certain. But the fact can be frequently demonstrated that functions are found distasteful and disrespectful in inferiors which superiors are not ashamed of in themselves. This fact takes on special significance with the transformation of society under absolutism, and therefore at absolutist courts, when the upper class, the aristocracy as a whole, has become, with degrees of hierarchy, a subservient and socially dependent class. This at first sight highly paradoxical phenomenon of an upper class that is socially extremely dependent will be discussed later in another context. Here we can only point out that this social dependence and its structure have decisive importance for the structure and pattern of affect restrictions. The examples contain numerous indications of how these restrictions are intensified with the growing dependence of the upper class. It is no accident that the first "peak of refinement" or "delicacy" in the manner of blowing the nose—and not only here—comes in the phase when the dependence and subservience of the aristocratic upper class is at its height, the period of Louis XIV (Examples H and I).

The dependence of the upper class also explains the dual aspect which the behavior patterns and instruments of civilization have at least in this formative stage. They express a certain measure of compulsion and renunciation, but they also immediately become a weapon against social inferiors, a means of distinction. Handkerchief, fork, plates, and all their related implements are at first luxury articles with a particular social prestige value (Example G).

The social dependence in which the succeeding upper class, the bourgeoisie, lives, is of a different kind, to be sure, from that of the court aristocracy, but tends to be greater and more compelling.

In general, we scarcely realize today what a unique and astonishing phenomenon a "working" upper class is. Why does it work? Why submit itself to this compulsion even though it is the "ruling" class and is therefore not commanded to do so? The question demands a more detailed answer than is possible in this context. What is clear, however, is the parallel to what has been said on the change in the instruments and forms of conditioning. During the stage of the court aristocracy, the restraint imposed on inclinations and emotions is based primarily on consideration and respect due to others and above all to social superiors. In the subsequent stage, renunciation and restraint of impulses is compelled far less by particular persons; expressed provisionally and approximately, it is now, more directly than before, the less visible and more impersonal compulsions of social interdependence, the division of labor, the market, and competition that impose restraint and control on the impulses and emotions. It is these pressures, and the corresponding manner of explanation and conditioning mentioned above, which make it appear that socially desirable behavior is voluntarily produced by the individual himself, on his own initiative. This applies to the regulation and restraint of drives necessary for "work"; it also applies to the whole pattern according to which drives are modeled in bourgeois industrial societies. The pattern of affect control, of what must and what must not be restrained, regulated, and transformed, is certainly not the same in this stage as in the preceding one of the court aristocracy. In keeping with its different interdependencies, bourgeois society applies stronger restrictions to certain impulses, while in the case of others aristocratic restrictions are simply continued and transformed to suit the changed situation. In addition, more clearly distinct national patterns of affect control are formed from the various elements. In both cases, in aristocratic court society as well as in the bourgeois societies of the nineteenth and twentieth centuries, the upper classes are socially constrained to a particularly high degree. The central role played by this increasing dependency of the upper classes as a motor of civilization will be demonstrated later.

THE CIVILIZING PROCESS

VII

On Spitting

Examples

Middle Ages

A

From *Stans puer in mensam*:[70]

27 Do not spit over or on the table.

37 Do not spit into the bowl when washing your hands.

B

From a *Contenence de table*:[71]

29 Do not spit on the table.

51 Do not spit into the basin when you wash your hands, but beside it.

C

From *The Book of Curtesye*:[72]

85 If thou spitt over the borde, or elles opon,
   thou schalle be holden an uncurtayse mon.

133 After mete when thou shall wasshe,
    spitt not in basyn, ne water thou dasshe.

D

From Zarncke, *Der deutsche Cato,* p. 137:

276 Do not spit across the table in the manner of hunters.

E

1530

From *De civilitate morum puerilium,* by Erasmus:

Turn away when spitting, lest your saliva fall on someone. If anything purulent falls to the ground, it should be trodden upon, lest it nauseate

---

someone. If you are not at liberty to do this, catch the sputum in a small cloth. It is unmannerly to suck back saliva, as equally are those whom we see spitting at every third word not from necessity but from habit.

F

1558

From *Galateo,* by Della Casa, quoted from the five-language edition (Geneva, 1609), p. 570:

It is also unseemly for someone sitting at table to scratch himself. At such a time and place you should also abstain as far as possible from spitting, and if it cannot be completely avoided it should be done politely and unnoticed.

I have often heard that whole peoples have sometimes lived so moderately and conducted themselves so honorably that they found spitting quite unnecessary. Why, therefore, should not we too be able to refrain from it just for a short time? [That is, during meals; the restriction on the habit applied only to mealtimes.]

G

1672

From Courtin, *Nouveau traité de civilité*, p. 273:

The custom we have just mentioned does not mean that most laws of this kind are immutable. And just as there are many that have already changed, I have no doubt that many of these will likewise change in the future.

Formerly, for example, it was permitted to spit on the ground before people of rank, and was sufficient to put one's foot on the sputum. Today that is an indecency.

In the old days you could yawn, provided you did not speak while doing so; today, a person of rank would be shocked by this.

H

1714

From an anonymous *Civilité française* (Liège, 1714), pp. 67, 41:

Frequent spitting is disagreeable. When it is necessary you should conceal it as much as possible, and avoid soiling either persons or their clothes, no matter who they are, nor even the embers beside the fire. And wherever you spit, you should put your foot on the saliva.

At the houses of the great, one spits into one's handkerchief. . . .

It ill becomes you to spit out of the window or onto the fire.

Do not spit so far that you have to look for the saliva to put your foot on it.

I

1729

From La Salle, *Les Règles de la bienséance et de la civilité chrétienne* (Rouen, 1729), p. 35:

You should not abstain from spitting, and it is very ill-mannered to swallow what should be spat. This can nauseate others.

Nevertheless, you should not become accustomed to spitting too often, and without need. This is not only unmannerly, but disgusts and annoys everyone. *When you are with well-born people,* and when you are in places that are kept clean, it is polite to spit into your handkerchief while turning slightly aside.

It is even good manners for everyone to get used to spitting into a handkerchief when in the houses of the great and in all places with waxed or parquet floors. But it is far more necessary to acquire the habit of doing so when in church, as far as is possible. . . . It often happens, however, that no kitchen or even stable floor is dirtier . . . than that of the church.

After spitting into your handkerchief, you should fold it at once, without looking at it, and put it into your pocket. You should take great care never to spit on your clothes, or those of others. . . . If you notice saliva on the ground, you should immediately put your foot adroitly on it. If you notice any on someone's coat, it is not polite to make it known; you should instruct a servant to remove it. If no servant is present, you should remove it yourself without being noticed. For good breeding consists in not bringing to people's attention anything that might offend or confuse them.

J

1774

From La Salle, *Les Règles de la bienséance et de la civilité chrétienne* (1774 ed.), p. 20. In this edition the chapter "On Yawning, Spitting, and Coughing," which covers four pages in the earlier editions, has shrunk to one page:

In church, in the houses of the great, and in all places where cleanliness reigns, you should spit into your handkerchief. It is an unpardonably gross habit of children to spit in the faces of their playmates. Such bad manners cannot be punished too severely; nor are those who spit out of windows, on walls and on furniture to be excused. . . .

K

1859

From *The Habits of Good Society*, p. 256:

Spitting is at all times a disgusting habit. I need say nothing more than—never indulge in it. Besides being coarse and atrocious, *it is very bad for the health.*

L

1910

From Cabanès, *Moeurs intimes*, p. 264:

Have you noticed that today we relegate to some discreet corner what our fathers did not hesitate to display quite openly?

Thus a certain intimate article of furniture had a place of honor . . . no one thought of concealing it from view.

The same is true of another piece of furniture no longer found in modern households, whose disappearance some will perhaps regret in this age of "bacillophobia": I am referring to the spittoon.

Some Comments on the Quotations on Spitting

1. Like the other groups of examples, the series of quotations about spitting shows very clearly that, since the Middle Ages, behavior has changed in a particular direction. In the case of spitting, the movement is unmistakably of the kind that we call "progress." Frequent spitting is even today one of the experiences that many Europeans find particularly unpleasant when traveling in the East or in Africa, together with the lack of "cleanliness." If they started out with idealized preconceptions, they call the experience disappointing, and find their feelings on the "progress" of Western civilization confirmed. No more than four centuries ago, this custom was no less widespread and commonplace in the West, as the examples show. Taken together, they give a particularly clear demonstration of the way in which the civilizing process took place.

2. The examples show a movement with the following stages: The Latin as well as the English, French, and German guides to table manners bear witness to the fact that in the Middle Ages it was not only a custom but also clearly a generally felt need to spit frequently. It is also entirely commonplace in the courts of the feudal lords. The only major restraint imposed is that one should not spit on or over the table but under it. Nor should one spit into the washbasin when cleaning mouth or hands, but beside it. These prohibitions are repeated in so

stereotyped a fashion in the *courtois* codes of manners that one can imagine the frequency of this instance of "bad manners." The pressure of medieval society on this practice never becomes so strong, nor the conditioning so compelling, that it disappears from social life. Here again we see the difference between social control in the medieval and the subsequent stages.

In the sixteenth century, social pressure grows stronger. It is demanded that sputum be trodden upon—at least if it contains purulence, says Erasmus, who here as always marks the transitional situation. And here again the use of a cloth is mentioned as a possible, not a necessary, way of controlling this habit, which is slowly becoming more distasteful.

The next step is shown clearly by Courtin's comment of 1672: "Formerly . . . it was permitted to spit on the ground before people of rank, and was sufficient to put one's foot on the sputum. Today that is an indecency."

Similarly, we find in the *Civilité* of 1714, intended for a wider audience: "Conceal it as much as possible, and avoid soiling either persons or their clothes. . . . At the houses of the great, one spits into one's handkerchief."

In 1729, La Salle extends the same precept to all places "that are kept clean." And he adds that in church, too, people ought to get used to using their handkerchiefs and not the floor.

By 1774 the whole practice, and even speaking about it, had become considerably more distasteful. By 1859 "spitting is at all times a disgusting habit." All the same, at least within the house, the spittoon, as a technical implement for controlling this habit in keeping with the advancing standard of delicacy, still has considerable importance in the nineteenth century. Cabanès, in 1910, reminds us that, like other implements (cf. Example L), it has slowly evolved from a prestige object to a private utensil.

Gradually this utensil too becomes dispensable. In large sections of Western society, even the need to spit from time to time seems to have disappeared completely. A standard of delicacy and restraint similar to that which Della Casa knew only from his reading of ancient writers, where "whole peoples . . . lived so moderately and . . . so honorably that they found spitting quite unnecessary" (Example F), has been attained once more.

3. Taboos and restrictions of various kinds surround the ejection of

saliva, like other natural functions, in very many societies, both "primitive" and "civilized." What distinguishes them is the fact that in the former they are always maintained by fear of other beings, even if only imaginary ones—that is, by external constraints—whereas in the latter these are transformed more or less completely into internal constraints. The prohibited tendencies (e.g., the tendency to spit) partly disappear from consciousness under the pressure of this internal restraint or, as it may also be called, the superego and the "habit of foresight." What remains behind in consciousness as the motivation of anxiety is some long-term consideration. So in our time the fear of spitting, and the feelings of shame and repugnance in which it is expressed, are concentrated about the more precisely defined and logically comprehensible idea of certain illnesses and their "causes," rather than around the image of magical influences, gods, spirits, or demons. But the series of examples also shows very clearly that rational understanding of the origins of certain diseases, of the danger of sputum as a carrier of illness, is neither the primary cause of fear and repugnance nor the motor of civilization, the driving force of the changes in behavior with regard to spitting.

At first, and for a long period, the retention of spittle is expressly discouraged. To suck back saliva is "unmannerly," says Erasmus (Example E). And as late as 1729, La Salle says: "You should not abstain from spitting" (Example I). For centuries there is not the faintest indication of "hygienic reasons" for the prohibitions and restrictions with which the tendency to spit is surrounded. Rational understanding of the "danger" of saliva is attained only at a very late stage of the change in behavior, and thus in a sense retrospectively, in the nineteenth century. And even then, the reference to what is indelicate and disgusting in such behavior still appears separately, alongside the reference to its ill effects on health: "Besides being coarse and atrocious, it is very bad for the health," Example K says of spitting.

It is well to establish once and for all that something which we know to be harmful to health by no means necessarily arouses feelings of distaste or shame. And conversely, something that arouses these feelings need not be at all detrimental to health. Someone who eats noisily or with his hands nowadays arouses feelings of extreme distaste without there being the slightest fear for his health. But neither the thought of someone reading by bad light nor the idea of poison gas, for example, arouses remotely similar feelings of distaste or shame, although the harmful consequences for health are obvious. Thus, disgust at the ejection of saliva intensifies, and the taboos surrounding it increase, long before people have a clear idea of the transmission of certain germs by saliva. What first arouses and increases the distasteful feelings and restrictions is a transformation of human relationships and dependencies. "Earlier it was permitted to yawn or spit openly; today, a person of rank would be shocked by it," Example G says, in effect. That is the kind of reason that people first give for increased restraint. Motivation from social consideration exists long before motivation from scientific insight. The king requires this restraint as a "mark of respect" from his courtiers. In court circles this sign of their dependence, the growing compulsion to be restrained and self-controlled, becomes also a "mark of distinction" that is immediately imitated below and disseminated with the rise of broader classes. And here, as in the preceding civilization-curves, the admonition "That is not done," with which restraint, fear, shame, and repugnance are inculcated, is connected only very late, as a result of a certain "democratization," to a scientific theory, to an argument that applies to all men equally, regardless of their rank and status. The primary impulse for this slow repression of an inclination that was formerly strong and widespread does not come from rational understanding of the causes of illness, but—as will be discussed in more detail later— from changes in the way people live together, in the structure of society.

4. The modification of the manner of spitting, and finally the more or less complete elimination of the need for it, is a good example of the malleability of psychic life. It may be that this need has been compensated by others (e.g., the need to smoke) or weakened by certain changes of diet. But it is certain that the degree of suppression which has been possible in this case is not possible with regard to many other drives. The inclination to spit, like that of looking at the sputum, mentioned in the examples, is replaceable; it now manifests itself only in children or in dream analyses, and its suppression is seen in the specific laughter that overcomes us when "such things" are spoken of openly.

Other needs are not replaceable or malleable to the same extent. And this raises the question of the limit of the transformability of the human personality. Without doubt, it is bound to certain regularities that may be called "natural." The historical process modifies it within these limits. The degree to which human life and behavior can be molded by historical processes remains to be determined in detail. At any rate, all this shows once again how natural and historical processes interact almost inseparably. The formation of feelings of shame and revulsion and advances in the threshold of delicacy are both at once natural and historical processes. These forms of feeling are manifestations of human nature under specific social conditions, and they react in their turn on the sociohistorical process as one of its elements.

It is difficult to see whether the radical contraposition of "civilization" and "nature" is more than an expression of the tensions of the "civilized" psyche itself, of a specific imbalance within psychic life produced in the recent stage of Western civilization. At any rate, the psychic life of "primitive" peoples is no less historically (i.e., socially) stamped than that of "civilized" peoples, even if the former are scarcely aware of their own history. There is no zero point in the historicity of human development, just as there is none in the sociality, the social interdependence among men. In both "primitive" and "civilized" peoples, there are socially induced prohibitions and restrictions, together with their psychic counterparts, socially induced anxieties, pleasure and displeasure, distaste and delight. At the least, therefore, it is not very clear what is meant when the so-called primitive standard is opposed as "natural" to the "civilized" as social and historical. So far as the psychical functions of men are concerned, natural and historical processes work indissolubly together.

VIII

On Behavior in the Bedroom

Examples

A

Fifteenth century
From *Stans puer in mensam*, an English book of table manners from the period 1463-1483:

---

215 And if that it forten so by
    nyght or Any tyme
That you schall lye with Any man
    that is better than you
Spyre hym what syde of the bedd
    that most best will ples hym,
And lye you on thi tother syde,
    for that is thi prow;
Ne go you not to bede before bot
    thi better cause the,
For that is no curtasy, thus seys
    doctour paler.

223 And when you arte in thi bed,
    this is curtasy,
Stryght downe that you lye with
    fote and hond.
When ze have talkyd what ze
    wyll, byd hym gode nyght in hye
For that is gret curtasy so schall
    thou understand.*

Let your better choose which side of the bed he'll lie on; don't go to bed first, till he asks you to (says Dr. Paler).

When you're both in bed, lie straight, and say "Good Night" when you've done your chat.

B

1530

From *De civilitate morum puerilium*, by Erasmus, ch. 12, "On the Bedchamber":

When you undress, when you get up, be mindful of modesty, and take care not to expose to the eyes of others anything that morality and nature require to be concealed.

If you share a bed with a comrade, lie quietly; do not toss with your body, for this can lay yourself bare or inconvenience your companion by pulling away the blankets.

*To facilitate comprehension, the old spelling is not reproduced exactly. The philologically accurate text can be found in *A Booke of Precedence*, p. 63.

C

1555

From *Des bonnes moeurs et honnestes contenances*, by Pierre Broë (Lyons, 1555):

If you share a bed with another man, keep still.

Take care not to annoy him or expose yourself by abrupt movements.

And if he is asleep, see that you do not wake him.

D

1729

From La Salle, *Les Règles de la bienséance et de la civilité chrétienne* (Rouen, 1729), p. 55:

You ought . . . neither to undress nor go to bed in the presence of any other person. Above all, unless you are married, you should not go to bed in the presence of anyone of the other sex.

It is still less permissible for people of different sexes to sleep in the same bed, unless they are very young children. . . .

If you are forced by unavoidable necessity to share a bed with another person of the same sex on a journey, it is not proper to lie so near him that you disturb or even touch him; and it is still less decent to put your legs between those of the other. . . .

It is also very improper and impolite to amuse yourself with talk and chatter. . . .

When you get up you should not leave the bed uncovered, nor put your nightcap on a chair or anywhere else where it can be seen.

E

1774

From La Salle, *Les Règles de la bienséance et de la civilité chrétienne* (1774 ed.) p. 31:

It is a strange abuse to make two people of different sex sleep in the same room. And if necessity demands it, you should make sure that the beds are apart, and that modesty does not suffer in any way from this commingling. Only extreme indigence can excuse this practice. . . .

If you are forced to share a bed with a person of the same sex, which seldom happens, you should maintain a strict and vigilant modesty. . . .

When you have awakened and had sufficient time to rest, you should get out of bed with fitting modesty and never stay in bed holding conversations or concerning yourself with other matters . . . nothing more clearly indicates indolence and frivolity; the bed is intended for bodily rest and for nothing else.

Some Comments on the Examples

1. The bedroom has become one of the most "private" and "intimate" areas of human life. Like most other bodily functions, sleeping has been increasingly shifted behind the scenes of social life. The nuclear family remains as the only legitimate, socially sanctioned enclave for this and many other human functions. Its visible and invisible walls withdraw the most "private," "intimate," irrepressibly "animal" aspects of human existence from the sight of others.

In medieval society this function had not been thus privatized and separated from the rest of social life. It was quite normal to receive visitors in rooms with beds, and the beds themselves had a prestige value related to their opulence. It was very common for many people to spend the night in one room: in the upper class, the master with his servants, the mistress with her maid or maids; in other classes, even men and women in the same room,[73] and often guests staying overnight.[74]

2. Those who did not sleep in their clothes undressed completely. In general, people slept naked in lay society, and in monastic orders either fully dressed or fully undressed according to the strictness of the rules. The rule of St. Benedict—dating back at least to the sixth century—required members of the order to sleep in their clothes and even to keep their belts on.[75] In the twelfth century, when their order became more prosperous and powerful and the ascetic constraints less severe, the Cluniac monks were permitted to sleep without clothes. The Cistercians, when striving for reform, returned to the old Benedictine rule. Special nightclothes are never mentioned in the monastic rules of this period, still less in the documents, epics, or illustrations left behind by secular society. This is also true for women. If anything, it was unusual to keep on day clothing in bed. It aroused suspicion that one might have some bodily defect—for what other reason should the body be hidden?—and in fact this usually was the case. In the *Roman de la violette*, for example, we hear the servant

ask her mistress in surprise why she is going to bed in her chemise, and the latter explains it is because of a mark on her body.[76]

This unconcern in showing the naked body, and the position of the shame frontier represented by it, are seen particularly clearly in bathing manners. It has been noted with surprise in later ages that knights were waited on in their baths by women; likewise, their night drink was often brought to their beds by women. It seems to have been common practice, at least in the towns, to undress at home before going to the bathhouse. "How often," says an observer, "the father, wearing nothing but his breeches, with his naked wife and children, runs through the streets from his house to the baths. . . . How many times have I seen girls of ten, twelve, fourteen, sixteen, and eighteen years entirely naked except for a short smock, often torn, and a ragged bathing gown at front and back! With this open at the feet and with their hands held decorously behind them, running from their houses through the long streets at midday to the baths. How many completely naked boys of ten, twelve, fourteen, and sixteen run beside them. . . ."[77]

This unconcern disappears slowly in the sixteenth and more rapidly in the seventeenth, eighteenth, and nineteenth centuries, first in the upper classes and much more slowly in the lower. Up to then, the whole mode of life, with its greater closeness of individuals, made the sight of the naked body, at least in the proper place, incomparably more commonplace than in the first stages of the modern age. "We reach the surprising conclusion," it has been said with reference to Germany, "that . . . the sight of total nakedness was the everyday rule up to the sixteenth century. Everyone undressed completely each evening before going to bed, and likewise no clothing was worn in the steambaths."[78] And this certainly applies not only to Germany. People had a less inhibited—one might say a more childish—attitude toward the body, and to many of its functions. Sleeping customs show this no less than bathing habits.

3. A special nightdress slowly came into use at roughly the same time as the fork and handkerchief. Like the other "implements of civilization," it made its way through Europe quite gradually. And like them it is a symbol of the decisive change taking place at this time in human beings. Sensitivity toward everything that came into contact with the body increased. Shame became attached to behavior that had previously been free of such feelings. The psychological process

which is already described in the Bible by—"and they saw that they were naked and were ashamed"—that is, an advance of the shame frontier, a thrust toward greater restraint—is repeated here, as so often in the course of history. The unconcern in showing oneself naked disappears, as does that in performing bodily functions before others. And as this sight becomes less commonplace in social life, the depiction of the naked body in art takes on a new significance. More than hitherto it becomes a dream image, an emblem of wish-fulfillment. To use Schiller's terms it becomes "sentimental," as against the "naïve" form of earlier phases.

In the courtly society of France—where getting up and going to bed, at least in the case of great lords and ladies, is incorporated directly into social life—nightdress, like every other form of clothing appearing in the communal life of man, takes on representational functions as it develops. This changes when, with the rise of broader classes, getting up and going to bed become intimate and are displaced from social life into the interior of the nuclear family.

The generations following World War I, in their books on etiquette, look back with a certain irony—and not without a faint shudder—at this period, when the exclusion of such functions as sleeping, undressing, and dressing was enforced with special severity, the mere mention of them being blocked by relatively heavy prohibitions. An English book on manners of 1936 says, perhaps with slight exaggeration, but certainly not entirely without justification: "During the Genteel Era before the War, camping was the only way by which respectable writers might approach the subject of sleep. In those days ladies and gentlemen did not go to bed at night—they retired. How they did it was nobody's business. An author who thought differently would have found himself excluded from the circulating library."[79] Here, too, there has been a certain reaction and relaxation since the war. It is clearly connected with the growing mobility of society, with the spread of sport, hiking, and travel, and also with the relatively early separation of young people from the family community. The transition from the nightshirt to pajamas—that is, to a more "socially presentable" sleeping costume—is a symptom of this. This change is not, as is sometimes supposed, simply a retrogressive movement, a recession of the feelings of shame or delicacy, or a release and de-control of instinctual urges, but the development of a form that fits both our advanced standard of delicacy and the specific situation in which present-day social life places the individual. Sleep is no longer so intimate and segregated as in the preceding stage. There are more situations in which people are exposed to the sight of strangers sleeping, undressing, or dressing. As a result, nightclothes (like underwear) have been developed and transformed in such a way that the wearer need not be "ashamed" when seen in such situations by others. The nightclothes of the preceding phase aroused feelings of shame and embarrassment precisely because they were relatively formless. They were not intended to be seen by people outside the family circle. On the one hand, the nightshirt of the nineteenth century marks an epoch in which shame and embarrassment with regard to the exposure of one's own body were so advanced and internalized that bodily forms had to be entirely covered even when alone or in the closest family circle; on the other hand, it characterizes an epoch in which the "intimate" and "private" sphere, because it was so sharply severed from the rest of social life, had not to any great extent been socially articulated and patterned. This peculiar combination of strongly internalized, compulsive feelings of delicacy, or morality, with a lack of social patterning with respect to the "spheres of intimacy"is characteristic of nineteenth-century society and not a little of our own.[80]

4. The examples give a rough idea of how sleep, becoming slowly more intimate and private, is separated from most other social relations, and how the precepts given to young people take on a specific moralistic undertone with the advance of feelings of shame. In the medieval quotation (Example A) the restraint demanded of young people is explained by consideration due to others, respect for social superiors. It says, in effect, "If you share your bed with a better man, ask him which side he prefers, and do not go to bed before he invites you, for that is not courteous." And in the French imitation of Johannes Sulpicius by Pierre Broë (Example C), the same attitude prevails: "Do not annoy your neighbor when he has fallen asleep; see that you do not wake him up, etc." In Erasmus we begin to hear a moral demand, which requires certain behavior not out of consideration for others but for its own sake: "When you undress, when you get up, be mindful of modesty." But the idea of social custom, of consideration for others, is still predominant. The contrast to the later period is particularly clear if we remember that these precepts, even those of Dr. Paler (Example A), were clearly directed to people who

went to bed undressed. That strangers should sleep in the same bed appears, to judge by the manner in which the question is discussed, neither unusual nor in any way improper even at the time of Erasmus.

In the quotations from the eighteenth century this tendency is not continued in a straight line, partly because it is no longer confined predominantly to the upper class. But in the meantime, even in other classes, it has clearly become less commonplace for a young person to share his bed with another: "If you are forced by unavoidable necessity to share a bed with another person . . . on a journey, it is not proper to lie so near him that you disturb or even touch him," La Salle writes (Example D). And: "You ought neither to undress nor go to bed in the presence of any other person."

In the 1774 edition, details are again avoided wherever possible. And the tone is appreciably stronger. "If you are forced to share a bed with a person of the same sex, which seldom happens, you should maintain a strict and vigilant modesty" (Example E). This is the tone of moral injunction. Even to give a reason has become distasteful to the adult. The child is made by the threatening tone to associate this situation with danger. The more "natural" the standard of delicacy and shame appears to adults and the more the civilized restraint of instinctual urges is taken for granted, the more incomprehensible it becomes to adults that children do not have this delicacy and shame by "nature." The children necessarily touch again and again on the adult threshold of delicacy, and—since they are not yet adapted—they infringe the taboos of society, cross the adult shame frontier, and penetrate emotional danger zones which the adult himself can only control with difficulty. In this situation the adult does not explain the demand he makes on behavior. He is unable to do so adequately. He is so conditioned that he conforms to the social standard more or less automatically. Any other behavior, any breach of the prohibitions or restraints prevailing in his society means danger, and a devaluation of the restraints imposed on himself. And the peculiarly emotional undertone so often associated with moral demands, the aggressive and threatening severity with which they are frequently upheld, reflects the danger in which any breach of the prohibitons places the unstable balance of all those for whom the standard behavior of society has become more or less "second nature." These attitudes are symptoms of the anxiety aroused in adults whenever the structure of their own instinctual life, and with it their own social existence and the social order in which it is anchored, is even remotely threatened.

A whole series of specific conflicts—above all, those between parents (usually ill-prepared for conditioning) and their children, conflicts arising with the advance of the shame-frontier and the growing distance between adults and children, and therefore largely founded on the structure of civilized society itself—are explained by this situation. The situation itself has been understood only relatively recently by society, first of all by small groups of professional educators. And only now, in the age that has been called the "century of the child," is the realization that, in view of the increased distance between them, children cannot behave like adults slowly penetrating the family circle with appropriate educational advice and instructions. In the long preceding period, the more severe attitude prevailed that morality and respect for taboos should be present in children from the first. This attitude certainly cannot be said to have disappeared today.

The examples on behavior in the bedroom give, for a limited segment, a certain impression of how late it really was that the tendency to adopt such attitudes reached its full development in secular education.

The line followed by this development scarcely needs further elucidation. Here, too, in much the same way as with eating, the wall between people, the reserve, the emotional barrier erected by conditioning between one body and another, grows continuously. To share a bed with people outside the family circle, with strangers, is made more and more embarrassing. Unless necessity dictates otherwise, it becomes usual even within the family for each person to have his own bed and finally—in the middle and upper classes—his own bedroom. Children are trained early in this isolation from others, with all the habits and experiences that this brings with it. Only if we see how natural it seemed in the Middle Ages for strangers and for children and adults to share a bed can we appreciate what a fundamental change in interpersonal relationships and behavior is expressed in our manner of living. And we recognize how far from self-evident it is that bed and body should form such psychological danger zones as they do in the most recent phase of civilization.

IX

Changes in Attitude Toward Relations Between the Sexes

1. The feeling of shame surrounding human sexual relations has increased and changed considerably in the process of civilization.[81] This manifests itself particularly clearly in the difficulty experienced by adults in the later stages of civilization in talking about these relations to children. But today this difficulty appears almost natural. It seems to be explained almost by biological reasons alone that a child knows nothing of the relations of the sexes, and that it is an extremely delicate and difficult task to enlighten growing girls and boys about themselves and what goes on around them. The extent to which this situation, far from being self-evident, is a further result of the civilizing process is only perceived if the behavior of people in a different stage is observed. The fate of Erasmus's renowned *Colloquies* is a good example.

Erasmus discovered that one of the works of his youth had been published without his permission in a corrupt form, with additions by others and partly in a bad style. He revised it and published it himself under a new title in 1522, calling it *Familiarum colloquiorum formulae non tantum ad linguam puerilem expoliandam, verum etiam ad vitam instituendam.*

He worked on this text, augmenting and improving it, until shortly before his death. It became what he had desired, not only a book from which boys could learn a good Latin style, but one which could serve, as he says in the title, to introduce them to life. The *Colloquies* became one of the most famous and widely read works of their time. As his treatise *De civilitate morum puerilium* did later, they went through numerous editions and translations. And like it, they became a schoolbook, a standard work from which boys were educated. Hardly anything gives a more immediate impression of the change in Western society in the process of civilization than the criticism to which this work was subjected by those who still found themselves obliged to concern themselves with it in the nineteenth century. An influential German pedagogue, Von Raumer, comments on it as follows in his *Geschichte der Pädagogik* (History of pedagogy):[82]

How could such a book be introduced in countless schools? What had boys to do with these satyrs? Reform is a matter for mature men. What sense were boys supposed to make of dialogues on so many subjects of which they understand nothing; conversations in which teachers are ridiculed, or between two women about their husbands, between a suitor and a girl he is wooing, or the colloquy "Adolescentis et Scorti" (The young man and the harlot). This last dialogue recalls Schiller's distich entitled "Kunstgriff" (The knack): "If you would please both the worldly and godly alike, paint them the joys of the flesh, but paint them the devil as well." Erasmus here paints fleshly lust in the basest way and then adds something which is supposed to edify. Such a book is recommended by the Doctor Theologiae to an eight-year-old boy, that he might be improved by reading it.

The work is indeed dedicated to the young son of Erasmus's publisher, and the father clearly felt no qualms at printing it.

2. The book met with harsh criticism as soon as it appeared. But this was not directed chiefly at its moral qualities. The primary target was the "intellectual," the man who was neither an orthodox Protestant nor an orthodox Catholic. The Catholic Church, above all, fought against the *Colloquies*, which certainly contain occasional virulent attacks on Church institutions and orders, and soon placed it on the Index.

But against this must be set the extraordinary success of the *Colloquies* and, above all, their introduction as a schoolbook. "From 1526 on," says Huizinga in his *Erasmus* (London, 1924, p. 199), "there was for two centuries an almost uninterrupted stream of editions and translations."

In this period, therefore, Erasmus's treatise must have remained a kind of standard work for a very considerable number of people. How is the difference between its viewpoint and that of the nineteenth-century critic to be understood?

In this work Erasmus does indeed speak of many things which with the advance of civilization have been increasingly concealed from the eyes of children, and which in the nineteenth century would under no circumstances have been used as reading matter for children in the way Erasmus desired and expressly affirmed in the dedication to his six- or eight-year-old godson. As the nineteenth-century critic stresses, Erasmus presents in the dialogues a young man wooing a girl. He shows a woman complaining about the bad behavior of her husband. And there is even a conversation between a young man and a prostitute.

Nevertheless, these dialogues bear witness, in exactly the same way as *De civilitate morum puerilium,* to Erasmus's delicacy in all questions relating to the regulation of instinctual life, even if they do not entirely correspond to our own standard. They even represent, measured by the standard of medieval secular society, and even by that of the secular society of his own time, a very considerable shift in the direction of the kind of restraint of instinctual urges which the nineteenth century was to justify above all in the form of morality.

Certainly, the young man who woos the girl in the colloquy "Proci et puellae" (Courtship) expresses very openly what he wants of her. He speaks of his love for her. When she resists, he tells her that she has drawn his soul half out of his body. He tells her that it is permissible and right to conceive children. He asks her to imagine how fine it will be when he as king and she as queen rule over their children and servants. (This idea shows very clearly how the lesser psychological distance between adults and children very often went hand in hand with a greater social distance.) Finally the girl gives way to his suit. She agrees to become his wife. But she preserves, as she says, the honor of her maidenhood. She keeps it for him, she says. She even refuses him a kiss. But when he does not desist from asking for one, she laughingly tells him that as she has, in his own words, drawn his soul half out of his body, so that he is almost dead, she is afraid that with a kiss she might draw his soul completely out of his body and kill him.

3. As has been mentioned, Erasmus was occasionally reproached by the Church, even in his own lifetime, with the "immorality" of the *Colloquies.* But one should not be misled by this into drawing false conclusions about the actual standard, particularly of secular society. A treatise directed against Erasmus's *Colloquies* from a consciously Catholic position, about which more will be said later, does not differ in the least from the *Colloquies* so far as unveiled references to sexual matters are concerned. Its author, too, was a humanist. The novelty of the humanists' writings, and particularly of those of Erasmus, is precisely that they do not conform to the standard of clerical society but are written from the standpoint of, and for, secular society.

The humanists were representatives of a movement which sought to release the Latin language from its confinement within the ecclesiastical tradition and sphere, and make it a language of secular society, at least of the secular upper class. Not the least important sign of the change in the structure of Western society, which has already been seen from so many other aspects in this study, is the fact that its secular constituents now feel an increasing need for a secular, scholarly literature. The humanists are the executors of this change, the functionaries of this need of the secular upper class. In their works the written word once again draws close to worldly social life. Experiences from this life find direct access to scholarly literature. This, too, is a line in the great movement of "civilization." And it is here that one of the keys to the "revival" of antiquity will have to be sought.

Erasmus once gave very trenchant expression to this process precisely in defending the *Colloquies*: "As Socrates brought philosophy from heaven to earth, so I have led philosophy to games and banquets," he says in the notes *De utilitate colloquiorum* that he appended to the *Colloquies* (1655 ed., p. 668). For this reason these writings may be correctly regarded as representing the standard of behavior of secular society, no matter how much their particular demands for a restraint of instincts and moderation of behavior may have transcended this standard and, represented in anticipation of the future, an ideal.

In *De utilitate colloquiorum,* Erasmus says with regard to the dialogue "Proci et puellae" mentioned above: "I wish that all suitors were like the one I depict and conversed in no other way when entering marriage."

What appears to the nineteenth-century observer as the "basest depiction of lust," what even by the present standard of shame must be veiled in silence particularly before children, appears to Erasmus and his contemporaries who help to disseminate this work as a model conversation, ideally suited to set an example for the young, and still largely an ideal when compared with what was actually going on around them.[83]

4. The case is similar with the other dialogues mentioned by Von Raumer in his polemic. The woman who complains about her husband is instructed that she will have to change her own behavior, then her husband's will change. And the conversation of the young man with the prostitute ends with his rejection of her disreputable mode of life. One must hear this conversation oneself to understand what Erasmus wishes to set up as an example for boys. The girl, Lucretia, has not seen the youth, Sophronius, for a long time. And she clearly invites him to do what he has come to the house to do. But he asks whether she

is sure that they cannot be seen, whether she has not a darker room. And when she leads him to a darker room he again has scruples. Is she really sure that no one can see them? "No one can see or hear us, not even a fly," she says. "Why do you hesitate?" But the young man asks: "Not even God? Not even the angels?"* And then he begins to convert her with all the arts of dialectics. He asks whether she has many enemies, whether it would not please her to annoy her enemies. Would she not annoy her enemies by giving up her life in this house and becoming an honorable woman? And finally he convinces her. He will secretly take a room for her in the house of a respectable woman, he will find a pretext for her to leave the house unseen. And at first he will look after her.

However "immoral" the presentation of such a situation (in a "children's book," of all places) must appear to an observer from a later period, it is not difficult to understand that from the standpoint of a different social standard and a different structure of feelings it could appear highly "moral" and exemplary.

The same line of development, the same difference in standards, could be demonstrated by any number of examples. The observer of the nineteenth and, to some extent, even of the twentieth century confronts the models and conditioning precepts of the past with a certain helplessness. And until we come to see that our own threshold of repugnance, our own structure of feelings, have developed—in a

---

*The text of this excerpt from the dialogue is as follows:

SOPHRONIUS: Nondum hic locus mihi videtur satis secretus.
LUCRETIA: Unde iste novus pudor? Est mihi museion,[84] ubi repono mundum meum, locus   adeo obscurus, ut vix ego te visura sim, aut te me.
SOPH.: Circumspice rimas omnes.
LUC.: Rima nulla est.
SOPH.: Nullus est in propinquo, qui nos exaudiat?
LUC.: Ne musca quidem, mea lux. Quid cunctaris?
SOPH.: Fallemus heic oculos Dei?
LUC.: Nequaquam: ille perspicit omnia.
SOPH.: Et angelorum?

SOPH.: This place doesn't seem secret enough to me. LUC.: How come you're so bashful all at once? Well, come to my private dressing room. It's so dark we shall scarcely see each other there. SOPH.: Examine every chink. LUC.: There's not a single chink. SOPH.: Is there nobody near to hear us? LUC.: Not so much as a fly, my dearest. Why are you hesitating? SOPH.: Can we escape the eye of God here? LUC.: Of course not; he sees everything. SOPH.: And the angels?

---

structured process—and are continuing to develop, it remains indeed almost incomprehensible from the present standpoint how such dia- logues could be included in a schoolbook or deliberately produced as reading matter for children. But this is precisely why our own stan- dard, including our attitude to children, should be understood as something which has developed.

More orthodox men than Erasmus did the same as he. To replace the *Colloquies,* which were suspected of heresy, other dialogues were written, as already mentioned, by a strict Catholic. They bear the title *Johannis Morisoti medici colloquiorum libri quatuor, ad Constan- tinum filium* (Basel, 1549). They are likewise written as a schoolbook for boys, since, as the author Morisotus says, one is often uncertain, in Erasmus's *Colloquies,* "whether one is listening to a Christian or a heathen." And in later evaluations of this opposing work from a strictly Catholic camp the same phenomenon appears.[85] It will suffice to introduce the work as it is reflected in a judgment from 1911:[86]

In Morisotus girls, maidens, and women play a still greater role than in Erasmus. In a large number of dialogues they are the sole speakers, and their conversations, which even in the first and second books are by no means always quite harmless, often revolve in the last two.[87] . . . around such risky matters that we can only shake our heads and ask: Did the stern Morisotus write this for his son? Could he be so sure that the boy would really only read and study the later books when he had reached the age for which they were intended? Admittedly, we should not forget that the sixteenth century knew little of prudery, and frequently enough presented its scholars with material in their exercise books that our pedagogues would gladly do without. But another question! How did Morisotus im- agine the use of such dialogues in practice? Boys, youths, and men could never use as a model for Latin speech a conversation in which there are only female speakers. Therefore Morisotus, no better than the despised Erasmus, has lost sight of the didactic purpose of the book.

The question is not difficult to answer.

5. Erasmus himself never "lost sight of his didactic purpose." His commentary *De utilitate colloquiorum* shows this quite unequivocal- ly. In it he makes explicit what kind of didactic purpose was attached to his "conversations" or, more exactly, what he wanted to convey to the young man. On the conversation of the young man with the harlot, for example, he says: "What could I have said that would have been more effective in bringing home to the young man the need for

modesty, and in bringing girls out of such dangerous and infamous houses?'' No, he never lost sight of his pedagogical purpose; he merely has a different standard of shame. He wants to show the young man the world as in a mirror; he wants to teach him what must be avoided and what is conducive to a tranquil life: "In senili colloquio quam multa velut in speculo exhibentur, quae, vel fugienda sunt in vita, vel vitam reddunt tranquillam!''

The same intention undoubtedly also underlies the conversations of Morisotus; and a similar attitude appears in many other educational writings of the time. They all set out to "introduce the boy to life,'' as Erasmus puts it.[88] But by this they meant the life of adults. In later periods there is an increasing tendency to tell and show children how they ought and ought not to behave. Here they are shown, by introducing them to life, how adults ought and ought not to behave. This is the difference. And one did not behave here in this way, there in that, as a result of theoretical reflection. For Erasmus and his contemporaries it was a matter of course to speak to children in this way. Even though subservient and socially dependent, boys lived very early in the same social sphere as adults. And adults did not impose upon themselves either in action or in words the same restraint with regard to the sexual life as later. In keeping with the different state of restraint of feelings produced in the individual by the structure of interpersonal relations, the idea of strictly concealing these drives in secrecy and intimacy was largely alien to adults themselves. All this made the distance between the behavioral and emotional standards of adults and children smaller from the outset. We see again and again how important it is for an understanding of the earlier psychic constitution and our own to observe the increase of this distance, the gradual formation of the peculiar segregated area in which people gradually come to spend the first twelve, fifteen, and now almost twenty years of their lives. Human biological development in earlier times will not have taken a very different course from today. Only in relation to this social change can we better understand the whole problem of "growing up'' as it appears today, and with it such particular problems as the "infantile residues'' in the personality structure of grown-ups. The more pronounced difference between the dress of children and adults in our time is only a particularly visible expression of this development. It, too, was minimal at Erasmus's time and for a long period thereafter.

6. To an observer from modern times, it seems surprising that

Erasmus in his *Colloquies* should speak at all to a child of prostitutes and the houses in which they live. In our phase of civilization it seems immoral even to acknowledge the existence of such institutions in a schoolbook. They certainly exist as enclaves even in the society of the nineteenth and twentieth centuries. But the fear and shame with which the sexual area of instinctual life, like many others, is surrounded from the earliest years, the "conspiracy of silence" observed on such matters in social discourse, are as good as complete. The mere mention of such opinions and institutions in social life is forbidden, and references to them in the presence of children are a crime soiling the childish soul, or at least a very grave error of conditioning.

In Erasmus's time it was taken equally for granted that children knew of the existence of these institutions. No one concealed them. At most they were warned about them. Erasmus does just that. If we read only the pedagogical books of the time, the mention of such social institutions can certainly appear as an idea emanating from an individual. If we see how the children actually lived with adults, and how scanty was the wall of secrecy between adults themselves and therefore also between adults and children, we comprehend that conversations like those of Erasmus and Morisotus relate directly to the standard of their times. They could reckon with the fact that children knew about all this; it was taken for granted. They saw it as their task as educators to show children how they ought to conduct themselves in the face of such institutions.

It may not seem to amount to very much to say that such houses were spoken about quite openly at the universities. All the same, people generally went to university a good deal younger than today. And it illustrates the theme of this whole chapter to point out that the prostitute was a topic even of comic public speeches at universities. In 1500 a master of arts at Heidelberg spoke "De fide meretricum in suos amatores" (On the fidelity of courtesans to their paramours), another "De fide concubinarum" (On the fidelity of concubines), a third "On the monopoly of the guild of swine," or "De generibus ebriosorum et ebrietate vitanda."[89]

And exactly the same phenomenon is apparent in many sermons of the time; there is no indication that children were excluded from them. This form of extramarital relationship was certainly disapproved in ecclesiastical and many secular circles. But the social prohibition was not yet imprinted as a self restraint in the individual to the extent that it was embarrassing even to speak about it in public. Society had not yet outlawed every utterance that showed that one knew anything about such things.

This difference becomes even clearer if one considers the position of venal women in medieval towns. As is the case today in many societies outside Europe, they have their own very definite place in the public life of the medieval town. There were towns in which they ran races on festival days.[90] They were frequently sent to welcome distinguished visitors. In 1438, for example, the protocols of the city accounts of Vienna read: "For the wine for the common women 96 Kreutzers. Item, for the women who went to meet the king, 96 Kreutzers for wine."[91] Or the mayor and council give distinguished visitors free access to the brothel. In 1434 the Emperor Sigismund publicly thanks the city magistrate of Bern for putting the brothel freely at the disposal of himself and his attendants for three days.[92] This, like a banquet, formed part of the hospitality offered to high-ranking guests.

The venal women form within city life a corporation with certain rights and obligations, like any other professional body. And like any other professional group, they occasionally defend themselves against unfair competition. In 1500, for example, a number of them go to the mayor of a German town and complain about another house in which the profession to which their house has the sole public rights is practiced. The mayor gives them permission to enter this house; they smash everything and beat the landlady. On another occasion they drag a competitor from her house and force her to live in theirs.

In a word, their social position was similar to that of the executioner, lowly and despised, but entirely public and not surrounded with secrecy. This form of extramarital relationship between man and woman had not yet been removed "behind the scenes."

7. To a certain extent, this also applies to sexual relations in general, even marital ones. Wedding customs alone give us an idea of this. The procession into the bridal chamber was led by the best men. The bride was undressed by the bridesmaids; she had to take off all finery. The bridal bed had to be mounted in the presence of witnesses if the marriage was to be valid. They were "laid together."[93] "Once in bed you are rightly wed," the saying went. In the later Middle Ages this custom gradually changed to the extent that the couple was allowed to lie on the bed in their clothes. No doubt these customs

varied somewhat between classes and countries. All the same, the old form was retained in Lübeck, for example, up to the first decade of the seventeenth century.[94] Even in the absolutist society of France, bride and bridegroom were taken to bed by the guests, undressed, and given their nightdress. All this is symptomatic of a different standard of shame concerning the relations of the sexes. And through these examples one gains a clearer perception of the specific standard of shame which slowly becomes predominant in the nineteenth and twentieth centuries. In this period, even among adults, everything pertaining to sexual life is concealed to a high degree and dismissed behind the scenes. This is why it is possible, and also necessary, to conceal this side of life for a long period from children. In the preceding phases the relations between the sexes, together with the institutions embracing them, are far more directly incorporated into public life. Hence it is more natural for children to be familiar with this side of life from an early age. From the point of view of conditioning, there is no need to burden this sphere with taboos and secrecy to the extent that becomes necessary in the later stage of civilization, with its different standard of behavior.

In aristocratic court society, sexual life was certainly a good deal more concealed than in medieval society. What the observer from a bourgeois-industrial society often interprets as the "frivolity" of court society is nothing other than this shift toward concealment. Nevertheless, measured by the standard of control of the impulses in bourgeois society itself, the concealment and segregation of sexuality in social life, as in consciousness, was relatively slight in this phase. Here, too, the judgment of later phases is often misled because standards, one's own and that of the court aristocracy, are viewed as absolute rather than as inseparable opposites, and because one's own standard is made the measure of all others.

In this society, too, the relative openness with which the natural stages in a process of development, functions are referred to among adults is matched by a greater freedom of speech and action in the presence of children. There are numerous examples of this. To take a particularly illustrative one, there lives at the court in the seventeenth century a little Mlle. de Bouillon who is six years old. The ladies of the court are wont to converse with her, and one day they play a joke on her: they try to persuade the young lady that she is pregnant. The little girl denies it. She defends herself. It is absolutely impossible, she says, and they argue back and forth. But then one day on waking up she finds a newborn child in her bed. She is amazed; and she says in her innocence, "So this has happened only to the Holy Virgin and me; for I did not feel any pain." Her words are passed round, and now the little affair becomes a diversion for the whole court. The child receives visits, as is customary on such occasions. The Queen herself comes to console her and to offer herself as godmother to the baby. And the game goes further: the little girl is pressed to say who is the father of the child. Finally, after a period of strenuous reflection, she reaches the conclusion that it can only be the King or the Count de Guiche, since they are the only two men who have given her a kiss.[95] Nobody takes this joke amiss. It falls entirely within the existing standard. No one sees in it a danger to the adaptation of the child to this standard, or to her spiritual purity, and it is clearly not seen as in any way contradicting her religious education.

8. Only very gradually, subsequently, does a stronger association of sexuality with shame and embarrassment, and a corresponding restraint of behavior, spread more or less evenly over the whole of society. And only when the distance between adults and children grows does "sexual enlightenment" become an "acute problem."

Above, the criticism of Erasmus's *Colloquies* by the well-known pedagogue Von Raumer was quoted. The picture of this whole curve of development becomes even more distinct if we see how the problem of sexual education, the adaptation of the child to the standard of his own society, posed itself to this educator. In 1857, Von Raumer published a short work called *The Education of Girls*. What he prescribes in it (p. 72) as a model behavior for adults in answering the sexual questions of their children was certainly not the only possible form of behavior at his time; nevertheless, it is highly characteristic of the standard of the nineteenth century, in the instruction of both girls and boys:

Some mothers are of the opinion, fundamentally perverse in my view, that daughters should be given insight into all family circumstances, even into the relations of the sexes, and initiated into things that will fall to their lot in the event that they should marry. Following the example of Rousseau, this view degenerated to the coarsest and most repulsive caricature in the philanthropist of Dessau. Other mothers exaggerate in the opposite direction by telling girls things which, as soon as they grow older, must reveal themselves as totally false. As in all other cases, this is reprehensible.

These things should not be touched upon at all in the presence of children, least of all in a secretive way which is liable to arouse curiosity. Children should be left for as long as is at all possible in the belief that an angel brings the mother her little children. This legend, customary in some regions, is far better than the story of the stork common elsewhere. Children, if they really grow up under their mother's eyes, will seldom ask forward questions on this point . . . not even if the mother is prevented by a childbirth from having them about her. . . . If girls should later ask how little children really come into the world, they should be told that the good Lord gives the mother her child, who has a guardian angel in heaven who certainly played an invisible part in bringing us this great joy. "You do not need to know nor could you understand how God gives children." Girls must be satisfied with such answers in a hundred cases, and it is the mother's task to occupy her daughters' thoughts so incessantly with the good and beautiful that they are left no time to brood on such matters. . . . A mother . . . ought only once to say seriously: "It would not be good for you to know such a thing, and you should take care not to listen to anything said about it." A truly well-brought-up girl will from then on feel shame at hearing things of this kind spoken of.

Between the manner of speaking about sexual relations represented by Erasmus and that represented here by Von Raumer, a civilization-curve is visible similar to that shown in more detail in the expression of other impulses. In the civilizing process, sexuality too is increasingly removed behind the scenes of social life and enclosed in a particular enclave, the nuclear family. Likewise, the relations between the sexes are isolated, placed behind walls in consciousness. An aura of embarrassment, the expression of a sociogenetic fear, surrounds this sphere of life. Even among adults it is referred to officially only with caution and circumlocutions. And with children, particularly girls, such things are, as far as possible, not referred to at all. Von Raumer gives no reason why one ought not to speak of them with children. He could have said it is desirable to preserve the spiritual purity of girls for as long as possible. But even this reason is only another expression of how far the gradual submergence of these impulses in shame and embarrassment has advanced by this time. It is now as natural not to speak of these matters as it was to speak of them in Erasmus's time. And the fact that both the witnesses invoked here, Erasmus and Von Raumer, were serious Christians who took their authority from God further underlines the difference.

THE CIVILIZING PROCESS

It is clearly not "rational" motives that underlie the model put forward by Von Raumer. Considered rationally, the problem confronting him seems unsolved, and what he says appears contradictory. He does not explain how and when the young girl should be made to understand what is happening and will happen to her. The primary concern is the necessity of instilling "modesty" (i.e., feelings of shame, fear, embarrassment, and guilt) or, more precisely, behavior conforming to the social standard. And one feels how infinitely difficult it is for the educator himself to overcome the resistance of the shame and embarrassment which surround this sphere for him. One detects something of the deep confusion in which this social development has placed the individual; the only advice that the educator is able to give mothers is to avoid contact with these things wherever possible. What is involved here is not the lack of insight or the inhibition of a particular person; it is a social, not an individual problem. Only gradually, as if through insight gained retrospectively, were better methods evolved for adapting the child to the high degree of sexual restraint, to the control, transformation, and inhibition of these drives that were indispensable for life in this society.

Von Raumer himself sees in a sense that this area of life ought not to be surrounded with an aura of secrecy "which is liable to arouse curiosity." But as this has become a "secret" area in his society, he cannot escape the necessity of secrecy in his own precepts: "A mother . . . ought only once to say seriously: 'It would not be good for you to know such a thing. . . .' " Neither "rational" motives nor practical reasons primarily determine this attitude, but rather the shame of adults themselves, which has become compulsive. It is the social prohibitions and resistances within themselves, their own superego, that makes them keep silent.

For Erasmus and his contemporaries, as we have seen, the problem is not that of enlightening the child on the relations of man and woman. Children find out about this of their own accord through the kind of social institutions and social life in which they grow up. As the reserve of adults is less, so too is the discrepancy between what is permitted openly and what takes place behind the scenes. Here the chief task of the educator is to guide the child, within what he already knows, in the correct direction—or, more precisely, the direction desired by the educator. This is what Erasmus seeks to do through conversations like that of the girl with her suitor or the youth with the prostitute. And the success of the book shows that Erasmus struck the right note for many of his contemporaries.

As in the course of the civilizing process the sexual drive, like many others, is subjected to ever stricter control and transformation, the problem it poses changes. The pressure placed on adults to privatize all their impulses (particularly sexual ones), the "conspiracy of silence," the socially generated restrictions on speech, the emotionally charged character of most words relating to sexual urges—all this builds a thick wall of secrecy around the adolescent. What makes sexual enlightenment—the breaching of this wall, which will one day be necessary—so difficult is not only the need to make the adolescent conform to the same standard of instinctual restraint and control as the adult. It is, above all, the personality structure of the adults themselves that makes speaking about these secret things difficult. Very often adults have neither the tone nor the words. The "dirty" words they know are out of the question. The medical words are unfamiliar to many. Theoretical considerations in themselves do not help. It is the sociogenetic repressions in them that resist speech. Hence the advice given by Von Raumer to speak on these matters as little as possible. And this situation is further exacerbated by the fact that the tasks of conditioning and "enlightenment" fall more and more exclusively to parents. The manifold love relationships between mother, father, and child tend to increase resistance to speaking about these questions, not only on the part of the child but also on that of the father or mother.

It is clear from this how the question of childhood is to be posed. The psychological problems of growing people cannot be understood if the individual is regarded as developing uniformly in all historical epochs. The problems relating to the child's consciousness and instinctual urges vary with the nature of the relations of children to adults. These relations have in each society a specific form corresponding to the peculiarities of its structure. They are different in chivalrous society from those in urban bourgeois society; they are different in the whole secular society of the Middle Ages from those of modern times. Therefore, the problems arising from the adaptation and molding of adolescents to the standard of adults—for example, the specific problems of puberty in our civilized society—can only be understood in relation to the historical phase, the structure of society as a whole, which demands and maintains this standard of adult

THE CIVILIZING PROCESS

behavior and this special form of relationship between adults and children.

9. A civilizing process analogous to that of "sexual enlightenment" could be shown in relation to marriage and its development in Western society. That monogamous marriage is the predominant institution regulating sexual relations in the West is undoubtedly correct in general terms. Nevertheless, the actual control and molding of sexual relations changes considerably in the course of Western history. The Church certainly fought early for monogamous marriage. But marriage takes on this strict form as a social institution binding on both sexes only at a late stage, when drives and impulses come under firmer and stricter control. For only then are extramarital relationships for men really ostracized socially, or at least subjected to absolute secrecy. In earlier phases, depending on the balance of social power between the sexes, extramarital relationships for men and sometimes also for women were taken more or less for granted by secular society. Up to the sixteenth century we hear often enough that in the families of the most honorable citizens the legitimate and illegitimate children of the husband are brought up together; nor is any secret made of the difference before the children themselves. The man was not yet forced socially to feel ashamed of his extramarital relationships. Despite all the countervailing tendencies that undoubtedly already exist, it is very often taken for granted that the bastard children are a part of the family, that the father should provide for their future and, in the case of daughters, arrange an honorable wedding. But no doubt this led more than once to "serious misunderstanding"[96] between the married couples.

The situation of the illegitimate child is not always and everywhere the same throughout the Middle Ages. For a long time, nevertheless, there is no trace of the tendency toward secrecy which corresponds later, in professional-bourgeois society, to the tendency toward a stricter confinement of sexuality to the relationship of one man to one woman, to the stricter control of sexual impulses, and to the stronger pressure of social prohibitions. Here, too, the demands of the Church cannot be taken as a measure of the real standard of secular society. In reality, if not always in law, the situation of the illegitimate children in a family differed from that of the legitimate children only in that the former did not inherit the status of the father nor in general his wealth, or at least not the same part of it as the legitimate children. That people in the upper class often called themselves "bastard" expressly and proudly is well enough known.[97]

Marriage in the absolutist court societies of the seventeenth and eighteenth centuries derives its special character from the fact that, through the structure of these societies, the dominance of the husband over the wife is broken for the first time. The social power of the wife is almost equal to that of the husband. Social opinion is determined to a high degree by women. And whereas society had hitherto acknowledged only the extramarital relationships of men, regarding those of the socially "weaker sex" as more or less reprehensible, the extramarital relationships of women now appear, in keeping with the transformation of balance of social power between the sexes, as legitimate within certain limits.

It remains to be shown in more detail how decisive this first increase in power changes or, if one likes, this first wave of emancipation of women in absolutist court society was for the civilizing process, for the advance of the frontier of shame and embarrassment and for the strengthening of social control over the individual. Just as the increased power changes, the social ascent of other social groups necessitated new forms of drive control for all at a level midway between those previously imposed on the rulers and the ruled respectively, so this strengthening of the social position of women signified (to express the point schematically) a decrease in the restrictions on their drives for women and an increase in the restrictions on their drives for men. At the same time, it forced both men and women to adopt a new and a stricter self-discipline in their relations with one another.

In the famous novel *La Princesse de Clèves,* by Madame de la Fayette, the Princess's husband, who knows his wife to be in love with the Duc de Nemours, says: "I shall trust only in you; it is the path my heart counsels me to take, and also my reason. With a temperament like yours, *by leaving you your liberty I set you narrower limits* than I could enforce."[98]

This is an example of the pressure toward self-discipline imposed on the sexes by this situation. The husband knows that he cannot hold his wife by force. He does not rant or expostulate because his wife loves another, nor does he appeal to his rights as a husband. Public opinion would support none of this. He restrains himself. But in doing so he expects from her the same self-discipline as he imposes on himself. This is a very characteristic example of the new constellation that comes into being with the diminishment of social inequality between the sexes. Fundamentally, it is not the individual husband who gives his wife this freedom. It is founded in the structure of society itself. But it also demands a new kind of behavior. It produces very specific conflicts. And there are certainly enough women in this society who make use of this freedom. There is plentiful evidence that in this courtly aristocracy the restriction of sexual relationships to marriage was very often regarded as bourgeois and socially unsuitable. Nevertheless, all this gives an idea of how directly a specific kind of freedom corresponds to particular forms and stages of social interdependence among human beings.

The nondynamic linguistic forms to which we are are still bound today oppose freedom and constraint like heaven and hell. From a short-term point of view, this thinking in absolute opposites is often reasonably adequate. For someone in prison the world outside the prison walls is a world of freedom. But considered more precisely, there is, contrary to what antitheses such as this one suggest, no such thing as "absolute" freedom, if this means a total independence and absence of social constraint. There is a liberation from one form of constraint that is oppressive or intolerable to another which is less burdensome. Thus the civilizing process, despite the transformation and increased constraint that it imposes on the emotions, goes hand in hand with liberations of the most diverse kinds. The form of marriage at the absolutist courts, symbolized by the same arrangement of living rooms and bedrooms for men and women in the mansions of the court aristocracy, is one of many examples of this. The woman was more free from external constraints than in feudal society. But the inner constraint which she had to impose on herself in accordance with the form of integration and the code of behavior of court society, and which stemmed from the same structural features of this society as her "liberation," had increased for women as for men in comparison to chivalrous society.

The case is similar if the bourgeois form of marriage of the nineteenth century is compared with that of the court aristocracy of the seventeenth and eighteenth centuries. In this later period the bourgeoisie as a whole is freed from the pressures of an absolutist estate society. Both bourgeois men and bourgeois women are now relieved of the external constraints to which they were subjected as second-rate people in the hierarchy of estates. But the intertwinement of trade and money, the growth of which had given them the social power to liberate themselves, has increased. In this respect, the social constraints on the individual are also stronger than before. The pattern of self-restraint imposed on the people of bourgeois society through their occupational work is in many respects different from the pattern imposed on the emotional life by the functions of court society. For many aspects of the "emotional economy", bourgeois functions—above all, business life—demand and produce greater self-restraint than courtly functions. Why the occupational work that became a general way of life with the rise of the bourgeoisie should necessitate a particularly strict disciplining of sexuality is a question in its own right. The connections between the personality structure and the social structure of the nineteenth century cannot be considered here. However, by the standard of bourgeois society, the control of sexuality and the form of marriage prevalent in court society appear extremely lax. Social opinion now severely condemns all extramarital relations between the sexes, though here, unlike the situation in court society, the social power of the husband is again greater than that of the wife, so that violation of the taboo on extramarital relationships by the husband is usually judged more leniently than the same offense by women. But both breaches must now be entirely excluded from official social life. Unlike those in court society, they must be removed strictly behind the scenes, banished to the realm of secrecy. This is only one of many examples of the increase in reserve and self-restraint which the individual now has to impose on himself.

10. The civilizing process does not follow a straight line. The general trend of change can be determined, as has been done here. On a smaller scale there are the most diverse crisscross movements, shifts and spurts in this or that direction. But if we consider the movement over large time spans, we see clearly how the compulsions arising directly from the threat of weapons and physical force gradually diminish, and how those forms of dependency which lead to the regulation of the affects in the form of self-control, gradually increase. This change appears at its most rectilinear if we observe the men of the upper class of the time—that is, the class composed first of warriors or knights, then of courtiers, and then of professional bourgeois. If the whole many-layered fabric of historical development is considered, however, the movement is seen to be infinitely more complex. In each phase there are numerous fluctuations, frequent

advances or recessions of the inward and outward constraints. An observation of such fluctuations, particularly those close to us in time, can easily obscure the general trend. One such fluctuation is present today in the memories of all: in the period following World War I, as compared to the prewar period, a "relaxation of morals" appears to have occurred. A number of constraints imposed on behavior before the war have weakened or disappeared entirely. Many things forbidden earlier are now permitted. And, seen at close quarters, the movement seems to be proceeding in the direction opposite to that shown here; it seems to lead to a relaxation of the constraints imposed on the individual by social life. But on closer examination it is not difficult to perceive that this is merely a very slight recession, one of the fluctuations that constantly arise from the complexity of the historical movement within each phase of the total process.

One example is bathing manners. It would have meant social ostracism in the nineteenth century for a woman to wear in public one of the bathing costumes commonplace today. But this change, and with it the whole spread of sports for men and women, presupposes a very high standard of drive control. Only in a society in which a high degree of restraint is taken for granted, and in which women are, like men, absolutely sure that each individual is curbed by self-control and a strict code of etiquette, can bathing and sporting customs having this relative degree of freedom develop. It is a relaxation which remains within the framework of a particular "civilized" standard of behavior involving a very high degree of automatic constraint and affect-transformation, conditioned to become a habit.

At the same time, however, we also find in our own time the precursors of a shift toward the cultivation of new and stricter constraints. In a number of societies there are attempts to establish a social regulation and management of the emotions far stronger and more conscious than the standard prevalent hitherto, a pattern of molding that imposes renunciations and transformation of drives on the individual with vast consequences for human life which are scarcely foreseeable as yet.

11. Regardless, therefore, of how much the tendencies may crisscross, advance and recede, relax or tighten on a small scale, the direction of the main movement—as far as it is visible up to now—is the same for all kinds of behavior. The process of civilization of the sex drive, seen on a large scale, runs parallel to those of other drives,

no matter what sociogenetic differences of detail may always be present. Here, too, measured in terms of the standards of the men of successive ruling classes, control grows ever stricter. The instinct is slowly but progressively suppressed from the public life of society. The reserve that must be exercised in speaking of it also increases.[99] And this restraint, like all others, is enforced less and less by direct physical force. It is cultivated in the individual from an early age as habitual self-restraint by the structure of social life, by the pressure of social institutions in general, and by certain executive organs of society (above all, the family) in particular. Thereby the social commands and prohibitions become increasingly a part of the self, a strictly regulated superego.

Like many other drives, sexuality is confined more and more exclusively, for both women and men, to a particular enclave, socially legitimized marriage. Social tolerance of other relationships, for both husband and wife, which was by no means lacking earlier, is suppressed increasingly, if with fluctuations. Every violation of these restrictions, and everything conducive to one, is therefore relegated to the realm of secrecy, of what may not be mentioned without loss of prestige or social position.

And just as the nuclear family only very gradually became, so exclusively, the only legitimate enclave of sexuality and of all intimate functions for men and women, so it was only at a late stage that it became the primary organ for cultivating the socially required control over impulses and behavior in young people. Before this degree of restraint and intimacy was reached, and until the separation of instinctual life from public view was strictly enforced, the task of early conditioning did not fall so heavily on father and mother. All the people with whom the child came into contact—and when intimization was less advanced and the interior of the house less isolated, they were often quite numerous—played a part. In addition, the family itself was usually larger and—in the upper classes—the servants more numerous in earlier times. People in general spoke more openly about the various aspects of instinctual life, and gave way more freely to their own impulses in speech and act. The shame associated with sexuality was less. This is what makes Erasmus's educational work quoted above so difficult for pedagogues of a later phase to understand. And so conditioning, the reproduction of social habits in the child, did not take place so exclusively behind closed doors, as it were, but far more directly in the presence of other people. A by no means untypical picture of this kind of conditioning in the upper class can be found, for example, in the diary of the doctor Jean Héroard, which records day by day and almost hour by hour the childhood of Louis XIII, what he did and said as he grew up.

It is not without a touch of paradox that the greater the transformation, control, restraint, and concealment of drives and impulses that is demanded of the individual by society, and therefore the more difficult the conditioning of the young becomes, the more the task of first instilling socially required habits is concentrated within the nuclear family, on the father and mother. The mechanism of conditioning, however, is still scarcely different than in earlier times. For it does not involve a closer supervision of the task, or more exact planning that takes account of the special circumstances of the child, but is effected primarily by automatic means and to some extent through reflexes. The socially patterned constellation of habits and impulses of the parents gives rise to a constellation of habits and impulses in the child; these may operate either in the same direction or in one entirely different from that desired or expected by the parents on the basis of their own conditioning. The interrelation of the habits of parents and children, through which the instinctive life of the child is slowly molded, is thus determined by nothing less than by "reason." Behavior and words associated by the parent with shame and repugnance are very soon associated in the same way by the children, through the parents' expressions of displeasure, their more or less gentle pressure; in this way the social standard of shame and repugnance is gradually reproduced in the children. But such a standard forms at the same time the basis and framework of the most diverse individual drive formations. How the growing personality is fashioned in particular cases by this incessant social interaction between the parents' and children's feelings, habits, and reactions is at present largely unforeseeable and incalculable to parents.

12. The tendency of the civilizing process to make all bodily functions more intimate, to enclose them in particular enclaves, to put them "behind closed doors," has diverse consequences. One of the most important, which has already been observed in connection with various other forms of drives, is seen particularly clearly in the case of the development of civilizing restraints on sexuality. It is the peculiar division in man which becomes more pronounced the more sharply

those aspects of human life that may be displayed in social life are divided from those that may not, and which must remain "intimate" or "secret." Sexuality, like all the other natural human functions, is a phenomenon known to everyone and a part of each human life. We have seen how all these functions are gradually charged with sociogenetic shame and embarrassment, so that the mere mention of them in society is increasingly restricted by a multitude of controls and prohibitions. More and more, people keep the functions themselves, and all reminders of them, concealed from one another. Where this is not possible—as in marriage, for example—shame, embarrassment, fear, and all the other emotions associated with these driving forces of human life are mastered by a precisely regulated social ritual and by certain concealing formulas that preserve the standard of shame. In other words, with the advance of civilization the lives of human beings are increasingly split between an intimate and a public sphere, between secret and public behavior. And this split is taken so much for granted, becomes so compulsive a habit, that it is hardly perceived in consciousness.

In conjunction with this growing division of behavior into what is and what is not publicly permitted, the personality structure is also transformed. The prohibitions supported by social sanctions are reproduced in the individual as self-controls. The pressure to restrain his impulses and the sociogenetic shame surrounding them—these are turned so completely into habits that we cannot resist them even when alone, in the intimate sphere. Pleasure promising drives and pleasure denying taboos and prohibitions, socially generated feelings of shame and repugnance, come to battle within him. This, as has been mentioned, is clearly the state of affairs which Freud tries to express by concepts such as the "superego" and the "unconscious" or, as it is not unfruitfully called in everyday speech, the "subconscious." But however it is expressed, the social code of conduct so imprints itself in one form or another on the human being that it becomes a constituent element of his individual self. And this element, the superego, like the personality structure of the individual as a whole, necessarily changes constantly with the social code of behavior and the structure of society. The pronounced division in the "ego" or consciousness characteristic of man in our phase of civilization, which finds expression in such terms as "superego" and "unconscious," corresponds to the specific split in the behavior which civilized society demands of its members. It matches the degree of regulation and restraint imposed on the expression of drives and impulses. Tendencies in this direction may develop in any form of human society, even in those which we call "primitive." But the strength attained in societies such as ours by this differentiation and the form in which it appears are reflections of a particular historical development, the results of a civilizing process.

This is what is meant when we refer here to the continuous correspondence between the social structure and the structure of the personality, of the individual self.

X

On Changes in Aggressiveness

The affect structure of man is a whole. We may call particular instincts by different names according to their different directions and functions, we may speak of hunger and the need to spit, of the sexual drive and of aggressive impulses, but in life these different instincts are no more separable than the heart from the stomach or the blood in the brain from the blood in the genitalia. They complement and in part supersede each other, transform themselves within certain limits and compensate for each other; a disturbance here manifests itself there. In short, they form a kind of circuit in the human being, a partial system within the total system of the organism. Their structure is still opaque in many respects, but their socially imprinted form is of decisive importance for the functioning of a society as of the individuals within it.

The manner in which impulses or emotional manifestations are spoken of today sometimes leads one to surmise that we have within us a whole bundle of different drives. A "death instinct" or a "self-assertive drive" are referred to as if they were different chemical substances. This is not to deny that observations of these different instincts in the individual may be extremely fruitful and instructive. But the categories by which these observations are classified must remain powerless in the face of their living objects if they fail to express the unity and totality of instinctual life, and the connection of each particular instinctual tendency to this totality. Accordingly, aggressiveness, which will be the subject of this chapter, is not a separable species of instinct. At most, one may speak of the "aggressive impulse'' only if one remains aware that it refers to a particular instinctual function within the totality of an organism, and that changes in this function indicate changes in the personality structure as a whole.

1. The standard of aggressiveness, its tone and intensity, is not at present exactly uniform among the different nations of the West. But these differences, which from close up often appear quite considerable, disappear if the aggressiveness of the "civilized" nations is compared to that of societies at a different stage of affect control. Compared to the battle fury of Abyssinian warriors—admittedly powerless against the technical apparatus of the civilized army—or to the frenzy of the different tribes at the time of the Great Migrations, the aggressiveness of even the most warlike nations of the civilized world appears subdued. Like all other instincts, it is bound, even in directly warlike actions, by the advanced state of the division of functions, and by the resulting greater dependence of individuals on each other and on the technical apparatus. It is confined and tamed by innumerable rules and prohibitions that have become self-constraints. It is as much transformed, "refined," "civilized," as all the other forms of pleasure, and its immediate and uncontrolled violence appears only in dreams or in isolated outbursts that we account for as pathological.

In this area of the affects, the theater of the hostile collisions between men, the same historical transformations has taken place as in all others. No matter at what point the Middle Ages stand in this transformation, it will again suffice here to take the standard of their secular ruling class, the warriors, as a starting point, to illustrate the overall pattern of this development. The release of the affects in battle in the Middle Ages was no longer, perhaps, quite so uninhibited as in the early period of the Great Migrations. But it was open and uninhibited enough compared to the standard of modern times. In the latter, cruelty and joy in the destruction and torment of others, like the proof of physical superiority, are placed under an increasingly strong social control anchored in the state organization. All these forms of pleasure, limited by threats of displeasure, gradually come to express themselves only indirectly, in a "refined" form. And only at times of social upheaval or where social control is looser (e.g., in colonial regions) do they break out more directly, uninhibitedly, less impeded by shame and repugnance.

2. Life in medieval society tended in the opposite direction. Rapine, battle, hunting of men and animals—all these were vital necessities which, in accordance with the structure of society, were visible to all. And thus, for the mighty and strong, they formed part of the pleasures of life.

"I tell you," says a war hymn attributed to the minstrel Bertran de Born,[100] "that neither eating, drinking, nor sleep has as much savor for me as to hear the cry 'Forwards!' from both sides, and horses without riders shying and whinnying, and the cry 'Help! Help!', and to see the small and the great fall to the grass at the ditches and the dead pierced by the wood of the lances decked with banners."

Even the literary formulation gives an impression of the original savagery of feeling. In another place Bertran de Born sings: "The pleasant season is drawing nigh when our ships shall land, when King Richard shall come, merry and proud as he never was before. Now we shall see gold and silver spent; the newly built stonework will crack to the heart's desire, walls crumble, towers topple and collapse, our enemies taste prison and chains. I love the melee of blue and vermilion shields, the many-colored ensigns and the banners, the tents and rich pavilions spread out on the plain, the breaking lances, the pierced shields, the gleaming helmets that are split, the blows given and received."

War, one of the *chansons de geste* declares, is to descend as the stronger on the enemy, to hack down his vines, uproot his trees, lay waste his land, take his castles by storm, fill in his wells, and kill his people. . . .

A particular pleasure is taken in mutilating prisoners: "By my troth," says the king in the same *chanson,* "I laugh at what you say, I care not a fig for your threats, I shall shame every knight I have taken, cut off his nose or his ears. If he is a sergeant or a merchant he will lose a foot or an arm."[101]

Such things are not only said in song. These epics are an integral part of social life. And they express the feelings of the listeners for whom they are intended far more directly than most of our literature. They may exaggerate in detail. Even in the age of chivalry money already had, on occasions, some power to subdue and transform the affects. Usually only the poor and lowly, for whom no considerable ransom could be expected, were mutilated, and the knights who commanded ransoms were spared. The chronicles which directly document social life bear ample witness to these attitudes.

They were mostly written by clerics. The value judgments they contain are therefore often those of the weaker group threatened by the warrior class. Nevertheless, the picture they transmit to us is quite genuine. "He spends his life," we read of a knight, "in plundering, destroying churches, falling upon pilgrims, oppressing widows and orphans. He takes particular pleasure in mutilating the innocent. In a single monastery, that of the black monks of Sarlat, there are 150 men and women whose hands he has cut off or whose eyes he has put out. And his wife is just as cruel. She helps him with his executions. It even gives her pleasure to torture the poor women. She had their breasts hacked off or their nails torn off so that they were incapable of work."[102]

Such affective outbursts may still occur as exceptional phenomena, as a "pathological" degeneration, in later phases of social development. But here no punitive social power existed. The only threat, the only danger that could instill fear was that of being overpowered in battle by a stronger opponent. Leaving aside a small elite, rapine, pillage, and murder were standard practice in the warrior society of this time, as is noted by Luchaire, the historian of thirteenth-century French society. There is little evidence that things were different in other countries or in the centuries that followed. Outbursts of cruelty did not exclude one from social life. They were not outlawed. The pleasure in killing and torturing others was great, and it was a socially permitted pleasure. To a certain extent, the social structure even pushed its members in this direction, making it seem necessary and practically advantageous to behave in this way.

What, for example, ought to be done with prisoners? There was little money in this society. With regard to prisoners who could pay and who, moreover, were members of one's own class, one exercised some degree of restraint. But the others? To keep them meant to feed them. To return them meant to enhance the wealth and fighting power of the enemy. For subjects (i.e., working, serving, and fighting hands) were a part of the wealth of the ruling class of that time. So prisoners were killed or sent back so mutilated that they were unfitted for war service and work. The same applied to destroying fields, filling in wells, and cutting down trees. In a predominantly agrarian society, in which immobile possessions represented the major part of property, this too served to weaken the enemy. The stronger affectivity of behavior was to a certain degree socially necessary. People behaved in a socially useful way and took pleasure in doing so. And it is entirely in keeping with the lesser degree of social control and constraint of instinctual life that this joy in destruction could sometimes give way, through a sudden identification with the victim, and doubtless also as an expression of the fear and guilt produced by the permanent precariousness of this life, to extremes of pity. The victor of today was defeated tomorrow by some accident, captured, and imperiled. In the midst of this perpetual rising and falling, this alternation of the human hunts of wartime with the animal hunts or tournaments that were the diversions of "peacetime," little could be predicted. The future was relatively uncertain even for those who had fled the "world"; only God and the loyalty of a few people who held together had any permanence. Fear reigned everywhere; one had to be on one's guard all the time. And just as people's fate could change abruptly, so their joy could turn into fear and this fear, in its turn, could give way, equally abruptly, to submission to some new pleasure.

The majority of the secular ruling class of the Middle Ages led the life of leaders of armed bands. This formed the taste and habits of individuals. Reports left to us by that society yield, by and large, a picture similar to those of feudal societies in our own times; and they show a comparable standard of behavior. Only a small elite, of which more will be said later, stood out to some extent from this norm.

The warrior of the Middle Ages not only loved battle, he lived in it. He spent his youth preparing for battle. When he came of age he was knighted, and waged war as long as his strength permitted, into old age. His life had no other function. His dwelling place was a watchtower, a fortress, at once a weapon of attack and defense. If by accident, by exception, he lived in peace, he needed at least the illusion of war. He fought in tournaments, and these tournaments often differed little from real battles.[103]

"For the society of that time war was the normal state," says Luchaire of the thirteenth century. And Huizinga says of the fourteenth and fifteenth centuries: "The chronic form which war was wont to take, the continuous disruption of town and country by every kind of dangerous rabble, the permanent threat of harsh and unreliable law enforcement . . . nourished a feeling of universal uncertainty."[104]

In the fifteenth century, as in the ninth or thirteenth, the knight still gives expression to his joy in war, even if it is no longer so open and intact as earlier.

"War is a joyous thing."[105] It is Jean de Bueil who says this. He has fallen into disfavor with the king. And now he dictates to his servant his life story. This is in the year 1465. It is no longer the completely free, independent knight who speaks, the little king in his domain. It is someone who is himself in service: "War is a joyous thing. We love each other so much in war. If we see that our cause is just and our kinsmen fight boldly, tears come to our eyes. A sweet joy rises in our hearts, in the feeling of our honest loyalty to each other; and seeing our friend so bravely exposing his body to danger in order to keep and fulfill the commandment of our Creator, we resolve to go forward and die or live with him and never leave him on account of love. This brings such delight that anyone who has not felt it cannot say how wonderful it is. Do you think that someone who feels this is afraid of death? Not in the least! He is so strengthened, so delighted, that he does not know where he is. Truly he fears nothing in the world!"

This is the joy of battle, certainly, but it is no longer the direct pleasure in the human hunt, in the flashing of swords, in the neighing of steeds, in the fear and death of the enemy—how fine it is to hear them cry "Help, help!" or see them lying with their bodies torn open![106] Now the pleasure lies in the closeness to one's friends, the enthusiasm for a just cause, and more than earlier we find the joy of battle serving as an intoxicant to overcome fear.

Very simple and powerful feelings speak here. One kills, gives oneself up wholly to the fight, sees one's friend fight. One fights at his side. One forgets where one is. One forgets death itself. It is splendid. What more?

3. There is abundant evidence that the attitude toward life and death in the secular upper class of the Middle Ages by no means always accords with the attitude prevalent in the books of the ecclesiastical upper class, which we usually consider "typical" of the Middle Ages. For the clerical upper class, or at least for its spokesmen, the conduct of life is determined by the thought of death and of what comes after, the next world.

In the secular upper class this is by no means so exclusively the case. However frequent moods and phases of this kind may.be in the life of every knight, there is recurrent evidence of a quite different attitude. Again and again we hear an admonition that does not quite accord with the standard picture of the Middle Ages today: do not let your life be governed by the thought of death. Love the joys of this life.

"Nul courtois ne doit blâmer joie, mais toujours joie aimer." (No *courtois* man should revile joy, he should love joy.)[107] This is a command of *courtoisie* from a romance of the early thirteenth century. Or from a rather later period: "A young man should be gay and lead a joyous life. It does not befit a young man to be mournful and pensive."[108] In these statements the chivalrous people, who certainly did not need to be "pensive," clearly contrast themselves to the clerics, who no doubt were frequently "mournful and pensive."

This far from life-denying attitude is expressed particularly earnestly and explicitly with regard to death in some verses in the *Distiche Catonis,* which were passed from generation to generation throughout the Middle Ages. That life is uncertain is one of the fundamental themes which recur in these verses:[109]

> To us all a hard uncertain life is given.

But this does not lead to the conclusion that one should think of death and what comes afterward, but rather:

> If you fear death you will live in misery.

Or in another place, expressed with particular clarity and beauty:[110]

> We well know that death shall come
> and our future is unknown:
> stealthy as a thief he comes,
> and body and soul he does part.
> So be of trust and confidence:
> be not too much afraid of death,
> for if you fear him overmuch
> joy you nevermore shall touch.

Nothing of the next life. He who allows his life to be determined by thoughts of death no longer has joy in life. Certainly, the knights felt themselves strongly to be Christians, and their lives were permeated by the traditional ideas and rituals of the Christian faith; but Christianity was linked in their minds, in accordance with their different social and psychological situation, with an entirely different scale of values from that existing in the minds of the clerics who wrote and read books. Their faith had a markedly different tenor and tone. It did not prevent them from savoring to the full the joys of the world; it did not hinder them from killing and plundering. This was part of their social function, an attribute of their class, a source of pride. Not to fear death was a vital necessity for the knight. He had to fight. The structure and tensions of this society made this an inescapable condition for the individual.

4. But in medieval society this permanent readiness to fight, weapon in hand, was a vital necessity not only for the warriors, the knightly upper class. The life of the burghers in the towns was characterized by greater and lesser feuds to a far higher degree than in later times; here, too, belligerence, hatred, and joy in tormenting others were more uninhibited than in the subsequent phase.

With the slow rise of a Third Estate, the tensions in medieval society were increased. And it was not only the weapon of money that carried the burgher upward. Robbery, fighting, pillage, family feuds—all this played a hardly less important role in the life of the town population than in that of the warrior class itself.

There is—to take one example—the fate of Mathieu d'Escouchy. He is a Picard, and one of the numerous men of the fifteenth century who wrote a "Chronicle."[111] From this "Chronicle" we would suppose him to be a modest man of letters who devoted his time to meticulous historical work. But if we try to find out something of his life from the documents, a totally different picture emerges.[112]

Mathieu d'Escouchy begins his carrer as magistrate as a councillor, juror, and mayor (prévot) of the town of Péronne between 1440 and 1450. From the beginning we find him in a kind of feud with the family of the procurator of the town, Jean Froment, a feud that is fought out in lawsuits. First it is the procurator who accuses d'Escouchy of forgery and murder, or of "excès et attemptaz." The mayor for his part threatens the widow of his enemy with investigation for magical practices. The woman obtains a mandate compelling d'Escouchy to place the investigation in the hands of the judiciary. The affair comes before the parliament in Paris, and d'Escouchy goes to prison for the first time. We find him under arrest six times subsequently, partly as defendant and once as a prisoner of war. Each time there is a serious criminal case, and more than once he sits in heavy chains. The contest of reciprocal accusations between the Froment and d'Escouchy families is interrupted by a violent clash in which Froment's son wounds d'Escouchy. Both engage cutthroats to take each other's lives.

THE CIVILIZING PROCESS

When this lengthy feud passes from our view, it is replaced by new attacks. This time the mayor is wounded by a monk. New accusations, then in 1461 d'Escouchy's removal to Nesle, apparently under suspicion of criminal acts. Yet this does not prevent him from having a successful career. He becomes a bailiff, mayor of Ribemont, procurator to the king at Saint Quintin, and is raised to the nobility. After new woundings, incarcerations, and expiation we find him in war service. He is made a prisoner of war; from a later campaign he returns home crippled. Then he marries, but this does not mean the beginning of a quiet life. We find him transported as a prisoner to Paris "like a criminal and murderer," accused of forging seals, again in feud with a magistrate in Compiègne, brought to an admission of his guilt by torture and denied promotion, condemned, rehabilitated, condemned once again, until the trace of his existence vanishes from the documents.

This is one of innumerable examples. The well-known miniatures from the "book of hours" of the Duc de Berry[113] are another. "People long believed," says its editor, "and some are still convinced today, that the miniatures of the fifteenth century are the work of earnest monks or pious nuns working in the peace of their monasteries. That is possible in certain cases. But, generally speaking, the situation was quite different. It was worldly people, master craftsmen, who executed these beautiful works, and the life of these secular artists was very far from being edifying." We hear repeatedly of actions which by the present standards of society would be branded as criminal and made socially "impossible." For example, the painters accuse each other of theft; then one of them, with his kinsmen, stabs the other to death in the street. And the Duc de Berry, who needs the murderer, must request an amnesty, a *lettre de rémission* for him. Yet another abducts an eight-year-old girl in order to marry her, naturally against the will of her parents. These *lettres de rémission* show us such bloody feuds taking place everywhere, often lasting for many years, and sometimes leading to regular battles in public places. And this applies to knights as much to merchants or craftsmen. As in all other countries with related social forms—for example, Ethiopia or Afghanistan today—the noble has bands of followers who are ready for anything. ". . . During the day he is constantly accompanied by servants and arms bearers in pursuit of his 'feuds.' . . . The *roturiers,* the citizens, cannot afford this luxury, but they have their 'relatives and friends' who come to their help, often in great numbers, equipped with every kind of awesome weapon that the local *coutumes,* the civic ordinances, prohibit in vain. And these burghers, too, when they have to avenge themselves, are *de guerre,* in a state of feud.''[114]

The civic authorities sought in vain to pacify these family feuds. The magistrates call people before them, order a cessation of strife, issue commands and decrees. For a time, all is well; then a new feud breaks out, an old one is rekindled. Two *associés* fall out over business; they quarrel, the conflict grows violent; one day they meet in a public place and one of them strikes the other dead.[115] An innkeeper accuses another of stealing his clients; they become mortal enemies. Someone says a few malicious words about another; a family war develops.

Not only among the nobility were there family vengeance, private feuds, vendettas. The fifteenth-century towns are no less rife with wars between families and cliques. The little people, too—the hatters, the tailors, the shepherds—were all quick to draw their knives. ''It is well known how violent manners were in the fifteenth century, with what brutality passions were assuaged, despite the fear of hell, despite the restraints of class distinctions and the chivalrous sentiment of honor, *despite the bonhomie and gaiety of social relations.*''[116]

Not that people were always going around with fierce looks, drawn brows, and martial countenances as the clearly visible symbols of their warlike prowess. On the contrary, a moment ago they were joking, now they mock each other, one word leads to another, and suddenly from the midst of laughter they find themselves in the fiercest feud. Much of what appears contradictory to us—the intensity of their piety, the violence of their fear of hell, their guilt feelings, their penitence, the immense outbursts of joy and gaiety, the sudden flaring and the uncontrollable force of their hatred and belligerence—all these, like the rapid changes of mood, are in reality symptoms of the same social and personality structure. The instincts, the emotions were vented more freely, more directly, more openly than later. It is only to us, in whom everything is more subdued, moderate, and calculated, and in whom social taboos are built much more deeply into the fabric of instinctual life as self-restraints, that this unveiled intensity of piety, belligerence, or cruelty appears as contradictory. Religion, the belief in the punishing or rewarding omnipotence of God, never has in itself a ''civilizing'' or affect-subduing effect. On the contrary, religion is always exactly as ''civilized'' as the society or class which upholds it. And because emotions are here expressed in a manner that in our own world is generally observed only in children, we call these expressions and forms of behavior "childish."

Wherever one opens the documents of this time, one finds the same: a life where the structure of affects was different from our own, an existence without security, with only minimal thought for the future. Whoever did not love or hate to the utmost in this society, whoever could not stand his ground in the play of passions, could go into a monastery; in worldly life he was just as lost as was, conversely, in later society, and particularly at court, the man who could not curb his passions, could not conceal and "civilize" his affects.

5. In both cases it is the structure of society that demands and generates a specific standard of emotional control. "We," says Luchaire, "with our peaceful manners and habits, with the care and protection that the modern state lavishes on the property and person of each individual," can scarcely form an idea of this other society.

At that time the country had disintegrated into provinces, and the inhabitants of each province formed a kind of little nation that abhorred all the others. The provinces were in turn divided into a multitude of feudal estates whose owners fought each other incessantly. Not only the great lords, the barons, but also the smaller lords of the manor lived in desolate isolation and were uninterruptedly occupied in waging war against their "sovereigns," their equals, or their subjects. In addition, there was constant rivalry between town and town, village and village, valley and valley, and constant wars between neighbors that seemed to arise from the very multiplicity of these territorial units.[117]

This description helps to see more precisely something which so far has been stated mainly in general terms, namely, the connection between social structure and personality structure. In this society there is no central power strong enough to compel people to restraint. But if in this or that region the power of a central authority grows, if over a larger or smaller area the people are forced to live in peace with each other, the molding of affects and the standards of the economy of instincts are very gradually changed as well. As will be discussed in more detail later, the reserve and "mutual consideration" of people increase, first in normal everyday social life. And the discharge of affects in physical attack is limited to certain temporal and spatial enclaves. Once the monopoly of physical power has passed to central authorities, not every strong man can afford the pleasure of physical attack. This is now reserved to those few legitimized by the central authority (e.g., the police against the criminal), and to larger numbers only in exceptional times of war or revolution, in the socially legitimized struggle against internal or external enemies.

But even these temporal or spatial enclaves within civilized society in which belligerence is allowed freer play—above all, wars between nations—have become more impersonal, and lead less and less to an affective discharge having the immediacy and intensity of the medieval phase. The necessary restraint and transformation of aggression cultivated in the everyday life of civilized society cannot be simply reversed, even in these enclaves. All the same, this could happen more quickly than we might suppose, had not the direct physical combat between a man and his hated adversary given way to a mechanized struggle demanding a strict control of the affects. Even in war in the civilized world, the individual can no longer give free rein to his pleasure, spurred on by the sight of the enemy, but must fight, no matter how he may feel, according to the commands of invisible or only indirectly visible leaders, against a frequently invisible or only indirectly visible enemy. And immense social upheaval and urgency, heightened by carefully concerted propaganda, are needed to re-awaken and legitimize in large masses of people the socially outlawed instincts, the joy in killing and destruction that have been repressed from everyday civilized life.

6. Admittedly, these affects do have, in a "refined," rationalized form, their legitimate and exactly defined place in the everyday life of civilized society. And this is very characteristic of the kind of transformation through which the civilization of the affects takes place. For example, belligerence and aggression find socially permitted expression in sporting contests. And they are expressed especially in "spectating" (e.g., at boxing matches), in the imaginary identification with a small number of combatants to whom moderate and precisely regulated scope is granted for the release of such affects. And this living-out of affects in spectating or even in merely listening (e.g., to a radio commentary) is a particularly characteristic feature of civilized society. It partly determines the development of books and the theater, and decisively influences the role of the cinema in our world. This transformation of what manifested itself originally as an active, often aggressive expression of pleasure, into the passive, more ordered

pleasure of spectating (i.e., a mere pleasure of the eye) is already initiated in education, in conditioning precepts for young people.

In the 1774 edition of La Salle's *Civilité,* for example, we read (p. 23): "Children like to touch clothes and other things that please them with their hands. This urge must be corrected, and they must be taught to touch all they see only with their eyes."

By now this precept is taken almost for granted. It is highly characteristic of civilized man that he is denied by socially instilled self-control from spontaneously touching what he desires, loves, or hates. The whole molding of his gestures—no matter how its pattern may differ among Western nations with regard to particulars—is decisively influenced by this necessity. It has been shown elsewhere how the use of the sense of smell, the tendency to sniff at food or other things, comes to be restricted as something animal-like. Here we see one of the interconnections through which a different sense organ, the eye, takes on a very specific significance in civilized society. In a similar way to the ear, and perhaps even more so, it becomes a mediator of pleasure, precisely because the direct satisfaction of the desire for pleasure has been hemmed in by a multitude of barriers and prohibitions.

But even within this transfer of emotions from direct action to spectating, there is a distinct curve of moderation and "humanization" in the transformation of affects. The boxing match, to mention only one example, represents a strongly tempered form of the impulses of aggressiveness and cruelty, compared with the visual pleasures of earlier stages.

An example from the sixteenth century may serve as an illustration. It has been chosen from a multitude of others because it shows an institution in which the visual satisfaction of the urge to cruelty, the joy in watching pain inflicted, emerges particularly purely, without any rational justification and disguise as punishment or means of discipline.

In Paris during the sixteenth century it was one of the festive pleasures of Midsummer Day to burn alive one or two dozen cats. This ceremony was very famous. The populace assembled. Solemn music was played. Under a kind of scaffold an enormous pyre was erected. Then a sack or basket containing the cats was hung from the scaffold. The sack or basket began to smolder. The cats fell into the fire and were burned to death, while the crowd reveled in their caterwauling.

Usually the king and queen were present. Sometimes the king or the dauphin was given the honor of lighting the pyre. And we hear that once, at the special request of King Charles IX, a fox was caught and burned as well.[118]

Certainly, this is not really a worse spectacle than the burning of heretics, or the torturings and public executions of every kind. It only appears worse because the joy in torturing living creatures shows itself so nakedly and purposelessly, without any excuse before reason. The revulsion aroused in us by the mere report of the institution, a reaction which must be taken as "normal" for the present-day standard of affect control, demonstrates once again the long term change of personality structure. At the same time, it enables us to see one aspect of this change particularly clearly: much of what earlier aroused pleasure arouses displeasure today. Now, as then, it is not merely individual feelings that are involved. The cat-burning on Midsummer Day was a social institution, like boxing or horse-racing in present-day society. And in both cases the amusements created by society for itself, are embodiments of a social standard of affects within the framework of which all individual patterns of affect regulation, however varied they may be, are contained; anyone who steps outside the bounds of this social standard is considered "abnormal." Thus, someone who wished to gratify his pleasure in the manner of the sixteenth century by burning cats would be seen today as "abnormal," simply because normal conditioning in our stage of civilization restrains the expression of pleasure in such actions through anxiety instilled in the form of self-control. Here, obviously, the same psychological mechanism is at work on the basis of which the long term change of personality structure has taken place: socially undesirable expressions of instinct and pleasure are threatened and punished with measures that generate and reinforce displeasure and anxiety. In the constant recurrence of displeasure aroused by threats, and in the habituation to this rhythm, the dominant displeasure is compulsorily associated even with behavior which at root may be pleasurable. In this manner, socially aroused displeasure and anxiety—nowadays represented, though by no means always and by no means solely, by the parents—fight with hidden desires. What has been shown here from different angles as an advance in the frontiers of shame, in the threshold of repugnance, in the standards of affect, has probably been set in motion by mechanisms such as these.

THE CIVILIZING PROCESS

It remains to be considered in more detail what change in the social structure actually triggered these psychological mechanisms, what change in external compulsions set in motion this "civilization" of affects and behavior.

XI

Scenes from the Life of a Knight

The question why men's behavior and emotions change is really the same as the question why their forms of life change. In medieval society certain forms of life had been developed, and the individual was bound to live within them, as knight, craftsman, or bondsman. In more recent society different opportunities, different forms of life were prescribed, to which the individual had to adapt. If he was of the nobility he could lead the life of a courtier. But he could no longer, even if he so desired (and many did), lead the less constrained life of a knight. From a particular time on, this function, this way of life was no longer present in the structure of society. Other functions, such as those of the guild craftsmen and the priest, which played an extraordinary part in the medieval phase, largely lost their significance in the total structure of social relations. Why do these functions and forms of life, to which the individual must adapt himself as to more or less fixed molds, change in the course of history? As has been mentioned, this is really the same question as why feelings and emotions, the structure of drives and impulses, and everything connected with them change.

A good deal has been said here on the emotional standards of the medieval upper class. To complement this, and at the same time to provide a link with the question of the causes of the change these standards underwent, we shall now add a short impression of the way in which knights lived, and thus of "social space" which society opened to individuals of noble birth, and within which it also confined them. The picture of this "social space," the image of the knight in general, became clouded in obscurity quite soon after what is called their "decline." Whether the medieval warrior was seen as the "noble knight" (only the grand, beautiful, adventurous, and moving aspects of his life being remembered) or as the "feudal lord," the oppressor of peasants (only the savage, cruel, barbaric aspects of his life being emphasized), the simple picture of the actual life of this class was usually distorted by values and nostalgia from the period of the observer. A few drawings, or at least descriptions of them, may help to restore this picture. Apart from a few writings, the works of sculptors and painters of the period convey particularly strongly the special quality of its atmosphere or, as we may call it, its emotional character, and the way it differs from our own, though only a few works reflect the life of a knight in its real context. One of the few picture books of this kind, admittedly from a relatively late period, between 1475 and 1480, is the sequence of drawings that became known under the not very appropriate title *Medieval House-Book.* The name of the artist who drew them is unknown, but he must have been very familiar with the knightly life of his time; moreover, unlike many of his fellow craftsmen, he must have seen the world with the eyes of a knight and largely identified with their social values. A not insignificant indication of this is his depiction on one sheet of a man of his own craft as the only craftsmen in courtly dress, as is the girl behind him, who places her arm on his shoulder and for whom he clearly expresses his sentiments. Perhaps it is a self-portrait.[119]

These drawings are from the late period of chivalry, the time of Charles the Bold and Maximilian, the last knight. We may conclude from the coats of arms that these two, or knights close to them, are themselves represented in one or another of the pictures. "There is no doubt," it has been said, "that we have . . . Charles the Bold himself or a Burgundian knight from his entourage before us."[120] Perhaps a number of the pictures of tournaments directly depict the jousting following the Feud of Neuss (1475), at the betrothal of Maximilian to Charles the Bold's daughter, Marie of Burgundy. At any rate, those we see before us are already people of the transitional age in which the knightly aristocracy is being gradually replaced by a courtly one. And a good deal that is reminiscent of the courtier is also present in these pictures. Nevertheless, they give, on the whole, a very good idea of the social space of a knight, of how he fills his days, of what he saw around him and how he saw it.

What do we see? Nearly always open country, hardly anything recalling the town. Small villages, fields, trees, meadows, hills, short stretches of river and, frequently, the castle. But there is nothing in these pictures of the nostalgic mood, the "sentimental" attitude to "nature" that slowly becomes perceptible not very long afterward, as the leading nobles have to forgo more and more frequently the relatively unbirdled life at their ancestral seats, and are bound increasingly tightly to the semiurban court and to dependence on kings or princes. This is one of the most important differences in emotional tone these pictures convey. In later periods the artist's consciousness sifts the material available to him in a very strict and specific way which directly expresses his taste or, more precisely, his affective structure. "Nature," the open country, shown first of all as merely a background to human figures, takes on a nostalgic glow, as the confinement of the upper class to the towns and courts increases and the rift between town and country life grows more perceptible. Or nature takes on, like the human figures it surrounds in the picture, a sublime, representative character. At any rate, there is a change in the *selection by feeling,* in what appeals to feeling in the representation of nature, and in what is felt as unpleasant or painful. And the same is true of the people depicted. For the public in the absolute court, much that really exists in the country, in "nature," is no longer portrayed. The hill is shown, but not the gallows on it, nor the corpse hanging from the gallows. The field is shown, but no longer the ragged peasant laboriously driving his horses. Just as everything "common" or "vulgar" disappears from courtly language, so it vanishes also from the pictures and drawings intended for the courtly upper class.

In the drawings of the *House-Book,* which give an idea of the structure of feeling of the late medieval upper class, this is not so. Here, all these things—gallows, ragged servants, laboring peasants— are to be seen in drawings as in real life. They are not emphasized in a spirit of protest, in the manner of later times, but shown as something very matter-of-fact, part of one's daily surroundings, like the stork's nest or the church tower. One is no more painful in life than the other, and so is not more painful in the picture. On the contrary, as everywhere in the Middle Ages, it is an inseparable part of the existence of the rich and noble that there also exist peasants and craftsmen working for them, and beggars and cripples with open hands. There is no threat to the noble in this, nor does he identify in any way with them; the spectacle evokes no painful feeling. And often enough the yokel and peasant are even the objects of pleasantries.

The pictures reveal the same attitude. First there is a sequence of drawings showing people under particular constellations. They are not grouped directly around the knight, but they make clear how and what he sees around him. Then comes a series of pages showing how a knight spends his life, his occupations and his pleasures. Measured by later times, they all bear witness to the same standard of repugnance and the same social attitudes.

At the beginning, for example, we see people born under Saturn. In the foreground a poor fellow is disemboweling a dead horse or perhaps cutting off the usable meat. His trousers have slipped down somewhat as he bends; part of his posterior is visible, and a pig behind him is sniffing at it. A frail old woman, half in rags, limps by supported on a crutch. In a small cave beside the road sits a wretch with his hands and feet in the stocks, and beside him a woman with one hand in the stocks, the other in fetters. A farm worker is toiling at a watercourse that vanishes between trees and hills. In the distance we see the farmer and his young son laboriously plowing the hilly field with a horse. Still further back a man in rags is led to the gallows, an armed man with a feather in his cap marching proudly beside him; at his other side a monk in his cowl holds out a large crucifix to him. Behind him ride the knight and two of his men. On the top of the hill stands the gallows with a body hanging from it, and the wheel with a corpse on it. Dark birds fly around; one of them pecks at the corpse.

The gallows is not in the least emphasized. It is there like the stream or a tree; and it is seen in just the same way when the knight goes hunting. A whole company rides past, the lord and lady often on the same horse. The deer vanish into a little wood; a stag seems to be wounded. Further in the background one sees a little village or perhaps the yard of a household—well, mill wheel, windmill, a few buildings. The farmer is seen plowing a field; he looks round at the deer, which are just running across his field. High up to one side is the castle; on the other, smaller hill opposite, wheel and gallows with a body, and birds circling.

The gallows, the symbol of the knight's judicial power, is part of the background of his life. It may not be very important, but at any rate, it is not a particularly painful sight. Sentence, execution, death—all these are immediately present in this life. They, too, have not yet been removed behind the scenes.

And the same is true of the poor and the laborers. "Who would plow our fields for us if you were all lords," asks Berthold von Regensburg in one of his sermons in the thirteenth century.[121] And elsewhere he says even more clearly: I shall tell you Christian folk

THE CIVILIZING PROCESS

how Almighty God has ordered Christendom, dividing it into ten kinds of people, ''and what kinds of services the lower owe the higher as their rulers. The first three are the highest and most exalted whom Almighty God himself chose and ordained, so that the other seven should all be subject to them and serve them.''[122] The same attitude to life is still found in these pictures from the fifteenth century. It is not distasteful, it is part of the natural and unquestioned order of the world that warriors and nobles have leisure to amuse themselves, while the others work for them. There is no identification of man with man. Not even on the horizon of this life is there an idea that all men are ''equal.'' But perhaps for that very reason the sight of the laborers has about it nothing shameful or embarrassing.

A picture of the manor shows the pleasures of the lords. A young lady of the nobility crowns her young friend with a wreath; he draws her to him. Another pair go walking in a close embrace. The old servant woman pulls an angry face at the love games of the young people. Nearby the servants are working. One of them sweeps the yard, another grooms the horse, a third scatters food for the ducks, but the maid waves to him from the window; he turns round, soon he will disappear into the house. Noble ladies at play. Peasant antics behind them. On the roof the stork clatters.

Then there is a small courtyard by a lake. On the bridge stands a young nobleman with his wife. Leaning on the balustrade they watch the servants in the water catching fish and ducks. Three young ladies are in a boat. Rushes, bushes, in the distance the walls of a small town.

Or we see workmen building a house in front of a wooded hill. The lord and lady of the castle look on. Tunnels have been driven into the little hill to quarry stones. Workmen are seen hewing the stones; others cart them away. Nearer to us, men are working on the half-finished building. In the foreground workmen are quarreling; they are about to stab and strike each other down. The lord of the castle stands not far from them. He shows his wife the angry scene; the complete calm of the lord and his wife is placed in sharp contrast to the excited gestures of the disputants. The rabble fight, the lord has nothing to do with it. He lives in another sphere.

It is not the events themselves, which in part are no different today, but above all the fact and the manner of their portrayal that underline the changed emotive condition. The upper classes of later phases did not have such things drawn. Such drawings did not appeal to their

feelings. They were not "beautiful." They did not form part of "art."
In later periods it is at most among the Dutch (who depict middle-
class, specifically uncourtly strata) that we find, for example, in the
work of Breughel a standard of repugnance that permits him to bring
cripples, peasants, gallows, or people relieving themselves into his
pictures. But the standard there is linked with very different social
feelings than in these pictures of the late medieval upper class.

Here, it is a matter of course that the laboring classes exist. They are
even indispensable figures in the landscape of knightly existence. The
lord lives in their midst. It does not shock him to see the servant
working beside him, nor does it shock him if the latter amuses himself
in his own way. On the contrary, it is an integral part of his self-esteem
to have these other people moving about him who are not like him,
whose master he is. This feeling is expressed again and again in the
drawings. There is scarcely one of them in which *courtois* occupations and gestures are not contrasted to the vulgar ones of the lower
classes. Whether he rides, hunts, loves, or dances, whatever the lord
does is noble and *courtois,* whatever the servants and peasants do
coarse and uncouth. The feelings of the medieval upper class do not
yet demand that everything vulgar should be suppressed from life and
therefore from pictures. It is gratifying for the nobles to know themselves different from others. *The sight of contrast heightens joy in
living;* and we should remember that, in a milder form, something of
the pleasure taken in such contrasts is still to be found, for example, in
Shakespeare. Wherever one looks at the heritage of the medieval
upper class, one finds this same attitude in an unrestrained form. The
further interdependence and the division of labor in society advance,
the more dependent the upper classes become on the other classes, and
the greater, therefore, becomes the social strength of these classes, at
least potentially. Even when the upper class is still primarily a warrior
class, when it keeps the other classes dependent chiefly through the
sword and the monopoly of weapons, some degree of dependence on
these other classes is certainly not entirely absent. But it is incomparably less; and less, too—as will be seen in more detail later—is the
pressure from below. Accordingly, the sense of mastery of the upper
class, its contempt for other classes, is far more open, and the pressure
on them to exercise restraint and to control their drives, is far less
strong.

Seldom has the matter-of-fact sense of mastery of this class, and its patriarchal contempt of others, been so vividly conveyed as in these drawings. This is expressed not only in the gesture with which the nobleman shows his wife the quarreling craftsmen and the workers in a kind of foundry who are holding their noses to ward off the foul vapors; not only where the lord watches his servants catching fish, or in the repeated depiction of the gallows with a corpse hanging from it; but also in the matter-of-fact and casual way in which the nobler gestures of the knight are juxtaposed to the coarse ones of the people.

There is a picture of a tournament. Musicians play. Fools cut clumsy capers. The noble spectators on their horses, often the lord and lady on the same horse, are conversing. The peasants, the citizens, the doctor, all recognizable by their dress, look on. The two knights, somewhat helpless in their heavy armor, wait at the center. Friends advise them. One of them is just being handed the long lance. Then the herald blows his trumpet. The knights charge at each other with their lances leveled. And in the background, contrasting to the *courtois* occupation of the masters, we see the vulgar pastimes of the people, a horse race accompanied by all kinds of nonsense. A man hangs onto the tail of one of the horses. The rider is furious. The others whip their horses and make off at a somewhat grotesque gallop.

We see a military camp. A circular barricade has been made with the gun carriages. Within it stand resplendent tents with their different coats of arms and banners, among them the imperial banner. At the center, surrounded by his knights, we see the king or even the emperor himself. A messenger on horseback is just bringing him a message. But at the gate of the camp, beggar women sit with their children, wringing their hands, while a man in armor on horseback brings in a fettered prisoner. Further back we see a peasant plowing his field. Outside the rampart, bones lie about, animal skeletons, a dead horse with a crow and a wild dog eating it. Close to a wagon a crouching servant relieves himself.

Or we see knights attacking a village under the sign of Mars. In the foreground, one of the soldiers is stabbing a prostrate peasant; on the right, apparently in a chapel, a second man is stabbed and his possessions are dragged away. On the roof the storks sit peacefully in their nest. Further back a peasant is trying to escape over the fence, but a knight on his horse holds him by the protruding tail of his shirt. A peasant woman cries out, wringing her hands. A peasant in fetters, doleful and wretched, is being beaten over the head by a knight on horseback. Further back horsemen are setting fire to a house; one of them drives off the cattle and strikes at the farmer's wife, who is trying to stop him; above, in the little tower of the village church, the peasants huddle together, and frightened faces look out of the window. In the far distance, on a small hill, stands a fortified monastery; behind the high walls one sees the church roof with a cross on it. Somewhat higher up, on a hill, a castle or another part of the monastery.

These are the ideas suggested to the artist by the sign of the god of war. The picture is wonderfully full of life. As in a number of the other drawings, one feels that something that has been really experienced is before one's eyes. One has this feeling because these pictures are not yet "sentimental," because they do not express the greater restraint of the emotions which from now on, for a long period, caused the art of the upper class to express more and more exclusively its wishful fantasies, and compelled it to suppress everything that conflicted with this advancing standard of repugnance. These pictures simply narrate how the knight sees and feels the world. The sifting of feeling, the grid placed on the affects which admits to the picture what is pleasurable and excludes what is painful or embarrassing, allows many facts to pass unimpeded which later attain expression only when a conscious or unconscious protest against the upper class censoring of drives is being expressed, and are then somewhat overemphasized. Here the peasant is neither pitiable nor a representative of virtue. Nor is he a representative of ugly vice. He is simply miserable and somewhat ridiculous, exactly as the knight sees him. The world centers around the knight. Hungry dogs, begging women, rotting horses, servants crouching against the ramparts, villages in flames, peasants being plundered and killed—all this is as much a part of the landscape of these people as are tournaments and hunts. So God made the world: some are rulers, the others bondsmen. There is nothing embarrassing about all this.

And the same difference in standard of feeling between even this late chivalrous society and the subsequent society of the absolute courts is also shown in the representation of love. There is a picture of people under the sign of Venus. Again we look far into the open country. There are little hills, a meandering river, bushes, and a small wood. In the foreground three or four pairs of young nobles, always a young lord and a young lady together; they walk in a circle to the

THE CIVILIZING PROCESS

sound of music, ceremoniously, elegantly, all with the long-toed, fashionable shoes. Their movements are measured and rounded; one noble has a large feather in his hat; others have garlands in their hair. Perhaps we are looking at a kind of slow dance. Behind stand three boys making music; there is a table with fruits and drinks and a young fellow leaning against it, who is to serve.

At the opposite side, enclosed by a fence and gate, is a little garden. Trees form a kind of bower, beneath which is an oval bathtub. In it sits a young man, naked, who grabs eagerly at a naked girl who is just climbing into the bath with him. As above, an old female servant who is bringing fruits and drinks surveys the love game of the young people with an angry face. And as the masters amuse themselves in the foreground, so do the servants in the background. One of them falls upon a maid who lies on the ground with her skirts already pulled up. He looks round once more to see whether there is anyone nearby. On the other side, two young fellows of the common people are dancing around, flinging their arms and legs like Morisco dancers; a third plays for them.

Or we see, likewise in the open country, a small stone bathhouse with a small yard in front of it surrounded by a stone wall. We can see a little beyond it. A path is indicated, bushes, a row of trees leading into the distance. In the yard young couples are sitting and walking about; one of them admires the fashionable fountains, others converse, one of the young men with a falcon on his hand. Dogs, a little monkey. Potted plants.

We can see into the bathhouse through a large, open, arched window. Two young men and a girl sit naked in the water, side by side, and talk. A second girl, already undressed, is just opening the door to climb into the water with them. In the large open vault of the bathhouse a boy sits playing something to the bathers on his guitar. Under the arch is a tap from which the water runs. In front of the little house, drinks are placed to cool in a small tub of water. On a table next to it are fruits and a goblet; at the table is a young man, a wreath in his hair and his head supported elegantly on his hands. Above, from the second floor of the bathhouse, a maid and a servant watch the masters enjoying themselves.

In this picture, as one can see, the erotic relation between man and woman is much more open than in the later phase, where it is hinted at in social life, as in pictures, in a way that is comprehensible to all but nevertheless half-concealed. Nakedness is not yet associated with shame to the extent that, to circumvent internal and external social controls, it can only appear in pictures sentimentally, as the costume, so to speak, of the Greeks and Romans.

But neither is the naked body depicted here in the way it sometimes appeared in later times, in "private drawings" passed secretly from hand to hand. These love scenes are anything but "obscene." Love is presented here like anything else in the life of the knight, tournaments, hunts, campaigns, or plunderings. The scenes are not particularly stressed; one does not feel in their representation anything of the violence, the tendency to excite or gratify a wish-fulfillment denied in life, characteristic of everything "obscene." This picture does not come from an oppressed soul; it does not reveal something "secret" by violating taboos. It seems quite carefree. Here, too, the artist drew what he must have seen himself often enough in life. And on account of this unconcern, this matter-of-factness with which, compared to our standard of shame and embarrassment, the relations between the sexes are presented, we call this attitude "naïve." Even in the *House-Book* we occasionally find a joke which is (to our taste) thoroughly coarse, as also in other artists of this phase—for example, Master E. F. and, perhaps copied from him, even in the popularizing "Master with the Banderoles."[123] And the adoption of such motifs by a popularizing copyist, who was possibly even a monk, indicates how different was the social standard of shame. These things are depicted with the same matter-of-factness as some detail of clothing. It is a joke, certainly a coarse one, if we like to call it that, but really no coarser than the joke the artist permits himself when he makes the shirttail of the plundered and fleeing peasant stick out so that the knight can catch hold of it, or when he gives the old servant surveying the love games of the young people an angry expression, as if mocking her for being too old for such dalliance.

All these are expressions of a society in which people gave way to drives and feelings incomparably more easily, quickly, spontaneously, and openly than today, in which the emotions were less restrained and, as a consequence, less evenly regulated and more liable to oscillate more violently between extremes. Within this standard of regulation of the emotions, which is characteristic of the whole secular society of the Middle Ages, of peasants as of knights, there were certainly considerable variations. And the people conforming to this standard were subjected to a large number of drive controls. But these were in a different direction; they were not of the same degree as in later periods, and they did not take the form of a constant, even almost automatic self-control. The kind of integration and interdependence in which these people lived did not compel them to restrain their bodily functions before each other or to curb their aggressive impulses, to the same extent as in the following phase. This applies to everyone. But of course, for the peasants the scope for aggression was more restricted than for the knight—restricted, that is, to his equals. For the knight, by contrast, aggression was less restricted outside his own class than within it, for here it was regulated by the code of chivalry. A socially generated restraint was at times imposed on the peasant by the simple fact that he had not enough to eat. This certainly represents a restriction of drives of the highest degree, which expresses itself in the whole behavior of a human being. But no one paid attention to this, and his social situation scarcely made it necessary for him to impose constraint on himself when blowing his nose or spitting or snatching food at table. In this direction, coercion in the knightly class was stronger. However uniform, therefore, the medieval standard of control of emotions appears in comparison to later developments, it contained considerable differences corresponding to the stratification of secular society itself, not to mention clerical society; these differences remain to be examined in detail. They are visible in these pictures, if the measured and sometimes even affected gestures of the nobles are compared to the clumsy movements of the servants and peasants.

The expressions of feeling of medieval people are, on the whole, more spontaneous and unrestrained than in the following period. But they are not unrestrained or without social molding in any *absolute* sense. In this respect there is no zero point. Man without restrictions is a phantom. Admittedly, the nature, strength, and elaboration of the prohibitions, controls, and dependencies change in a hundred ways, and with them the tension and equilibrium of the emotions, and likewise the degree and kind of gratification that the individual seeks and finds.

Taken together, these pictures give a certain impression of where the knight sought and found gratification. At this time he may already live more frequently at court than earlier. But castle and manor, hill, stream, fields and villages, trees and woods still form the background of his life; they are taken for granted and regarded quite without sentimentality. Here he is at home, and here he is the master. His life is divided essentially between war, tournaments, hunts, and love.

But in the fifteenth century itself, and more so in the sixteenth, this changes. At the semiurban courts of princes and kings, partly from elements of the old nobility and partly from new rising elements, a new aristocracy forms with a new social space, new functions, and accordingly a different emotional structure.

People feel this difference themselves and express it. In 1562 a man named Jean du Peyrat translates Della Casa's book on manners into French. He gives it the title *Galatée ou la maniere et fasson comme le gentilhomme se doit gouverner en toute compagnie* (Galateo, or the manner in which the gentleman should conduct himself in all company). And even in this title the increased compulsion now imposed on the nobles is clearly expressed. But Peyrat himself, in his introduction, explicitly stresses the difference between the demands that life used to make on the knight and those which are now made on the noblemen by life in court:

> The entire virtue and perfection of the gentleman, your lordship, does not consist in correctly spurring a horse, handling a lance, sitting straight in one's armor, using every kind of weapon, behaving modestly among ladies, or in the pursuit of love: for this is another of the exercises attributed to the gentleman. There is, in addition, service at table before kings and princes, the manner of adjusting one's language toward people according to their rank and quality, their glances, gestures, and even the smallest signs or winks they might give.

Here, exactly the same things are enumerated as constituting the customary virtue, perfection, and activities of the noble as in the pictures of the *House-Book:* feats of arms and love. Contrasted to them are the additional perfections and the new sphere of life of the nobleman in the service of a prince. A new constraint, a new, more extensive control and regulation of behavior than the old knightly life made either necessary or possible, is now demanded of the nobleman. These are consequences of the new, increased dependence in which the noble is now placed. He is no longer the relatively free man, the master in his own castle, whose castle is his homeland. He now lives at court. He serves the prince. He waits on him at table. And at court he lives surrounded by people. He must behave toward each of them in exact accordance with their rank and his own. He must learn to adjust his gestures exactly to the different ranks and standing of the people at court, to measure his language exactly, and even to control his eyes exactly. It is a new self-discipline, an incomparably stronger reserve that is imposed on people by this new social space and the new ties of interdependence.

The attitude whose ideal form was expressed by the concept of *courtoisie* is giving way to another expressed more and more by the concept of *civilité.*

The translation of *Galateo* by Jean du Peyrat represents this transitional period linguistically as well. Up to 1530 or 1535 the concept of *courtoisie* predominates more or less exclusively in France. Toward the end of the century the concept of *civilité* slowly gains precedence, without the other being lost. Here, about the year 1562, the two are used together without any noticeable precedence of one or the other. In his dedication Peyrat says: "Let this book, which treats the instruction of a young courtier and gentleman, be protected by him who is as the paragon and mirror of others in *courtesy, civility,* good manners, and praiseworthy customs."

The man to whom these words are addressed is that very Henri de Bourbon, Prince of Navarre, whose life most visibly symbolizes this transition from the chivalrous to the courtly man and who, as Henri IV, was to be the direct executor of this change in France, being obliged, often against his will, to compel or even condemn to death those who resisted, those who did not understand that from free lords and knights they were to become dependent servants of the king.[124]

Appendices

Appendix I

Introduction to the 1968 Edition

I

In thinking and theorizing about the structure and controls of human affects nowadays, we are usually content to use as evidence observations from the more developed societies of today. We thus proceed from the tacit assumption that it is possible to construct theories about the affect structures of man in general on the basis of studies of people in a specific society that can be observed here and now—our own. However, there are numerous relatively accessible observations which point to the conclusion that the standard and pattern of affect controls in societies at different stages of development, and even in different strata of the same society, can differ. Whether we are concerned with the development of European countries, which has lasted for centuries, or with the so-called "developing countries" in other parts of the world, we are constantly confronted by observations which give rise to the following question: how and why, in the course of the overall transformations of society which take place over long time spans and in a particular direction—for which the term "development" has been adopted—is the affectivity of human behavior and experience, the control of individual affects by external and internal constraints, and in this sense the structure of all forms of human expression altered in a particular direction? Such changes are indicated in everyday speech by such statements as that the people of our own society are more "civilized" than they were earlier, or that those of other societies are more "uncivilized" (or even more "barbaric") than those of our own. The value judgments contained in such statements are obvious; the facts to which they relate are less so. This is partly because empirical investigations of long-term transformations of personality structures, and especially of affect controls, give rise at the present stage of sociological research to very considerable difficulties. At the forefront of sociological interest at present are relatively short-term processes, and usually only problems relating to a given state of society. Long-term transformations of social structures, and therefore of personality structures as well, have by and large been lost to view.

The present study is concerned with these long-term processes. Understanding of it may be aided by a brief indication of the various kinds of such processes. To begin with, two main directions in the structural changes of societies may be distinguished: those tending toward increased differentiation and integration, and those tending toward decreased differentiation and integration. In addition, there is a third type of social process, in the course of which the structure of a society or of its particular aspects is changed, but without a tendency toward either an increase or a decrease in the level of differentiation and integration. Finally, there are countless changes in a society which do not involve a change in its structure. This account does not do justice to the full complexity of such changes, for there are numerous hybrid forms, and often several types of change, even in opposite directions, can be observed simultaneously in the same society. But for the present, this brief outline of the different types of change suffices to indicate the problems with which this study is concerned.

This first volume addresses itself above all to the question of whether the supposition, based on scattered observations, that there are long-term changes in the affect and control structures of people in particular societies—changes which follow one and the same direction over a large number of generations—can be confirmed by reliable evidence and proved to be factually correct. This volume therefore contains an account of sociological procedures and findings, the best-known counterpart of which in the physical sciences is the experiment and its results. It is concerned with the discovery and elucidation of what actually takes place in the as yet unexplored field of inquiry to which our questions relate: the discovery and definition of factual connections.

The demonstration of a change in human affect and control structures taking place over a large number of generations in the same direction—to state it briefly, the increased tightening and differentiation of controls—gives rise to a further question. Is it possible to relate this long-term change in personality structures with long-term structural changes in society as a whole, which likewise tend in a particular direction, toward a higher level of social differentiation and integration? The second volume is concerned with these problems.

For these long-term structural changes of society, empirical evidence is likewise lacking. It has therefore been necessary to devote a part of the second volume to the discovery and elucidation of factual connections in this second area. The question is whether a structural change of society as a whole, tending toward a higher level of differentiation and integration, can be demonstrated with the aid of reliable empirical evidence. This proves possible. The process of the formation of nation states, discussed in the second volume, is an example of this kind of structural change.

Finally, in a provisional sketch of a theory of civilization, a model is evolved to show the possible connections between the long-term change in human personality structures toward a consolidation and differentiation of affect controls, and the long-term change in the social structure toward a higher level of differentiation and integration—for example, toward a differentiation and prolongation of the chains of interdependence and a consolidation of "state controls."

II

It can readily be seen that in adopting an approach directed at factual connections and their explanation (that is, an empirical and theoretical approach concerned with long-term structural changes of a specific kind, or "developments"), we take leave of the metaphysical ideas which connect the concept of development either to the notion of a mechanical necessity or to that of a teleological purpose. The concept of civilization, as the first chapter of this volume shows, has often been used in a semimetaphysical sense and has remained highly nebulous until today. Here, the attempt is made to isolate the factual core to which the current prescientific notion of the civilizing process refs. This core consists primarily of the structural change in people toward an increased consolidation and differentiation of their affect controls, and therefore both of their experience (e.g., in the form of an advance in the threshold of shame and revulsion) and of their behavior (e.g., in the differentiation of the implements used at table). The next task posed by the demonstration of such a change in a specific direction over many generations is to provide an explanation. A sketch of one is to be found, as already mentioned, at the end of the second volume.

But with the aid of such an investigation we likewise take leave of the theories of social change predominant today, which in the course of time have taken the place in sociological inquiry of an earlier one centered on the old, semimetaphysical notion of development. As far as can be seen, these current theories scarcely ever distinguish in an unambiguous way between the different types of social change briefly mentioned earlier. In particular, there is still a lack of theories based on empirical evidence to explain the type of long-term social changes which take the form of a process and, above all, of a development.

When I was working on this book it seemed quite clear to me that I was laying the foundation of an undogmatic, empirically based sociological theory of social processes in general and of social development in particular. I believed it quite obvious that the investigation, and the concluding model of the long-term process of state formation to be found in the second volume, could serve equally as a model of the long-term dynamic of societies in a particular direction, to which the concept of social development refers. I did not believe at that time that it was necessary to point out explicitly that this study was neither of an "evolution" in the nineteenth-century sense of an automatic progress, nor of an unspecific "social change" in the twentieth-century sense. At that time this seemed so obvious that I omitted to mention these theoretical implications explicitly. The introduction to the second edition gives me the opportunity to make good this omission.

III

The comprehensive social development studied and presented here through one of its central manifestations—a wave of advancing integration over several centuries, a process of state formation with the complementary process of advancing differentiation—is a figurational change which, in the to-and-fro of contrary movements, maintains, when surveyed over an extended time span, a constant direction through many generations. This structural change in a specific direction can be demonstrated as a fact, regardless of how it is evaluated. The factual proof is what matters here. The concept of social change by itself does not suffice, as an instrument of research, to take account of such facts. A mere change can be of the kind observable in clouds or smoke rings: now they look like this, now like that. A concept of social change that does not distinguish clearly between changes that relate to the structure of a society and those that do not—and, further, between structural changes without a specific direction and those which follow a particular direction over many generations, e.g., toward greater or lesser complexity—is a very inadequate tool of sociological inquiry.

The situation is similar with a number of other problems dealt with here. When, after several preparatory studies which enabled me both to investigate documentary evidence and to explore the gradually unfolding theoretical problems, the way to a possible solution became clearer, I was made aware that this study brings somewhat nearer to resolution the intractable problem of the connection between individual psychological structures (so-called personality structures) and figurations formed by large numbers of interdependent individuals (social structures). It does so because it approaches both types of structure not as fixed, as usually happens, but as changing, and as interdependent aspects of the same long-term development.

IV

If the various academic disciplines whose subject matter is touched on by this study—including, above all, the discipline of sociology— had already reached the stage of scientific maturity at present enjoyed by many of the natural sciences, it might have been expected that a carefully documented study of long-term processes, such as those of civilization or state formation, with the theoretical proposals developed from it, would be assimilated, either in its entirety or in some of its aspects, after thorough testing and discussion, after critical sifting of all unsuitable or disproved content, to that discipline's stock of empirical and theoretical knowledge. Since the advance of scholarship depends in large measure on interchange and cross-fertilization between numerous colleagues and on the continuous development of the common stock of knowledge, it might have been expected that thirty years later this study would either have become a part of the standard knowledge of the discipline or have been more or less superseded by the work of others and laid to rest.

Instead, I find that a generation later this study still has the character of a pioneering work in a problematic field which today is hardly less in need than it was thirty years ago, of the simultaneous investigation on the empirical and theoretical plane that is to be found here. Understanding of the urgency of the problems discussed here has grown. Everywhere gropings in the direction of these problems are observable. There is no lack of later attempts to solve problems to whose solution the empirical documentation in these two volumes, and the concluding sketch of a theory of civilization, endeavor to contribute. I do not believe these later attempts to have been successful.

To exemplify this, it must suffice to discuss the way in which the man who at present is widely regarded as the leading theoretician of sociology, Talcott Parsons, attempts to pose and solve some of the problems dealt with here. It is characteristic of Parsons's theoretical approach to attempt to dissect analytically into their elementary components, as he once expressed it,[1] the different types of society in his field of observation. He called one particular type of elementary component "pattern variables." These pattern variables include the dichotomy of "affectivity" and "affective neutrality." His conception can best be understood by comparing society to a game of cards: every type of society, in Parsons's view, represents a different "hand." But the cards themselves are always the same; and their number is small, however diverse their faces may be. One of the cards with which the game is played is the polarity between affectivity and affective neutrality. Parsons originally conceived this idea, he tells us, in analysing Tönnies's society types *Gemeinschaft* (community) and *Gesellschaft* (society). "Community," Parsons appears to believe, is characterized by affectivity and "society" by affective neutrality. But in determining the differences between different types of society, and between different types of relationship within one and the same society, he attributes to this "pattern variable" in the card game, as to the others, a wholly general meaning. In the same context. Parsons addresses himself to the problem of the relation of social structure to personality.[2] He indicates that while he had previously seen them merely as closely connected and interacting "human action systems," he can now state with certainty that in a theoretical sense they are different phases or aspects of one and the same fundamental action system. He illustrates this by an example, explaining that what may be considered on the sociological plane as an institutionalization of affective neutrality is essentially the same as what may be regarded on the level of personality as "the imposition of renunciation of immediate gratification in the interests of disciplined organization and the longer-run goals of the personality."

It is perhaps useful for an understanding of this study to compare this later attempt to solve such problems with the earlier one reprinted in unchanged form here. The decisive difference in scientific approach, and in the conception of the objectives of sociological theory, is evident from even this short example of Parsons's treatment of similar problems. What in this book is shown with the aid of extensive empirical documentation to be a process, Parsons, by the static nature of his concepts, reduces retrospectively, and it seems to me quite unnecessarily, to states. Instead of a relatively complex process whereby the affective life of people is gradually moved toward an increased and more even control of affects—but certainly not toward a state of total affective neutrality—Parsons presents a simple opposition between two states, affectivity and affective neutrality, which are supposed to be present to different degrees in different types of society, like different quantities of chemical substances. By reducing to two different states what was shown empirically in *The Civilizing Process* to be a process and interpreted theoretically as such, Parsons deprives himself of the possibility of discovering how the distinguishing peculiarities of different societies to which he refers are actually to be explained. So far as is apparent, he does not even raise the question of explanation. The different states denoted by the antitheses of the "pattern variables" are, it seems, simply given. The subtly articulated structural change toward increased and more even affect control that may be observed in reality disappears in this kind of theorizing. Social phenomena in reality can only be observed as evolving and having evolved; their dissection by means of pairs of concepts which restrict the analysis to two antithetical states represents an unnecessary impoverishment of sociological perception on both empirical and theoretical levels.

Certainly, it is the task of every sociological theory to clarify the characteristics that all possible human societies have in common. The concept of the social process, like many others used in this study, has precisely this function. But the basic categories selected by Parsons seem to me arbitrary to a high degree. Underlying them is the tacit, untested, and seemingly self-evident notion that the objective of every scientific theory is to reduce everything variable to something invariable, and to simplify all complex phenomena by dissecting them into their individual components.

The example of Parsons's theory suggests, however, that theorizing in the field of sociology is complicated rather than simplified by a systematic reduction of social processes to social states, and of complex, heterogeneous phenomena to simpler, seemingly homogeneous components. This kind of reduction and abstraction could be justified as a method of theorizing only if it led unambiguously to a clearer and deeper understanding by men of themselves as societies and as individuals. Instead of this we find that the theories formed by such methods, like the epicycle theory of Ptolemy, require needlessly complicated auxiliary constructions to make them agree with the observable facts. They often appear like dark clouds from which here and there a few rays of light touch the earth.

V

One example of this, which will be discussed more fully later, is Parsons's attempt to develop a theoretical model of the relation between personality structures and social structures. In this undertaking two not very compatible ideas are frequently thoroughly confused: the notion that individual and society—"ego" and "social system"—are two entities existing independently of each other, with the individual regarded as the actual reality and society treated as an epiphenomenon; and the notion that the two are different but inseparable planes of the universe formed by men. Furthermore, concepts like "ego" and "social system" and all those related to them, which refer to men as individuals and as societies, are applied by Parsons—except when he is using psychoanalytical categories—as if the normal condition of both could be considered as an unalterable state. This study cannot be properly understood if the view of what is actually observable in human beings is blocked by such notions. It cannot be understood if we forget that concepts such as "individual" and "society" do not relate to two objects existing separately but to different yet inseparable aspects of the same human beings, and that both aspects (and human beings in general) are normally involved in a structural transformation. Both have the character of processes, and there is not the slightest necessity, in forming theories about human beings, to abstract from this process-character. Indeed, it is indispensable that the concept of process be included in sociological and other theories relating to human beings. As is shown in this study, the relation between individual and social structures can only be clarified if both are investigated as changing, evolving entities. Only then is it possible to develop models of their relationship, as is done here, which are in some agreement with the demonstrable facts. It can be stated with complete certainty that the relation between what is referred to conceptually as the "individual" and as "society" will remain incomprehensible so long as these concepts are used as if they represented two separate bodies, and even bodies normally at rest, which only come into contact with one another afterwards as it were. Without ever saying so clearly and openly, Parsons and all sociologists of the same persuasion undoubtedly envisage those things to which the concepts "individual" and "society" refer as existing separately. Thus—to give only one example—Parsons adopts the notion already developed by Durkheim that the relation between "individual" and "society" is an "interpenetration" of the individual and the social system. However such an "interpenetration" is conceived, what else can this metaphor mean than that we are concerned with two different entities which first exist separately and then subsequently "interpenetrate"?[3]

This makes clear the difference between the two sociological approaches. In this study the possibility of discerning more precisely the connection between individual structures and social structures results from a refusal to abstract from the process of their evolution as from something incidental or "merely historical." For the structures of personality and of society evolve in an indissoluble interrelationship. It can never be said with certainty that the people of a society *are* civilized. But on the basis of systematic investigations referring to demonstrable evidence, it can be said with a high degree of certainty that some groups of people have *become* more civilized, without necessarily implying that it is better or worse, has a positive or negative value, to become more civilized. Such a change in personality structures can, however, be shown without difficulty to be a specific aspect of the development of social structures. This is attempted in what follows.

It is not particularly surprising to encounter in Parsons, and in many other contemporary sociological theoreticians, a tendency to reduce processes to states even when these writers are explicitly concerned with the problem of social change. In keeping with the predominant trend in sociology, Parsons takes as his starting point the hypothesis that every society normally exists in a state of unchanging equilibrium which is homeostatically preserved. It changes, he supposes, when this normal state of social equilibrium is disturbed by, for example, a violation of the social norms, a breach of conformity.ᐟ Social change thus appears as a phenomenon resulting from the accidental, externally activated malfunction of a normally well-balanced social system. Moreover, the society thus disturbed strives, in Parsons's view, to regain its state of rest. Sooner or later, as he sees it, a different "system" with a different equilibrium is established, which once again maintains itself more or less automatically, despite oscillations, in the given state. In a word, the concept of social change refers here to a transitional state between two normal states of changelessness, brought about by malfunction. Here, too, the difference between the theoretical approaches represented by this study and by Parsons and his school emerges very distinctly. The present study upholds the idea, based on abundant documentary material, that change is a normal characteristic of society. A structured sequence of continuous change serves here as the frame of reference for investigating states located at particular points in time. In prevailing sociological opinion, conversely, social situations treated as if they normally existed in a state of rest serve as the frame of reference for all change. Thus a society is regarded as a "social system," and a "social system" as a "system in a state of rest." Even when a relatively differentiated, "highly developed" society is involved, the attempt is often made to consider it as at rest and self-contained. It is not regarded as an integral part of the inquiry to ask how and why this highly developed society has developed to this state of differentiation. In keeping with the static frame of reference of the predominant system-theories, social changes, processes, and developments, which include the development of a state or a civilizational process, appear merely as something additional, a mere "historical introduction" the investigation and explanation of which may very well be dispensed with in coming to an understanding of the "social system" and its "structure" and "functions," as they may be observed here and now from a short-term viewpoint. These conceptual tools themselves—including concepts like "structures" and "function," which serve as the badge of the contemporary sociological school of "structural functionalists"— bear the stamp of this specific mode of thinking, which reduces processes to states. Of course, their originators cannot entirely dismiss the idea that the "structures" and "functions" of the social "unit" or its "parts," which they picture as states, move and change. But the problems which thus come into view are reconciled with the static mode of thought by encapsulating them in a special chapter with the title "Social Change," as though the phenomenon were supplementary to the problems of the normally unchanging system. In this way "social change" itself is treated as an attribute of a state of rest. In other words, the basic, state-orientated attitude is reconciled with empirical observations of social change by introducing into the theoretical waxworks of motionless social phenomena a few more equally motionless figures with labels like "social change" or "social process." In this way the problems of social change are in a sense frozen and rendered innocuous to state-oriented sociology. So it happens that the concept of "social development" has almost completely vanished from the sight of contemporary sociological theorists—paradoxically, in a phase of social development when, in actual social life and partly also in empirical sociological research, people are concerning themselves more intensely and consciously than ever before with problems of social development.

VI

In writing an introduction to a book that on both the theoretical and the empirical side is squarely opposed to widespread tendencies in contemporary sociology, one has a certain obligation to tell the reader clearly and unequivocally how and why the problems posed here, and the steps taken to solve them, differ from those of the predominant type of sociology, and particularly from those of theoretical sociology. To do this, one cannot entirely evade the question how it is to be explained that sociology, for whose leading nineteenth-century representatives the problems of long-term social processes were of primordial interest, should in the twentieth century have become a sociology of states to such an extent that the investigation of long-term social processes has as much as disappeared from its research activity. Within the scope of this introduction I cannot presume to discuss this displacement of the center of interest of sociological research, and the radical change in the entire sociological manner of thinking connected with it, with the thoroughness they deserve. But the problem is too important for an understanding of what follows, and beyond that for the further development of sociology, to be passed over in complete silence. I shall therefore confine myself to picking out a few elements from the complex of conditions responsible for this regression in the intellectual apparatus of sociology and the concomitant narrowing of its field of inquiry.

The most obvious reason why awareness of the significance of problems of long-term social change, of the sociogenesis and development of social formations of all kinds has been largely lost to sociologists, and why the concept of development has fallen into disrepute among them, is to be found in the reaction of many sociologists—above all, the leading theoreticians of the twentieth century—to certain aspects of the outstanding sociological theories of the nineteenth century. It has been shown that the theoretical models of long-term social development elaborated in the nineteenth century by men like Comte, Spencer, Marx, Hobhouse, and many others rested in part on hypotheses determined primarily by the political and philosophical ideals of these men and only secondarily by their relation to facts. Later generations had a much larger and constantly increasing supply of facts at their disposal. Reexamination of the classical nineteenth-century theories of development in light of the more comprehensive findings of subsequent generations made many aspects of the earlier process-models appear questionable or at any rate in need of revision. Many of the sociological pioneers' articles of faith were no longer accepted by twentieth-century sociologists. These included, above all, the belief that the development of society is necessarily a development for the better, a movement in the direction of progress. This belief was emphatically rejected by many later sociologists in accordance with their own social experience. They could see more clearly in retrospect that the earlier models of development comprised a mixture of relatively fact-based and of ideological notions.

In a mature discipline one might, first of all, have set about the task of revising and correcting the earlier models of development. One might have tried, in this situation, to ascertain which aspects of the old theories could be used as a basis for further research in light of the more comprehensive factual knowledge now available, and which should find their place as expressions of time-bound political or philosophical prejudice, with a suitable tombstone, in the graveyard of dead doctrines.

Instead, an extremely sharp reaction against the type of sociological theory concerned with long-term social processes set in. The study of the long-term development of society was almost universally decried, and the center of sociological interest moved, in a radical reaction against the older type of theory, to the investigation of data on society conceived as normally existing in a state of rest and equilibrium. Hand in hand with this went the hardening of a collection of stereotyped arguments against the older sociological theories and many of their central concepts, particularly that of social development. As these sociologists did not trouble to distinguish between the fact-based and the ideological elements in the concept of development, the whole discussion of long-term social processes, particularly developmental processes, was henceforth associated with one or another of the nineteenth-century systems of belief, and so, above all, with the notion that social development, whether proceeding in a straight line without conflict or dialectically with conflict, must automatically be a change for the better, a movement in the direction of progress. From then on it appeared almost old-fashioned to occupy oneself with questions of social development. It is sometimes said that generals, in planning strategy for a new war, take the strategy of the old one as their model. To assume without question that concepts like "social development" or "long-term social processes" inevitably include the old idea of progress is to proceed in a similar way.

We find, therefore, in the framework of sociology, an intellectual development involving a radical swing of the pendulum from a one-sided position to an opposite position no less one-sided. A phase in which sociological theorists primarily sought models of long-term social development has been succeeded by one in which they are primarily concerned with models of societies in a state of rest and immutability. If research was once founded on a Heraclitean kind of basic assumption that all is in flux (with the difference that it was taken almost for granted that the flow was in the direction of improvement), it is based now on an Eleatic idea. The Eleatics, it is said, imagined the flight of an arrow as a series of states of rest; actually, it seemed to them, the arrow does not move at all. For at every given moment it is in a particular place. The assumption of many present-day sociological theorists that societies are usually to be found in a state of equilibrium, so that the long-term social development of mankind appears as a chain of static social types, is strongly reminiscent of the Eleatic conception of the flight of an arrow. How can this swing of the pendulum from one extreme to the other in the development of sociology be explained?

At first sight it seems that the decisive reason for the change in the theoretical orientation of sociology is a reaction of scientists protesting in the name of the scientific character of their research against the interference of political and philosophical ideas in the theory of their subject. Exponents of contemporary sociological theories of state are themselves often inclined to this interpretation. On closer examination, however, it is found to be inadequate. The reaction against the sociology of development predominant in the nineteenth century was not directed simply against the primacy of ideals, the dominance of preconceived social doctrines, in the name of scientific objectivity. It was not simply the expression of a concern to pull aside the veil of short-lived notions of what society ought to be, in order to perceive the real dynamics and functioning of society itself. In the last analysis it was a reaction against the primacy of *particular* ideals in sociological theory, in the name of others partly opposed to them. If in the nineteenth century specific conceptions of what ought to be or of what was desired—specific ideological conceptions—led to a central interest in the development of society, in the twentieth century other conceptions of what ought to be or is desirable—other ideological conceptions—led to the pronounced interest among leading sociological theorists in the state of society as it is, to their neglect of problems of the dynamics of social formations, and to their lack of interest in problems of long-term processes and in all the opportunities of explanation that the investigation of such problems provides.

This sharp change in the character of social ideals, encountered here in the development of sociology, is not an isolated phenomenon. It is symptomatic of a more comprehensive change in the ideals predominant in the countries in which the main work of sociology is concentrated. This change points, in turn, to a specific transformation that has been taking place in the nineteenth and twentieth centuries in the internal and external relations of the older, developed industrial states. It must suffice here—as a summary of a more extensive inquiry—to indicate briefly the main outline of this transformation. This will facilitate understanding of sociological studies which, like the present one, give a central place to the investigation of long-term processes. The purpose is not to attack other ideals in the name of one's own, but to seek a better understanding of the structure of such processes themselves and to emancipate the theoretical framework of sociological research from the primacy of social ideals and doctrines. For we can only elicit sociological knowledge which is sufficiently adequate to be of use in solving the acute problems of society if, when posing and solving sociological problems, we cease giving precedence to preconceived notions of what the solutions ought to be over the investigation of what is.

VII

In the industrializing countries of the nineteenth century in which the first great pioneering works of sociology were written, the voices expressing the social beliefs, ideals, hopes, and long-term goals of the rising industrial classes gradually gained the advantage over those seeking to preserve the existing social order in the interests of the established courtly-dynastic, aristocratic, or patrician power elites. It was the former who, in keeping with their situation as the rising classes, had high expectations of a better future. And as their ideal l‖ y not in the present but in the future, they were particularly interested in the dynamics, the development of society. In conjunction with one or another of these rising industrial classes, the sociologists of the time sought confirmation that the development of mankind would move in the direction of their wishes and hopes. They did so by exploring the direction and the driving forces of social development hitherto. In this activity they undoubtedly brought to light a very considerable amount of adequate knowledge on the problems of social development. But it is often very difficult in retrospect to distinguish between specific heteronomous doctrines filled with short-lived, time-bound ideals and those conceptual models which have significance independently of these ideals, solely with regard to verifiable facts.

On the other side, in the nineteenth century, were to be heard the voices of those who for one reason or another opposed the transformation of society through industrialization, whose social faith was

---

oriented toward conservation of the existing heritage, and who held up, against what they took to be the deteriorating present, their ideal of a better past. They represented not only the preindustrial elites of the dynastic states but also broader working groups—above all, those engaged in agriculture and handicrafts, whose traditional livelihoods were being eroded by advancing industrialization. They were the opponents of all those who spoke from the standpoint of the two rising industrial classes, the industrial and commercial bourgeoisie and the industrial working class, and who, in keeping with the rising situation of these classes, drew their inspiration from a belief in a better future, the progress of mankind. Thus, in the nineteenth century, the chorus of voices was split between those extolling a better past and those celebrating a better future.

Among the sociologists whose image of society was oriented toward progress and a better future are to be found, as we know, spokesmen of the two industrial classes. They include men like Marx and Engels, who identified themselves with the industrial working class; and they include bourgeois sociologists like Comte at the beginning of the nineteenth century or Hobhouse at the end. The spokesmen for the two rising industrial classes took confidence in the thought of the future improvement of the human condition, even if what they envisaged as improvement and progress varied widely depending on their class. It is of no small importance to realize how intense the interest in the problems of social development in the nineteenth century was, and to ask on what this interest was founded, if one is to understand why the belief in progress waned in the twentieth century and why, correspondingly, interest among sociologists in the problems of long-term social development declined.

But to understand this shift it is not sufficient, as has already been indicated, to consider only class figurations, the social relationships within states. The rise of industrial classes within the industrializing states of Europe in the nineteenth century went hand in hand with the continuing rise of these nations themselves. In that century these nations drove each other by constant rivalry to a greater increase of their predominance over less developed nations than ever before. Not only the classes within them but also these state-societies in their totality were rising, expanding social formations.

One might be tempted to attribute the belief in progress in European writing in the centuries preceding the twentieth primarily to the progress in science and technology. But that is an insufficient explanation. How little the experience of scientific and technological progress alone gives rise to an idealization of progress, to a confident faith in the continuous improvement of the human condition, is shown clearly enough by the twentieth century. The actual degree and tempo of progress in science and technology in this century exceed that in the preceding centuries very considerably. Likewise, the standard of living of the masses in the countries of the first wave of industrialization has been higher in the twentieth century than in preceding centuries. The state of health has improved; life expectancy has increased. But in the total chorus of the time, the voices of those who affirm progress as something valuable, who see in the improvement of the condition of men the centerpiece of a social ideal, and who believe confidently in the better future of mankind, have become appreciably fewer than in preceding centuries. On the other side of the choir, the voices of those who cast doubt on all these developments, who see no geat promise of a better future for mankind or even for their own nation, and whose central social faith concentrates instead on the present as the highest value, on the conservation of their own nation, on the idealization of its existing social form or even of its past, its heritage and its traditional order, are increasing in the twentieth century and gradually becoming ever louder. In the preceding centuries, in which actual progress was already very palpable yet still slow and relatively limited, the idea of further, future progress had the character of an ideal toward which its adherents were striving and which possessed high value precisely as an ideal. In the twentieth century, when actual progress in science, technology, health, the standard of living, and not least in the reduction of inequality between people exceeds by far, in the older industrial nations, the progress in all previous centuries, progress has ceased for many people to be an ideal. The voices of those who doubt all this actual progress are growing more numerous.

The reasons for this change are manifold. Not all need be considered here. The recurrent wars, the incessant danger of war, and the threat of nuclear and other new scientific weapons certainly contribute to this coincidence of accelerating progress, particularly in the scientific and technical fields, with diminishing confidence in the value of this progress and of progress in general.

But the contempt heaped in the twentieth century on the preceding centuries' "shallow" belief in progress or their notion of a progressive development of human society; the obstructions blocking sociologists' view of problems of long-term social processes; the almost complete disappearance of the concept of social development from sociological texts—these and other symptoms of an extreme swing of the intellectual pendulum are not sufficiently explained by the upheavals of war and related phenomena. To understand them, we must also take account of specific changes in the twentieth century in the overall internal structure and international position of the great industrial nations of the nineteenth century.

Within these nations the representatives of the two industrial classes, the industrial bourgeoisie and the industrial working class, now establish themselves firmly against the earlier dynastic-aristocratic military power elites as the ruling groups in their states. The two industrial classes hold each other in an often precarious and always unstable balance of tensions, with the established working class still in the weaker position, but slowly gaining strength. The rising classes of the nineteenth century, who still had to fight within their states against the traditional dynastic elite, and for whom development, progress, a better future was not only a fact but also an ideal of great emotional significance, have become in the course of the twentieth century the more or less established industrial classes whose representatives are installed institutionally as the ruling or co-ruling groups. Partly as partners, partly as opponents, the representatives of the industrial bourgeoisie and the established industrial working class now form the primary elite in the nations of the first wave of industrialization. Accordingly, alongside class-consciousness and class ideals, and partly as a disguise for them, national consciousness and the ideal of their own nation as the highest value play an increasing role within the two industrial classes—first of all in the industrial bourgeoisie, but increasingly in the industrial working class as well.

Seen as an ideal, however, the nation turns attention to what already exists. Since representatives of the two powerful and populous industrial classes now have access to positions of power in the state, the nation, organized as a state, appears emotionally and ideologically as the highest value in its present condition. Moreover, it appears— emotionally and ideologically—as eternal, immutable in its essential features. Historical changes affect only externals; the people, the nation, so it appears, do not change. The English, German, French, Italian, and all other nations are, for those who constitute them, everlasting. In their "essence" they are always the same, whether we are speaking of the tenth or the twentieth century.

Furthermore, it was not only the two industrial classes within the older industrial nations which changed, once and for all, in the course of the twentieth century. The rise of the European nations and of their offshoots in other parts of the world, which had gone on for centuries, also came slowly to a standstill in our own. To be sure, their actual lead over non-European nations (with few exceptions) at first remained large; for a time it even increased. But the idea had formed and established itself in the age of the unchallenged ascendancy of the European nations, as among all powerful and ruling groups in the world, that the power they were able to wield over other nations was the expression of an eternal mission bestowed on them by God or nature or historical destiny, the expression of a superiority over those less powerful which was founded in their very essence. This idea of their own self-evident superiority, deeply rooted in the self-image of the older industrial nations, has been profoundly shaken by the actual course of development in the twentieth century. The reality-shock suffered when a national ideal collides with social reality has been absorbed by each nation in a different way, according to its own development and the specific nature of its national self-image. For Germany the more comprehensive significance of this collision was first concealed by the more direct shock of the military defeats. But it is indicative both of the solidity of the old national ideals and of the relative autonomy of this development as a whole that even in the victorious countries of the second European-American war there were, at first, immediately after the victory had been won, as far as can be determined, only very few people who realized how radically and fundamentally the military conflicts between two groups of relatively highly developed countries would reduce the power of this class of countries as a whole over the less developed countries, a reduction which had been prepared for some time. As is often the case, this sudden diminution in their power found the previously mighty countries unprepared and bewildered.

The actual opportunities for progress, for a better future, are—leaving aside the regressive possibilities of war—still very great for the older industrial nations. But in relation to their traditional national self-images, in which the idea of their own national civilization or culture is usually ensconced as the highest value of mankind, the future is disappointing. The idea of the unique nature and value of one's own nation often serves as legitimation for that nation's claim to lead all other nations. It is this self-image, this claim to leadership by the older industrial nations, that has been shaken in the second half of the twentieth century by what is still a very limited increase in power among the poorer, previously dependent and partly subjugated pre-industrial societies in other parts of the world.[5]

In other words, this reality-shock, insofar as it affects the emotive value of the present state of a nation in regard to its future possibilities, merely reinforces a tendency already present in national feeling present what the nation is and always has been, its eternal, unalterable heritage, possesses a far greater emotive value, as a means of self-legitimation and as an expression of the national scale of values and the national ideal, than any promise or ideal located in the future. The "national ideal" draws attention away from what changes to the enduring and the immutable.

This aspect of the transformation taking place in the European states, and in a number of closely related non-European states as well, has been matched by specific changes in the realm of ideas and in the modes of thought of intellectuals. In the eighteenth and nineteenth centuries, philosophers and sociologists who spoke of "society" were usually thinking of "bourgeois society"—that is, aspects of social life that seemed to lie beyond the dynastic and military aspects of the state. In keeping with their situation and their ideals as spokesmen for groups which were by and large excluded from access to the central positions of state power, these men, when talking of society, usually had in mind a human society transcending all state frontiers. With the extensive assumption of state power by representatives of the two industrial classes, and with the corresponding development of national ideals in these two classes and particularly in their representative ruling elites, this conception of society was changed in sociology as well.

In society at large, the various class ideals of the industrial classes increasingly mingle and interpenetrate with national ideals. Certainly, conservative and liberal national ideals show a different nuance of nationalism than do socialist or communist ones. But such nuances influenced only marginally, if at all, the broad outline of the change that took place in the attitude toward state and nation of the established industrial classes, including their political and intellectual spokesmen, when these classes, ceasing to be groups excluded from central state power, became groups truly constituting the nation, whose leaders themselves represented and exercised state power. It accords with this development that many twentieth-century sociologists, when speaking of "society," no longer have in mind (as did their predecessors) a "bourgeois society" or a "human society" beyond the state, but increasingly the somewhat diluted ideal image of a nation-state. Within their general conception of society as something abstracted from the reality of the nation-state, the above-mentioned political and ideological nuances are again to be found. Among the leading sociological theorists of the twentieth century, conservative and liberal as well as socialist and communist shades are to be found in the image of society. Since, in the twentieth century, American sociology has taken over for a time the leading role in the development of theoretical sociology, the dominant type of sociological theory of this period reflects the specific character of its predominant national ideal, within which conservative and liberal features are not so sharply divided, or felt to be so antithetical, as in some European nation-states, particularly Germany.[6]

In sociological discussions, and in philosophical debates as well, the rejection of certain aspects of the sociological theories of the nineteenth century—above all, their orientation toward social development and the concept of progress—is often presented as based solely on the factual inadequacy of these theories. The short survey that has been given here of one of the main structural tendencies of the development of relations within and between the older industrial nations throws into sharper relief certain ideological aspects of this rejection. In accordance with the concept of ideology developed within the Marxian tradition, one might seek to explain the ideological aspects of the neglect of social development, and the preoccupation with the state of social systems, dominant in recent sociological theories solely by reference to the ideals of classes whose hopes, wishes, and ideals are related not to the future but to the conservation of the existing order. But this class-explanation of the social beliefs and ideals implicit in sociological theory is no longer sufficient in the twentieth century. In this period we must also take account of the development of national ideals transcending social classes in order to understand the ideological aspects of sociological theories. The integration of the two industrial classes into a state structure previously ruled by numerically very small preindustrial minorities; the rise of both classes to a position in which their representatives play a more or less dominant role in the state, and in which even the weaker sectors of the industrial workers can no longer be ruled without their consent; and the resulting stronger identification of both classes with the nation—all these factors give special impetus, in the social attitudes of this time, to the belief in one's own nation as one of the highest values in human life. The lengthening and multiplication of chains of interdependence between states, and the heightening of specific tensions and conflicts between states resulting from this, the momentous national wars and the ever-present danger of war—all these factors contribute to the growth of nation-centered patterns of thought.

It is the convergence of these two intrastate and interstate lines of development in the older industrial nations that has weakened the ideal of progress, the orientation of faith and desire toward a better future and therefore also toward an image of the past considered as development. Combined, the two lines of development cause this type of ideal to be replaced by others directed at conserving and defending the existing order. They relate to something that is felt to be immutable and realized in the present—the eternal nation. The voices proclaiming belief in a better future and the progress of mankind as their ideal make way, as the dominant section in the mixed social chorus of the time, for the voices of those who give precedence to the value of what exists and, above all, to the timeless value of their own nations, for which, in the succession of great and small wars, many people have lost their lives. This is—sketched in its main outline—the overall structural development which is reflected in the development of theories of society. Theories which reflect the ideals of rising classes in expanding industrial societies are replaced by theories dominated by the ideals of more or less established classes in highly developed societies whose growth has reached or passed its peak.

As an example of this type of sociological theory, it may suffice to cite one of its representative concepts, that of the "social system," as used by Parsons, but certainly not by him alone. It expresses very clearly the way in which a "society" is now conceived. A "social system" is a society "in equilibrium." Small oscillations of this equilibrium do occur, but normally society exists in a state of rest. All its parts, in this conception, are normally harmoniously attuned to one another. All individuals belonging to it are normally attuned by the same kind of socialization to the same norms. All are normally well-integrated, respect the same values in their actions, fulfill their prescribed roles without difficulty. Conflicts between them do not normally occur; these, like changes in the system, are manifestations of malfunction. In short, the image of society represented theoretically by this concept of the social system reveals itself on closer inspection to be the ideal image of a nation: all the people belonging to it obey the same norms on the basis of the same socialization, uphold the same values, and thus live normally in well-integrated harmony with one another. In the conception of the "social system" that we have before u|, in other words, the image of the nation as community can be discerned. It is tacitly assumed that within such a "system" there is a relatively high degree of equality between people, for integration rests on the same socialization of people, on the uniformity of their values and norms throughout the entire system. Such a "system" is therefore a construction abstracted from a democratically conceived nation-state. From whatever side this construction is considered, the distinction between what the nation is and what the nation ought to be is blurred. Just as in the nineteenth-century sociological models of development the desired social process was presented (mingled with realistic observations) as a fact, so in the twentieth-century sociological models of a normally unchanging "social system" the desired ideal of a harmonious integration of all parts of the nation is also presented (mingled with realistic observations) as something that exists, a fact. But in the former case it is the future, in the latter the present, the nation-state existing here and now, that is idealized.

A mixture of "is" and "ought," of factual analyses and normative postulates, relating primarily to a society of a very definite type, a nation-state conceived in broadly egalitarian fashion, thus presents itself as the centerpiece of a theory which claims to be capable of serving as a model for the scientific investigation of societies in all times and places. One need only raise the question of whether and how far such sociological theories—derived primarily from present-day, more or less democratic nation-state societies which presuppose a high degree of integration of people into the "social system" as something both self-evident and desirable, and which therefore, imply a relatively advanced stage of social democratization—are applicable to societies at different stages of development, and which are less centralized and democratized, in order to perceive the weakness of a general theory of society from the church-steeple perspective of the present state of our own society. If such models of a "social system" are tested for their suitability as theoretical tools for the scientific investigation of a society with a high percentage of slaves or unfree subjects, or of feudal or hierarchical states—that is, societies in which not even the same laws apply to all people, not to speak of the same norms and values—it is quickly seen how present-centered these sociological models of systems conceived as states actually are.

What has been illustrated here by the "social" system example could be shown without difficulty to apply to other concepts of dominant contemporary sociology. Concepts like "structure," "function," "norm," "integration," and "role" all represent in their current forms attempts to conceptualize certain aspects of human societies by abstracting from their dynamics, their genesis, their character as a process, their development. The rejection of the nineteenth-century ideological understanding of these dynamic aspects of society that has taken place can therefore be seen not only as a criticism of these ideological aspects in the name of a scientific concern with fact, but above all as a criticism of earlier ideals that no longer correspond to present social conditions and experience and have therefore been rejected in the name of later ideals. This replacement of one ideology by another[7] explains the fact that it is not simply the ideological elements in the nineteenth-century sociological concept of development that have been called into question, but the concept of development itself, the very consideration of problems of long-term social development, of sociogenesis and psychogenesis. In a word, the baby has been thrown out with the bathwater.

The present study, which concerns itself once again with social processes, may be better understood if this development of theoretical sociology is kept in mind. The tendency to condemn the social ideologies of the nineteenth century from the standpoint of those of the twentieth appears to preclude the idea that long-term processes might be made the object of investigation without an ideological motive— that is, without the author, under the pretense of speaking of what is or was, speaking in reality of what he believes and wishes ought to be. If the present study has any significance at all, this results not least from its opposition to this mingling of what is and what ought to be, of scientific analysis and ideal. It points to the possibility of freeing the study of society from its bondage to social ideologies. This is not to say that an investigation of social problems which excludes political and philosophical ideas means renouncing the possibility of influencing the course of political events through the results of sociological research. The opposite is the case. The usefulness of sociological research as a tool of social practice is increased if the researcher does not deceive himself by projecting what he desires, what he believes ought to be, into his investigation of what is and has been.

VIII

To understand the blockage which the predominant modes of thinking and feeling place in the way of the investigation of long-term changes of social structure and personality structure—and thus in the way of an understanding of this book—it is not enough to trace the development of the image of men as societies, the image of society. It is also necessary to keep in mind the development of the image of men as individuals, the image of the personality. As has been mentioned, one of the peculiarities of the traditional image of man is that people often speak and think of individuals and societies as if these were two phenomena existing separately—of which, moreover, one is often considered "real" and the other "unreal"—instead of two different aspects of the same human being.

This curious aberration of thinking, too, cannot be understood without a glance at its implicit ideological content. The splitting of the image of humanity into an image of man as individual and an image of men as societies has widely ramifying roots. One branch is a very characteristic split in the values and ideals encountered, on close inspection, in all the more developed nation-states, and perhaps most pronounced in nations with a strong liberal tradition. In the development of the value systems of all such nation-states, one finds, on the one hand, a strand which sees society as a whole, the nation, as the highest value; and, on the other, a strand which posits the wholly self-sufficient, free individual, the "closed personality," as the highest value. It is not always easy to harmonize these two "highest values" with one another. There are situations in which the two ideals are plainly irreconcilable. But usually this problem is not squarely faced. People talk with great warmth of the freedom and independence of the individual, and with equal warmth of the freedom and independence of their own nation. The first ideal arouses the expectation that the individual member of a nation-state, despite his community and interdependence with others, can reach his decisions in an entirely self-sufficient way, without regard to others; the second arouses the expectation—fulfilled particularly in war but often enough in peacetime, too—that the individual should and must subordinate everything belonging to him, even his life, to the survival of the "social whole."

This split in the ideals, this contradiction in the ethos by which people are brought up, finds expression in the theories of sociology. Some of these theories take as their starting point the independent, self-sufficient individual as the "true" reality, and therefore as the true object of social science; others start with the independent social totality. Some theories attempt to harmonize the two conceptions, usually without indicating how it is possible to reconcile the idea of an absolutely independent and free individual with that of an equally independent and free "social totality," and often without clearly perceiving the problem. The reflection of this unresolved inner division between the two ideals is seen above all in the theories of sociologists whose national ideal has a conservative-liberal tinge. Max Weber's theoretical work—if not his empirical work—and the theories of his successor Talcott Parsons are examples of this.

It may suffice as illustration to return once more to what has already been said about Parsons's conception of the relation of individual and society, of the "individual actor" and the "social system." One description of their relation is contained in the metaphor of "interpenetration," which shows clearly the important role played by the idea of the separate existence of the two human aspects. The reification of the ideal therefore finds expression in this conceptual edifice not only in the notion of the social system as a specific ideal image of the nation, but also in that of the individual actor, the "ego," as an ideal image of the free individual existing independently of all others. In both cases the theorist's ideal image is changed unawares under his hands into a fact, something that actually exists. For with regard to the image of the individual, too, what in the mind of the theorist ought to be, the image of the absolutely free and independent individual, is treated as if it were the image of what the individual actually is.

Now this is certainly not the place to fathom the reasons for this widely disseminated split in thinking about human beings. But the concern of the present study cannot properly be understood so long as the problems of the civilizing process are approached with the notions of the individual that have just been mentioned. In the course of this process the structures of the individual human being are changed in a particular direction. This is what the concept of "civilization," in the factual sense in which it is used here, actually means. The image current today of the individual as an absolutely independent and self-sufficient being is difficult to reconcile with the facts adduced here. It obstructs understanding of the long-term processes which people undergo on both the individual and social planes. Parsons uses on occasion, to illustrate his image of the personality, the old metaphor of the personality of the human actor as a "black box,"[8] i.e., a closed container "inside" which certain individual processes take place. The metaphor is taken from the toolbox of psychology. It basically means that all that can be observed scientifically in a human being is his behavior. We can observe what the "black box" does. But what goes on inside the box, what is also termed the "soul" or "mind"—the "ghost in the machine," as an English philosopher called it[9]—is not an object of scientific investigation. One cannot avoid, in this context, exploring in more detail an image of the individual which plays a considerable role in the human sciences today and thus also contributes to the neglect of long-term changes in human beings in the course of social development as a subject of research.

The image of the individual as an entirely free, independent being, a "closed personality" who is "inwardly" quite self-sufficient and separate from all other people, has behind it a long tradition in the development of European societies. In classical philosophy this figure comes onto the scene as the epistemological subject. In this role, as *homo philosophicus,* the individual gains knowledge of the world "outside" him in a completely autonomous way. He does not need to learn, to take this knowledge from others. The fact that he came into the world as a child, the whole process of his development to adulthood and as an adult, is neglected as immaterial by this image of man. In the development of mankind it took many thousands of years for people to learn to understand the relations between natural events, the course of the stars, rain and sun, thunder and lightning, as manifestations of a blind, impersonal, purely mechanical and regular sequence of causal connections. But the "closed personality" of *homo philosophicus* apparently perceives this mechanical and regular causal chain as an adult simply by opening his eyes, without needing to learn anything about it from others, and quite independently of the stage of knowledge reached by society. The process—the individual human being as a process in growing up, human beings together as a process in the development of mankind—is reduced in thought to a state. The individual opens his eyes as an adult and not only recognizes autonomously here and now, without learning from others, what all these objects are that he perceives; he not only knows immediately what he is to classify as animate and inanimate, as mineral, vegetable, or animal; but he also knows directly here and now that they are linked causally in accordance with natural laws. The question for philosophers is merely whether he gains this knowledge of causal connections here and now on the basis of his experience—whether, in other words, these connections are a property of the observable facts "outside" him—or the connections are something rooted in the nature of human reason and superadded from "inside" the human being to what flows into him from "outside" through the sense organs. If we start from this image of man, from the *homo philosophicus* who was never a child and seemingly came into the world an adult, there is no way out of the epistemological impasse. Thought steers helplessly back and forth between the Scylla of positivism and the Charybdis of apriorism. It does so precisely because what is actually observable as a process, a development of the social macrocosm within which the development of the individual microcosm can also be observed, is reduced in thought to a state, an act of perception taking place here and now. We have here an example of how closely the inability to conceive long-term social processes (i.e., structured changes in the figurations formed by large numbers of interdependent human beings) or to understand the human beings forming such figurations is connected to a certain type of image of man and of self-perception. People to whom it seems self-evident that their own self (or their ego, or whatever else it may be called) exists, as it were, "inside" them, isolated from all the other people and things "outside," have difficulty assigning significance to all those facts which indicate that individuals live from the first in interdependence with others. They have difficulty conceiving people as relatively but not absolutely autonomous and interdependent individuals forming changeable figurations with one another. Since the former self-perception seems self-evident to those subscribing to it, they cannot easily take account of facts which show that this kind of perception is itself limited to particular societies, that it comes into being in conjunction with certain kinds of interdependencies, of social bonds between people—in short, that it is a structural peculiarity of a specific stage in the development of civilization, corresponding to a specific stage of differentiation and individualization of human groups. If one grows up in the midst of such a group, one cannot easily imagine that there could be people who do not experience themselves in this way as entirely self-sufficient individuals cut off from all other beings and things. This kind of self-perception appears as obvious, a symptom of an eternal human state, simply the normal, natural, and universal self-perception of all human beings. The conception of the individual as *homo clausus*, a little world in himself who ultimately exists quite independently of the great world outside, determines the image of man in general. Every other human being is likewise seen as a *homo clausus*; his core, his being, his true self appears likewise as something divided within him by an invisible wall from everything outside, including every other human being.

But the nature of this wall itself is hardly ever considered and never properly explained. Is the body the vessel which holds the true self locked within it? Is the skin the frontier between "inside" and "outside"? What in man is the capsule, and what the encapsulated? The experience of "inside" and "outside" seems so self-evident that such questions are scarcely ever posed; they seem to require no further examination. One is satisfied with the spatial metaphor of "inside" and "outside," but one makes no serious attempt to locate the "inner" in space; and although this omission to investigate one's own presuppositions is hardly appropriate to scientific procedure, this preconceived image of *homo clausus* commands the stage not only in society at large but also in the human sciences. Its derivatives include not only the traditional *homo philosophicus,* the image of man of classical epistemology, but also *homo oeconomicus, homo psychologicus, homo historicus,* and not least *homo sociologicus* in his present-day version. The images of the individual of Descartes, of Max Weber, and of Parsons and many other sociologists are of the same provenance. As philosophers did before them, many sociological theorists today accept this self-perception, and the image of the individual corresponding to it, as the untested basis of their theories. They do not detach themselves from it in order to confront it and call its aptness into question. Consequently, this kind of self-perception and image of the individual often coexists unchanged with attempts to abolish the reduction to states. In Parsons, for example, the static image of the ego, the individual actor, the adult abstracted from the process of growing up, coexists unmediated with the psychoanalytical ideas that he has taken over in his theory—ideas which relate not to the state of adulthood but to the process of becoming adult, to the individual as an open process in indissoluble interdependence with other individuals. As a result, the ideas of social theorists constantly find themselves in blind alleys from which there seems no way out. The individual—or, more precisely, what the present concept of the individual refers to—appears again and again as something existing "outside" society. What the concept of society refers to appears again and again as something existing outside and beyond individuals. One seems to have the choice only between theoretical approaches which present the individual as the truly existent beyond society, the truly "real" (society being seen as an abstraction, something not truly existing), and other theoretical approaches which posit society as a "system," a "social fact *sui generis*," a reality of a peculiar type beyond individuals. At most one can—as is occasionally done in an apparent solution to the problem—juxtapose the two conceptions unconnectedly, that of the individual as *homo clausus*, as ego, as individual beyond society, and that of society as a system outside and beyond individuals. But the incompatibility of these two conceptions is not thereby disposed of. In order to pass beyond this dead end of sociology and the social sciences in general, it is necessary to make clear the inadequacy of both conceptions, that of the individual outside society and, equally, that of a society outside individuals. This is difficult as long as the sense of the encapsulation of the self within itself serves as the untested basis of the image of the individual, and as long as, in conjunction with this, the concepts "individual" and "society" are understood as if they related to unchanging states.

The conceptual trap in which one is continually being caught by these static notions of "individual" and "society" can only be prized open if, as is done here, these notions are developed further, in conjunction with empirical investigations, in such a way that the two concepts are made to refer to processes. But this development is initially blocked by the extraordinary conviction carried in European societies since roughly the Renaissance by the self-perception of human beings in terms of their own isolation, the severance of their own "inside" from everything "outside." In Descartes the perception of the isolation of the individual, who finds himself confronted as a thinking ego within his own head by the entire external world, is somewhat weakened by the idea of God. In contemporary sociology the same basic experience finds theoretical expression in the acting ego, which finds itself confronted with people "outside" as "others." Apart from Leibnizian monadology, there is in this philosophico-sociological tradition scarcely a single approach to the problem that sets out from the basis of a multiplicity of interdependent human beings. Leibniz, who did just that, only managed to do so by bringing his version of *homo clausus*, the "windowless monads," in relation to one another by a metaphysical construction. All the same, monadology represents an early advance in the direction of precisely the kind of model that is urgently in need of further development in sociology today. The decisive step Leibniz took was an act of self-distantiation, which enabled him to entertain the idea that one might experience oneself not as an "ego" confronting all other people and things, but as a being among others. It was characteristic of the prevalent kind of experience in that whole period that the geocentric world-picture of the preceding age was superseded only in the area of inanimate nature by a world-picture demanding from the subject of experience a higher degree of self-detachment, a removal of oneself from the center. In men's reflection on themselves the geocentric world-picture was to a large extent preserved in the egocentric one that replaced it. At the center of the human universe, or so it appeared, stood each single human being as an individual completely independent of all others.

Nothing is more characteristic of the unquestioning way in which even today, in thinking about human beings, the separate individual is taken as the starting point than the fact that one does not speak of *homines sociologiae* or *oeconomiae* when talking of the image of man in the social sciences, but always of the image of the single human being, the *homo sociologicus* or *oeconomicus*. From this conceptual starting point, society presents itself finally as a collection of individuals completely independent of each other, whose true essence is locked within them and who therefore communicate only externally and from the surface. One must call on the help of a metaphysical solution, as Leibniz did, if, starting from windowless, closed, human and extrahuman monads, one is to justify the notion that interdependence and communication between them, or the perception by human beings of interdependence and communications, are possible. Whether we are dealing with human beings in their role as "subject" confronting the "object," or in their role as "individual" confronting "society," in both cases the problem is presented as if an adult human being, completely isolated and self-sufficient—that is, in a form reflecting the prevalent self-perception of people in the modern age crystallized in an objectifying concept—constitutes the frame of reference. What is discussed is his relation to something "outside" himself conceived (like the isolated human being) as a state, to "nature" or to "society." Does this something exist? Or is it only produced by a mental process, or at any rate founded primarily on a mental process?

IX

Let us try to make clear what the problem actually is that is being discussed here. We are not concerned with calling into doubt the authenticity of the self-perception that finds expression in the image of man as *homo clausus* and its many variations. The question is whether this self-perception, and the image of man in which it is usually crystallized quite spontaneously and without reflection, can serve as a reliable starting point for an attempt to gain adequate understanding of human beings—and therefore also of oneself—regardless of whether this attempt is philosophical or sociological. Is it justified—that is the question—to place at the foundation of philosophical theories of perception and knowledge, and of sociological and other theories in the human sciences, as a self-evident assumption incapable of further explanation, the sharp dividing line between what is "inside" man and the "external world," a division which often appears directly given in self-awareness, and furthermore has put down deep roots in European intellectual and linguistic traditions, without a critical and systematic examination of its validity?

This conception has had, for a certain period of human development, an extraordinary persistence. It is found in the writings of all groups whose powers of reflection and whose self-awareness have reached the stage at which people are in a position not only to think but also to be conscious of themselves, and to reflect on themselves, as thinking beings. It is already found in Platonic philosophy and in a number of other schools of philosophy in antiquity. The idea of the "self in a case," as already mentioned, is one of the recurrent *leitmotifs* of modern philosophy, from the thinking subject of Descartes, Leibniz's windowless monads, and the Kantian subject of knowledge (who from his aprioristic shell can never quite break through to the "thing in itself") to the more recent extension of the same basic idea of the entirely self-sufficient individual: beyond the perspective of thought and perception as reified into "understanding" (*Verstand*) and "reason" (*Vernunft*), to the whole "being" of man, his "existence" in the various versions of existentialist philosophy; or to his action as the starting point of the social theory of Max Weber, for example, who—entirely in keeping with the above-mentioned split—made the not wholly successful attempt to distinguish between "social action" and "nonsocial action," i.e., presumably "purely individual action."

But one would gain only a very inadequate idea of the nature of this self-perception and this image of man if they were understood merely as ideas set forth in scholarly writings. The windowlessness of the monads, the problems surrounding *homo clausus*, which a man like Leibniz tries to make at least more bearable by a speculative solution showing the possibility of relationships between monads, is today accepted as self-evident not only by scholars. Expressions of this self-perception are found in a less reflected form in imaginative literature—for example, in Virginia Woolf's lament over the incommunicability of experience as the cause of human solitude. Its expression is found in the concept of "alienation," used more and more frequently within and outside literature in the most diverse variations in recent decades. It would be not uninteresting to ascertain more systematically whether and how far gradations and variations of this type of self-perception extend to the various elite groups and the broader strata of more developed societies. But the examples cited suffice to indicate how persistent and how much taken for granted in the societies of modern Europe is the feeling of people that their own "self," their "true identity," is something locked away "inside" them, severed from all other people and things "outside"—although, as has been mentioned, no one finds it particularly simple to show clearly where and what the tangible walls or barriers are which enclose this inner self as a vessel encloses its contents, and separate it from what is "outside." Are we here concerned, as it often appears, with an eternal, fundamental experience of all human beings accessible to no further explanation, or with a type of self-perception which is characteristic of a certain stage in the development of the figurations formed by people, and of the people forming these figurations?

In the context of this book the discussion of this complex of problems has a twofold significance. On the one hand, the civilizing process cannot be understood so long as one clings to this type of self-perception and regards the image of man as *homo clausus* as self-evident, not open to discussion as a source of problems. On the other hand, the theory of civilization developed in this study offers a procedure for solving these problems. The discussion of this image of man serves in the first place to improve understanding of the ensuing study of the civilizing process. It is possible, however, that one might gain a better understanding of this introductory discussion from the vantage point of the end of the book, from a more comprehensive picture of the civilizing process. It will suffice here to indicate briefly the connection between the problems arising from the concept of *homo clausus* and the civilizing process.

One can gain a clear idea ot this connection relatively simply by first looking back at the change in people's self-perception that was influenced by the abandonment of the geocentric world-picture. Often this transition is presented simply as a revision and extension of knowledge about the movements of the stars. But it is obvious that this changed conception of the figurations of the stars would not have been possible had not the prevailing image of man been seriously shaken on its own account, had not people become capable of perceiving themselves in a different light than before. Of primary importance for human beings everywhere is a mode of experience by which they place themselves at the center of public events, not just as individuals but as groups. The geocentric world-picture is the expression of this spontaneous and unreflecting self-centeredness of men, which is still encountered unequivocally today in the ideas of people outside the realm of nature, e.g., in natiocentric sociological modes of thought or those centered on the isolated individual.

The geocentric experience is still accessible to everyone as a plane of perception even today. It merely does not constitute the dominant plane of perception in public thought. When we say, and indeed "see," that the sun rises in the east and goes down in the west, we spontaneously experience ourselves and the earth on which we live as the center of the cosmos, as the frame of reference for the movements of the stars. It was not simply new discoveries, a cumulative increase in knowledge about the objects of human reflection, that were needed to make possible the transition from a geocentric to a heliocentric world-picture. What was needed above all was an increased capacity in men for self-detachment in thought. Scientific modes of thought cannot be developed and become generally accepted unless people renounce their primary, unreflecting, and spontaneous attempt to understand all their experience in terms of its purpose and meaning for themselves. The development that led to more adequate knowledge and increasing control of nature was therefore, considered from one aspect, also a development toward greater self-control by men.

It is not possible to go into more detail here about the connections between the development of the scientific manner of acquiring knowledge of objects, on the one hand, and the development of new attitudes of men toward themselves, new personality structures, and especially shifts in the direction of greater affect control and self-detachment, on the other. Perhaps it will contribute to an understanding of these problems if one recalls the spontaneous, unreflecting self-centeredness of thought that can be observed at any time among children in our own society. A heightened control of the affects, developed in society and learned by the individual, and above all a heightened degree of autonomous affect control, was needed in order for the world-picture centered on the earth and the people living on it to be overcome by one which, like the heliocentric world-picture, agreed better with the observable facts but was at first far less satisfying emotionally; for it removed man from his position at the center of the universe and placed him on one of many planets circling about the center. The transition from an understanding of nature legitimized by a traditional faith to one based on scientific research, and the shift in the direction of greater affect control that this transition involved, thus represents one aspect of the civilizing process examined from other aspects in the following study.

But at that particular stage in the development of these more object-related than self-related conceptual instruments for exploring extra-human nature, it was apparently not possible to include in the investigation, and to reflect upon, this civilizational shift itself, the move toward stronger and more "internalized" self-control that was taking place within man himself. What was happening to human beings as they increased their understanding of nature remained at first inaccessible to scientific insight. It is not a little characteristic of this stage of self-consciousness that the classical theories of knowledge representing it are concerned far more with the problems of the object of knowledge than with the subject of knowledge, with object-perception than with self-perception. But if the latter is not included from the start in posing epistemological problems, then this very posing leads to an impasse of equally inadequate alternatives.

The development of the idea that the earth circles round the sun in a purely mechanical way in accordance with natural laws—that is, in a way not in the least determined by any purpose relating to mankind, and therefore no longer possessing any great emotional significance for men—presupposed and demanded at the same time a development in human beings themselves toward increased emotional control, a greater restraint of their spontaneous feeling that everything they experience and everything that concerns them takes its stamp from them, is the expression of an intention, a destiny, a purpose relating to themselves. Now, in the age that we call "modern," men reach a stage of self-detachment that enables them to conceive of natural processes as an autonomous sphere operating without intention or purpose or destiny in a purely mechanical or causal way, and having a meaning or purpose for themselves only if they are in a position, through objective knowledge, to control it and thereby give it a meaning and a purpose. But at this stage they are not yet able to detach themselves sufficiently from themselves to make their own self-detachment, their own affect restraint—in short, the conditions of their own role as the subject of the scientific understanding of nature—the object of knowledge and scientific enquiry.

Herein lies one of the keys to the question of why the problem of scientific knowledge took on the form of classical European epistemology familiar today. The detachment of the thinking subject from his objects in the act of cognitive thought, and the affective restraint that is demanded, did not appear to those thinking about it at this stage as an act of distancing but as a distance actually present, as an eternal condition of spatial separation between a mental apparatus apparently locked "inside" man, an "understanding" or "reason," and the objects "outside" and divided from it by an invisible wall.

If we saw earlier how ideals can turn unawares in thought into something actually existing, how "ought" becomes "is," we are here confronted with a reification of a different kind. The act of conceptual distancing from the objects of thought that any more emotionally controlled reflection involves—which scientific observations and thought demand in particular, and which at the same time makes them possible—appears to self-perception at this stage as a distance actually existing between the thinking subject and the objects of his thought. And the greater restraint of affect-charged impulses in the face of the objects of thought and observation, which accompanies every step toward increased conceptual distancing, appears here in people's self-perception as an actually existing cage which separates and excludes the "self" or "reason" or "existence," depending on the point of view, from the world "outside" the individual.

The fact that, and in part the reason why, from the late Middle Ages and the early Renaissance on, there was a particularly strong shift in individual self-control—above all, in self-control acting independently of external agents as a self-activating automatism, revealingly said today to be "internalized"—is presented in more detail from other perspectives in the following study. The transformation of interpersonal external compulsion into individual internal compulsion, which now increasingly takes place, leads to a situation in which many affective impulses cannot be lived out as spontaneously as before. The autonomous individual self-controls produced in this way in social life, such as "rational thought" or the "moral conscience," now interpose themselves more sternly than ever before between spontaneous and emotional impulses, on the one hand, and the skeletal muscles, on the other, preventing the former with greater severity from directly determining the latter (i.e., action) without the permission of these control mechanisms.

That is the core of the structural change and the structural peculiarities of the individual which are reflected in self-perception, from about the Renaissance onward, in the notion of the individual "ego" in its locked case, the "self" divided by an invisible wall from what happens "outside." It is these civilizational self-controls, functioning in part automatically, that are now experienced in individual self-perception as a wall, either between "subject" and "object" or between one's own "self" and other people ("society").

The shift in the direction of greater individualization that took place during the Renaissance is well enough known. This study gives a somewhat more detailed picture of this development in terms of personality structure. At the same time, it points to connections that have not yet been properly clarified. The transition from the experience of nature as landscape standing opposed to the observer, from the experience of nature as a perceptual object separated from its subject as if by an invisible wall; the transition from the intensified self-perception of the individual as an entirely self-sufficient entity independent and cut off from other people and things—these and many other phenomena of the time bear the structural characteristics of the same civilizational shift. They all show marks of the transition to a further stage of self-consciousness at which the inbuilt self-control of the affects grows stronger and reflective detachment greater, while the spontaneity of affective action diminishes, and at which people feel these peculiarities of themselves but do not yet detach themselves sufficiently from them in thought to make themselves the object of investigation.

We thus come somewhat closer to the center of the structure of the individual personality underlying the self-experience of *homo clausus.* If we ask once again what really gives rise to this concept of the individual as encapsulated "inside" himself, severed from everything existing outside him, and what the capsule and the encapsulated really stand for in human terms, we can now see the direction in which the answer must be sought. The firmer, more comprehensive and uniform restraint of the affects characteristic of this civilizational shift, together with the increased internal compulsions that, more implacably than before, prevent all spontaneous impulses from manifesting themselves directly and motorically in action, without the intervention of control mechanisms—these are what is experienced as the capsule, the invisible wall dividing the "inner world" of the individual from the "external world" or, in different versions, the subject of cognition from its object, the "ego" from the "other," the "individual" from "society." What is encapsulated are the restrained instinctual and affective impulses denied direct access to the motor apparatus. They appear in self-perception as what is hidden from all others, and often as the true self, the core of individuality. The term "the inner man" is a convenient metaphor, but it is a metaphor that misleads.

There is good reason for saying that the human brain is situated within the skull and the heart within the rib cage. In these cases we can say clearly what is the container and what is contained, what is located within walls and what outside, and of what the dividing walls consist.

But if the same figures of speech are applied to personality structures they become inappropriate. The relation of instinct controls to instinctive impulses, to mention only one example, is not a spatial relationship. The former do not have the form of a vessel containing the latter within it. There are schools of thought that consider the control mechanisms, conscience or reason, as more important, and there are others which attach greater importance to instinctual or emotional impulses. But if we are not disposed to argue about values, if we restrict our efforts to the investigation of what is, we find that there is no structural feature of man that justifies our calling one thing the core of man and another the shell. Strictly speaking, the whole complex of tensions, such as feeling and thought, or spontaneous behavior and controlled behavior, consists of human activities. If instead of the usual substance-concepts like "feeling" and "reason" we use activity-concepts, it is easier to understand that while the image of "outside" and "inside," of the shell of a receptacle containing something inside it, is applicable to the physical aspects of a human being mentioned above, it cannot apply to the structure of the personality, to the living human being as a whole. On this level there is nothing that resembles a container—nothing that could justify metaphors like that of the "inside" of a human being. The intuition of a wall, of something "inside" man separated from the "outside" world, however genuine it may be as an intuition, corresponds to nothing in man having the character of a real wall. One recalls that Goethe once expressed the idea that nature has neither core nor shell and that in her there is neither inside nor outside. This is true of human beings as well.

On the one hand, therefore, the theory of civilization which the following study attempts to develop helps us to see the misleading image of man in what we call the modern age as less self-evident, and to detach ourselves from it, so that work can begin on an image of man oriented less by one's own feelings and the value judgments attached to them than by men as the actual objects of thought and observation. On the other hand, a critique of the modern image of man is needed for an understanding of the civilizing process. For in the course of this process the structure of individual human beings changes; they become "more civilized." And so long as we see the individual human being as by nature a closed container with an outer shell and a core concealed within it, we cannot comprehend how a civilizing process embracing many generations is possible, in the course of which the personality structure of the individual human being changes without the nature of human beings changing.

This must suffice here as an introduction to the reorientation of individual self-consciousness and to the resulting development of the image of man, without which any ability to conceive a civilizing process or a long-term process involving social and personality structures is largely blocked. So long as the concept of the individual is linked with the self-perception of the "ego" in a closed case, we can hardly conceive "society" as anything other than a collection of windowless monads. Concepts like "social structure," "social process," or "social development" then appear at best as artificial products of sociologists, as "ideal-typical" constructions needed by scientists to introduce some order, at least in thought, into what appears in reality to be a completely disordered and structureless accumulation of absolutely independent individual agents.

As can be seen, the actual state of affairs is the exact converse. The notion of individuals deciding, acting, and "existing" in absolute independence of one another is an artificial product of men which is characteristic of a particular stage in the development of their self-perception. It rests partly on a confusion of ideals and facts, and partly on a reification of individual self-control mechanisms—of the severance of individual affective impulses from the motor apparatus, from the direct control of bodily movements and actions.

This self-perception in terms of one's own isolation, of the invisible wall dividing one's own "inner" self from all the people and things "outside," takes on for a large number of people in the course of the modern age the same immediate force of conviction that the movement of the sun around an earth situated at the center of the cosmos possessed in the Middle Ages. Like the geocentric picture of the physical universe earlier, the egocentric image of the social universe is certainly capable of being conquered by a more realistic, if emotionally less appealing picture. The emotion may or may not remain: it is an open question how far the feeling of isolation and alienation is attributable to ineptitude and ignorance in the development of individual self-controls, and how far to structural characteristics of advanced societies. Just as the public predominance of emotionally less appealing images of a physical universe not centered on the earth did not entirely efface the more private self-centered experience of the sun as circling around the earth, the ascendancy of a more objective image of man in public thinking may not necessarily efface the more private ego-centered experience of an invisible wall dividing one's own "inner world" from the world "outside." But it is certainly not impossible to dislodge this experience, and the image of man corresponding to it, from its self-evident acceptance in research in the human sciences. Here and in what follows one can see at least the beginnings of an image of man that agrees better with unhindered observations of human beings, and for this reason facilitates access to problems which, like those of the civilizing process or the state-building process, remain more or less inaccessible from the standpoint of the old image of man, or which, like the problem of the relation of individuals to society, continually give rise from that standpoint to unnecessarily complicated and never entirely convincing solutions.

The image of man as a "closed personality" is here replaced by the image of man as an "open personality" who possesses a greater or lesser degree of relative (but never absolute and total) autonomy vis-à-vis other people and who is, in fact, fundamentally oriented toward and dependent on other people throughout his life. The network of interdependencies among human beings is what binds them together. Such interdependencies are the nexus of what is here called the figuration, a structure of mutually oriented and dependent people. Since people are more or less dependent on each other first by nature and then through social learning, through education, socialization, and socially generated reciprocal needs, they exist, one might venture to say, only as pluralities, only in figurations. That is why, as was stated earlier, it is not particularly fruitful to conceive of men in the image of the individual man. It is more appropriate to envisage an image of numerous interdependent people forming figurations (i.e., groups or societies of different kinds) with each other. Seen from this basic standpoint, the rift in the traditional image of man disappears. The concept of the figuration has been introduced precisely because it expresses what we call "society" more clearly and unambiguously than the existing conceptual tools of sociology, as neither an abstraction of attributes of individuals existing without a society, nor a "system" or "totality" beyond individuals, but the network of interdependencies formed by individuals. It is certainly quite possible to speak of a social system formed of individuals. But the undertones associated with the concept of the social system in contemporary sociology make such an expression seem forced. Furthermore, the concept of the system is prejudiced by the associated notion of immutability.

What is meant by the concept of the figuration can be conveniently explained by reference to social dances. They are, in fact, the simplest example that could be chosen. One should think of a mazurka, a minuet, a polonaise, a tango, or rock 'n'roll. The image of the mobile figurations of interdependent people on a dance floor perhaps makes it easier to imagine states, cities, families, and also capitalist, communist, and feudal systems as figurations. By using this concept we can eliminate the antithesis, resting finally on different values and ideals, immanent today in the use of the words "individual" and "society." One can certainly speak of a dance in general, but no one will imagine a dance as a structure outside the individual or as a mere abstraction. The same dance figurations can certainly be danced by different people; but without a plurality of reciprocally oriented and dependent individuals, there is no dance. Like every other social figuration, a dance figuration is relatively independent of the specific individuals forming it here and now, but not of individuals as such. It would be absurd to say that dances are mental constructions abstracted from observations of individuals considered separately. The same applies to all other figurations. Just as the small dance figurations change— becoming now slower, now quicker—so too, gradually or more suddenly, do the large figurations which we call societies. The following study is concerned with such changes. Thus, the starting point of the study of the process of state formation is a figuration made up of numerous relatively small social units existing in free competition with one another. The investigation shows how and why this figuration changes. It demonstrates at the same time that there are explanations which do not have the character of causal explanations. For a change in a figuration is explained partly by the endogenous dynamic of the figuration itself, the immanent tendency of a figuration of freely competing units to form monopolies. The investigation therefore shows how in the course of centuries the original figuration changes into another, in which such great opportunities of monopoly power are linked with a single social position—kingship—that no occupant of any other social position within the network of interdependencies can compete with the monarch. At the same time, it indicates how the personality structures of human beings also change in conjunction with such figurational changes .

Many questions that deserve consideration in an introduction have had to be left aside here; otherwise, the introduction would have become a separate volume. Limited as they are, however, these reflections show perhaps that an understanding of the following study requires a fairly extensive reorientation in the sociological thought and imagination predominant today. To detach oneself from the idea of oneself and of every individual human being as *homo clausus* is certainly not easy. But without detachment from this notion, one cannot possibly understand what is meant when a civilizing process is referred to as a transformation of individual structures. Similarly, it is not easy so to develop one's own imaginative capacity that one is able to think in figurations, and, moreover, in figurations whose normal characteristics include a tendency to change, sometimes even in a specific direction.

In this introduction I have endeavored to discuss some fundamental problems which, had they not been discussed, would have stood in the way of an understanding of this book. The ideas expressed are not all simple, but I have attempted to present them as simply as I could. I hope they may facilitate and deepen the understanding, and perhaps also the pleasure, afforded by this book.

Leicester   N.E.
July, 1968

Appendix II

Foreign Language Originals of the Exemplary Extracts and Verses

Medieval Manners
(p. 60)

"Dem vrumen soltu volgen,
dem boesen wis erbolgen."[8]

"Svenne dîn gesinde dich
erzürne, lieber sun, sô sich
daz dir werde iht sô gâch
daz dich geriuve dar nâch."[9]

"Kein edeler man selbander sol
mit einem leffel sufen niht;
daz zimet hübschen liuten wol,
den dicke unedellich geschiht."[10]

"Sümliche bizent ab der sniten
und stozents in die schüzzel wider
nach geburischen siten;
sülh unzuht legent diu hübschen niden."[11]

"Etlicher ist also gemuot,
swenn er daz bein genagen hat,
daz erz wider in die schüzzel tuot;
daz habet gar für missetat."[12]

"Der riuspet, swenne er ezzen sol,
und in daz tischlach sniuzet sich,
diu beide ziment niht gar wol,
als ich des kan versehen mich."[13]

"Swer ob tem tische sniuzet sich,
ob er ez ribet an die hant,

der ist ein gouch, versihe ich mich,
dem ist niht besser zuht bekannt.''[14]

"Swer snudet als ein wazzerdahs,
so er izzet, als etlicher phliget,
und smatzet als ein Beiersahs,
wie gar der sich der zuht verwiget.''[15]

"Ir sült die kel ouch jucken niht,
so ir ezrt, mit blozer hant;
ob ez aber also geschiht,
so nemet hovelich daz gewant.''[16]

"In diu oren grifen niht enzimt
und ougen, als etlicher tuot,
swer den unflat von der nasen nimt,
so er izzet, diu driu sint niht guot.''[17]

"ich hoere von sümlichen sagen
(ist daz war, daz zimet übel),
daz si ezzen ungetwagen;
den selben müezen erlamen die knübel.''[18]

"man sol ouch ezzen alle frist
mit der hant diu engegen ist;
sitzt der gesell ze der rehten hant,
mit der tenken iz zehant;
man sol sich geren wenden
daz man ezz mit beiden henden.''[20]

"Schaffe vor swaz dir sî nôt
daz du iht sitzest schamerôt.''[22]

The Problem of the Change of Behavior at the Renaissance
(p. 70)

"Ne mangue mie je te commande,
avant que on serve de viande,
car il sembleroit que tu feusses
trop glout, ou que trop fain eüsses.''
....
"Vuiddier et essever memoire
aies ta bouche, quant veulz boire.''[32]

On Behavior at Table
(p. 84)

A.

Thirteenth century

Daz ist des tanhausers getiht und ist guod hofzuht.

1   Er dünket mich ein zühtic man,
der alle zuht erkennen kan,
der keine unzuht nie gewan
und im der zühte nie zeran.

2   Der zühte der ist also vil
und sint ze manegen dingen guot;
nu wizzent, der in volgen wil,
daz er vil selten missetuot.
....

25   Swenne ir ezzt, so sit gemant,
daz ir vergezzt der armen niht;
so wert ir gote vil wol erkant,
ist daz den wol von iu geschiht.

On v. 25 c.f. the first rule of Bonvicino da Riva:

La primiera è questa:
che quando tu è a mensa,
del povero bexognoxo
imprimamenté inpensa.

From *Ein spruch der ze tische kêrt:*

313   Mit der schüzzel man niht sûfen sol,
mit einem lefel, daz stât wol.

315   Swer sich über die schüzzel habt,
und unsüberlicben snabt
mit dem munde, als ein swin,
der sol bi anderm vihe sîn.

33   Kein edeler man selbander sol
mit einem leffel sufen niht;
daz zimet hübschen liuten wol,
den dicke unedellich geschiht.

37   Mit schüzzeln sufen niemen zimt,
swie des unfuor doch maneger lobe,
der si frevellichen nimt
und in sich giuzet, als er tobe.

41   Und der sich über die schüzzel habet,
     so er izzet, als ein swin,
     und gar unsuberliche snabet,
     und smatzet mit dem munde sin . . .

45   Sümliche bizent ab der sniten
     und stozents in die schüzzel wider

319   swer sniubet als ein lahs,
     unde smatzet als ein dahs,
     und rüsset sô er ezzen sol,
     diu driu dinc ziment niemor wol.

In the *Curtesien* of Bonvicino da Riva:

     La sedexena apresso con veritae:
     No sorbilar dra bocha quando tu mangi con cugial;
     Quello fa sicom bestia, chi con cugial sorbilia
     Chi doncha à questa usanza, ben fa s'el se dispolia.

         or

In *The Book of nurture and school of good manners:*

201   And suppe not lowde of thy Pottage
     no tyme in all thy lyfe.

On v. 45 c.f. *Ein spruch der ze tische kêrt:*

346   Swer diu bein benagen hât,
     und wider in die schüzzel tuot,
     dâ sîn die höveschen vor behuot.

         or

From *Quisquis es in mensa:*

     In disco racta non sit bucella redacta.

     nach geburischen siten;
     sülh unzuht legent die hübschen nider.

49   Etlicher ist also gemuot,
     swenn er daz bein genagen hat,
     daz erz wider in die schüzzel tuot;
     daz habet gar für missetat.

53   Die senf und salsen ezzent gern,
     die sulen des vil flizic sin,
     daz si den unflat verbern
     und stozen niht die vinger drin.

57   Der riuspet, swenne er ezzen sol,
     und in daz tischlach sniuzet sich,
     diu beide ziment niht gar wol,
     als ich des kan versehen mich.

---

65   Der beide reden und ezzen wil,
        diu zwei werc mit einander tuon,
        und in dem slaf wil reden vil,
        der kan vil selten wol geruon.

69   Ob dem tische lat daz brehten sin,
        so ir ezzet, daz sümliche tuont,
        dar an gedenkent, friunde min,
        daz nie kein site so übele stuont.

        ....

81   Ez dünket mich groz missetat,
        an sweme ich die unzuht sihe,
        der daz ezzen in dem munde hat
        und die wile trinket als ein vihe.

85   Ir sült niht blasen in den tranc,
        des spulgent sümeliche gern;
        daz ist ein ungewizzen danc,
        der unzuht solte man enbern.

94   E daz ir trinkt, so wischt den munt,
        daz ir besmalzet niht den tranc;
        diu hovezuht wol zimt alle stunt
        und ist ein hovelich gedanc.

105   Und die sich uf den tisch legent,
        so si ezzent, daz enstet niht wol;
        wie selten die die helme wegent,
        da man frouwen dienen sol.

109   Ir sült die kel ouch jucken niht,
        so ir ezzt, mit blozer hant;
        ob ez aber also geschiht,
        so nemet hovelich daz gewant.

113   Und jucket da mit, daz zimt baz,
        denn iu diu hant unsuber wirt;
        die zuokapher merkent daz,
        swer sülhe unzuht niht verbirt.

117   Ir sült die zende stüren niht
        mit mezzern, als etlicher tuot,
        und als mit manegem noch geschiht;
        swer des phliget, daz ist niht guot.

125   Swer ob dem tisch des wenet sich,
        daz er die gürtel witer lat,
        so wartent sicherliche uf mich,
        er ist niht visch biz an den grat.

129   Swer ob dem tische sniuzet sich,
ob er ez ribet an die hant,
der ist ein gouch, versihe ich mich,
dem ist niht bezzer zuht bekant.

141   Ich hoere von sümlichen sagen
(ist daz war, daz zimet übel),
daz si ezzen ungetwagen;
den selben müezen erlamen die knübel!

157   In diu oren grifen niht enzimt
und ougen, als etlicher tuot,
swer den unflat von der nasen nimt,
so er izzet, diu driu sint niht guot.

B.

Fifteenth century

From *S'ensuivent les contenances de la table*:

I

Enfant qui veult estre courtoys
Et à toutes gens agreable,
Et principalement à table,
Garde ces rigles en françois.

II

Enfant soit de copper soigneux
Ses ongles, et oster l'ordure,
Car se l'ordure il y endure,
Quant ilz se grate yert roingneux.

III

Enfant d'honneur, lave tes mains
A ton lever, à ton disner,
Et puis au supper sans finer;
Ce sont trois foys à tous le moins.

XII

Enfant, se tu es bien sçavant,
Ne mès pas ta main le premier
Au plat, mais laisse y toucher
Le maistre de l'hostel avant.

XIII

Enfant, gardez que le morseau
Que tu auras mis en ta bouche
Par une fois, jamais n'atouche,
Ne soit remise en ton vaisseau.

XIV

Enfant, ayes en toy remors
De t'en garder, se y as failly,

Et ne presentes à nulluy
Le morseau que tu auras mors.

XV

Enfant, garde toy de maschier
En ta bouche pain ou viande,
Oultre que ton cuer ne demande,
Et puis apres le recrascher.

XVII

Enfant, garde qu'en la saliere
Tu ne mettes point tes morseaulx
Pour les saler, ou tu deffaulx,
Car c'est deshonneste maniere.

XXIV

Enfant, soyes tousjours paisible,
Doulx, courtois, bening, amiable,
Entre ceulx qui sierront à table
Et te gardes d'estre noysibles.

XXVI

Enfant, se tu faiz en ton verre
Souppes de vin aucunement,
Boy tout le vin entierement,
ou autrement le gecte à terre.

XXXI

Enfant se tu veulx en ta pence
Trop excessivement bouter
Tu seras constraint à rupter
Et perdre toute contenance.

XXXIV

Enfant garde toy de frotter
Ensamble tes mains, ne tes bras
Ne à la nappe, ne aux draps
A table on ne se doit grater.

C.

1530

From *De civilitate morum puerilium*, by Erasmus of Rotterdam:

Mantile si datur, aut humero sinistro aut bracchio laevo imponito.

Cum honoratioribus accubiturus, capite prexo, pileum relinquito.

A dextris sit poculum et cultellus escarius rite purgatus, ad laevam panis.

Quidam ubi vix bene consederint, mox manus in epulas conjiciunt. Id luporum est . . .

Primus cibum appositum ne attingito, non tantum ob id quod arguit avidum, sed quod interdum cum periculo conjunctum est, dum qui fervidum inexploratum recipit in os, aut expuere cogitur, aut si deglutiat, adurere gulam, utroque ridiculus aeque ac miser.

Aliquantisper morandum, ut puer assuescat affectui temperare.

Digitos in jusculenta immergere, agrestium est: sed cultello fuscinave tollat quod vult, nec id ex toto eligat disco, quod solent liguritores, sed quod forte ante ipsum jacet, sumat.

Quod digitis excipi non potest, quadra excipiendum est.

Si quis e placenta vel artorcrea porrexit aliquid, cochleari aut quadra excipe, aut cochleare porrectum accipe, et inverso in quadram cibo, cochleare reddito.

Si liquidius est quod datur, gustandum sumito et cochleare reddito, sed ad mantile extersum.

Digitos unctos vel ore praelingere, vel ad tunicam, extergere, pariter incivile est: id mappa potius aut mantili faciendum.

D.

1558

From *Galateo*, by Giovanni della Casa, Archbishop of Benevento, quoted from the five-language edition (Geneva, 1609), p. 68:

Was meynstu würde dieser Bischof und seine edle Gesellschaft (il Vescove e la sua nobile brigata) denen gesagt haben, die wir bisweilen sehen wie die Säwe mit dem rüssel in der suppen ligen und ihr gesicht nit einmal auffheben und ihre augen, viel weniger die hände nimmermehr von der speise abwenden, die alle beyde backen auffblasen gleich als ob sie in die Trommete bliesen oder ein fewer auffblasen wolten, die nicht essen sondern fressen und die kost einschlingen, die ihre Hände bey nahe bis an den Elbogen beschmutzen und demnach die servieten also zu richten, dass unflätige küchen oder wischlumpen viel reiner sein möchten.

Dennoch schämen sich diese unfläter nit mit solchen besudelten servieten ohn unterlass den schweiss abzuwischen (der dann von wegen ihrs eilenden und ubermessigen fressens von irem haüpt über die stirn und das angesicht bis auff den hals häufig herunter trüpffet) ja auch wol die Nase so offt es inen gelicht darin zu schneutzen.

E.

1560

From a *Civilité* by C. Calviac:

L'enfant estant assis, s'il ha une serviette devant luy sur son assiette, il la prendra et la mettra sur son bras ou espaule gauche, puis il mettra son pain de costé gauche, le cousteau du costé droit, comme le verre aussi, s'il le veut laisser sur la table, et qu'il ait la commodité de l'y tenir sans offenser personne. Car il pourra advenir qu'on ne sçaurait tenir le verre à table ou du costé droit sans empescher par ce moyen quelqu'un.

Il fault que l'enfant ait la discrétion de cognoistre les circonstances du lieu où il sera. En mangeant . . . il doit prendre le premier qui luy viendra en main de son tranchoir.

Que s'il y a des sauces, l'enfant y pourra . . . tremper honnestement et sans tourner de l'autre costé après qu'il l'aura tremper de l'un . . .

Il est bien nécessaire à l'enfant qu'il apprenne dès sa jeunesse à despécer un gigot, une perdrix, un lapin et choses semblables.

C'est une chose par trop ords que l'enfant présente une chose après l'avoir rongée, ou celle qu'il ne daigneroit manger, si ce n'est à son serviteur.

Il n'est non plus honneste de tirer par la bouche quelque chose qu'on aura jà mâchée, et la mettre sur le tranchoir; si ce n'est qu'il advienne que quelquefoys il succe la moelle de quelque petit os, comme par manière de passe temps en attendant la desserte, car après l'avoir succé il le doit mettre sur son assiette, comme aussi les os des cerises et des prunes et semblables, pour ce qu'il n'est point bon de les avaler ny de les jecter à terre.

L'enfant ne doit point ronger indécentement les os, comme font les chiens.

Quant l'enfant voudra du sel, il en prendra avec la poincte de son cousteau et non point avec les trois doigs;

Il faut que l'enfant couppe sa chair en menus morceaux sur son tranchoir . . . et ne faut point qu'il porte la viande à la bouche tantost d'une main, tantost de l'autre, comme les petits qui commencent à manger; mais que tousjours il le face, avec la main droicte, en prenant honnestement le pain ou la chair avec troys doigs seulement.

Quant à la manière de mâcher, elle est diverse selon les lieux ou pays où on est. Car les Allemans mâchent la bouche close, et trouvent laid de faire autrement. Les Françoys au contraire ouvrent à demy la bouche, et trouvent la procédure des Allemans peu ord. Les Italiens y procèdent fort mollement, et les François plus rondement et en sorte qu'ils trouvent la procédure des Italiens trop délicate et précieuse.

Et ainsi chacune nation ha quelque chose de propre et différent des autres. Pourquoy l'enfant y pourra procéder selon les lieux et coustumes d'iceux où il sera.

Davantage les Allemans usent de culières en mangeant leur potage et toutes les choses liquides, et les Italiens des fourchettes. Et les Françoys de l'un et de l'autre, selon que bon leur semble et qu'ilz en ont la commodité. Les Italiens se plaisent aucunement à avoir chacun son cousteau. Mais les Allemans ont cela en singulière recommandation, et tellement qu'on leur fait grand desplaisir de le prendre devant eux ou de leur demander. Les François au contraire: toute une pleine table de personnes se servont de deux ou trois cousteaux, sans faire difficulté de le demander, ou prendre, ou le bailler s'ilz l'ont. Par quoy, s'il advient que quelqu'un demande son cousteau à l'enfant, il luy doit bailler après l'avoir nettoyé à sa serviette, en tenant la poincte en sa main et présentant le manche à celuy qui le demande: car il seroit deshonneste de la faire autrement.

F.

Between 1640 and 1680
From *Chanson des Marquis de Coulanges*[51]:

> Jadis le potage on mangeoit
> Dans le plat, sans cérémonie,
> Et sa cuillier on essuyoit
> Souvent sur la poule bouillie.
> Dans la fricassée autrefois
> On saussait son pain et ses doigts.
>
> Chacun mange présentement
> Son potage sur son assiette;
> Il faut se servir poliment
> Et de cuillier et de fourchette,
> Et de temps en temps qu'un valet
> Les aille laver au buffet.

G.

1672
From Antoine de Courtin, *Nouveau traité de civilité:*

P. 127. Si chacun prend au plat, il faut bien se garder d'y mettre la main, que les plus qualifiez ne l'y ayent mise les premiers; n'y de prendre ailleurs qu'à l'endroit du plat, qui est vis à vis de nous: moins encore doit-on prendre les meilleurs morceaux, quand même on seroit le dernier à prendre.

Il est nécessaire aussi d'observer qu'il faut toûjours essuyer vostre cuillere quand, après vous en estre servy, vous voulez prendre quelque chose dans un autre plat, y ayant des gens si delicats qu'ils ne voudroient pas manger du potage où vous l'auriez mise, après l'avoir portée à la bouche.

Et même si on est à la table de gens bien propres, il ne suffit pas d'essuyer sa cuillere; il ne faut plus s'en servir, mais en demander une autre. Aussi sert—on à present en bien des lieux des cuilleres dans des plats, qui ne servent que pour prendre du potage et de la sauce.

Il ne faut pas manger le potage au plat, mais en mettre proprement sur son assiette; et s'il estoit trop chaud, il est indecent de souffler à chaque cuillerée; il faut attendre qu'il soit refroidy.

Que si par malheur on s'estoit brûlé, il faut le souffrir si l'on peut patiemment et sans le faire paroître: mais si la brûlure estoit insupportable comme il arrive quelquefois. il faut promptement et avant que les autres s'en apperçoivent, prendre son assiette d'une main, et la porter contre sa bouche, et se couvrant de l'autre main remettre sur l'assiette ce que l'on a dans la bouche, et le donner vistement par derriere à un laquais. La civilité veut que l'on ait de la politesse, mais elle ne pretend pas que l'on soit homicide de soy-même. Il est tres indecent de toucher à quelque chose de gras, à quelque sauce, à quelque syrop etc. avec les doigts, outre que cela en même—temps vous oblige à deux ou trois autres indecences, l'une est d'essuyer frequemment vos mains à vostre serviette, et de la salir comme un torchon de cuisine; en sorte qu'elle fait mal au coeur à ceux qui la voyent porter à la bouche, pour vous essuyer. L'autre est de les essuyer à vostre pain, ce qui est encore tres—malpropre; et la troisième de vous lécher les doigts, ce qui est le comble de l'impropreté.

P. 273 . . . comme il y en a beaucoup (sc. usages) qui ont déja changé, je ne doute pas qu'il n'y en ait plusieurs de celles-cy, qui changeront tout de même à l'avenir.

Autrefois on pouvoit . . . tremper son pain dans la sausse, et il suffisoit pourvu que l'on n'y eût pas encore mordu; maintenant ce seroit une espece de rusticité.

Autrefois on pouvoit tirer de sa bouche ce qu'on ne pouvoit pas manger, et le jetter à terre, pourvu que cela se fist adroitement; et maintenant ce seroit une grande saleté . . .

H.

1717

From François de Callières, *De la science du monde et des connoissances utiles à la conduite de la vie*:

P. 97. En Allemagne et dans les Royaumes du Nord, c'est une civilité et une bienséance pour un Prince de boire le premier à la santé de celui ou de ceux qu'il traite, et de leur faire presenter ensuite le même verre, ou le même gobelet, rempli d'ordinaire de même vin; et ce n'est point parmi eux un manque de politesse de boire dans le même verre, mais une marque de franchise et d'amitié; les femmes boivent aussi les premieres, et donnent ensuite, ou font porter leur verre avec le même vin, dont elles ont bû à la santé de celui à qui elles se sont adressées, sans que cela passe pour une faveur particulière comme parmi nous . . .

Je ne sçaurois approuver (p. 101)—n'en déplaise a Messieurs les Gens du Nort—cette maniere de boire dans le même verre, et moins encore sur le reste des Dames, cela a un air de malpropreté, qui me feroit souhaiter qu'ils témoignassent leur franchise par d'autres marques.

I.

1714

From an anonymous *Civilité française* (Liège, 1714?):

P. 48. Il n'est pas . . . honnête d'humer sa soupe quand on se serviroit d'écuelle si ce n'étoit que ce fut dans la famille aprés en avoir pris la plus grande partie avec la cuilliére.

Si le potage est dans un plat portez-y la cuilliére à votre tour sans vous précipiter.

Ne tenez-pas toujours votre couteau à la main comme font les gens de village; il suffit de le prendre lorsque vous voulez vous en servir.

Quand on vous sert de la viande, il n'est pas séant de la prendre avec la main; mais il faut présenter votre assiette de la main gauche en tenant votre fourchette ou votre couteau de la droite.

Il est contre la bienséance de donner à flairer les viandes et il faut se donner bien de garde de les remettre dans le plat après les avoir flairées. Si vous prenez dans un plat commun ne choisissez pas les meilleurs morceaux. Coupez avec le couteau après que vous aurez arrété la viande qui est dans le plat avec la fourchette de laquelle vous vous servirez pour porter sur votre assiette ce que vous aurez coupé, ne prenez donc pas la viande avec la main . . .

Il ne faut pas jetter par terre ni os ni coque d'oeuf ni pelure d'aucun fruit.

Il en est de méme des noyaux que l'on tire plus honnétement de la bouche avec les deux doigts qu'on ne les crache dans la main.

J.

1729

From La Salle, *Les Règles de la bienséance et de la civilité chrétienne* (Rouen, 1729):

Des choses dont on doit se servir lorsqu'on est à Table (p. 87).

On doit se servir à Table d'une serviette, d'une assiette, d'un couteau, d'une cuillier, et d'une fourchette: il serait tout à fait contre l'honnêteté, de se passer de quelqu'une de toutes ces choses en mangeant.

C'est à la personne la plus qualifée de la compagnie à déplier sa serviette la premiere, et les autres doivent attendre qu'elle ait déplié la sienne, pour déplier la leur. Lorsque les pesonnes sont à peu prés égales, tous la déplient ensemble sans cérémonie.

Il est malhonneste de se servir de sa serviette pour s'essuier le visage; il l'est encore bien plus de s'en frotter les dents et ce serait une faute des plus grossieres contre la Civilité de s'en servir pour se moucher . . . L'usage qu'on peut et qu'on doit faire de sa serviette lorsqu'on est à Table, est de s'en servir pour nettoïer sa bouche, ses lévres et ses doigts quand ils sont gras, pour dégraisser le couteau avant que de couper du Pain, et pour nettoïer la cuiller, et la fourchette après qu'on s'en est servi.

Lorsque les doits sont fort gras, il est á propos de les dégraisser d'abord avec un morceau de pain, qu'il faut ensuite laisser sur l'assiette avant que de les essuïer a sa serviette, afin de ne la pas beaucoup graisser, et de ne la pas rendre malpropre.

Lorsque la cuillier, la fourchette ou le couteau sont sales, ou qu'ils sont gras, il est trés mal honnète de les lecher, et il n'est nullement séant de les essuïer, ou quelqu'autre chose que ce soit, avec la nape, on doit dans ces occasions, et autres semblables, se servir de la serviette et pour ce qui est de la nape, il faut avoir égard de la tenir toújours fort propre, et de n'y laisser tomber, ni eau, ni vin, ni rien qui la puisse salir.

Lorsque l'assiette est sale, on doit bien se garder de la ratisser avec la cuillier, ou la fourchette, pour la rendre nette, ou de nettoïer avec ses doigts son assiette, ou le fond de quelque plat: cela est trés indécent, il faut, ou n'y pas toucher, ou si on a la commodité d'en changer, se la faire déservir, et s'en faire aporter une autre.

Il ne faut pas lorsqu'on est à Table tenir toújours le couteau á la main, il suffit de le prendre lorsqu'on veut s'en servir.

Il est aussi trés incivil de porter un morceau de pain à la bouche aïant le couteau á la main; il l'est encore plus de l'y porter avec la pointe du couteau. Il faut observer la mème chose en mangeant des pommes, des poires ou quelques autres fruits.

Il est contre la Bienséance de tenir la fourchette ou la cuillier á plaine main, comme si on tenoit un bàton; mais on doit toújours les tenir entre ses doights.

On ne doit pas se servir de la fourchette pour porter à sa bouche des choses liquides
. . . c'est la cuiller qui est destinée pour prendre ces sortes de choses.

Il est de l'honnèteté de se servir toujours de la fourchette pour porter de la viande á sa bouche, car la Bien-séance ne permet pas de toucher avec les doigts à quelque chose de gras, à quelque sauce, ou á quelque sirop; et si quelqu'un le faisoit, il ne pouoit se dispenser de commettre ensuite plusieurs autres incivilitez: comme seroit d'essuïer souvent ses doigts à sa serviette, ce qui la rendroit fort sale et fort malpropre, ou de les essuïer à son pain, ce qui seroit très incivil, ou de lècher ses doigts, ce qui ne peut être permis á une personne bien née et bien élevée.

K.

1774
From La Salle, *Les Règles de la bienséance et de la civilité chrétienne* (1774 ed.) p. 45ff.:

La serviette qui est posée sur l'assiette, étant destinée à préserver les habits des taches ou autres malpropretés inséparables des repas, il faut tellement l'étendre sur soi qu'elle couvre les devants du corps jusques sur les genoux, en allant au-dessous du col et non la passant en dedans du même col. La cuillier, la fourchette et le couteau doivent toujours être placée à la droite.

La cuiller est destinée pour les choses liquides, et la fourchette pour les viandes de consistance.

Lorsque l'une ou l'autre est sale, on peut les nettoyer avec sa serviette, s'il n'est pas possible de se procurer un autre service; il faut éviter de les assuyer avec la nappe, c'est une malpropreté impardonnable.

Quand l'assiette est sale, il faut en demander une autre; ce seroit une grossiéreté révoltante de la nettoyer avec les doigts avec la cuiller, la fourchette et le couteau.

Dans les bonnes tables, les domestiques attentifs changent les assiettes sans qu'on les en avertissent.

Rien n'est plus mal-propre que de se lécher les doigts, de toucher les viandes, et de les porter à la bouche avec la main, de remuer les sauces avec le doigt, ou d'y tremper le pain avec la fourchette pour la sucer.

On ne doit jamais prendre du sel avec les doigts. Il est très ordinaire aux enfants d'entasser morceaux sur morceaux, de retirer même de la bouche ce qu'ils y ont mis et qui est maché, de pousser les morceaux avec les doigts. Rien n'est plus mal honnête. . . . porter les viandes au nez, les flairer, ou les donner à flairer est une autre impolitesse qui attaque le Maître de la table; et s'il arrive que l'on trouve quelque malpropreté dans les aliments, il faut les retirer sans les montrer.

L.

1780?
From an anonymous work, *La Civilité honete pour les enfants* (Caen, n.d.) p.35:

. . . Après, il mettra sa serviette sur lui, son pain à gauche et son couteau à droite, pour couper la viande sans le rompre. Il se donnera aussi de garde de porter son couteau à sa bouche. Il ne doit point avoir ses mains sur son assiette. . . . il ne doit point non plus s'accouder dessus, car cela n'appartient qu'à des gens malades ou vieux.

Le sage Enfant s'il est avec des Supérieurs mettra le dernier la main au plat . . .
. . . après si c'est de la viande, la coupera proprement avec son couteau et la mangera avec son pain.

C'est une chose rustique et sale de tirer de sa bouche la viande qu'on a déjà mâchée et la mettre sur son assiette. Aussi ne faut-il jamias remettre dans le plat ce qu'on en a osté.

M.

1786

From a conversation between the poet Delille and Abbé Cosson:

Dernièrement, l'abbé Cosson, professeur de belles lettres au collége Mazarin, me parla d'un dîner où il s'étoit trouvé quelques jours auparavant avec des gens de la cour . . . à Versailles.

Je parie, lui dis-je, que vous avez fait cent incongruités.

—Comment donc, reprit vivement l'abbé Cosson, fort inquiet. Il me semble que j'ai fait la même chose que tout le monde.

—Quelle présomption! Je gage que vous n'avez rien fait comme personne. Mais voyons, je me bornerai au dîner. Et d'abord que fîtes-vous de votre serviette en vous mettant à table?

—De ma serviette? Je fis comme tout le monde; je la déployai, je l'étendis sur moi et l'attachai par un coin à ma boutonnière.

—Eh bien mon cher, vous êtes le seul qui ayez fait cela; on n'étale point sa serviette, on la laisse sur ses genoux. Et comment fîtes-vour pour manger votre soupe?

—Comme tout le monde, je pense. Je pris ma cuiller d'une main et ma fourchette de l'autre . . .

—Votre fourchette, bon Dieu! Personne ne prend de fourchette pour manger sa soupe . . . Mais dites-mois quelque chose de la manière dont vous mangeâtes votre pain.

—Certainement à la manière de tout le monde: je la coupai proprement avec mon couteau.

—Eh, on rompt son pain, on ne le coupe pas . . . Avançons. Le café, comment le prîtes-vous?

—Eh, pour le coup, comme tout le monde; il était brûlant, je le versai par petites parties de ma tasse dans ma soucoupe.

—Eh bien, vous fîtes comme ne fit sûrement personne: tout le monde boit son café dans sa tasse, et jamais dans sa soucoupe . . .

Changes in Attitude Toward the Natural Functions
(p. 129)

A.

Fifteenth Century

From *S'ensuivent les contenances de la table*:

VIII.

Enfant, prens de regarder peine
Sur le siege où tu te sierras
Se aucune chose y verra
Qui soit deshonnete ou vilaine

B.

From *Ein spruch der ze tische kêrt*[81]:

329   Grîf ouch niht mit blôzer hant
        Dir selben under dîn gewant.

C.

1530

From *De civilitate morum puerilium*, by Erasmus of Rotterdam:

Incivile est eum salutare, qui reddit urinam aut alvum exonerat . . .

Membra quibus natura pudorem addidit retegere citra necessitatem procul abesse debet ab indole liberali. Quin ubi necessitas huc cogit, tamen id quoque decente verecundia faciendum est, etiam si nemo testis adsit. Nunquam enim non adsunt angeli, quibus in pueris gratissimus est pudicitiae comes custosque pudor.

Lotium remorari valetudini perniciosum, secreto reddere verecundum. Sunt qui praecipiant ut puer compressis natibus ventris flatum retineat. Atqui civile non est, dum urbanus videri studes morbum accersere. Si licet secedere, solus id faciat. Sin minus, iuxta vetustissimum proverbium: Tussi crepitum dissimulet. Alioqui cur non eadem opera praecipiunt ne aluum deijciant, quum remorari flatum periculosius sit, quam alvum stringere.

Morbum accersere: Audi Coi senis de crepitu sententiam . . . Si flatus sine crepitu sonituque excernitur optimus. Melius tamen est, ut erumpat eum sonitu quam si condatur retineaturque. Atqui adeo utile hic fuerit devorare pudorem, ut corpus redimas, ut consilio omnium medicorum sic nates comprimas, quemadmodum apud epigrammatarium Aethon, qui quamvis in sacro sibi caverit crepando, tamen compressis natibus Iovem salutat. Parasitica, et illorum qui ad supercilinin stant, vox est; Didici comprimere nates.

Tussi crepitum dissimulare: Tussire se simulant, qui pudoris gratia nolunt crepitum audiri. Lege Chiliades; Tussis pro crepitu.

Quum remorari flatum perniciosus sit: Extant Nicarchi versus epigrammatum libro secundo. . . . quibus pestiferam retenti crepitus vim describit, sed quia omnium manibus teruntur non duxi adscribendos.

D.

1558

From *Galateo*, by Giovanni della Casa, Archbishop of Benevento:

Uber das stehet es einem sittsamen, erbahrn mensch nicht an (Similmente non si conviene a Gentilhuomo costumatè apparecchiarsi alle necessità naturali . . .), dass er sich zu natürlicher notdurft in andrer Leute gegenwertigkeit rüste und vorbereite oder nach dem er solches verrichtet sich in ihrer gegenwertigkeit widerum nestele und bekleide. So wird auch ein solcher nach seiner aus heimlichen orten wiederkunfft für ehrliche gesellschaft die hände nicht waschen, nach dem die ursache darumb er sich wäschet der leut gedancken eine unfläterey für die augen stellt. Ist auch eben umb derselbigen ursach willen kein feine gewohnheit, wenn einem auf der Gassen etwas abscheuliches, wie es sich wol bisweilen zuträgt, fürkommet, statim ad comitem se convertat eique illam monstrat.

Multo minus decebit alteri re foetidam, ut olfaciat porrigere, quod nonnunquam facere aliqui solent atque adeo urgere, quum etiam naribus aliorum rem illam grave olentem admovent et inquiunt: Odorare amabo quantopere hoec foeteat; quum potius dicendum esset: Quia foctet, noli odorari.

E.

1570

From the Wernigerode Hofordnung of 1570:

Dass nicht männiglich also unverschämt und ohn alle Scheu, den Bauern gleich, die nicht zu Hofe oder bei einigen ehrbaren, züchtigen Leuten gewesen, vor das Frauenzimmer,

Hofstuben und andrer Gemach Thüren oder Fenster seine Nothdurft ausrichte, sondern in jeder sich jederziet und—ort vernünftiger, züchtiger und ehrerbietiger Wort und Geberde erzeige und verhalte.

F.

1589

From the Brunswick Hofordnung of 1589:

Dergleichen dass niemand, der sei auch wer er wolle, unter, nach oder vor den Mahlzeiten, spät oder früh, die Wendelsteine, Treppen, Gänge and Gemächer mit dem Urin oder anderm Unflath verunreinigen, sondern wegen solcher Nothdurft an gebührliche, verordnete Orte gehen thue.

H.

1694

From the correspondence of the Duchess of Orléans:

L'odeur de la boue est horrible. Paris est un endroit affreux; les rues y ont une si mauvaise odeur qu'on ne peut y tenir; l'extrême chaleur y fait pourrir beaucoup de viande et de poisson et ceci, joint à la foule des gens qui . . . dans les rues, cause une odeur si détestable qu'il n y a pas moyen de la supporter.

I.

1729

From La Salle, *Les Règles de la bienséance et de la civilité chrétienne* (Rouen, 1729), p. 45ff.:

Il est de la Bienséance, et de la pudeur de couvrir toutes les parties du Corps, hors la teste et les mains. On doit éviter avec soin, et autant qu'on le peut, de porter la main nuë sur toutes les parties du Corps qui ne sont pas ordinairement découvertes; et si on est obligé de les toucher, il faut que ce soit avec beaucoup de précaution. Il est à propos de s'accoutumer à souffrir plusieurs petites incommoditez sans se tourner, frotter, ni gratter . . .

Il est bien plus contre la Bienséance et l'honnesteté, de toucher, ou de voir en une autre personne, particulierement si elle est de sexe différent, ce que Dieu défend de regarder en soi. Lorsqu'on a besoin d'uriner, il faut toujours se retirer en quelque lieu écarté: et quelques autres besoins naturels qu'on puisse avoir, il est de la Bienséance (aux Enfants mesmes) de ne les faire que dans des lieux oú on ne puisse pas estre apperçú.

It est très incivil de laisser sortir des vens de son Corps, soit par haut, soit par bas, quand mesme ce seroit sans faire aucun bruit, lorsqu'on est en compagnie; et il est honteux et indécent de le faire d'une maniere qu'on puisse estre entendu des autres.

Il n'est jamais séant de parler des parties du Corps qui doivent estre cachées, ni de certaines nécessitez du Corps ausquelles la Nature nous a assujetti, ni mesme de les nommer.

J.

1731

From Johann Christian Barth, *Die galanthe Ethica*, in welcher gezeiget wird, wie sich ein junger Mensch bey der galanten Welt sowohl durch manierliche Werke als complaisante Worte recommandiren soll. Allen Liebhabern der heutigen Politesse zu sonderbarem Nutzen and Vergnügen ans Licht gestellet. (Dresden and Leipzig, 1731), p. 288:

Gehet man bey einer Person vorbey, welche sich erleichtert, so stellet man sich, als ob man solches nicht gewahr würde, und also ist es auch wider die Höflichkeit, selbige zu begrüssen.

K.

1774

From La Salle, *Les Règles de la bienséance et de la civilité chrétienne*, p. 24:

Il est de la bienséance et de la pudeur de couvrir toutes les parties du corps, hors de la tête et les mains.

Pour les besoins naturels il est de la bienséance (aux enfants même) de n'y satisfaire que dans des lieux ou on ne soit pas apperçu.

Il n'est jamais séant de parler des parties du corps qui doivent toujours être cachées, ni de certaines nécessités du corps auxquelles la nature nous a assujettis, ni même de les nommer.

L.

1768

Letter from Madame du Deffand to Madame de Choiseul, 1768:

Je voudrais, chère grand'maman, venir peindre, ainsi qu'au grand-abbé, quelle fut ma surprise, quand hier matin on m'apporte, sur mon lit, un grand sac de votre part. Je me hâte de l'ouvrir, j'y fourre la main, j'y trouve des petits pois . . . et puis un vase . . . je le tire bien vite: c'est un pot de chambre. Mais d'une beauté, d'une magnificence telles, que mes gens tout d'une voix disent qu'il en fallait faire une saucière. Le pot de chambre a été en représentation hier toute la soirée et fit l'admiration de tout le monde. Les pois . . . furent mangés sans qu'il en restât un seul.

On Blowing One's Nose
(p. 143)

A.

Thirteenth Century

Bonvesin de la Riva (Bonvicino da Riva) *De le zinquanta cortexie da tavola:*

(a)

La desetena apresso si è:
quando tu stranude,
Over ch'el te prende la tosse,
guarda con tu làvori
In oltra parte te volze,
ed è cortexia inpensa,
Azò che dra sariva no
zesse sor la mensa.

(b)

Pox la trentena è questa:
zaschun cortese donzello
Che se vore mondà lo naxo,
con li drapi se faza bello;

Chi mangia over chi menestra,
no de'sofià con le die;
Con li drapi da pcy se monda
vostra cortexia.

B.

From *Ein spruch der ze tische kêrt:*

323   Swer in daz tischlach sniuzet sich,
       daz stât niht wol, sicherlich.

C.

From *S'ensuivent les contenances de la table:*

XXXIII

Enfant se ton nez est morveux,
Ne le torche de la main nue,
De quoy ta viande est tenue.
Le fait est vilain et honteux.

D.

From A. Cabanès, *Moeurs intimes du temps passé* (Paris, 1910) p. 101:

Au quinzième siècle, on se mouchait encore dans les doigts et les sculpteurs de l'époque n'ont pas craint de reproduire ce geste, passablement réaliste, dans leur monuments.

E.

1530
From *De civilitate morum puerilium*, by Erasmus, ch. 1:

Pileo aut veste emungi, rusticanum, bracchio cubitove, salsamentariorum, nec multo civilius id manu fieri, si mox pituitam vesti illinas. Strophiolis excipere narium recrementa, decorum; idque paulisper averso corpore, si qui adsint honoratiores.
Si quid in solum dejectum est emuncto duobus digitis naso, mox pede proterendum est.
[From the scholia:]
Inter mucum et pituitam parum differentiae est, nisi quod mucum crassiores, pituitam fluidas magis sordes interpretantur. Strophium et strophiolum, sudarium et sudariolum, linteum et linteolum confundunt passim Latini scriptores.

G.

558
From *Galateo*, by Giovanni della Casa:

P. 72: Du solt dein fatzenetlein niemand, überreichen als ob es new gewaschen were . . . (non offerirai il suo mocichino . . .).

P. 44: Es gehöret sich auch nicht, wenn du die nase gewischet hast, dass du das schnuptuch auseinander ziehest und hineinguckest gleich als ob dir perlen und rubinen vom gehirn hätte abfallen mögen.

P. 618: . . . Was soll ich dann nun von denen sagen . . . die ihr fatzolet oder wischtüchlein im mund umbhertragen? . . .

G.

From Cabanès, *Mœurs intimes du passé* (Paris 1910):

(a)
P. 103: Martial d'Auvergne, les "Arrêts d'amour":
. . . à fin qu'elle l'eut en mémoire, il s'advisa de luy faire faire un des plus beaulx et riches mouchoirs, où son nom estoit en lettres entrelacées, le plus gentement du monde, car il estoit attaché à un beau cueur d'or, et franges de menues pensées.

(b)
P. 168: 1594 Henry IV demandait à son valet de chambre combien il avait de chemises et celui-ci répondait: Une douzaine, Sire, encore i en a-t-il de déschirées.—Et de mouchoirs, dit le roi, est-ce pas huit que j'ai?—Il n'i en a pour reste heure que cinq, dist-il. (Lestoil, Journal d'Henri IV.)

"Cinq mouchoirs d'ouvrage d'or, d'argent et soye, prisez cent escuz."

(c)
P. 102: Au seizième siècle, dit Monteil, en France comme partout, le petit peuple se mouche sans mouchoir; mais, dans la bourgeoisie, il est reçu qu'on se mouche avec la manche. Quant aux gens riches, ils portent dans la poche un mouchoir; aussi, pour dire qu'un homme a de la fortune, on dit qu'il ne se mouche pas avec la manche.

H.

1672
From Antoine de Courtin, *Nouveau traité de civilité*:

P. 134. Se moucher avec son mouchoir à découvert et sans se couvrir de sa serviette, en essuyer la sueur du visage . . . sont des saletez á faire soulever le coeur à tout le monde.
Il faut éviter de bâiller, de se moucher et de cracher. Si on y est obligé en des lieux que l'on tient proprement, il faut le faire dans son mouchoir, en se détournant le visage et se couvrant de sa main gauche, et ne point regarder après dans son mouchoir.

I.

1694
From Ménage, *Dictionnaire étymologique de la langue française*:

Mouchoir à moucher:
Comme ce mot de moucher donne une vilaine image, les dames devroient plutost appeler ce mouchoir, de poche, comme on dit mouchoir de cou, que mouchoir à moucher.

J.

1714
From an anonymous *Civilité française* (Liège, 1714):

P. 41: Gardez-vous bien de vous moucher avec les doigts ou sur la manche comme les enfans, mais servez-vous de votre mouchoir et ne regardez pas dedans aprés vous être mouché.

K.

1729

From La Salle, *Les Règles de la bienséance et de la civilité chrétienne* (Rouen, 1729):

Du nez et de la maniere de se moucher et d'éternuer (p. 23).

Il est trés mal honneste de foüiller incessament dans les narines avec le doigt, et il est encore bien plus insuportable de porter ensuite dans la bouche ce qu'on a tiré hors des narines . . .

Il est vilain de se moucher avec la main nuë, en la passant dessous le Nez, ou de se moucher sur sa manche, ou sur ses habits. C'est une chose trés contraire à la Bienséance, de se moucher avec deux doigts, et puis jeter l'ordure á terre, et d'essuier ensuite ses doigts avec ses habits; on sçait combien il est mal séant de voir de telles mal-propretés sur des habits, qui doivent toújours être trés propres, quelques pauvres qu'ils soient.

Il y en a quelques-uns qui mettent un doigt contre le Nez, et qui ensuite en soufflant du Nez, poussent à terre l'ordure qui est dedans; ceux qui en usent ainsi sont des gens qui ne sçavent ce que c'est d'honnêteté.

Il faut toújours se servir de son mouchoir pour se moucher, et jamais d'autre chose, et en le faisant se couvrir ordinairement le Visage de son chapeau.

On doit éviter en se mouchant de faire du bruit avec le Nez . . . Avant que de se moucher, il est indécent d'estre longtems à tirer son mouchoir: c'est manquer de respect à l'égard des personnes avec qui on est, de le déplier en différends endroits, pour voir de quel côté on se mouchera; il faut tirer son mouchoir de sa poche, sans qu'il paroisse, et se moucher promptement, de manier qu'on ne puisse presque pas ester aperçú des autres.

On doit bien se garder, aprés qu'on s'est mouché, de regarder dans son mouchoir; mais il est à propos de le plier aussitôt, et le remettre dans sa poche.

L.

1774

From La Salle, *Les Règles de la bienséance et de la civilité chrétienne:*

Tout mouvement volontaire du nez, soit avec la main, soit autrement, est indécent et puérile; porter les doigts dans les narines est une malpropreté qui revolte, et en y touchant trop souvent, il arrive, qu'il s'y forme des incommodités, dont on serssent longtemps.

Les enfants sont assez dans l'usage de tomber dans ce défaut; les parents doivent les en corriger avec soin.

Il faut observer, en se mouchant, toutes les regles de la bienséance et de la propreté.

M.

1797

From La Mésangère, *Le voyageur de Paris* (1797), vol. 2, p. 95:

On faisait un art de moucher il y a quelques années. L'un imitait le son de la trompette, l'autre le jurement du chat; le point de perfection consistait à ne faire ni trop de bruit ni trop peu.

On Spitting
(p.153)

Middle Ages

A.

From *Stans puer in mensam* (*The Babees Book* v. 2, p. 32.):

27   nec ultra mensam spueris nec desuper unquam
          nec carnem propriam verres digito neque scalpes

37   Si sapis extra vas expue quando lavas

B.

From a *Contenence de table* (*The Babees Book* v. 2, p. 7.):

29   Ne craiche par dessus la table,
          Car c'est chose desconvenable

51   Cellui qui courtoisie a ch'er
          Ne doit pas ou bacin crachier,
          Fors quant sa bouche et ses mains leve,
          Ains mette hors, qu'aucun ne greve

D.

From Zarncke, *Der Deutsche Cato*, p. 137:

          Wirff nit nauch půrschem sin
          Die spaichei über den tisch hin

E.

1530
From *De civilitate morum puerilium*, by Erasmus:

Aversus expuito, ne quem conspuas aspergasve. Si quid purulentius in terram rejectum erit, pede, ut dixi, proteratur, ne cui nauseam moveat. Id si non licet, linteolo sputum excipito. Resorbere salivam, inurbanum est, quemadmodum et illud quod quosdam videmus non ex necessitate, sed ex usu, ad tertium quodque verbum expuere.

F.

1558
From *Galateo*, by Giovanni della Casa:

P. 570: Es stehet auch übel, dass sich einer, da er am Tisch sitzet, krauet: Ja an dem Ort und zu solcher Zeit sol sich einer so viel es müglich auch dess auswerfens enthalten, und so man es ja nicht ganz umbgehen könte, so sol man es doch auff eine höfliche Weise und unvermercket thun.

Ich habe offt gehöret, dass für zeiten ganze völcker so mass gelebet, und sich so dapfer geübet, dass sie des aussprünzen durchaus nit bedürffet haben. Wie solten dann wir uns auch nit eine geringe zeit desselben enthalten können.

G.

1672
From Antoine de Courtin, *Nouveau traité de civilité*:

P. 273: . . . Cet usage dont nous venons de parler ne permet pas que la pluspart de ces sortes de loix soient immuables. Et comme il y en a beaucoup qui ont déja changé, je ne doute pas qu'il n'y en ait plusieurs de celles-cy, qui changeront tout de même à l'avenir.

Autrefois, par exemple, il estoit permis de cracher à terre devant des personnes de qualité, et il suffisoit de mettre le pied dessus; à present c'est une indecence.

Autrefois on pouvoit bâiller et c'estoit assez, pourvu que l'on ne parlast pas en bâillant; à present une personne de qualité s'en choqueroit.

H.

1714
From an anonymous *Civilité française* (Liège, 1714):

P. 67: Le cracher frequent est desagréable; quand il est de nécessité on doit le rendre moins visible que l'on peut et faire en sorte qu'on ne crache ni sur les personnes, ni sur les habits de qui que ce soit, ni même sur les tisons étant auprés du feu. Et en quelque lieu que l'on crache, on doit mettre le pied sur le crachat.

Chez les grands on crache dans son mouchoir.

P. 41: Il est de mauvaise grace de cracher par la fenétre dans la rue ou sur le feu.

Ne crachez point si loin qu'il faille aller chercher le crachat pour mettre le pied dessus.

I.

1729
From La Salle, *Les Règles de la bienséance et de la civilité chrétienne* (Rouen, 1729):

P. 35: On ne doit pas s'abstenir de cracher, et c'est une chose trés indécente d'avaler ce qu'on doit cracher; cela est capable de faire mal au coeur aux autres.

Il ne faut pas cependant s'accoútumer á cracher trop souvent, et sans nécessité: cela est non seulement trés malhonnête; mais cela dégoute et incommode tout le monde. Quand on se trouve avec des personnes de qualité et lorsqu'on est dans des lieux au'on tient propres, il est de l'honnêteté de cracher dans son mouchoir, en se tournant un peu de côté.

Il est même de la Bienséance que chacun s'accoútume à cracher dans son mouchoir, lorqu'on est dans les maison des Grands et dans toutes les places qui sont, ou cirées, ou parquetées; mais il est bien plus nécessaire de prendre l'habitude de le faire lorsqu'on est dans l'Eglise autant qu'il est possible . . . cependant il arrive souvent qu'il n'y a point de pavé de Cuisine, ou même d'Ecurie plus sale . . . que celui de l'Eglise . . .

Après avoir craché dans son mouchoir, il faut le plier aussitòt, sans le reagrder, et le mettre dans sa poche. On doit avoir beaucoup d'égard de ne jamais cracher sur ses habits, ni sur ceux des autres . . . Quand on aperçoit à terre quelque gros Crachat, il faut aussitòt mettre adroitement le pied dessus. Si on en remarque sur l'habit de quelqu'un, il n'est pas bien séant de le faire connoistre: mais il faut avertir quelque domestique de aller óter: et s'il n'y en a point, il faut l'óter soi-méme, sans qu'on s'en apercoive: car il est de l'honnèteté de ne rien faire paroitre á l'égard de qui que ce soit, qui lui puisse faire peine: ou lui donner de la confusion.

J.

1774

From La Salle, *Les Règles de la bienséance et de la civilité chrétienne* (1774):

P. 20: Dans l'Eglise, chez les Grands et dans tous les endroits où regnent la propreté, il faut cracher dans son mouchoir. C'est une grossiéreté impardonnable dans les enfants, que celle qu'ils contractent en crachant au visage de leurs camarades: on ne saurait punir trop sévérement ces incivilités; on ne peut pas plus excuser ceux qui crachent par les fenêtres, sur les murailles et sur les meubles . . .

L.

1910

From Augustin Cabanès, *Moeurs intimes*:

P. 264: Avez-vous observé que nous reléguons aujourd'hui dans quelque coin discret ce que nos pères n'hésitaient pas à étaler au grand jour?

Ainsi certain meuble intime occupait une place d'honneur . . . on ne songeait pas à le dérober aux regards.

Il en était de même d'un autre meuble, qui ne fait plus partie du mobilier moderne et dont, par ce temps de "bacillophobie," d'aucuns regretteront peutêtre la disparition: nous voulons parler du crachoir.

On Behavior in the Bedroom
(p. 160)

B.

1530

From *De civilitate morum querilium* (ch. XII de cubiculo) by Erasmus:

Sive cum exuis te, sive cum surgis, memor verecundiae, cave ne quid nudes aliorum oculis quod mos et natura tectum esse voluit.

Si cum sodali lectum habeas communem, quietus jaceto, neque corporis jactatione vel te ipsum nedes, vel sodali detractis palliis sis molestus.

C.

1555

From *Des bonnes moeurs et honnestes contenances*, Lyon, 1555, by Pierre Broe:

Et quand viendra que tu seras au lit
Après soupper pour prendre le délit
d'humain repos aucques plaisant some
si auprès de toi est couché quelque home
Tien doucement tous tes membres à droyt
Alonge toy, et garde à son endroyt

de le facher alor aucunement
pour te mouvoyr ou tourner rudement
par toy ne soyent ces membres descouvers
te remuant ou faisant tours divers:
Et si tu sens qu'il soit ja someillé
Fay que par toy il ne soyt esueillé.

D.

1729
From La Salle, *Les Règles de la bienséance et de la civilité chrétienne* (Rouen, 1729):

P. 55: On doit . . . ne se deshabiller, ni coucher devant personne; l'on doit surtout, à moins qu'on ne soit engagé dans le Mariage, ne pas se coucher devant aucune personne d'autre sexe.

Il est encore bien moins permis à des personnes de sexe différent, de coucher dans un même lit, quand ce ne serait que des Enfants fort jeunes . . .

Lorsque par une nécessité indispensable, on est contraint dans un voïage de coucher avec quelque autre de mesme séxe, il n'est pas bien-séant de s'en aprocher si fort, qu'on puisse non seulement s'incommoder l'un l'autre, mais mesme se toucher; et il l'est encore moins de mettre ses jambes entre celles de la personne avec qui on est couché . . .

Il est aussi trés indécent et peu honnète, de s'amuser á causer, á badiner . . .

Lorsqu'on sort du lit, il ne faut pas le laisser découvert ni mettre son bonnet de nuit sur quelque siége, ou en quelqu'autre endroit d'oú il puisse être aperçú.

E.

1774
From La Salle, *Les Règles de la bienséance et de la civilité chrétienne* (1774) p. 31:

C'est un étrange abus de faire coucher des personnes de différents sexes dans une même chambre; et si la nécessité y oblige, il faut bien faire ensorte que les lits soient séparés, et que la pudeur ne souffre en rien de ce mélange. Une grande indigence peut seule excuser cet usage . . .

Lorsqu'on se trouve forcé de coucher avec une personne de même sexe, ce qui arrive rarement, il faut s'y tenir dans une modestie sévere et vigilante . . .

Dès que l'on est éveillé, et que l'on a pris un temps suffisant pour le repos, il faut sortir du lit avec la modestie convenable, et ne jamais y rester á tenir des conversations ou vaquer à d'autres affaires . . . rien n'annonce plus sensiblement la paresse et la légéreté; le lit est destiné au repos du corps et non á toute autre chose.

Changes in the Aggressive Impulse
(p. 190)

"Sint uns allen ist gegeben
ein harte ungewissez leben"

"Wildu vürhten den tôt,
sô muostu leben mit nôt."

"Man weiz wol daz der tôt geschiht,
man weiz ab sîner zuokunft niht:
er kumt geslichen als ein diep
und scheidet leide unde liep.
Doch habe du guote zuoversiht
vürhte den tôt ze sêre niht
vürhtestu in ze sêre
du gewinnest vreude nie mêre."

Notes

Chapter One

1. Oswald Spengler, *The Decline of the West* (London, 1926), p. 21: "Each Culture has its own new possibilities of self-expression which arise, ripen, decay, and never return. . . . These cultures, sublimated life-essences, grow with the same superb aimlessness as the flowers of the field. They belong, like the plants and the animals, to the living Nature of Goethe, and not to the dead Nature of Newton."

2. The whole question of the evolution of the concepts *Kultur* and *Zivilisation* needs a fuller examination than is possible here, where the problem can only be briefly introduced. Nevertheless, a few notes may support the ideas in the text.

It could be demonstrated that in the course of the nineteenth century, and particularly after 1870, when Germany was both strong in Europe and a rising colonial power, the antithesis between the two words diminished considerably at times, "culture" referring, as it does today in England and to some extent in France, to only a particular area or a higher form of civilization. Thus, for example, Friedrich Jodl, in his *Die Kulturgeschichtschreibung* (Halle, 1878, p. 3), defines "general cultural history" as "the history of civilization" (cf. also ibid., p. 25).

G. F. Kolb, in his *Geschichte der Menschheit und der Cultur* (1843; a later edition is entitled *Cultur-Geschichte der Menschheit*) includes in his concept of culture the idea of progress that is generally excluded from it today. He bases his conception of *Kultur* explicitly on Buckle's concept of *Zivilisation*. But, as Jodl states (*Die Kulturgeschichtschreibung*, p. 36), his ideal "takes its essential features from modern conceptions and demands with regard to political, social, and religious freedom, and could easily be included in a party-political program."

In other words, Kolb is a "progressive," a liberal from the pre-1848 period, a time when the concept of *Kultur* also approached the Western concept of civilization.

All the same, the 1897 edition of Meyer's *Konversationslexikon* still states: "Civilization is the stage through which a barbaric people must pass in order to attain higher *Kultur* in industry, art, science, and attitudes."

However near the German concept of *Kultur* sometimes seems to come to the French and English concept of civilization in such statements, the feeling that *Zivilisation* is a second-rate value in comparison to *Kultur* never entirely disappears in Germany even in this period. It is an expression of Germany's self-assertion against the Western countries which regard themselves as the standard-bearers of civilization, and of the tension between them. Its strength changes with the degree and kind of this tension. The history of the German concepts *Zivilisation* and *Kultur* is very closely interrelated with the history of relations between England, France, and Germany. Its underlying constituents are certain political circumstances which persist throughout many phases of development, emerging in the psychological makeup of Germans as in their concepts—above all, those expressing their self-image.

Cf. also Conrad Hermann, *Philosophie der Geschichte* (1870), in which France is referred to as the country of "civilization," England as that of "material culture," and Germany as that of "ideal *Bildung*." The term "material culture," current in England and France, has virtually disappeared from ordinary German usage, if not quite from scholarly terminology. The concept of *Kultur* has merged completely in ordinary speech with what is here called *ideale Bildung*. The ideals of *Kultur* and *Bildung* were always closely related, although the reference to objective human accomplishments gradually became more prominent in the concept of *Kultur*.

3. On the problem of the intelligentsia, see in particular K. Mannheim, *Ideology and Utopia: An Introduction to the Sociology of Knowledge* (London, 1936). On the same subject, see also K. Mannheim, *Man and Society in an Age of Reconstruction* (London, 1940), and H. Weil, *Die Entstehung des Deutschen Bildungsprinzips* (Bonn, 1930), ch. 5.

4. *Grosses vollständiges Universal-Lexikon aller Wissenschaften und Künste* (Leipzig and Halle; Joh. H. Zedler, 1736). (All italics in the quotation are the author's.) Cf. also the article on "The Courtier":

"A person serving in a respected position at the court of a prince. Court life has always been described on the one hand as dangerous, on account of vacillating princely favor, the many envious parties, secret slanderers, and open enemies, and on the other as depraved, on account of the idleness, lasciviousness, and luxury frequently encountered there.

"There have, however, at all times been courtiers who prudently avoided these pitfalls and vigilantly escaped the temptations to wickedness, and so represented worthy examples of happy and virtuous courtiers. Nonetheless it is not said without reason that 'close to Court is close to the Devil.' "

Cf. also the article "Court": "If all subjects were deeply convinced that they honored their princes on account of their inward merits, there would be no need of outward pomp; as it is, however, the great part of their subjects remain attached to externals. A prince remains the same whether he walks alone or attended by a great company; nevertheless, there is no lack of examples where the prince attracted little or no attention when going alone among his subjects, but was received quite differently when acting in accordance with his position. For this reason it is necessary that the prince have servants not only to rule the land but also for outward appearance and for his own service."

Similar ideas were already expressed in the seventeenth century, e.g., in the *Discurs v. d. Höfflichkeit* (1665); cf. E. Cohn, *Gesellschaftsideale und Gesellschaftsroman des 17 Jahrhunderts,* (Berlin, 1921), p. 12. The German contraposition of "outward courtesy" and "inward merit" is as old as German absolutism and as the social weakness of the German bourgeoisie vis-à-vis the courtly circles of this period, a weakness that is to be understood not least in relation to the particular strength of the German bourgeoisie in the preceding phase.

5. Quoted in Aronson, *Lessing et les classics français* (Montpellier, 1935), p. 18.

6. E. de Mauvillon, *Lettres françoises et germaniques* (London, 1740), p. 430.

7. Ibid., p. 427.

8. Ibid., pp. 461-462.

9. Reprinted in the *Deutsche Literatur-denkmale* (Heilbronn, 1883), vol. 16.

10. Cf. Arnold Berney, *Friedrich der Grosse* (Tübingen, 1934), p. 71.

11. Cf. Hettner, *Geschichte der Literatur im 18 Jahrhundert*, vol. 1, p. 10. "It is undeniable that French drama is in its innermost essence court-drama, the drama of etiquette. The prerogative of being a tragic hero is tied to the strictest court etiquette."

12. G. E. Lessing, *Briefe aus dem zweiten Teil der Schriften* (Göschen, 1753); quoted in Aronson, *Lessing*, p. 161.

13. This and the following references are from Lamprecht, *Deutsche Geschichte* (Freiburg, 1906), vol. 8, pt. 1, p. 195.

14. Mauvillon, *Lettres*, pp. 398f.

15. Sophie de la Roche, *Geschichte des Fräulein von Sternheim* (1771; Berlin: Kuno Ridderhoff, 1907).

16. From Herder's *Nachlass*, vol. 3, pp. 67-68.

17. Sophie de la Roche, *Fräulein von Sternheim*, p. 99.

18. Ibid., p. 25.

19. Ibid., p. 90.

20. Caroline von Wolzogen, *Agnes von Lilien* (pub. in Schiller's *Horen*, 1796; pub. as book, 1798). A short fragment is reprinted in *Deutsche National-Literatur* (Berlin and Stuttgart), vol. 137, pt. 2; quotation from p. 375.

21. Ibid., p. 363.

22. Ibid., p. 364.

23. *Grimms Wörterbuch*, article on "Hofleute."

24. Ibid.

25. Brunot, in his *Histoire de la langue française,* cites the use of the word *civilisation* by Turgot. But it does not appear quite certain that Turgot himself used this word. It proved impossible to find it in a search of his works, with one exception: in the table of contents to the editions by Dupont de Nemours and by Schelle. But this table was probably produced not by Turgot but by Dupont de Nemours. If, however, one looks not for the word but for the idea and meaning, sufficient material is indeed to be found in Turgot in 1751. And it is perhaps not idle to point this out as an example of how a certain idea forms in the minds of people from certain experiences, and then gradually a special word becomes associated with this idea, this conceptual area.
It is no accident that in his edition of Turgot, Dupont de Nemours gives as the contents of

the section mentioned: *"La civilisation et la nature."* This section contains the early idea of civilization to which the word was later gradually attached.

An introductory letter to the publisher of the *Lettres d'une péruvienne,* Madame de Graffigny, gives Turgot the opportunity to express his ideas on the relation of the "savage" to the *homme policé* (*Oeuvres de Turgot,* ed. G. Schelle [Paris, 1913], vol. 1, p. 243). The *péruvienne* ought to consider, he says, "the reciprocal advantages of the savage and the *homme policé.* To prefer the savage is a ridiculous declamation. Let her refute it, let her show that the vices we take to be the product of *politesse* are innate to the human heart."

A few years later, Mirabeau was to use the more comprehensive and dynamic term *civilisation* in the same sense as Turgot here uses the term *politesse,* though with the opposite evaluation.

26. On this and subsequent points, see J. Moras, *Ursprung und Entwicklung des Beriffs Zivilisation in Frankreich (1756-1830),* in *Hamburger Studien zu Volkstum und Kultur der Romanen* (Hamburg, 1930), vol. 6, p. 38.

27. Ibid., p. 37.

28. Ibid., p. 36.

29. Cf. Lavisse, *Histoire de France* (Paris, 1910), vol. 9, pt. 1, p. 23.

30. Cf. Moras, *Ursprung,* p. 50.

31. Baron d'Holbach, *Système sociale ou principes naturels de la morale et de la politique* (London, 1774), vol. 3, p. 113; quoted in Moras, *Ursprung,* p. 50.

32. Baron d'Holbach, *Système,* p. 162.

33. Voltaire, *Siècle de Louis XIV,* in *Oeuvres Complètes* (Paris: Garnier Frères, 1878), vol. 14, pt. 1, p. 516.

Chapter Two

1. S. R. Wallach, *Das abendländische Gemeinschaftsbewusstsein im Mittelalter* (Leipzig and Berlin, 1928); *Beiträge zur Kultur-geschichte des Mittelalters und der Renaissance,* ed. W. Goetz, vol. 34, pp. 25-29. Here "Latins" refers to Latin Christianity, i.e., the West in general.

2. The *Bibliotheca Erasmiana* (Ghent, 1893) records 130 editions or, more precisely, 131, including the text of 1526 which unfortunately was unavailable to me, so that I am unaware how far it coincides with subsequent editions.

After the *Colloquies,* the *Moriae encomium,* the *Adagia,* and *De duplici copia verborum ac rerum commentarii, De civilitate* achieved the highest number of editions of Erasmus's own writings. (For a table of numbers of editions of all works by Erasmus, cf. Mangan, *Life, Character and Influence of Desiderius Erasmus of Rotterdam* [London, 1927], vol. 2, pp. 396ff.) If account is taken of the long series of writings more or less closely related to Erasmus's civility-book, and so of the wide radius of its success, its significance as compared to his other writings must doubtless be estimated still more highly. An idea of the direct impact of his books is given by noting which of them were translated from scholarly language into popular languages. There is as yet no comprehensive analysis of this. According to M. Mann, *Erasme et les débuts de la réforme française* (Paris, 1934), p. 181, the most surprising thing—as far as France is concerned—is "the preponderance of the books of instruction or piety over those of entertainment or satire. The *Praise of Folly*, the *Colloquies* . . . have scarcely any place in this list. . . . It was the *Adages*, the *Preparation for Death* and the *Civility in Boys* that attracted translators and that the public demanded." A similar success analysis for German and Dutch regions would probably yield somewhat different results. It may be supposed that the satirical writings had a somewhat greater success there (cf. note 30 below).

The success of the Latin edition of *De civilitate* was certainly considerable. Kirchhoff (in *Leipziger Sortimentshändler im 16 Jahrhundert*; quoted in W. H. Woodward, *Desiderius Erasmus*, [Cambridge, 1904], p. 156, n. 3) ascertains that in the three years 1547, 1551, and 1558 no less than 654 copies of *De civilitate* were in stock, and that no other book by Erasmus was listed in such numbers.

3. Compare the notice on the writings on civility by A. Bonneau in his edition of the *Civilité puérile* (see n. 35 below).

4. Despite its success in his own time, this work has received relatively little attention in the Erasmus literature of more recent times. In view of the book's theme, this is only too understandable. This theme—manners, etiquette, codes of conduct—however informative on the molding of people and their relations, is perhaps of only limited interest for historians of ideas. What Ehrismann says of a *Hofzucht* (Court discipline) in his *Geschichte der deutschen Literatur bis zum Ausgang des Mittelalters,* vol. 6, pt. 2, p. 330, is typical of a scholarly evaluation frequently encountered in this field: "A book of instruction for youths of noble birth. Not raised to the level of a teaching on virtue."

In France, however, books of courtesy from a particular period—the seventeenth century—have received increasing attention for some time, stimulated no doubt by the work of D. Parodie cited in n. 98, and above all by the comprehensive study by M. Magendie, *La politesse mondaine* (Paris, 1925). Similarly, the study by B. Groethuysen, *Origines de l'esprit bourgeois en France* (Paris, 1927), also takes literary products of a more or less average kind as a starting point in tracing a certain line in the changes in people and the modification of the social standard (cf., e.g., pp. 45ff.).

The material used in Chapter Two of this study is a degree lower, if we may put it that way, than that in the works just mentioned. But perhaps they, too, show the significance this "slight" literature has for an understanding of the great changes in the structure of people and their relations.

5. Reprinted in part in A. Franklin, *La vie privée d'autrefois: les repas,* (Paris, 1889), pp. 164, 166, which has numerous other quotations on this subject.

6. Reprinted in *The Babees Book,* ed. Frederick Furnivall (London, 1868), pt. 2; for further English, Italian, French, and German books of this genre, cf. Early English Text Society, Extra Series, no. 8, ed. F. J. Furnivall (London, 1869), including *A Booke of Precedence* and others. The molding of the young nobleman through service at the house of one of the "great" of his country is expressed particularly clearly in these English books of conditioning. An Italian observer of English customs, writing about the year 1500, remarks that the English probably adopted this practice because one is served better by strangers than by one's own children. "Had they had their own children at home, they would have been

obliged to give them the same food as they had prepared for themselves." (See the introduction to *A Fifteenth-Century Courtesy-Book,* ed. R. W. Chambers [London, 1914], p. 6). Nor is it without interest that the Italian observer of about 1500 stresses that "the English, you see, are great epicures."

For a number of further references, see M. and C. H. B. Quennel, *A History of Everyday Things in England* (London, 1931), vol. 1, p. 144.

7. Edited by F. J. Furnivall (see n. 6 above). For information on the German literature of this genre, with references to the corresponding literature in other languages, cf. G. Ehrismann, *Geschichte,* vol. 6, pt. 2 (speech, p. 326; table disciplines, p. 328); P. Merker and W. Stammler, *Reallexikon der deutschen Literaturgeschichte,* vol. 3, entry on table disciplines (P. Merker); and H. Teske, *Thomasin von Zerclaere* (Heidelberg, 1933), pp. 122ff.

8. For the German version used here, see Zarncke, *Der deutsche Cato* (Leipzig, 1852).

9. Ibid, p. 39, v. 223.

10. Tannhäuser, *Die Hofzucht,* in *Der Dichter Tannhäuser,* ed. J. Siebert (Halle, 1934), p. 196, vv. 33f.

11. Ibid., vv. 45f.

12. Ibid., vv. 49f.

13. Ibid., vv. 57f.

14. Ibid., vv. 129f.

15. Ibid., vv. 61f.

16. Ibid., vv. 109f.

17. Ibid., vv. 157f.

18. Ibid., vv. 141f.

19. Zarncke, *Der deutsche Cato,* p. 136.

20. Ibid., p. 137, vv. 287f.

21. Ibid., p. 136, vv. 258f.

22. Ibid., vv. 263f.

23. Tannhäuser, *Hofzucht,* vv. 125f.

24. Glixelli, *Les Contenances de table.*

25. *The Babees Book* and *A Booke of Precedence* (see n. 6).

26. Cf. A. von Gleichen Russwurm, *Die gothische Welt* (Stuttgart, 1922), pp. 320ff.

27. See A. Cabanès, *Moeurs intimes du temps passé,* (Paris, 1910), 1st series, p. 248.

28. Ibid., p. 252.

29. A. Bömer, *Anstand und Etikette in den Theorien der Humanisten,* in *Neue Jahrbücher für das Klassische Altertum* 14 (Leipzig, 1904).

30. Characteristic of the German burgher way of giving precepts on manners at the end of the Middle Ages and in the Renaissance is the *grobianische Umkehrung* (boorish inversion). The writer ridicules "bad" conduct by appearing to recommend it. Humor and satire, which later gradually recede in the German tradition, or at least become second-rank values, are in this phase of German burgher society notably dominant.

The satirical inversion of precepts can be traced back as a specifically urban, burgher form of instilling manners at least as far as the fifteenth century. The recurrent precept not to fall greedily on the food is heard, for example, in a little poem of this time, "Wie der maister sein nun lernet" (in Zarncke, *Der deutsche Cato,* p. 148):

> Gedenk und merk waz ich dir sag
> wan man dir die kost her trag
> so bis der erst in der schizzel;
> gedenk und scheub in deinen drizzel
> als groz klampen als ain saw.

Remember, when the food is brought in be the first to the dish; stuff large chunks down your throat like a pig.

The precept not to search about for a long time in the common dish recurs here in the following version:

> Bei allem dem daz ich dir ler
> grab in der schizzel hin und her
> nach dem aller besten stuck;
> daz dir gefall, daz selb daz zuck,
> und leg erz auf dein teller drat;
> acht nicht wer daz für übel hat.

What I teach is, dig about for the best piece in the dish; snatch the piece you like best and put it on your plate, and care nothing for those who disapprove.

In Kaspar Scheidt's German translation of the *Grobianus* (Worms, 1551; reprinted in *Neudruck deutscher Literaturwerke des 16 und 17 Jahrhunderts,* nos. 34 and 35 [Halle, 1882], p. 17, vv. 223f.), the instruction to wipe one's nose in good time appears as follows:

> Es ist der brauch in frembden landen
> Als India, wo golt verhanden
> Auch edel gstein und perlin göt
> Dass mans an d'nasen hencken thut.
> Solch gut hat dir das gluck nit bschert
> Drum hor was zu deinr nasen hort:
> Ein wuster kengel rechter leng

Auss beiden lochern aussher heng,
Wie lang eisz zapffen an dem hauss,
Das ziert dein nasen uberausz.

It is the custom in foreign countries where gold, jewels, and pearls are found to hang them on the nose.
As we are less fortunate, hear what you should wear on your nose: a long filthy trickle hanging from both nostrils, like icicles from a house—that would admirably adorn your nose.

Doch halt in allen dingen moss,
Dass nit der kengel werd zu gross:
Darumb hab dir ein solches mess,
Wenn er dir fleusst biss in das gfress
Und dir auff beiden lefftzen leit,
Dann ist die nass zu butsen zeit.
Auff beide ermel wüsch den rotz,
Dasz wer es seh vor unlust kotz.

Yet keep a measure in all things, and when the trickle grows too long and runs all over mouth and lips, the time to clean your nose has come.
Wipe the snot on both your sleeves that all who see may vomit with disgust.

Obviously, this account is intended as an instructive deterrent. Inscribed on the title page of the Worms edition of 1551 one reads:

Lisz wol disz buchlin offt und vil
Und thu allzeit das widerspil

Read this booklet often, and always do the opposite.

To elucidate the specifically burgher character of this book, the dedication of the Helbach edition of 1567 may be quoted:
Dedicated "by Wendelin Helbach, the unworthy vicar of Eckhardtschausen, to the honorable and learned gentlemen Adamus Lonicerus, doctor of medicine and city doctor of Frankfurt am Main, and Johannes Cnipius Andronicus, citizen thereof, my gracious lords and good friends."
The long title of the Latin *Grobianus* itself may give a certain basis for assessing the time at which the concept of *civilitas,* in Erasmus's sense and probably in the wake of his book, begins to spread in the Latin-writing German intellectual stratum. In the title of the 1549 *Grobianus,* this word does not yet occur. There we read: "Iron . . . Chlevastes Studiosae Juventuti. . . ." In the 1552 edition the same passage contains the word *civilitas:* "Iron episcoptes studiosae iuventuti civilitatem optat." And so it remains until the edition of 1584. To a 1661 edition of the *Grobianus* an extract from Erasmus's *De civilitate morum puerilium* is appended.
Finally, a new translation of the *Grobianus* of 1708 is inscribed: "Written with poetic pen for the discourteous Monsieur Blockhead, and presented for the merriment of all judicious and *civilized* minds." In this translation much is said in a milder tone and in a far more veiled manner. With increasing "civilization," the precepts of a past phase, which for all their satire were meant very seriously, become merely a subject for laughter, which symbolizes both the superiority of the new phase and a slight violation of its taboos

31. *The Babees Book*, p. 344.

32. Glixelli, *Les Contenances* (Romania), vol. 47, p. 31, vv. 133ff.

33. François de Callières, *De la science du monde et des connoissances utiles à la conduite de la vie* (Brussels, 1717), p. 6.

34. Arthur Denecke, "Beiträge zur Entwicklungsgeschichte des gesellschaftlichen Anstandsgefühls," in *Zeitschrift fur Deutsche Kulturgeschichte*, ed. C. Meyer, New Series, vol. 2, no. 2 (Berlin, 1892), p. 175. quotes the following precepts as new in Erasmus: "If up to now we have acquainted ourselves with the ideas on table manners prevalent in the higher circles of the common people, in Erasmus's famous book *De civilitate morum puerilium* we are given precepts for good behavior in a prince. . . . The following lessons are new: If you are given a napkin at table you should lay it over the left shoulder or arm. . . . Erasmus also says: You should sit bareheaded at table, if the custom of the country does not forbid it. You should have your goblet and knife on the right of your plate, the bread on the left. The latter should not be broken but cut. It is improper and also unhealthy to begin the meal by drinking. It is loutish to dip your fingers into the broth. Of a good piece offered to you, take only a part and pass the rest to the person offering it, or the person next to you. Solid foods offered to you should be taken with three fingers or on your plate; liquids offered on a spoon | hould be taken with the mouth, but the spoon should be wiped before it is returned. If food offered to you is not wholesome, under no circumstances say, 'I cannot eat that,' but excuse yourself politely. Every man of refinement must be adept at carving every kind of roast meat. You may not throw bones and leavings onto the floor. . . . To eat meat and bread together is healthy. . . . Some people gobble while eating. . . . A youth should speak at table only when necessary. . . . If you are giving a meal yourself, apologize for its meagerness and, at all costs, do not list the prices of the various ingredients. Everything is offered with the right hand.

"It may be seen that, despite the caution of the educator of princes and despite the refinement of some details, broadly the same spirit is present in these precepts as in the middle-class table disciplines. . . . Similarly, Erasmus's teaching differs primarily from the other social forms of conduct only in the wide scope of the precepts intended for the other circles, since he is concerned at the least to give an account exhaustive for that time."

This quotation complements the earlier considerations to some extent. Unfortunately, Denecke limits his comparison to German table disciplines. To confirm his findings, a comparison would be needed with books of courtesy in French and English, and above all with the behavior-precepts of earlier humanists.

35. Cf. *"La civilité puérile" par Erasme de Rotterdam, précédé d'une notice sur les libres de civilité depuis le XVI siècle par Alcide Bonneau* (Paris, 1877):

"Did Erasmus have models? Obviously, he did not invent *savoir-vivre*, and long before him the general rules had been laid down. . . . Nonetheless, Erasmus is the first to have treated the subject in a special and complete manner; none of the authors just quoted had envisaged civility or, if you will, propriety as capable of providing the subject of a separate study. They had formulated precepts here and there, which naturally related to education, morality, fashion, or hygiene. . . ."

A similar observation is made on Giovanni della Casa's *Galateo* (first edition together with other pieces by the author, 1558) in the introduction by I. E. Spingarn (p. xvi) to an edition entitled *Galateo of Manners and Behavior* (London, 1914).

It is perhaps of service to further work to point out that there already existed in English literature in the fifteenth century longer poems (published by the Early Text Society) treating behavior in getting dressed, at church, at table, etc., almost as comprehensively as Erasmus's treatise. It is not impossible that Erasmus knew something of these poems on manners.

What is certain is that the theme of education for boys had a considerable degree of topicality in humanist circles in the years preceding the appearance of Erasmus's little book. Quite apart from the verses *De moribus in mensa servandis* by Johannes Sulpicius, there appeared—to mention only a few—Brunfels's *Disciplina et puerorum institutio* (1525), Hegendorff's *De instituenda vita* (1529), and S. Heyden's *Formulae puerilium colloquiorum* (1528). Cf. Merker and Stammler, *Reallexikon*, entry on table disciplines.

36. Latin table discipline, *Quisquis es in mensa*, V, 18, in Glixelli, *Les Contenances*, p. 29.

37. Caxton's *Book of Curtesye*, Early English Text Society, Extra Series, no. 3, ed. F. J. Furnivall (London, 1868), p. 22.

38. Della Casa, *Galateo*, pt. 1, chs. 1, 5.

39. Caxton's *Book of Curtesye*, p. 45, v. 64.

40. In the American behaviorist literature a number of terms have been precisely defined that, with some modifications, are useful and even indispensable in investigating the past. These include "socializing the child" (cf., e.g., J. B. Watson, *Psychological Care of Infant and Child*, p. 112) and "habit formation" and "conditioning" (cf. Watson, *Psychology from the Standpoint of a Behaviorist*, p. 312).

41. Tannhäuser, *Hofzucht*, pp. 195ff.

42. Zarncke, *Der Deutsche Cato*, pp. 138ff.

43. Cf. *The Babees Book*, p. 76.

46. Ibid., p. 302.

47. Ibid., pt. 2, p. 32.

48. Ibid.

49. Ibid., pt. 2, p. 8.

50. Cf. A. Franklin, *Les Repas*, pp. 194f.

51. Ibid., p. 42.

52. Ibid., p. 283.

53. Dom. Bouhours, *Remarques nouvelles sur la langue française* (Paris, 1676), vol. 1, p. 51.

54. François de Callières, *Du bon et du mauvais usage dans les manières de s'exprimer. Des facons de parler bourgeoises; en quoy elles sont differentes de celles de la cour* (Paris,

1694), p. 12: "Then a footman came to inform the lady that Monsieur Thibault the younger was asking to see her. 'Very well,' said the lady. 'But before admitting him I must tell you who M. Thibault is. He is the son of a bourgeois friend of mine in Paris, one of those rich people whose friendship is sometimes useful to people of rank in lending them money. The son is a young man who has studied with the intention of entering a public office, but who needs to be purged of the bad grace and language of the bourgeoisie.' "

55. Andressen and Stephan, *Beiträge zur Geschichte der Gottdorffer Hof- und Staatsverwaltung von 1594-1659* (Kiel, 1928), vol. 1, p. 26 n. 1.

56. Leon Sahler, *Montbéliard à table. Mémoires de la Société d'Emulation de Montbéliard* (Montbéliard, 1907), vol. 34, p. 156.

57. Cf. Andressen and Stephan, *Beiträge*, vol. 1, p. 12.

58. Cf. Platina, *De honesta voluptate et valitudine* (1475), bk. 6, p. 14. The whole "civilizational curve" is clearly visible in a letter to the editor with the title "Obscurities of Ox-Roasting," published by the *Times* of London on May 8, 1937, shortly before the coronation ceremonies, and obviously suggested by the memory of similar festivities in the past: "Being anxious to know, as many must be at such a time as this, how best to roast an ox whole, I made inquiries about the matter at Smithfield Market. But I could only find that nobody at Smithfield knew how I was to obtain, still less to spit, roast, carve and consume an ox whole. . . . The whole matter is very disappointing." On May 14, on the same page of the *Times*, the head chef at Simpsons in the Strand gives instructions for roasting an ox whole, and a picture in the same issue shows the ox on a spit. The debate, which continued for some time in the columns of the *Times*, gives a certain impression of the gradual disappearance of the custom of roasting animals whole, even on occasions when an attempt is being made to preserve traditional forms.

59. Gred Freudenthal, *Gestaltwandel der bürgerlichen und proletarischen Hauswirtschaft mit besonderer Berücksichtigung des Typenwandels von Frau und Familie von 1760 bis zur Gegenwart*, diss. Frankfurt am Main (Würzburg, 1934).

60. See Andressen and Stephan, *Beiträge*, vol. 1, p. 10, which also contains the information that the use of the fork only began to penetrate the upper strata of society in the north at the beginning of the seventeenth century.

61. Cf. Zarncke, *Der deutsche Cato*, p. 138.

62. See Kurt Treusch von Buttlar, "Das tägliche Leben an den deutschen Fürstenhöfen des 16 Jahrhunderts," in *Zeitschrift für Kulturgeschichte* (Weimar, 1897), vol. 4, p. 13 n.

63. Ibid.

64. Cf. *The Babees Book*, p. 295.

65. Quoted in Cabanès, *Moeurs*, p. 292.

66. The best and briefest guide to the subject is A. Franklin, *Les Soins de la toilette* (Paris, 1877), and, above all, the same author's *La Civilité* (Paris, 1908), vol. 2, where a number of instructive quotations are assembled in an appendix. Some of what the writer

says must be read critically, however, since he does not always distinguish fully between what is typical of a particular time and what is regarded as exceptional.

67. Mathurin Cordier, *Colloquiorum scholasticorum libri quatuor* (Paris, 1568), bk. 2, colloquium 54 (*Exemplum ad pueros in simplici narratione exercendos*).

68. Some not easily accessible material is to be found in De Laborde, *Le Palais Mazarin* (Paris, 1816). See, for example, n. 337: "Is it necessary to go into details? The almost political role played throughout this epoch [seventeenth century] by the night commode allows us to speak of it without false shame and to say that people were reduced to this utensil and the Provençal *passarès*. One of Henri IV's mistresses, Madame de Verneuil, wished to have her chamber pot in her bedroom, which would be an impropriety in our day but at that time was no more than a slightly nonchalant liberty."

The important information in these notes also needs careful scrutiny if one is to gain a perspective of the standards of the various classes. One means of tracing these standards would be a precise study of inventories of estators' estates. Regarding the extract on nose-blowing we may note here, for example, that Erasmus left behind—so far as can be ascertained today—the astonishingly high number of thirty-nine handkerchiefs, but only one golden and one silver fork; see *Inventarium über die Hinterlassenschaft des Erasmus*, ed. L. Sieber (Basel, 1889), reprinted in *Zeitschrift für Kulturgeschichte* (Weimar, 1897), vol. 4, pp. 434ff.

A wealth of interesting information is contained in Rabelais's *Gargantua and Panta-gruel*. On the subject of "natural functions," for example, see bk. 1, ch. 13.

69. Georg Brandes quotes this passage of the memoirs in his book *Voltaire* (Berlin, n.d.), vol. 1, pp. 340f., and comments on it as follows: "It does not embarrass her to be seen naked by a servant; she did not consider him as a man in relation to herself as a woman."

70. *The Babees Book*, pt. 2, p. 32.

71. Ibid., pt. 2, p. 7.

72. Ibid., p. 301f.

73. Cf. Rudeck, *Geschichte der öffentlichen Sittlichkeit* (Jena, 1887), p. 397.

74. T. Wright, *The Home of Other Days* (London, 1871), p. 269.

75. Otto Zöckler, *Askese und Mönchstum* (Frankfurt, 1897), p. 364.

76. T. Wright, *Home*, p. 269; also Cabanès, *Moeurs intimes*, 2d series, p. 166. See also G. Zappert, *Uber das Badewesen in mittelalterlicher und späterer Zeit*, in *Archiv für Kunde österr, Geschichtsquellen* (Vienna, 1859), vol. 21. On the role of the bed in the household, see G. G. Coulton, *Social Life in Britain* (Cambridge, 1919), p. 386, where the scarcity of beds and the unquestioning use of beds by several people is briefly and clearly demonstrated.

77. Quoted in M. Bauer, *Das Liebesleben in der deutschen Vergangenheit* (Berlin, 1924), p. 208.

78. Rudeck, *Geschichre der öffentlichen Sittlichkeit*, p. 399.

79. Dr. Hopton and A. Balliol, *Bed Manners* (London, 1936), p. 93.

80. There is certainly no lack of reactions against pajamas. An American expression of this, of interest particularly for its argumentation, is as follows (from *The People*, July 26, 1936):

"Strong men wear no pyjamas. They wear night-shirts and disdain men who wear such effeminate things as pyjamas. Theodore Roosevelt wore night-shirts. So did Washington, Lincoln, Napoleon, Nero and many other famous men.

"These arguments in favour of the night-shirt as against pyjamas are advanced by Dr. Davis of Ottawa, who has formed a club of night-shirt wearers. The club has a branch in Montreal and a strong group in New York. Its aim is to re-popularise the night-shirt as a sign of real manhood."

This speaks clearly for the spread of the use of pajamas in the relatively short period since the war.

It is still clearer that the use of pajamas by women has been receding again for some time. What replaces them is clearly a derivative of the long evening dress and an expression of the same social tendencies, including a reaction against the "masculinization" of women and a tendency toward sharper social differentiation, as well as the simple need for a certain harmony between evening and night costume. For precisely this reason, a comparison between this new nightdress and that of the past shows particularly clearly what has here been called the undeveloped state of the intimate sphere. This nightdress of our days is far more like a dress and far better formed than the earlier one.

81. M. Ginsberg, *Sociology* (London, 1934), p. 118: "Whether innate tendencies are repressed, sublimated or given full play depends to a large extent upon *the type of family life and the traditions of the larger society*. . . . Consider, for example, the difficulty of determining whether the aversion to incestuous relationships has an instinctive basis, or of disentagling the genetic factors underlying the various forms of sexual jealousy. The inborn tendencies, in short, have a certain *plasticity* and their mode of expression, repression or sublimation is, in varying degrees, socially conditioned."

The present study gives rise to very similar ideas. It attempts, above all in the conclusion to the second volume, to show that the molding of instinctual life, including its compulsive features, is a function of social interdependencies that persist throughout life. These dependencies of the individual vary in structure according to the structure of society. To the variations in this structure correspond the differences in personality structure that can be observed in history.

It might be recalled at this point that related observations are recorded very unambiguously in Montaigne's *Essays* (bk. 1, ch. 23):

> The laws of conscience that we say are born of nature, are born of custom; anyone holding in inner veneration the opinions and manners approved and accepted around him cannot disregard them without remorse or observe them without applause. It seems to me that the power of custom was very well understood by the originator of the fable of the village woman who, having acquired at birth the habit of caressing and carrying about with her a calf, and continuing to do so ever after, was still carrying it, by virtue of custom, when the animal was fully grown. . . . *Usus efficacissimus rerum omnium magister.* . . . Through custom as often as through illness, says Aristotle, women pull out their hair, bite their nails, eat coals and earth, and as much by custom as by nature males consort with males.

Particularly consonant with the findings of the present study is the idea that "remorse," and thus the psychic structure referred to here on Freudian lines, if with a slightly different meaning, as the superego, is imprinted on the individual by the society in which he grows up—in a word, that this superego is sociogenetic.

In this connection it scarcely needs to be said, but is perhaps worth emphasizing explicitly, how much this study owes to the discoveries of Freud and the psychoanalytical school. The connections are obvious to anyone acquainted with psychoanalytical writings, and it did not seem necessary to point them out in particular instances, especially because this could not have been done without lengthy qualifications. Nor have the not inconsiderable differences between the whole approach of Freud and that adopted in this study been stressed explicitly, particularly as the two could perhaps after some discussion be made to agree without undue difficulty. It seemed more important to build a particular intellectual perspective as clearly as possible, without digressing into disputes at every turn.

82. Von Raumer, *Geschichte der Pädagogik* (Stuttgart, 1857), pt. 1, p. 110.

83. On all these questions, cf. Huizinga, *Erasmus* (New York and London, 1924), p. 200: "What Erasmus really demanded of the world and mankind, how he pictured to himself that passionately desired, purified Christian society of good morals, fervent faith, simplicity and moderation, kindliness, toleration and peace—this we can nowhere else find so clearly and well expressed as in the *Colloquia.*"

84. "Museion," says the 1665 edition, is the word for a secret room.

85. The bewilderment of the later observer is no less when he finds himself confronted by morals and customs of the earlier phase which express a different standard of shame. This applies particularly to medieval bathing manners. In the nineteenth century it seems at first completely incomprehensible that medieval people were not ashamed to bathe naked together in large numbers, and often both sexes together.

Alwin Schultz, *Deutsches Leben im XIV und XV Jahrhundert* (Vienna, 1892), pp. 68f., says on this question:

> We possess two interesting pictures of such a bathhouse. *I should like to say in advance that I consider the pictures exaggerated, and that in my view the medieval predilection for coarse, earthy jokes has been accommodated by them.*
>
> The Breslau miniature shows us a row of bathtubs in each of which a man and a woman sit facing each other. A board laid across the tub serves as a table, and is covered by a pretty cloth on which are fruit, drinks, etc. The men have a headcloth and wear a loincloth, the women are adorned with coiffure, necklace, etc., but are otherwise quite naked. The Leipzig miniature is similar, except that the tubs are separate; over each of them there is a kind of awning, with curtains that can be drawn. Behavior in these bathhouses was not unduly decorous, and decent women no doubt kept away from them. Usually, however, the sexes were certainly segregated; the city fathers would never have tolerated such an open flouting of all decency.

It is not without interest to see how the affective condition and the standard of repugnance of his own time put into the author's mouth the supposition that "usually . . . the sexes were certainly segregated," even though the historical evidence that he himself produces points rather to the opposite conclusion. Compare to this the matter of fact and simply descriptive attitude toward these differences of standard in P. S. Allen, *The Age of Erasmus* (Oxford, 1914), pp. 204ff.

86. See A. Bömer, *Aus dem Kampf gegen die Colloquia familiara des Erasmus*, in *Archiv für Kulturgeschichte* (Leipzig and Berlin, 1911), vol. 9, pt. 1, p. 32.

87. A. Bömer writes here: "In the last two books, intended for mature and old men." But the whole book is dedicated by Morisotus to his young son; the whole book was conceived as a schoolbook. In it Morisotus discusses the different stages of life. He introduces grown-ups to the child, men and women, young and old alike, so that the child can see and learn to understand them, and see what good and bad behavior are in this world. The notion that certain parts of this work were intended to be read solely by women or solely by old men is clearly put into the mind of the author by his understandable perplexity in face of the idea that all this might once have been intended as reading matter for children.

88. It is of importance for an understanding of this whole question that the age of marriage in this society was lower than that of later times.

"In this period," writes R. Köbner of the late Middle Ages, "man and woman often marry very young. The Church gives them the right to marry as soon as they have reached sexual maturity, and this right was often exercised. Youths marry between 15 and 19, girls between 13 and 15. This custom has always been regarded as a characteristic peculiarity of the society of that time." See R. Köbner, *Die Eheauffassung des ausgehenden Mittelalters*, in *Archiv für Kulturgeschichte*, (Leipzig and Berlin, 1911), vol. 9, no. 2. For copious information and documentation on child marriages, see Early English Text Society, Orig. Series, no. 108, ed. F. J. Furnivall (London, 1897), including *Child-Marriages, Divorces and Ratifications*, etc. There the possible marriageable age is given as fourteen for boys and twelve for girls (p. xix).

89. F. Zarncke, *Die deutsche Universität im Mittelalter* (Leipzig, 1857), Beitrag 1, pp. 49ff.

90. Bauer, *Das Liebesleben*, p. 136.

91. W. Rudeck, *Geschichte der öffentlichen Sittlichkeit in Deutschland* (Jena, 1897), p. 33.

92. Ibid., p. 33.

93. K. Schäfer, "Wie man früher heiratete," *Zeitschrift für deutsche Kulturgeschichte* (Berlin, 1891), vol. 2, no. 1, p. 31.

94. W. Rudeck, p. 319.

95. Brienne, *Mémoires*, vol. 2, p. 11; quoted in Laborde, *Palais Mazarin*, n. 522.

96. F. von Bezold, "Ein Kölner Gedenkbuch des XVI Jahrhunderts," in *Aus Mittelalter und Renaissance* (Munich and Berlin, 1918), p. 159.

97. W. Rudeck, p. 171, Allen, *Age of Erasmus*, p. 205; A. Hyma, *The Youth of Erasmus* (University of Michigan Press, 1930), pp. 56f. See also Regnault, *La condition juridique du bâtard au moyen âge* (Pont Audemer, 1922), where, however, the legal rather than the actual position of the bastard is considered. Common law often takes a not very benevolent attitude toward the bastard. It is a question that remains to be investigated whether common law thus expresses the actual social opinion of different strata or only the opinion of a particular stratum.

It is sufficiently known that as late as the seventeenth century, at the French royal court, the legitimate and illegitimate children were brought up together. Louis XIII, for example, hates his half-sister. Even as a child he says the following of his half-brother: "I like my little sister better than [him] because he has not been in mama's belly with me, as she has."

98. D. Parodie, "L'honnête homme et l'idéal moral du XVIIe et du XVIIIe siècle," *Revue pédagogique* (1921), vol. 78, no. 2, pp. 94ff.

99. Cf., e.g., Peters, "The Institutionalised Sex-Taboo," in Knight, Peters, and Blanchard, *Taboo and Genetics*, p. 181.

A study of 150 girls made by the writer in 1916/17 showed a taboo on thought and discussion among well-bred girls of the following subjects, which they characterice as "indelicate," "polluting" and "things completely outside the knowledge of a lady."
    1. Things contrary to custom, often called "wicked" and "immoral."
    2. Things "disgusting" such as bodily functions, normal as well as pathological, and all the implications of uncleanliness.
    3. Things uncanny, that "make your flesh creep," and things suspicious.
    4. Many forms of animal life, which it is a commonplace that girls will fear or which are considered unclean.
    5. Sex differences.
    6. Age differences.
    7. All matters relating to the double standard of morality.
    8. All matters connected with marriage, pregnancy, and childbirth.
    9. Allusions to any part of the body except head and hands.
    10. Politics.
    11. Religion.

100. A. Luchaire, *La societé française au temps de Philippe-Auguste* (Paris, 1909), p. 273.

101. Ibid., p. 275.

102. Ibid., p. 272.

103. Ibid., p. 278.

104. I. Huizinga, *Herbst des Mittelalters, Studien über Lebens und Geistesform des 14 und 15 Jahrhunderts in Frankreich und in den Niederlanden* (Munich, 1924), p. 32.

105. From *"Le Jouvencel" Lebensgeschichte des Ritters Jean de Bueil*, ed. Kervyn de Lettenhove, in Chastellain, *Oeuvres*, vol. 8; quoted in Huizinga, *Herbst*, p. 94.

106. See p. xxx.

107. H. Dupin, *La courtoisie au moyen âge* (Paris, 1931), p. 79.

108. Ibid., p. 77.

109. Zarncke, *Der deutsche Cato*, pp. 36f., vv. 167f., 178ff.

110. Ibid., p. 48, vv. 395ff.

111. Huizinga, *Herbst,* pp. 32ff.

112. L. Mirot, *Les d'Orgemont, leur origine, leur fortune, etc.* (Paris, 1913); P. Champion, *François Villon. Sa vie et son temps* (Paris, 1913) vol. 2, pp. 230ff., quoted in Huizinga, *Herbst,* p. 32.

113. P. Durrieu, *Les très belles heures de Notre Dame du Duc Jean de Berry* (Paris, 1922), p. 68.

114. Ch. Petit-Dutaillis, *Documents nouveaux sur les moeurs populaires et le droit de vengeance dans les Pays-Bas au XV siècle* (Paris, 1908), p. 47.

115. Ibid., p. 162.

116. Ibid., p. 5.

117. Luchaire, *La societé française* pp. 278f.

118. For further details on this, see A. Franklin, *Paris et les Parisiens au seizième siècle* (Paris, 1921), pp. 508f.

119. Th. Bossert mentions in his introduction to the *House-Book* (p. 20) an engraving by the same artist in which he "ridicules the newfangled nobility, the craving of bourgeois for coats of arms and knightly practices." This may point in the same direction.

120. Introduction to *Das Mittelalterliche Hausbuch,* ed. H. T. Bossert and W. Storck (Leipzig, 1912), pp. 27ff.

121. Berthold von Regensburg, *Deutsche Predigten,* ed. Pfeiffer and Strobl, (Vienna, 1862-1880), vol. 1, fourteen, p. 7.

122. Ibid., vol. 1, one hundred forty-one, pp. 24ff.

123. Max Lehrs, *Der Meister mit den Bandrollen* (Dresden, 1886), pp. 26ff.

124. We shall now consider by way of a note a special problem arising from the material on the civilization of behavior which was not included in the text, partly for reasons of space and partly because it did not seem to contribute anything essentially new to the understanding of the main outline of civilization. Yet this problem deserves some attention. The relation of Western people to *cleanliness,* to *washing* and *bathing,* shows, over a long time span, the same transformational curve as has been examined in the text from many other sides. The impulse toward regular cleaning and constant bodily cleanliness does not derive in the first place from clearly defined hygienic insight, from a clear or, as we say, "rational" understanding of the danger of dirt to health. The relation to washing, too, changes in conjunction with the transformation of human relationships mentioned in the text and to be considered in more detail in the next volume.

At first it is taken for granted that people should clean themselves regularly only out of respect for others, especially social superiors, i.e., for social reasons, under the pressure of more or less perceptible external compulsions. Regular washing is omitted, or limited to the minimum demanded by immediate personal well-being, when such external compulsions are absent, when the social position does not demand it. Today, washing and bodily cleanliness are instilled in the individual from an early age as a kind of automatic habit, so that it gradually more or less disappears from his consciousness that he washes and disciplines himself to constant cleanliness out of regard for others and, at least originally, at the instigation of others, i.e., for reasons of external compulsion. He washes by self-compulsion even if no one else is present who might censure or punish him for not doing so. If he omits to do so, it is today—as it was not earlier—an expression of a not wholly successful conditioning to the existing social standard. The same change in behavior and in affective life that emerged in the investigation of other civilizational curves is seen here also. Social relations are transformed so that compulsions exerted by people on one another are changed into more and more pronounced self-compulsions in the individual; the formation of the superego is consolidated. It is, in a word, that sector of the individual representing the social code, his own superego, which today constrains the individual to wash and clean himself regularly. The mechanism becomes perhaps even clearer if we remember that today many men shave even if there is no social obligation to do so, simply from habit, because they feel discomfited by their superego if they do not, even though such an omission is quite certainly not detrimental to health. Regular washing with soap and water is another such "compulsive action" cultivated in our society by the nature of our conditioning and consolidated in our consciousness by hygienic, "rational" explanations.

It may suffice in this connection to document this change by evidence from another observer. I. E. Spingarn says in the introduction to an English translation of Della Casa's *Galateo* (The Humanist Library, ed. L. Einstein, [London, 1914], vol. 8, p. xxv): "Our concern is only with secular society, and there we find that cleanliness was considered only in so far as it was a social necessity, if indeed then; as an individual necessity or habit it scarcely appears at all. Della Casa's standard of social manners applies here, too: cleanliness was dictated by the need of pleasing others, and not because of any *inner* demand of individual instinct. . . . All this has changed. Personal cleanliness, because of its complete acceptance as an individual necessity has virtually ceased to touch the problem of social manners at any point." The curve of change is expressed here all the more clearly because the observer takes the standard of his own society—the *inner* desire for cleanliness—as given, without asking how and why it emerged from the other standard in the course of history. Today, indeed, it is in general only children who wash and clean themselves only under external pressure and direct compulsion from outside, out of regard for others on whom they depend. In adults, as we have said, this behavior is now gradually becoming a self-compulsion, a personal habit. Formerly, however, it was produced in adults, too, by direct external compulsion. We here meet again with what was earlier called the *fundamental law* of sociogenesis. The history of a society is mirrored in the history of the individual within it. The individual must pass through anew, in abbreviated form, the civilizing process that society as a whole has passed through over many centuries; for he does not come "civilized" into the world.

One further point in this civilization-curve deserves some attention. It appears, from the accounts of a number of observers, as if people in the sixteenth and seventeenth centuries were, if anything, less "clean" than in the preceding centuries. Such observations, when tested, are found to be correct in at least one way; it appears that the use of water as a means of bathing and cleaning declined somewhat in the transition to modern times, at least if life in the upper classes is considered. If the change is examined in this way, a simple explanation presents itself that certainly needs more exact confirmation. It was well enough known at the end of the Middle Ages that one could contract diseases, even fatal ones, in the bathhouses. To understand the effect of such a discovery, one must place oneself within the consciousness of this society, in which causal connections, in this case the nature of the transmission of disease and infection, were still somewhat vague. What could be imprinted on consciousness was the simple fact: water baths are dangerous, one can poison oneself in them. For it was in this way, as a kind of poisoning, that human reason at this time assimilated the mass infections, the plagues that swept through society in numerous waves. We know and understand the terrible fear which seized people in the face of such plagues. It was a fear that could not, as at our stage of social experience, be limited and guided into certain channels by exact knowledge of the causal connections and therefore of the limits of the danger. And it is very possible that at that time the use of water, particularly warm water for bathing purposes, was associated with a relatively indistinct fear of this kind which greatly exaggerated the real danger.

But if in a society at that stage of experience an object or piece of behavior is associated with fear in this way, it can be a long while before this fear and its symbols, the corresponding prohibitions and resistances, recede again. In the course of generations the memory of the original cause of the fear may very well disappear. What remains alive in the consciousness of people is perhaps only a feeling transmitted from one generation to another that danger is connected to the use of water, and a general discomfort, a feeling of distaste for this custom that is constantly socially reinforced. Thus we find in the sixteenth century, for example, pronouncements like this:

> Estuves et bains, je vous en prie
> Fuyès-les, ou vous en mourrés.

Flee sweating-rooms and baths, I beg you, or you will die.

This is said by a doctor, Guillaume Bunel, in 1513, among other pieces of advice against the plague (*Oeuvre excellente et a chascun désirant soy de peste préserver*, reprinted by Ch. J. Richelet [Le Mans, 1836]). We need only observe from our own standpoint how in his advice right and fantastically wrong ideas are mingled together to understand the effects of a fear less limited than our own. And in the seventeenth and even the eighteenth century we still constantly find warnings against the use of water, since it is harmful to the skin or one might catch a cold, among other "reasons." It looks indeed like a slowly ebbing wave of fear; but at the present state of research this is certainly only a hypothesis.

All the same, the hypothesis shows one thing quite clearly: how such phenomena *could* be explained. And it thereby demonstrates a fact that is highly characteristic of the whole civilizing process. This process takes place in conjunction with a progressive limitation of outward dangers, and so with a limitation and channeling of fear of such external dangers. These outward dangers of human life become more calculable, the paths and scope of human fears more regulated. Life sometimes seems to us uncertain enough today, but this bears no comparison with the insecurity of the individual in medieval society. The greater control of sources of fear that is slowly established in the transition to our social structure is indeed one of the most elementary preconditions for the standard of conduct that we express by the concept of "civilization." The armor of civilized conduct would crumble very rapidly if, through a change in society, the degree of insecurity that existed earlier were to break in upon us again, and if danger became as incalculable as it once was. Corresponding fears would soon burst the limits set to them today.

However, one specific form of fear does grow with the increase of civilization: the half-unconscious "inner" fear of a breaching of the restrictions imposed on civilized men.

Some concluding ideas on this subject are to be found at the end of the second volume in the "Sketch of a Theory of Civilization."

Notes on the 1968
Introduction

1. Talcott Parsons, *Essays in Sociological Theory* (Glencoe, 1963), pp. 359f.
2. Ibid., p. 359.
3. T. Parsons, *Social Structure and Personality* (Glencoe, 1963), pp. 82, 258f.
4. The idea that social change should be understood in terms of a change of structure through a malfunction of a normally stable state of social equilibrium is to be found in numerous places in Parsons's work; c.f., for example, T. Parsons and N. J. Smelser, *Economy and Society* (London, 1957), pp. 247f. Similarly, in Robert K. Merton, *Social Theory and Social Structure* (Glencoe, 1959), p. 122, an ideal social state (though one apparently understood as real) in which there are no contradictions and tensions is counterposed to another in which these social phenomena, evaluated as "dysfunctional," exert a pressure toward "change" on a social structure normally free of tension and immutable.

The problem being put forward for discussion here, as can be seen, is not identical with the problem traditionally discussed in terms of the concepts "static" and "dynamic." The traditional discussion often involves the question of which method is preferable in examining social phenomena, one limiting the inquiry to a particular time segment or one involving the study of more extended processes. Here, in contrast, it is not the sociological method or even the sociological selection of problems as such which is under discussion, but the conceptions of society, of human figurations, underlying the use of the various methods and types of problem selection. What is said here is not directed against the possibility of sociologically investigating short-term social conditions, this type of problem being an entirely legitimate and indispensable kind of sociological inquiry. What is said here is directed against a certain type of theoretical conception, often but by no means necessarily associated with empirical sociological investigations of states. It is quite certainly possible to undertake empirical investigations of states while using models of social changes, processes, and developments of one kind or another as a theoretical frame of reference. The debate on the relation between "social statics" and "social dynamics" suffers from insufficiently clear differentiation between the empirical investigation of short-term sociological problems and the methods of inquiry appropriate to them, on the one hand, and the theoretical models by which—explicitly or not—one is guided in posing the problems and in presenting the results of the inquiry, on the other. Merton's use of the terms "static" and "dynamic" in the passage cited above shows very clearly this insufficient capacity to differentiate, as when he says that within the framework of a sociological theory of function the gap between statics and dynamics can be bridged by the consideration that discrepancies, tensions, and antitheses are "dysfunctional" in terms of the existing "social system," and therefore signify malfunction, but are "instrumental" from the point of view of change.

5. The tendencies of the European nations to greater unification may certainly derive a good part of their driving force from the consolidation and extension of chains of interdependencies, above all in the economic and military spheres; but it was the shock to the traditional national self-images of the European countries that gave rise in all these nations to a disposition to adapt their own attitudes—hesitantly and tentatively, at least in the beginning—toward greater functional interdependence, despite the natiocentric tradition. The difficulty of this undertaking lies precisely in the fact that, as a result of the natiocentric socialization of children and adults, each of these nations occupies the dominant emotional position among its own people, whereas the larger transnational formation which is evolving possesses at first only a "rational" but hardly an emotional significance for them.

6. This difference deserves a more extensive comparative investigation than is possible

here. But in general terms it can be explained in a few words. It is connected with the kind and extent of the value of preindustrial power elites which pass into the values of the industrial strata and their representatives as they come into power.

In countries like Germany (but also in other countries on the European continent) a type of bourgeois conservatism can be observed which is determined to a very high degree by the values of the preindustrial dynastic-agrarian-military power elites. These values include a very pronounced depreciation of everything that is referred to as the "world of commerce" (i.e., trade and industry) and an unequivocally higher value attached to the state, the "social whole" as against the individual. Wherever such values play a prominent part in the conservatism of industrial classes, they understandably contain a perceptible antiliberal tendency. In this tradition negative feelings are attached to the high estimation of the individual personality and of individual initiative and to the correspondingly lower evaluation of the "state" totality, in other words, to the values of a commercial world pleading for free competition.

In countries where members of the preindustrial agrarian elite kept less emphatically aloof in their practical life and in their values from commercial operations and from all those earning their livelihood by such operations, and where the power of princes and court circles as centers of the state was limited, as in England, or nonexistent, as in America, the rising bourgeois groups, in their gradual ascent to become the dominant class, evolved a type of conservatism which—apparently—was highly compatible with the ideals of nonintervention by the state, of the freedom of the individual, and therefore with specifically liberal values. More will be said in the text about some of the specific difficulties of this liberal-conservative nationalism, this apparently unproblematic simultaneous assertion of the "individual" and of the nation as the highest value.

7. The superseding of an ideology oriented toward the future by one oriented toward the present is sometimes concealed by an intellectual sleight of hand that can be recommended to any sociologist interested in the study of ideologies as a prime example of the subtler kind of ideology formation. The orientation of the various natiocentric ideologies toward the existing order as the highest ideal sometimes produces the result that exponents of such values—particularly but by no means exclusively exponents of their conservative-liberal shades—posit their own attitudes simply as nonideological statements of fact and restrict the concept of ideology to those kinds of ideologies which are directed at changing the existing order, particularly within the state. An example of this conceptual masking of one's own ideology in the development of German society is the well-known ideology of *Realpolitik*. This argument starts from the idea, conceived as a statement of fact, that in international politics every nation actually exploits its potential power in its own national interest in an entirely ruthless and unrestricted way. This apparent statement of fact served to justify a particular natiocentric ideal, a modern version of the Machiavellian ideal, which states that national policy ought to be pursued in the international field without consideration for others, solely in one's own national interest. This ideal of *Realpolitik* is in fact unrealistic because every nation is actually dependent on others.

A similar train of thought is found in more recent times—and, in keeping with American tradition, in a somewhat more moderate form—in a book by an American sociologist, Daniel Bell, bearing the revealing title *The End of Ideology* (New York, 1961). Bell, too, starts from the assumption that the power struggle between organized groups in the pursuit of their own advantage is a fact. He concludes from this fact, much like the advocates of German *Realpolitik,* that the politician, in pursuing the power goals of his own group, ought to intervene without ethical commitment in the power struggles of different groups. At the same time, Bell claims that this program does not have the character of a profession of political faith, of a preconceived value system, i.e., an ideology (ibid., p. 279). He attempts to limit this concept solely to political doctrines directed at changing the existing order. He forgets that it is possible to treat the existing order not only as a simple fact but as a value underpinned by emotions, as an ideal, as something that ought to be. He does not distinguish between a scientific investigation of what is and an ideological defense of what is (as the embodiment of a highly valued ideal). It is quite obvious that Bell's ideal is the state that he describes as a fact.

"Democracy," writes another American sociologist, Seymour Martin Lipset, "is not only or even primarily a means through which different groups can attain their ends or seek the good society; it is the good society itself in operation" *(Political Man,* New York, 1960, p. 403). Lipset later modified this statement to some extent. But this and other pronouncements by leading American sociologists are examples of how little even the most intelligent representatives of American sociology are in a position to withstand the extraordinarily strong pressure toward intellectual conformity in their society, and of how much this situation impairs their critical faculties. As long as this is the case, as long as natiocentric values and ideals dominate the theorizing of leading American sociologists to such a degree, as long as they fail to realize that sociology can no more be conducted from a primarily national point of view than physics, their predominant influence represents a not inconsiderable danger for the worldwide development of sociology. As can be seen, "the end of ideology" is not yet in sight among sociologists.

Incidentally, something similar would probably have to be said about Russian sociology if it had a similarly dominant influence. But as far as I am aware, while there are in the U.S.S.R. a growing number of empirical sociological investigations, there is as yet scarcely a theoretical sociology. This is understandable, for its place is taken in the Soviet Union not so much by the system of Marx and Engels as by a Marxist intellectual edifice raised to the status of a creed. Like the dominant American theory of society, the Russian theory is a natiocentric mental construct. From this side, too, the end of ideology is quite certainly not in sight in sociological theorizing. But that is no reason not to strive to the utmost to bring nearer the end of this continuous self-deception, this constant masking of short-term social ideals as eternally valid sociological theories.

8. T. Parsons, *Societies: Evolutionary and Comparative Perspectives* (Englewood Cliffs, N.J., 1966), p. 20: "This process occurs inside that 'black box,' the personality of the actor."

9. Gilbert Ryle, *The Concept of Mind* (London, 1949).

INDEX

V

Voltaire, François Marie, 14, 20, 28, 36, 46, 48, 103, 111
  Brutus, 14
  Discours sur la Tragédie, 14
  Zaïre, 103
Von Raumer, 169-170, 172, 179-180, 181-82
  Education of Girls, 179-180, 181-82
  Geschichte der Pädagogik, 169, 172

W

Washing, 57, 64-65; *see also* Cleanliness
Weber, Max, xv, 246, 249, 253
Weste, Richard, 131
  Book of Demeanor, 131-32
Winkelmann, 20
Wolff, 20
Wolzogen, Caroline von, 24
  Agnes von Lilien, 24-25
Women, role of, 184-87
Woolf, Virginia, 253
Work, 152

Z

Zarncke, 153
  Der deutsche Cato, 153
Zedler Universal Lexicon, 9-10
Zirklaria, Thomasin von, 61, 66
  Höflichkeit, 61, 66
  Italian Guest, 61, 66
Zivilisation, 4, 6, 9, 29-30, 34; *see also Kultur*

. . . we must meantime occupy ourselves with a less resplendent, but still meritorious, task, namely, to level the ground and to render it sufficiently secure for moral edifices of these majestic dimensions. For this ground has been honeycombed by subterranean workings which reason, in its confident but fruitless search for hidden treasures, has carried out in all directions, and which threaten the security of the superstructures.

—Kant

MOLE EDITIONS
An Editorial Statement

Our series MOLE EDITIONS would like to show a possible way out of a quandary. Though social science and social history cannot exist without theoretical foundations, there exists today no adequate philosophy and no comprehensive social theory capable of informing research without imposing dogmatic distortions. Realizing the intimate interdependence of theory and practice in the social, intellectual and political processes, the editors of MOLE EDITIONS think that the present dilemma is rooted in the inadequacy of the answers provided by theory and in the inability of narrow empirical research to ask questions which could solicit meaningful explanations—as though there were only quick answers or no answers at all, with the enjoyment of detail destroyed in either case.

A possible manner of confronting this impasse—and the general malaise that extends from everyday life to intellectual discourse—would not seem to lie in yet another program, yet another grand scheme. Rather, it seems more useful to examine the history of theory itself, rediscovering the roots of the problems which have produced the impasse, concentrating simultaneously on the details of social, political and cultural history so as to let these details speak for themselves. Through this retrieval, we hope to be able to arrive at new, more adequate, theoretical frameworks. We are therefore prepared to entertain a more contemplative scholarly sensibility and to rework material which has either been ignored or has escaped the grasp of inherited theories. We hope that this will help to restore some of the pleasure that social science lost when its mode of discourse was divorced from literature.

MOLE EDITIONS
Available in 1977

Pierre Clastres	Society against the State	$12.95 cloth
Norbert Elias	The Civilizing Process: Vol. 1	$15.00 cloth
Dolf Sternberger	Panorama of the 19th Century	$15.00 cloth

In active preparation for 1978

Reinhart Koselleck	Enlightenment and Hypocrisy	$12.95 cloth
Wolf Lepenies	The End of Natural History	$12.95 cloth
Norbert Elias	The Civilizing Process: Vol. II	
Robert Jaulin	The White Peace	
Wolfgang Schivelbusch	The Industrialized Traveller	

In active preparation for 1979

Pierre Clastres	Chronicles of the Guayaki Indians

DATE DUE

28 June 78			
JUL 1 3 1978			
JUL 1 1 2003			
GAYLORD			PRINTED IN U.S.A